RUSSIA AND GERMANY REBORN

RUSSIA AND GERMANY REBORN

UNIFICATION, THE SOVIET COLLAPSE, AND THE NEW EUROPE

Angela E. Stent

PRINCETON UNIVERSITY PRESS   PRINCETON, NEW JERSEY

Copyright © 1999 by Princeton University Press
Published by Princeton University Press, 41 William Street,
Princeton, New Jersey 08540
In the United Kingdom: Princeton University Press, Chichester, West Sussex

Library of Congress Cataloging-in-Publication Data

Stent, Angela.
Russia and Germany reborn : unification, the Soviet collapse, and
the new Europe / Angela E. Stent.
p.   cm.
Includes bibliographical references and index.
ISBN 0-691-05965-9 (cl : alk. paper)
1. Soviet Union—Foreign relations—Germany. 2. Germany—Foreign relations—Soviet
Union. 3. Russia (Federation)—Foreign relations—Germany. 4. Germany—Foreign
relations—Russia (Federation). 5. Germany—History—Unification, 1990. 6. National
security—Europe. 7. World politics—1989–   I. Title.
DK67.5.G3S77   1999
327.47043—dc21   98-3532   CIP

This book has been composed in Galliard

Princeton University Press books are printed on acid-free paper
and meet the guidelines for permanence and durability of the
Committee on Production Guidelines for Book Longevity of the
Council on Library Resources

http://pup.princeton.edu

Printed in the United States of America

10 9 8 7 6 5 4 3 2 1

To Ronnie, Danny, Alex, and Rebecca

And in Loving Memory of Gabi

Contents

Preface

BETWEEN October 1989 and December 1991, the two communist states that defined and symbolized the Cold War—the Soviet Union and the German Democratic Republic—collapsed. After forty years of East-West confrontation and a series of major crises over Berlin, East Germany expired with a bang while the USSR went out with a whimper. East Germany was absorbed into the Federal Republic of Germany, which in turn was thrust into a new role in Europe—one for which it was unprepared. The Russians, by contrast, lost both their internal and external empires as the Soviet Union broke into fifteen independent states, of which the Russian Federation was by far the largest. The disappearance of the GDR and the USSR, the rebirth of Russia, and the unification of Germany have had a profound impact on European security and the entire structure of international relations. United Germany is a rising power, destined to lead the European continent once its own process of unification is complete. Russia will also shape European developments in the next century. But its major source of leverage for the foreseeable future will be its weakness, its ability to disrupt European stability. It will be a constant concern to its neighbors because of its potentially lethal combination of political instability, a nuclear arsenal with an uncertain future, and difficulties in adjusting to the loss of empire. Whatever happens, however, geography and history will ensure that Germany will play an important role in Russia's future, whether Russia continues on the democratic path or whether it moves toward authoritarian rule. Developments in Russia will also affect Germany's security, particularly if Russia does not remain on its present path. Between them, Russia and Germany will do much to determine the fate of postcommunist Europe.

The interaction between Russia and Germany, one of the defining international relationships of the twentieth century, will continue to influence the architecture of Europe and its future security in the twenty-first century. It is a relationship that we need to better understand as we contemplate the world of the next millennium. Germany played a major role in both the rise and fall of Soviet power. The Rapallo treaty of 1922 was midwife to the infant Soviet state's birth as a European power and its entry into the world of international diplomacy. German unification in 1990 was the final act in the decline and fall of the USSR's imperial system; it sounded the death knell for Soviet power in Eastern Europe and ultimately for the Soviet Union itself. Throughout the Soviet period, therefore, Germany played a significant role in both facilitating the growth of Soviet power and finally hastening its collapse. Today, united Germany continues to play a major role in Russia, partly because of the unification treaties and partly because relations with Russia will remain central to the ongoing redefinition of Germany's national interests. Similarly, Russia will continue to view Germany as its most important European partner. These bilateral interests have survived the death of communism and the unification of Germany. The environment in which these interests are defined and pursued has, however, greatly changed.

This book places the dramatic and unexpected events surrounding German unification and the end of the Cold War in their broader historical context. It asks why and how these profound and unanticipated changes happened. It chronicles the twenty-five years of German-Soviet and German-Russian relations that changed the face of Europe, and examines the rebirth of two new states—Germany and Russia—which continue to struggle with historical legacies that inevitably shape their present and future interactions. The book highlights the central role that Germany occupied in Soviet foreign policy prior to unification and the USSR's significance for East and West Germany. It explains the decision-making process within the Soviet Union during the dramatic years of unification, 1989–91, and the role of Germany and the United States in influencing this process. It explores a great puzzle: why and how Moscow assented to what had always been depicted as its worst postwar political nightmare—a united Germany in NATO. It analyzes the evolution of bilateral postunification Russo-German relations in the context of major multilateral debates about future European security architecture, and it discusses prospects for a future European security system in which Russia could play an active and constructive role. Looking toward the next century, it suggests different scenarios for understanding the future of Russo-German relations in Europe based both on patterns of interaction that have emerged in this century and on developments at which we can at present only guess.

There are three main themes in this book. The first is the centrality of the triangular Soviet–East German–West German relationship in defining the politics of the Cold War. Konrad Adenauer once said that his nightmare was Potsdam. By this he meant a U.S.–Soviet condominium to divide Germany and keep it weak. But for the USSR the major postwar nightmare was a revived Germany looking and marching east. In the attempt to prevent this from happening, the Kremlin created the GDR—a state that never enjoyed popular legitimacy and whose most successful industry was spying, not only on West Germany, but on its own people. By 1970, the Soviet leadership came to what proved to be a highly erroneous conclusion, namely, that the GDR was stable enough to pursue rapprochement with West Germany. This had a negative impact on the

GDR-Soviet relationship because détente with West Germany created instability in the GDR. By this point, the Soviet Union was already launched on its own détente policy with West Germany, but events did not turn out as Moscow had anticipated. Contrary to the Kremlin's expectations, détente with West Germany undermined not only the stability of East Germany, but Eastern Europe as well. Once the USSR decided it would no longer use force to maintain its empire in Eastern Europe, the Soviet bloc quickly collapsed. Even after the collapse, the complex legacies of past relations continues to shape the expectations of the new Russia, the new Germany, and the states that lie between them.

The second theme is how Germany was united and how the decision-making process within the Kremlin operated during this period. In 1989, officials in neither German state nor the USSR believed that German unification was desirable or feasible. Yet within nine months, the Soviet Union experienced its most dramatic reversal of fortune in the postwar era: the GDR disappeared, and a united Germany became a full member of NATO. A major thesis of this book is that the Soviet Union initially did not intend or expect either of these developments to occur. Gorbachev and his advisors mistakenly believed that reform communism or some form of left-wing social democracy was possible in East Germany, a belief they also held about the Soviet Union. But between the ouster of East German boss Erich Honecker in October 1989 and the assent to full German NATO membership in July 1990, the Soviet leadership was constantly forced to respond to events over which it had little control—events it had unwittingly helped bring about by eschewing the use of force. In retrospect, what is remarkable is the ineptness of the negotiating strategy, and the lack of forethought or clear definitions of interest or goals on the Soviet side, given how central the existence of the GDR was to its postwar foreign policy.

Even as the entire structure of its foreign and security policy crumbled after the Berlin wall came down, the USSR had no strategy for dealing with the fast-moving events, but pursued an almost entirely reactive policy. The Soviet leadership finally agreed to make the best out of a situation that was antithetical to its interests by bargaining for substantial German economic concessions in return for accepting German political conditions—an arrangement that was designed to ensure German involvement in the USSR for a long time and guaranteed Germany a premier role in the post-Soviet states after the collapse of communism. Thus, Gorbachev and his foreign minister Eduard Shevardnadze, as they presided over the collapse of the USSR, also brought about the rebirth of Germany as a major power. They were the reluctant midwives to two new states, Russia and united Germany.

The third theme is the impact of German unification and Soviet disintegration on post-communist European security. The legacy of the Soviet period is still present in relations between Russia and Germany, and traditional ways of interaction have survived the collapse of the system that initially produced them; yet German perceptions have caught up with reality more rapidly than have those in Russia. With the end of the Warsaw Pact and the emergence of post-communist, democratizing states in east-central Europe, a political and security vacuum has developed in the heart of the continent. Germany is anxious to fill it in a multilateral context through enlarging the European Union and NATO, while Moscow is wary of any expansion of Western structures that excludes Russia. Thus, the core issue is how to reconcile the competing pressures from east-central Europe and the westernmost former Soviet republics in a way that enhances, rather than weakens, European security.

This rethinking of European security will be directly affected by the developing relationship between Germany and Russia. Yet that relationship itself is intimately linked to the search for new national identities in both Germany and Russia, a process that holds both promise and great risk. The rediscovery and distortion of ethnic and national identities in postcommunist Europe has already produced disastrous wars in the Balkans and parts of the former Soviet Union. The process of Russia rediscovering its identity could also lead to greater instability on Germany's borders and to a possible exacerbation of nationalist sentiment within Germany.

For Russia and Germany, the redefinition of identity is connected to the search for a usable past. Neither country has natural borders and both have historically expanded at the expense of their neighbors' liberty and sovereignty in an attempt to increase their security and power. The Germans have come much further in overcoming their twentieth-century history than have the Russians. In the heterogeneous patchwork that is contemporary Russia, it may take decades to digest and overcome the legacy of Stalinism and develop a democratic, nonexpansionist national identity, as opposed to an imperial one. The ability of the next generation in Russia and Germany to integrate and transcend history and develop a bilateral relationship whose psychopolitical basis has moved beyond the Second World War and the Cold War is a precondition for the evolution of a productive Russian-German relationship in the twenty-first century. Europe's future will in large measure depend on whether this process succeeds.

The book is based on interviews conducted with officials, politicians, scholars, and those in the private sector in the former Soviet Union, Germany, Britain, and the United States. The interviewees include President Mikhail Gorbachev; participants in the negotiations that led to German unification, including the Two-Plus-Four talks; and officials who are involved in the post-Soviet German-Russian relationship and NATO enlargement. The book also uses documents from the SED (East German) party archives in East Berlin, as well as numerous German and Russian sources. Many of the participants in the events described below have written their memoirs, from President Gorbachev, Chancellor Kohl, and Prime Minister Thatcher to Foreign Ministers Shevardnadze and Genscher and Secretary of State James Baker, as well as numerous Gorbachev advisors and other German and American officials. Each has his or her own—sometimes contradictory—perspective on these events. I have taken these memoirs into account in the book, providing an evaluation and synthesis of their perspectives. Since most of the key participants have published their reminiscences and some of the archives have been opened, we will probably not know much more about the process of unification until the German Foreign Ministry opens the rest of its archives and until the Russians make both their party and Foreign Ministry archives more systematically available. This book moves beyond the unification period, however. No book on German unification that has so far been published has explored the development of Russo-German ties since unification or their role in broader questions of European security.

Vladimir Ilyich Lenin, once wrote:

> Russia and Germany are two chickens in one egg. One of them, which is much weaker but more mobile, has the thin skin of the Romanov Regime. The other chicken sits in a steel shell; it is weak, not very mobile, and cannot break through the shell quickly. And so it has come to pass that our two states embody the living reality of two forms of today's human civilization: German capitalism has the most highly developed technology, the highest labor productivity, organizational skills, precision, and great efficiency, from which we must learn. Above all, we must understand that it is necessary to learn from the Germans.[1]

Nearly a century after this was written, many Russians still believe that they must learn both politically and economically from Germany's postwar experiences if Russia is to make a successful transition from communism to a viable democratic, postimperial market society. Russia and Germany, interconnected on many different levels, have enjoyed an intense and contradictory historical relationship. Since unification the relationship has improved but it is in transition, hovering between past and future. Generational change will also have a major impact on future ties. The generation whose consciousness was shaped by World War II—of which Gorbachev, Yeltsin, and Kohl are the last representatives—is fading from the political scene. How will younger Russians and Germans, unburdened by the experience of the war, view each other? Their actions and responses will determine how Russia and Germany interact in the future. It remains to be seen whether the lessons of the twentieth century will enable Russia and Germany to coexist in a more peaceful twenty-first century.

Acknowledgments

I AM GRATEFUL to a number of organizations that assisted me in developing my ideas and meeting those involved in the decisions that form the core of this book. The Harvard Russian Research Center and its former director, Adam Ulam, provided me with a Mellon Fellowship, as well as intellectual stimulation and congenial colleagues, at the start of this project. The Aspen Institute in Berlin, under the leadership of the late Shephard Stone, invited me to become a member of an American-German Young Leaders Group. Over the half-decade we met in Berlin and elsewhere, we hammered out many issues at the heart of this book. I particularly benefited from discussions with Ron Asmus, J. D. Bindenagel, Dan Hamilton, Wolfgang Ischinger, James McAdams, and Bruce Scott. I thank the International Research and Exchanges Board for including me in the first (and last) American-Soviet workshop on Eastern Europe. Our meetings in Washington and Moscow, during the crucial years of the late 1980s, gave me invaluable insights into the evolution of Gorbachev's policies. The German Marshall Fund of the United States sent me as an academic observer to the first free elections in the GDR, in March 1990, an experience that enabled me to understand the momentous changes that were taking place there. The Council on Foreign Relations Task Force "Should NATO Expand?" influenced the evolution of my views on questions of European security, as did Women in International Security's conferences in Prague, Tallinn, and Washington on ethnic conflict and European security. The American Council on Germany and the Atlantik-Brücke also provided stimulating forums for the discussion of transatlantic Ostpolitik.

A number of foundations and research institutes assisted me in this project. I gratefully acknowledge the financial support of the German Marshall Fund of the United States, the National Council for Soviet and East European Research, and the John D. and Catherine T. Macarthur Foundation's Program on Peace and International Cooperation. I thank the International Research and Exchanges Board for supporting me during my stay at the Soviet Academy of Science's Institute for World Economy and International Relations in Moscow. Georgetown University and its Department of Government enabled me to complete the research and writing during two sabbaticals. Thanks also to Cambridge Energy Research Associates for opening up new vistas in Russia.

I thank the many people who agreed to be interviewed in Bonn, Berlin, London, Moscow, and Washington, some off the record but most on the record. The names of the latter will be found in the bibliography. Some of them talked to me several times as I was writing the book. Their willingness to speak and discuss openly some of these complex events added immensely to the written sources. Thanks also to Beate Lindemann and Lilia Shevtsova for their advice and for helping arrange some of these interviews in Bonn and Moscow.

I have also been fortunate to have had the support of excellent research assistants. My thanks go to Gabriel Al-Salem for his sleuth work in Berlin; Jennifer Long; Michele Raffino, who was instrumental in helping me complete the book; Leslie Sherman; and Cheri Woodworth.

I thank the following for their helpful comments on my manuscript: Thane Gustafson, Karl Kaiser, Catherine Kelleher, F. Stephen Larrabee, Immo Stabreit, R. W. Stent, and Steven Szabo. I also thank the political science and law editor at Princeton University Press, Malcolm Litchfield, for his encouragement through several versions of the manuscript, and Gavin Lewis for his excellent copyediting. Thanks also to my agent, Georges Borchardt, for his patience and support.

Above all, I thank my husband, Daniel Yergin, for his support and encouragement over many years and his insistence on high quality and clarity of prose. And gratitude too to my children, Alex and Rebecca, whose humor, patience, and unvarnished questions helped me keep sight of what was really important.

Abbreviations and Transliteration

BIOST	Bundesinstitut für ostwissenschaftliche und internationale Studien (Federal Institute for Eastern and International Studies)
CDU	Christlichdemokratische Union (Christian Democratic Union)
CFE	Conventional Forces in Europe
CIS	Commonwealth of Independent States
CMEA	Council for Mutual Economic Assistance
COCOM	Coordinating Committee
CPSU	Communist Party of the Soviet Union
CSCE	Conference on Security and Cooperation in Europe
CSU	Christlichsoziale Union (Christian Social Union)
DIW	Deutsches Institut für Wirtschaftsforschung (German Institute for Economic Research)
EC	European Community
EU	European Union
FAZ	*Frankfurter Allgemeine Zeitung*
FBIS	Foreign Broadcast Information Service
FDP	Freie Demokratische Partei (Free Democratic Party)
FRG	Federal Republic of Germany
GDR	German Democratic Republic
GRU	Chief Intelligence Directorate, Soviet General Staff
INF	Intermediate-range nuclear forces
MEMO	*Mirovaia ekonomika i mezhdunarodnie otnoshenie*
NIS	Newly Independent States
NVA	Nationale Volksarmee (National People's Army)
NZZ	*Neue Zürcher Zeitung*
OSCE	Organization for Security and Cooperation in Europe
PDS	Partei des Demokratischen Sozialismus (Party of Democratic Socialism)
PfP	Partnership for Peace
REF/RL	Radio Free Europe/Radio Liberty
SAP	Bundesarchiv, Bonn. Stiftung der Parteien und Massenorganisationen der DDR
SDI	Strategic Defense Initiative
SED	Sozialistische Einheitspartei Deutschlands (Socialist Unity Party)

SPD   Sozialdemokratische Partei Deutschlands (Social
             Democratic Party of Germany)
SZ   *Süddeutsche Zeitung*

Names of Russian people and places mentioned in the text are given in
the most widely used English transliterations in each case. Names of
Russian authors of works in English and German cited in the notes are
given as they appear on the title pages, as German and English
transliterations differ. Names of authors and titles of works in Russian
cited in the notes are given in Library of Congress transliteration, as are
occasional Russian words and phrases appearing in the text.

RUSSIA AND GERMANY REBORN

One

Comrades in Misfortune:
The USSR and Germany, 1917–1970

History goes in zigzags and makes detours.
Today, the Germans not only represent bestial
imperialism, but also the principle of discipline,
organization, harmonious cooperation in the
most advanced industrial country, and strict
accounting and control. And it is precisely
here that we are deficient.
  (*V. I. Lenin, May 1918*)[1]

The GDR? What does it amount to, this
GDR? It's not even a real state. It's only kept
in being by Soviet troops, even if we do call it
the "German Democratic Republic."
  (*Lavrentii Beria, 1953*)[2]

Russia and Germany before the Revolution

It is impossible to understand current ties between Russia and Germany
and the shadow they cast over Central Europe without examining the
rich, ambiguous, and compelling mutual historical relationship of the
two nations. On the Russian side, the complexity of these ties has been
part of a wider ambivalence about whether Russia is part of Europe,
whose destiny lies with the secular, post-Enlightenment, materialist West,
or whether it is a unique Eurasian country, whose natural allies are to be
found in the more spiritual East. This was the classic debate between
Slavophiles and Westernizers, a debate that has been revived in post-Soviet Russia and continues to influence relations with the West. Germans,
too, have historically shared a similar, although less sharply defined, ambivalence about whether they belong to eastern or western Europe. Some
Germans have traditionally felt a kinship with those elements of Slavic
culture that reject Western Enlightenment values, viewing Germany as a
central or eastern, as opposed to western, European country—part of
Mitteleuropa. As Germany's capital moves from Bonn to Berlin—a mere
fifty kilometers from Poland—these debates have been revived, and affect

contemporary German discussions about united Germany's future place in the world and its preference for integration with the West, rather than the East.

The contours of the twentieth-century Russian-German relationship were in place well before the 1917 Revolution and continued to influence the evolution of their ties throughout the Soviet period. In the prerevolutionary period, Germany was a more important influence on Russia than vice versa, playing both an economic and a political role.

Peter the Great first brought Germans to Russia to assist in developing the economy. But he, like many of his successors, and like some in the current Russian leadership, was ambivalent about whether Russia should remain involved with the West after it had reaped Europe's technical assistance: "We need Europe for a few decades," he said. "Later we must turn our backs on it."[3] Of course, whenever Russia turned its back on the West, it fell behind technologically. Indeed, Catherine the Great was more convinced than Peter of the need to import Germans to modernize Russia; she created a large German immigrant colony on the Volga which developed Russia's agriculture. The future of the descendants of these German immigrants has been an issue between the Russian and German governments.

There were also a significant number of aristocratic Germans who were important in Russian political life. The house of Romanov intermarried with the German nobility. Catherine the Great herself was German, as was the last tsarina, Alexandra Fyodorovna. After Russia acquired the Baltic states in the eighteenth century, the Baltic German nobility played a disproportionately large role in the administration of the Russian empire and in Russian intellectual life compared to the percentage of the population they represented. About one-third of high government officials were of German origin at a time when Germans formed about 1 percent of Russia's population.[4] The Russian minister who negotiated the Franco-Russian entente of 1893, Count Vladimir Lambsdorf, was a Baltic German, one of whose descendants later negotiated major Soviet–West German trade treaties for Bonn and another of whom became the first German ambassador to postcommunist Latvia in 1991.

German philosophy and political ideas also influenced the Russian intelligentsia, attracting both the right and the left. German idealist philosophy came to Russia in the eighteenth century and influenced the growth of Slavophilism. However, the Slavophiles, even though they admired German philosophy, did not necessarily admire the Germans. As Ivan Kireevsky, a leading Slavophile who studied with Schelling and Hegel, wrote in 1830, "On the entire globe, there is no nation worse, more soulless, dull and vexing than the Germans."[5] There were other meetings of minds between Germans and Russians in the late nineteenth century, particularly between German and Russian anti-Semites. Both the German kaiser and the Russian tsar regarded the Jews as the agents of capitalism and socialism and both were impressed by the forged *Protocols of the Elders of Zion*.[6]

It was not only the Russian Right that was influenced by German ideas. The Russian revolutionaries' ideology was, of course, shaped by Marx and Engels, although it was also influenced by indigenous Russian populism.[7] One could argue that in his Russification of Marxism, Lenin significantly distorted Marx's ideas; nevertheless, the impact of German revolutionary thought on the Russian revolutionaries was considerable. Moreover, the other major current of nineteenth century German Marxism, social democracy, also had an enduring impact on the Bolsheviks, even though it never took root in prerevolutionary Russia. Lenin and his colleagues viewed German social democracy as their main rival for the loyalty of the international working class and the major threat to the success of world revolution. Stalin's suicidal policy between 1928 and 1934 of encouraging the German Communists to join with the Nazis to combat the Social Democrats was a product of his distorted Bolshevik mentality.

Germany not only influenced Russian domestic policy but was also a major challenge for Russian diplomacy. Russia has confronted a "German question" for centuries, but the problem became more acute after the creation of the Bismarckian Reich. Germany lay in the center of Europe, the *Mittellage*, with no clearly defined borders, and its growing industrial and military strength fueled expansionist ambitions. Between Russia and Germany lay east-central Europe, sandwiched between two restless powers, both of whom had designs on the lands that separated them. Russia viewed Germany both as a rival in east-central Europe and as a threat to the Russian heartland, perceptions that intensified after it had been attacked twice by Germany in the twentieth century. It pursued a policy of domination of east-central Europe more consistently than did Germany and was more successful—especially after World War II—in achieving its aims. Control of east-central Europe was viewed not only as a means of increasing Soviet power, but also of protecting the USSR from another attack by Germany. Russian and Soviet leaders, therefore, largely perceived their security through a German lens—the weaker Germany was and the further its borders were from Moscow, the better for Russia's stability. The shape and fate of Germany were an *Existenzfrage* for Russian and Soviet leaders.

In the nineteenth century, Russia and postunification Germany enjoyed periods of both cooperation and conflict. Throughout all these diplomatic maneuvers, Germany became Russia's most important economic partner and remained so irrespective of the vagaries of diplomacy. Their mutual trade was always complementary and remains so today. Russia exported raw materials and imported German machinery. Germany was always more important to Russia than vice versa. From 1858 to 1872, imports from Germany formed 28 percent of Russian imports and exports to Germany 16 percent of Russian exports. From 1868 to 1872, the figures were 44 percent and 24 percent respectively; and in 1913, when they reached their height, 47 and 29 percent. In 1923, they were 25 and 30 percent and in 1932, 47 and 18 percent.[8] Germany was not only Russia's major source of manufactures; it was also its most important technological partner, particularly when Russia began to modernize seriously under Sergei Witte. By the time of the Bolshevik Revolution, therefore, there were few areas of Russian domestic politics or foreign policy where Germany did not have significant impact, even if much of the Russian nobility preferred French language and culture to German.

After the outbreak of World War I the Bolsheviks viewed the German imperial government as both an enemy and a source of help—after all, it enabled Lenin to return to Russia. When the Bolsheviks took over, therefore, the new Russian leaders placed their hopes on Germany, anticipating that a revolution in the country of Marx's birth would ensure their own tenure in power. They were, of course, sorely disappointed by the lack of successful revolutions in Germany.

Russia and Germany before the Cold War

The failure of the German uprisings in 1919 ensured that Bolshevik Russia would have to survive by itself, without international socialist support. Nevertheless, in the 1920s, Germany played a key role in enabling the Soviet Union to become a diplomatic player in Europe and in building up Soviet military strength. The USSR likewise facilitated Germany's rearmament. The two pariahs in the international system, the "comrades in misfortune" as Winston Churchill called them, who had been excluded from the Versailles settlement, began their clandestine military cooperation in 1921 and continued it until Hitler came to power. The Germans were thereby enabled to evade restrictions on their rearmament imposed by the Versailles settlement and the Russians to rebuild their military industry and their armed forces with the assistance of a more technologically advanced country.[9] The official diplomatic breakthrough, of course, came at Rapallo in 1922, when the Soviet commissar of foreign affairs, Georgi Chicherin, managed to persuade the reluctant German Foreign Minister Walter Rathenau to sign a separate German-Soviet treaty instead of an agreement with the Western powers who were negotiating in nearby Locarno.

The Treaty of Rapallo itself was rather innocuous. It provided merely for the resumption of full diplomatic relations, the cancellation of mutual claims, and the granting of most-favored-nation status, and it was separate from the secret military collaboration. Yet it symbolized for the Western powers the ultimate act of perfidy—the Soviet state, in its first diplomatic triumph, making a separate deal with Germany, persuading Germany to reject its western and eastern neighbors and collaborate with Russia to the detriment of European security. Rapallo was subsequently praised by Soviet writers as a model for future cooperation and was criticized by the West as an example of nefarious secret dealing, so much so that when Chancellor Helmut Kohl negotiated with Mikhail Gorbachev (without the participation of Germany's allies) the deal that enabled a united Germany to remain in NATO, the specter of Rapallo was once again raised. Rapallo as a metaphor has, therefore, played an important role in shaping the attitudes of Germany's and Russia's neighbors in the twentieth century. It also represented for the postwar Soviet *Germanisty* (German experts) an ideal model for the future.[10] It has provided a powerful historical image, used by critics and admirers alike to resurrect fears from a bygone era when issues of the future of European security are discussed.

During the Weimar Republic, economic ties between Germany and the USSR were a major factor in the growth of Soviet industrial strength. Germany was a far more important trade partner for the Soviet Union than vice versa, because of the limited market for Soviet raw material exports: imports from Germany, on the other hand, were particularly significant during the first Five Year Plan, when they constituted half of all Russian imports. During this period, the Soviets developed a solid respect for German industrial imports and the German business class developed a continuing interest in the Soviet market that revived after the chilliest days of the Cold War.[11]

When Hitler came to power in January 1933, Foreign Minister Vyacheslav Molotov declared that there was no reason for change in Soviet policy toward Germany. The Soviet leadership had read Hitler's writings and knew that the essential elements of Nazi ideology included anti-Semitism, anticommunism, a disdain for Slavs, and the belief that Russia was part of Germany's rightful *Lebensraum*.[12] Yet at this point they failed to appreciate how different Nazism was from other right-wing movements. Moreover, Stalin may well not have realized that the German dictator believed in his ideology more than did the Soviet dictator. When the Soviets finally began to realize the potential danger, they closed down the German military bases, began to pursue a policy of collective security with the West, and in 1934 reversed the previous Comintern line equating Nazis and Social Democrats, urging the formation of popular fronts between communists, Socialists, and other antifascist forces. The history of Soviet relations with the Nazis prior to 1939 involved both attempts to contain the spread of German power and the knowledge that, in order to stay out of a European war, which the USSR was ill-equipped to fight, there were good reasons for once again making a separate deal with the Germans. Moreover, domestic factors played a major role in defining Soviet policy. Between 1936 and 1939 the purges were in full swing, the entire Bolshevik old guard and the top military officers were killed, millions of Soviet citizens perished in camps, and Stalin remained obsessed with destroying any conceivable rival source of power.

As the danger of war mounted, and the Western Powers failed to stop Hitler's expansion, Stalin negotiated both with the British and French and with the Germans in 1938 and 1939. The traditional Soviet argument (and that of some Western revisionist historians) until the Gorbachev era was that Stalin genuinely desired an alliance with the British and the French, but that their dilatory tactics and anticommunism forced him to turn to the Nazis and sign an agreement with them in August 1939. Western scholars largely disagreed, maintaining that, from Stalin's point of view, a nonaggression pact with Germany was clearly preferable. An alliance with France and Britain would have involved the USSR in actual fighting, whereas a nonaggression pact would enable the Soviet Union to stay out of the hostilities altogether or at least buy time until it had to fight. Moreover, the Soviets would be able to take back lost territory from Poland—the "bastard of Versailles" as Molotov called it—and gain new territory.

Since the flowering of glasnost under Gorbachev and the opening of previously secret archives, Soviet historians have convincingly argued the mainstream Western case. They have shown that Stalin quite clearly preferred the German option to an alliance with Britain and France against the Nazis. Talks on improving bilateral trade ties began in earnest in 1937 and were at first a surrogate for political dialogue.[13] When the political dialogue picked up in 1939, Stalin was able to ensure that the Soviet Union not only stayed out of the war but also, by the secret protocols that were only very reluctantly released by Gorbachev toward the end of his tenure, acquired the Baltic states and parts of Poland and Rumania. The forced return to Germany of German communists, who had taken refuge in the USSR and who were subsequently to perish at the hands of the Nazis, was a small price to pay for this increase of territory and noninvolvement in the war.[14]

Stalin's refusal to heed the warnings of American, British, and even his own officials that a German attack was imminent was the ultimate testimony to his failure to understand Hitler and Nazism.[15] Despite this, as well as the generally cooperative Soviet-German ties of the interwar years, once the invasion took place, Stalin managed to tap a deep reservoir of anti-German and nationalist feeling amongst the Soviet population. It is quite remarkable that, after over a decade of social upheaval, famine, economic dislocation, and purges, Stalin was able to rally his people to fight and ultimately defeat the Germans. When "Death to the German Invader!" replaced "Proletarians of the World Unite!" on the masthead of *Pravda*, it was a sign that the Soviet leaders realized that the fear of the Germans, so deep in traditional Russian political culture, would come to their aid.

During the "Great Patriotic War," as the Soviets called it, the full force of the Soviet propaganda machine was unleashed on reinforcing the enemy image of Germany, as was the Nazi propaganda apparatus targeted on demonizing Russians. With 27 million Soviet citizens killed in the war and millions more who experienced great privations during the Nazi occupation, and with German memories of the brutal way in which the victorious Soviet soldiers treated them in 1945, the experiences of the period between 1941 and 1945 left deep scars on both sides. The image of the bad West German, successor to the Nazis, was a constant in Soviet media and popular culture right through the Brezhnev era, although officially East Germans were portrayed as "good" Germans who had had nothing to do with fascism. East Germans likewise portrayed the Soviets officially as liberators and benefactors. The reality, of course, was quite different.

The USSR and the Two Germanies

After the division of Germany, the USSR's German problem became much more complex. Between 1949 and 1990, the Kremlin's major challenge was calibrating its policies toward the two German states in such a way as to enhance Soviet security in both parts of Europe. The Federal Republic was the most important country in Western Europe, the key to Soviet strategy—the greatest challenge, but also the greatest prize. Despite periodic Soviet warnings about the dangers of German revanchism, the FRG did not present a physical threat to the USSR. The USSR was immeasurably more powerful militarily than was the FRG, and there were Soviet troops on West Germany's borders, and not vice versa. Nevertheless, West Germany challenged Soviet security for two reasons: it was the United States' key NATO ally and therefore central to the effectiveness of the Western alliance; and it was the only western country that maintained a persistent interest in a close relationship with an Eastern-bloc country, the German Democratic Republic. Its stated aim from 1949 to 1989 was to overcome the division of Germany, so it represented a potential threat to Moscow's sphere of influence in Europe. But West Germany also held some attraction for Moscow. If the dual Soviet strategy of containing German influence in Eastern Europe and wooing the FRG away from the United States had succeeded and the NATO alliance had been seriously weakened, the potential military and political threat from Europe to the Soviet heartland would have significantly diminished. No other European country affected Soviet security so directly.

The Kremlin sought to use the German problem to further its goals in east-central Europe. The West German danger initially served as a pretext for legitimizing Moscow's hegemony. After all, if there were no Germany to contain and no West German "revanchism," there would be no need for the Warsaw Pact. But playing up the German danger ultimately was counterproductive to Soviet interests in Europe after 1970. The Soviets had created and sustained an enemy image of Germany that made it difficult to accept the FRG as a reliable partner without diluting an important control mechanism both domestically and in Eastern Europe.

By the mid-1970s, most of east-central Europe had a favorable view of West Germany. The experience of thirty years of Soviet domination and the desire to find an alternative to Moscow-style communism dimmed memories of German behavior during the Second World War and led East Europeans to emphasize their common links with European—as opposed to Eurasian—culture. The intelligentsia in these countries revisited their links with German civilization and liberal traditions, contrasting these with Russia's lack of experience with the Enlightenment, Reformation, or other modern "civilizing" movements.[16] Just as the demonization of Germany, based on the Nazi experience, had initially facilitated Soviet control over east-central Europe, the de-demonization of West Germany after 1970 was a major factor contributing toward the unraveling of that control.

Moscow's German Problem before Détente

The Federal Republic

In 1945, the major Soviet preoccupation was to prevent any future German attack; hence the imposition of Soviet-controlled governments in a ring of buffer states between Germany and the USSR.[17] But did Moscow favor the division of Germany *ab initio*? Most Soviet writers and officials denied that they ever wanted Germany divided and blamed the West for the division. As veteran Soviet Foreign Minister Andrei Gromyko wrote in his memoirs, "All Germans, wherever they live, should remember that the Soviet Union never wanted the dismemberment of Germany. It was the USA and Britain who at the three-power Allied conferences proposed tearing Germany apart."[18] Stalin was at least ambivalent about the future of Germany. Newly released documents suggest that from the beginning he favored a united, neutral, communist Germany.[19] But, failing that, he insisted on partition. It is unlikely that in 1945, the USSR would have agreed to a solution to the German problem that denied the Soviets control over some part of Germany and access to what remained of its economic resources.

After the creation of the FRG and GDR in 1949, the major Soviet goal was to retain control over the GDR and create a viable government there. The main German problem was an *East* German problem. But there was also a *West* German problem, because Moscow unsuccessfully tried to prevent the FRG from joining NATO, and offered a reunification deal in 1952 to forestall West German military integration into the West.[20] Once the Soviet offer was rejected, Stalin told his East German comrades to "Organize your own state. The line of demarcation between East and West Germany must be seen as a frontier and not as a simple border but as a dangerous one."[21]

For the first twenty years of its existence, West Germany was a revisionist country. It refused to recognize the postwar boundaries of Europe, including the incorporation of former German territories into the USSR, Poland, and Czechoslovakia. And it refused to recognize East Germany or to have diplomatic relations with any country that did (except the USSR), although it developed a significant economic relationship with the GDR.[22] This was the essence of what the Soviets termed "revanchism." Although the specter of revanchism was useful to Moscow in justifying the need for the Warsaw Pact, it also challenged the weak legitimacy of the GDR by denying it international recognition. Moscow therefore sought to gain West German recognition of Eastern Europe as a means of enhancing the GDR's stability. In addition, from the late 1950s onwards, the USSR's political goals regarding West Germany were supplemented by a consistent economic goal: to gain as much as possible from its economic ties with Bonn and to separate bilateral economic from political ties. Moscow sought to reverse the post-1945 freeze on trade ties and restore the profitable pre–World War II links involving the exchange of German manufactures and technology for Russian raw materials.[23]

Nevertheless, from 1949 to 1969, Soviet policy toward the Federal Republic was largely confrontational. The Soviets accused the West Germans of being heirs to the Nazi state, and a satellite of the imperialist United States. Of course, West German policy toward the Soviet Union was largely confrontational too. Adenauer, the Rhineland Catholic who was suspicious of Prussia and its traditional links with the East, was more interested in Westpolitik (integration with the West) than Ostpolitik (rapprochement with the East). His major goal was to secure West Germany's full membership in the Western alliance.

There was one curious episode suggesting a possible change in Soviet policy, and that was Khrushchev's proposed visit to West Germany in 1964.[24] After bullying and blustering during the 1958–61 Berlin crisis, when the USSR tried to force West Berlin into becoming an independent entity, cut off from ties to Bonn, the Kremlin changed its tune in 1964. Khrushchev let it be known that he would visit the Federal Republic and there were rumors of Soviet-FRG deals in the making that were partly inspired by the obvious animosity between Khrushchev and Walter Ulbricht, the veteran East German leader.[25] The latter, a staunch supporter of the Stalinist system ever since his years conspiring in the corridors of the Comintern Hotel Lux in Moscow in the 1930s and 1940s, was aghast at the undisciplined reformer in the Kremlin and his interest in talking to Bonn, which would not even recognize East Berlin. We shall never know what Khrushchev's real plans were, because he was ousted a few days before his visit. There was a critical debate within the foreign policy elite over whether to adopt new initiatives toward West Germany, but the Soviet leadership decided that this was premature.[26]

By 1969, all that had changed. With growing economic problems at home and a realization of the benefits offered by a rapprochement with the West, Brezhnev decided to embark on détente. He was eager to deal with the two Western leaders who held the key to an East-West rapprochement, Richard Nixon and Willy Brandt. These two men, one who made his name as an anticommunist investigator while a congressman, the other a long-time socialist and opponent of Nazism, both outsiders in their respective societies, came to power just as the Soviets were reorienting their policies. Vietnam and the growing Sino-Soviet split provided the impetus for the Americans and the Russians to begin talks. For the Germans, it was a question of movement and rehabilitation. The confrontational Ostpolitik of the CDU had brought few concrete gains. It was time to change German policy.

The German Democratic Republic

The GDR was created by the Soviet Union and owed its entire existence to it. When Moscow decided in 1989 not to prop up the regime any more, it quickly collapsed. Nevertheless, it served three main functions for the Soviets: as the most important buffer state guaranteeing Soviet security; as a vital source of economic and technological assistance to the Soviet economy; and as one of the most loyal replicas of the Soviet political system, offering ideological and institutional legitimacy for the Soviet model.

The Kremlin pursued two major goals toward the GDR, one connected with Soviet Blokpolitik (policy toward Eastern Europe) and one connected with its Westpolitik (policy toward the Western alliance). Control of the GDR was a vital component of Soviet Blokpolitik, yet the Soviet attitude toward the GDR was from the outset ambivalent. Although the GDR was viewed as the linchpin of the Soviet security system in Europe, the Kremlin realized from the beginning that the GDR was an artificial state, dependent on Moscow for its continued survival. This gave Moscow considerable leverage over the GDR leadership, but also induced it to make concessions to East Berlin which it would not have made to Prague or Warsaw. According to Yuli Kvitsinsky, who began his long political career in the Soviet embassy in East Berlin, "Moscow mothered [the GDR] like a small child—most GDR functionaries were convinced that they could permit themselves any mistake in politics without fearing a loss of power. Moscow would rush to their assistance at the decisive moment and use every means possible to keep the GDR, because without it, all the Soviet positions in Europe would be lost."[27]

But East Germany also presented opportunities for Soviet Westpolitik. Moscow dangled the prospect of closer intra-German ties both to manipulate the GDR and to entice the FRG into developing a special relationship with the Soviet Union that might distance Bonn from the United States. In this asymmetrical relationship, the USSR had more to offer the two German states than either had to offer the Soviet Union,[28] but the danger of this dual policy—which became apparent in the 1980s—was that Soviet encouragement of the intra-German relationship might lead to an intra-German rapprochement that destabilized the GDR and lessened the Kremlin's control over it.

Moscow's opportunities for initiatives in its triangular German policy were limited by its concerns about the GDR's legitimacy. Given the inherent instability of the GDR, the Soviets sought to strengthen its domestic legitimacy and promote a socialist German identity. They also realized that strengthening the GDR's international legitimacy might reinforce its domestic legitimacy, and therefore pressed for international recognition of the GDR. Thus, securing West German recognition of East Germany was a major goal for the Soviets. But in fact the achievement of international legitimacy undermined the GDR's domestic legitimacy because, in the process of normalizing German-German relations, the GDR became more vulnerable to West German influence. This was a general phenomenon throughout the Eastern bloc: during the height of the Cold War, communist states were virtually isolated from the West, thus facilitating Soviet control, whereas détente ultimately undermined that control.

Once Stalin had decided that the creation of a loyal East German state took precedence over experiments with a united Germany whose future political orientation would be uncertain, Soviet policy toward the GDR became more consistent. In 1953, after Stalin's death, the German question became an issue in the ensuing power struggle. Soviet leaders blamed the ruling SED for provoking the unrest that led to the June 1953 uprising by trying to build socialism too quickly. In a conversation with the SED leadership shortly before the uprising, Soviet leaders said that they would strengthen their military presence in the GDR and would continue to fight Adenauer's "bourgeois clique," possibly utilizing the West German SPD in this endeavor.[29] But Lavrentii Beria, Stalin's last secret police chief, disagreed with his colleagues about the need to strengthen East Germany and is alleged to have suggested renouncing the GDR.[30] Beria was subsequently tried in secret and shot. But in any case, after the uprising Moscow had little choice but to keep the loyal through unpopular Walter Ulbricht in power to prevent the GDR from disintegrating. Although the USSR continued to discuss German unification with the Western Powers, the emphasis had shifted: until the construction of the Berlin Wall in August 1961, the preservation of East Germany, not the wooing of West Germany, determined Soviet policy.

The growing instability in the GDR prompted Khrushchev to take more drastic measures to secure East Germany's continuing viability, this time using Berlin as a pressure point. With its open borders providing an easy means of escape for the rising tide of refugees from East to West, the city dramatically symbolized the GDR's lack of legitimacy. Moscow's 1958 Berlin ultimatum, largely Khrushchev's initiative, demanded that West Berlin become an independent, demilitarized city, severing its links to Bonn. Documents from the archives show that Khrushchev played a major role in drafting the ultimatum and giving detailed instructions to the East Germans as to how the demands were to be carried out.[31] However, Khrushchev's gambit failed and, with the resumption in 1960 of the forced collectivization drive, the emigration situation assumed catastrophic proportions, reaching a peak of two thousand East German refugees arriving in West Berlin per day. Because this spelled near-term economic and ultimate political disaster for the GDR regime, the Soviets opted, as they had in 1953, for supporting Ulbricht, and they built the Wall. This marked an important turning point in Soviet-German relations: by saving the Ulbricht regime, and hence the GDR, the Wall ultimately enabled the Soviets to pursue a more flexible policy toward both Germanies.

By 1970, the USSR had achieved its main goals toward the GDR. It had created a loyal, dependent buffer state whose economy was a constant source of support for the USSR, whose army played an important role in the Warsaw Pact, and which identified itself ideologically with the Soviet Union. It was a staunch supporter of the Warsaw Pact invasion of

Czechoslovakia in 1968, because Alexander Dubček's government represented a double threat: reform socialism domestically which, Ulbricht felt, would undermine his power, and a willingness to deal with "realistic" forces in West Germany, at a time when Ulbricht insisted that no socialist country should deal with the FRG before it was willing to recognize the GDR.[32] After the invasion of Czechoslovakia, however, the Soviet Union's interests diverged from those of the GDR. Having made clear through the invasion that Moscow could control the pace of political reform in Eastern Europe, the Kremlin now felt able to pursue broader interests and sell accommodation with the West on its own terms—policies that ultimately threatened Ulbricht's position because they fell short of his demand for full international recognition of the GDR by all countries, including the Federal Republic.

The Legacies of the Past

The contradictory history of Russo-German and Soviet-German relations has left three major legacies, all of which continue to play a role in the postcommunist period. The first is a powerful one and, even in the nuclear age, as relevant as in the nineteenth century. It is the legacy of geography and resources and their impact on both countries' national identities and national interests. The lack of natural frontiers and complementarity of their economies inevitably produced both cooperation and confrontation.

Between Germany's first and second unification, from 1871 to 1990, its struggle to develop its own national identity and international role had a major effect on its neighbors in Europe. The European continent suffered two devastating wars in this century as Germany pursued its quest for a national and international role commensurate with its perceived power. Indeed, Germany was only able to finally emerge as a status quo state with a democratic, European identity after it was unified and Soviet power collapsed.

Russia's current and future search for a viable national identity and international role may well become the twenty-first century's counterpart to Germany's twentieth-century search. Its unresolved relationship with its neighbors and uncertain domestic politics have the potential to engulf Europe in more insecurities, even if its intentions, unlike those of Germany in an earlier age, are not malevolent. As an English observer wrote of Germany in 1906 (and the same might be said of Russia today), "Suspicious of all sentimentalities in foreign affairs, we have always acknowledged that *from the German point of view* the aims of German foreign policy are entirely justified. The only objection to them is that in no point of the world can they be realized without threatening the security and independence of existing states or destroying their present order. That is not the fault of the German nation, it is its misfortune."[33]

Russia's security, like Germany's, cannot be separated from Europe's security, precisely because of its geographic location and its resources. Russia is indeed a European power and will inevitably influence European developments, as it has for centuries. Germany's role will be much greater than it was in its period of limited sovereignty during the Cold War because it is now free to pursue its interests in the East in a way that was impossible while east-central Europe was communist.

The second legacy is that of cooperation between Russia and Germany. This partnership has had a positive impact both on Russia and on its neighbors, in particular in the economic, scientific, and cultural fields. The positive aspects of historic Russo-German ties have encouraged Germans and Russians in the postcommunist period to anticipate much more intense economic, political, and technological cooperation as a major factor guaranteeing the successful outcome of Russia's transition.

But other aspects of Russo-German cooperation have also historically had less benign effects. Rapallo, the secret military cooperation during the 1920s, the Molotov-Ribbentrop Pact, and Soviet–East German intelligence and military collaboration in repressing their own populations and those in other countries show that Russo-German collaboration has sometimes been a product of cynicism and purely instrumental need, of shared pragmatic interests that overrode other differences and were destructive of their populations' and neighbors' security. This historical legacy continues to raise concerns in Europe and in the United States that, despite major differences in the German and Russian domestic systems, they might be tempted to join forces in the pursuit of national interests to the detriment of their neighbors. These fears may well be unfounded, but they are a reminder of the power of historical analogies.

The third legacy is that of German-Russian enmity, which has produced two world wars in this century and which made the divided city of Berlin the most tense outpost of the Cold War. Soviet–West German relations prior to 1970 were also characterized by confrontation and tension and created fears among both populations about the other side's aggressive intentions. Russian concerns today, however, focus more on German abandonment than on German attack. Likewise, Germany fears not Russia's military might, but its weakness. Thus, of all the legacies, that of German-Russian antagonism seems the least important today. Nevertheless, it also reminds Europe that conflict between Russia and Germany can be even more devastating than cynical collaboration.

In an age when we are witnessing the rebirth of history in every postcommunist country, with its negative and violent aspects as well as its more benign ones, the ghosts of the past inevitably haunt the German-Russian relationship. Will an economically strong, politically united Germany achieve through economic means in the twenty-first century what it was unable to achieve through military means in the twentieth century, namely the domination of Europe? Will it reopen the territorial questions that the Second World War resolved? Will a new *Drang nach Osten* inevitably arise from the power vacuum created by a weak central Europe, a disorganized Russia, and a retreating United States? Will Russia, despite its weakness, revive its expansionist ambitions and seek to reincorporate the states of the former Soviet Union? Domestic developments within Germany and Russia, plus the evolution of postcommunist central Europe, will largely determine which legacy predominates in the next century.

Two

Prelude to Unification:
Moscow and Bonn in the Détente Era

We have troops in your country. Erich, I'm
telling you openly, never forget this: the GDR
can't exist with its power and strength without
us, without the Soviet Union. Without us
there is no GDR. . . . I want to tell you this
openly, as Communist to Communist: [the
GDR] shows a certain arrogance toward other
socialist states, their experience, methods and
leadership, etc. It is also arrogant toward us.
That disturbs us, that must be changed, you
must change it.
 (*Leonid Brezhnev to Erich Honecker, 1970*)[1]

I beg you to ask Comrade Ilyich Brezhnev
openly whether it is worth destabilizing the
GDR and shattering our peoples' trust in the
party and state leadership for the sake of two
million tonnes of oil.
 (*Conversation between Erich Honecker and
 Konstantin Rusakov, 1981*)[2]

Castro. We have a Communist party, but we
 have not yet built socialism. You have a
 Socialist Unity Party and you are already
 building communism.
Honecker. That's the dialectic. . . . There are
 different paths to communism. . . . We have
 now developed to the point where we think
 about communism. You thought about
 communism first and called your party
 communist.
Castro. It's Karl Marx's fault.
 (*Conversation between Honecker and Castro,
 1980*)[3]

THE USSR entered the 1970s with great expectations, at the height of its power. Having achieved military parity with the United States, enjoying what appeared to be a growing economy and endless reserves of oil and gas, and with a vigorous Brezhnev having established himself as the clear leader in the Kremlin, the Soviet Union, it seemed, confronted few obstacles it could not overcome. This self-confidence encouraged the Kremlin to enter into détente with West Germany, to remind the East Germans that East Berlin had to follow Moscow's orders, and to embark on various Third World adventures once détente with the United States was also under way. But by the end of the decade, an overextended Soviet Union, with a declining economy, restless East European populations, and an aging and infirm Kremlin leadership that had become increasingly rigid, had retrenched on détente. By this time, it was impossible to reconstruct the previous relationship with Eastern Europe, especially with East Germany, where the USSR had been the clear master. The Brezhnev regime was ultimately unable to calibrate its relationship with the two German states in a way that served Soviet interests in both countries. In particular, the rise and decline of détente with West Germany created the framework that determined how unification was achieved.

Soviet–West German Détente: Soviet Expectations

The impetus for Soviet–West German détente came from Willy Brandt, the first postwar West German chancellor who was willing to recognize the European status quo. The FRG initiated negotiations, accepted Soviet terms, and thereby made possible the normalization of relations.[4] But it is important to recall that the Soviets put feelers out to West Germany even before Brandt's election in September 1969.[5] The reasons for the change in Soviet policy were both domestic and international. In 1968, the Soviets had invaded Czechoslovakia because they feared the long-term consequences for their control of Eastern Europe of the dynamic, liberalizing movement that came to be known as the Prague Spring. Having reasserted its traditional *droit de regard* through the Brezhnev Doctrine, the Kremlin now felt that it could embark on a more flexible policy toward the West without endangering its hegemony in Eastern Europe. Moreover, there was a personal dimension to these initiatives. Soviet participants in the discussions that ultimately led to détente argue that when Brezhnev first came to power, he was weak, viewed as a transitional leader, and understood little about foreign policy. But he decided that an assertive, successful foreign policy would boost his chances of remaining in power.[6] Détente became Brezhnev's own personal policy, the basis of his rise to *primus inter pares* status among the collective leadership, to the detriment of domestic change.

What did the Soviets expect to gain from détente with the Federal Republic? They hoped that West Germany would finally cease to be a revisionist power, and hence would ratify the European status quo, thereby legitimizing their hegemony over Eastern Europe. West German recognition of the post-1945 borders was a high priority for both the Soviets and the GDR, since it would help to stabilize the GDR by finally bestowing recognition by the FRG which was the precondition for international acceptance. Moscow also anticipated that the FRG would develop a long-term stake in close bilateral ties with the Soviet Union. After all, the USSR held the key to intra-German ties. This was the ultimate lever that the Kremlin possessed in pursuit of its objectives toward the FRG. The West German political interest in détente would reinforce, the Kremlin hoped, its willingness to intensify economic ties with the Soviets, thereby creating vested interests in West Germany in a long-term cooperative relationship. In this way the Kremlin sought to move West German policy closer to that of the USSR without undermining the GDR; and Soviet expectations of détente were partly linked to their Blokpolitik.

But Soviet policy toward the FRG was also part of Moscow's Westpolitik. The Soviets expected that by developing an independent stake in closer ties to the USSR, West Germany might be induced to weaken its links with the United States and the Western alliance. Moreover, the Soviets hoped to gain greater access to West German public opinion as the number of links between the two countries multiplied. They could encourage "progressive" and "peace-loving" elements within West German society, thereby intensifying existing public dissatisfaction with the United States resulting mainly from the Vietnam conflict.

Clearly, the Kremlin did not expect to realize all of these objectives simultaneously or to their full extent. Nevertheless, those who supported Brezhnev expected that at a minimum, the USSR would finally gain FRG recognition of the borders of Eastern Europe and some improvement in political and economic ties. Still, a rapprochement with Bonn carried one significant risk: since the FRG now presented itself as a state committed to East-West reconciliation, with no territorial claims on Eastern Europe, it would become more difficult for the Soviets to justify the need for the Warsaw Pact. Détente with West Germany was not without potential costs for Soviet control in Eastern Europe.

The Brandt Era

The stages of German-Soviet relations from 1969 to 1985 were largely defined by the three administrations in Bonn—those of Willy Brandt, Helmut Schmidt, and Helmut Kohl. There was continuity in Brezhnev's policies from 1969 to 1982, followed by uncertain signals under the ailing Andropov and Chernenko, with changes coming only after Mikhail Gorbachev's accession. It is useful to divide the analysis of détente into two distinct areas of concern for the Kremlin—Soviet–West German relations and the influence of the FRG's *Deutschlandpolitik* (policy toward the GDR) on GDR-Soviet relations. Both of these had an impact on how unification was achieved.

Brandt's Ostpolitik

In 1967, the Kremlin had indicated that the Social Democrat and former Nazi exile Willy Brandt would be a preferable partner in any negotiations, and that his election would help to override the objections of those in the Soviet leadership who opposed a rapprochement with Bonn.[7] As West German foreign minister, Brandt had introduced a number of policies designed to improve ties with the Soviets and with Eastern Europe. He and his advisor Egon Bahr agreed that the Ostpolitik of previous German administrations was bankrupt. The refusal to recognize the postwar division of Europe and the ostracism of the GDR had not brought the FRG any nearer to overturning the results of Yalta and Potsdam. Brandt's Ostpolitik was one of resignation, a recognition that the FRG had to accept the division of Europe if it were to play a more credible world role. Yet he was never willing to admit that a settlement with the Soviets would freeze the status quo in Europe. Rather, he espoused Bahr's 1963 formula of *Wandel durch Annäherung* or "change through rapprochement," which argued that a recognition of the geographical status quo was a prerequisite to the eventual overcoming of the political status quo.[8] Bahr was widely criticized both at the time and subsequently for harboring illusions in this respect, but the events of 1989 bore out some of his predictions. However, what Brandt and Bahr envisaged was liberalization through stabilization, whereas what happened in the GDR was liberation through destabilization.[9]

The Soviet–West German Renunciation of Force Treaty was signed with pomp and circumstance in the Great Hall of the Kremlin on August 12, 1970. The two sides undertook not to use force in bilateral relations and "to respect without restriction the territorial integrity of all states of

Europe within their present frontiers"; but the FRG insisted, in a letter appended to the treaty and grudgingly accepted by the Soviets, that the treaty did not conflict with Germany's political obligation to seek reunification.[10] The signing of the treaty was only the beginning of a hard-fought and bitter process in West Germany to secure ratification. Although Rainer Barzel, head of the CDU, challenged Brandt in the 1972 election, claiming that he had sold out to the Soviets and East Europeans by ceding territories that had once been part of Germany and terming Bahr's negotiations a "criminal act," privately he acknowledged that, had his party been in power in 1970, it would have negotiated a similar treaty.[11] While the various Ostpolitik treaties with the USSR, Poland, Czechoslovakia, and the GDR were being negotiated, Brandt and Brezhnev developed a close relationship. At one point, Brezhnev is said to have expressed sympathy for the West German desire for reunification.[12]

Brandt had early on realized that Soviet economic problems had impelled Brezhnev to mend fences with his erstwhile Western antagonists. Since West German industry was interested in intensifying ties with a traditional trade partner, he was able to utilize economic incentives as a means of encouraging Soviet cooperation during the negotiations.[13] In 1970, West Germany signed the first of several agreements involving the export of Soviet natural gas in return for West German pipeline equipment and credits.

Under Willy Brandt, West German public opinion also became more favorably disposed toward the Soviets. Although there was strong opposition to the Eastern treaties among conservative voters, the results of the 1972 election showed that a majority supported the rapprochement with the Soviet Union and Eastern Europe.[14] The treaties with the USSR, Poland, Czechoslovakia, and the GDR rehabilitated West Germany in world public opinion, showing that the heirs of the Third Reich were seriously interested in reconciliation. Although Willy Brandt's emotional gesture of falling to his knees at the Warsaw Ghetto monument in 1970 irked some older, conservative Germans (and Polish Communists) it was a positive symbol for much of the rest of the world. By the end of Brandt's tenure in office, the majority of West Germans believed in the necessity of continuing détente with the Soviet Union and Eastern Europe. This was largely because the Soviets had prevailed upon their East German ally to embark on a rapprochement with the Federal Republic.

Ulbricht's Departure and Soviet-GDR Relations

The primary motivation behind Brandt's Ostpolitik was a desire to improve ties with East Germany, thereby making life more tolerable for its citizens and lessening the human costs of the division of Germany. (Brandt himself did not believe that unification was likely in the foreseeable future, but he wanted to attenuate the worst aspects of division.) The Renunciation of Force Treaty was a means to that end, an acknowledgment that all roads to East Berlin had to lead initially through Moscow.

Moscow responded to the West German initiatives by informing the East Germans that they should move toward normalizing ties with West Germany. At this point, Soviet Westpolitik took precedence over Blokpolitik. Moscow was willing to risk problems with the GDR in order to achieve its overriding goal of détente with West Germany. But the Soviet decision to respond favorably to West German initiatives precipitated a two-year crisis in Soviet-GDR relations and ultimately led to Ulbricht's fall—an event that took place in a manner surprisingly similar to the way in which Ulbricht's main antagonist, Erich Honecker, was himself ousted eighteen years later.

Soviet-GDR tensions over the future of West German–Soviet relations had begun to surface publicly in March 1969. At a conference celebrating the fiftieth anniversary of the founding of the Comintern, Politburo members and guardians of ideological orthodoxy Mikhail Suslov and Boris Ponomarev refuted the Stalinist theory that social democracy was the chief enemy of communism, an obvious olive branch to the West German SPD, which was already engaged in a dialogue with the Soviets. Ulbricht, however, defended the Comintern's 1928 equation of social democracy with "social fascism." The exchange clearly represented more than an esoteric dialogue about the theoretical nature of social democracy.[15] In 1969, as in 1989, the East German leader felt that Moscow was negotiating a deal with Bonn that would undermine East Berlin's position. Newly released documents show that Ulbricht was not in principle opposed to rapprochement with the FRG, but wanted to negotiate intra-German détente on his own terms, not those of Moscow.[16] He was dismayed by the prospect of a Soviet–West German détente which fell short of full de jure West German recognition of East Germany and unconditional acceptance of the GDR's borders. As he pointed out to Soviet Foreign Minister Gromyko, it was quite possible for West Germany to recognize post-1945 European borders in general without recognizing the GDR-FRG border, and he warned that the West German concept of "intra-German relations" was inherently unequal,[17] because it implied that the border between the two Germanies was unique and not one that separated two states fully sovereign in international law.

When it became clear that the Kremlin was pushing ahead with its policies, Ulbricht tried to link up with opponents of Brezhnev's détente policy in the Kremlin, particularly Politburo member and head of the

Ukrainian party Pyotr Shelest.[18] He stalled the Berlin negotiations as much as he could, but to no avail.[19] Ulbricht ultimately challenged not only Moscow's right to dictate the course of East German foreign policy, but also the supremacy of the Soviet model of socialism. At the Twenty-fourth CPSU Congress in March 1971, he invoked his personal acquaintance with Lenin, pointing out that his "Soviet comrades also had things to learn." He announced his intention to unveil a comprehensive program for "the developed social system of socialism," throwing down the gauntlet to the Soviet leadership by claiming that the GDR was an advanced socialist society, perhaps more advanced than the USSR.[20] As in 1989, here was a GDR leader contemptuous of the USSR's claims to superiority, who felt threatened by what he considered the Kremlin's overly conciliatory policy toward West Germany. But his colleagues, who had grown increasingly frustrated by his dictatorial leadership style, jumped at the chance to oust him, claiming to be more loyal to the Soviet Union than he was.

New documents from the SED archives reveal that Ulbricht's ouster was largely a product of domestic East German maneuvering, but that the Kremlin supported it because of Ulbricht's recalcitrant approach to Soviet-FRG relations. Indeed, Erich Honecker prepared an extensive collection of documents on Ulbricht's fall in the late 1980s in order to convey to his colleagues the message that he, too, had once been the architect of a palace coup and was therefore too savvy to allow a similar plot against him to succeed. In an attack on Ulbricht circulated after a Central Committee meeting in 1970, Honecker accused Ulbricht of a litany of sins which sound remarkably similar to criticisms made of Honecker himself in 1989: Ulbricht was arrogant toward the Soviet Union and unwilling to view it as the GDR's model; removed from reality and unaware of the real situation within the GDR; neglectful of the Politburo and over reliant on the advice of his own personal aide; and an exponent of economic policies that were detrimental to the GDR's well-being.[21]

At first, Brezhnev was not eager to back the revolt against Ulbricht. In July 1970, Brezhnev acknowledged in a letter to Honecker that Ulbricht was old, in poor health, and difficult, but he warned Honecker against taking precipitous action against the East German leader because it could disrupt relations with other socialist countries.[22] A month later, in the presence of both Ulbricht and Honecker, Brezhnev warned explicitly against infighting within the SED, stressing the importance of the party's unity,[23] and the East Germans agreed to heed his admonition.

By January 1971, however, most of the SED Politburo had decided that it was time to oust Ulbricht. They wrote a letter to the Soviet Politburo designed to persuade Brezhnev that the time for prevarication was over, and that the agreement they had made in Moscow in August 1970 could no longer continue. They not only accused Ulbricht of pursuing domestic economic policies opposed to the GDR's interests, but highlighted his opposition to the Kremlin's policies toward the FRG, hinting that the USSR's entire relationship with West Germany could be undermined by Ulbricht's actions. Stressing Ulbricht's opposition to Soviet policies, they asked Brezhnev to persuade Ulbricht to resign on grounds of age and ill health.[24] By this time, Ulbricht's obstruction of the four-power talks on normalizing the situation in Berlin had persuaded the Kremlin that he had to go. In a talk to party workers in Leipzig in November 1970, he had said (contrary to what Gromyko had previously discussed with him) that there was no difference between the West German CDU-CSU and the SPD, that Brandt and his colleagues were out to undermine the GDR, and that the GDR must be given a role in the Berlin negotiations.[25] This threatened the success of Brezhnev's Westpolitik, which focused on dealing with the SPD and excluding both German states from the four-power Berlin negotiations. In May 1971, Ulbricht resigned and Erich Honecker replaced him. Shortly thereafter, the four-power Berlin talks culminated in the conclusion of the September 1971 Quadripartite Agreement on Berlin.[26]

Brezhnev's attitude toward the intra-German dialogue was ambivalent. In the summer of 1970, he made it clear that despite the improvement of ties with the FRG, "there can be no rapprochement [*Annäherung*] between the GDR and the FRG. . . . The GDR . . . is the result of World War II, it is our achievement, which was achieved with the sacrifice of the Soviet people, with the blood of Soviet soldiers. . . . Without the Soviet Union there is no GDR."[27] However, he also realized that negotiations between the two German states were a prerequisite for the diplomatic recognition of the GDR.

The *Grundvertrag*, or Basic Treaty between the FRG and GDR was signed in 1972 after a period of intense negotiations.[28] Both Germanies agreed to recognize each other, albeit in different ways. Whereas the GDR recognized the FRG as a separate state *tout court*, West Germany treated East Germany, in Brandt's formula, as "a separate state within the same nation." In economic terms, West Germany's insistence on a special relationship with East Germany proved to be advantageous. Inner-German trade was considered domestic trade, making the GDR a de facto member of the European Community. No other communist country had such an advantageous relationship and it was the result of this curious recognition formula. Moreover, since trade was conducted on the basis of bilateral clearing, the GDR did not have to expend one pfennig of hard currency on it. But politically, the special intra-German formulation was a constant source of GDR frustration, especially when the USSR did not support GDR claims to full sovereignty with anything more than rhetoric.

In the absence of full diplomatic relations between the GDR and FRG, however, the recognition formula agreed on by the Soviets and West Germans left a great deal of ambiguity in the intra-German relationship and created the preconditions for the undermining of the GDR regime. Ultimately, the Kremlin accepted de facto as opposed to de jure recognition of the GDR. What counted for Moscow was that the GDR gain some form of recognition. But West Germany's less than full recognition did not materially affect Soviet security interests in Eastern Europe as Brezhnev defined them at that time.

The Basic Treaty's major positive effect for the Soviets was the GDR's belated entry into the international community. Prior to 1972, only communist states and a handful of radical Third World nations had recognized it. Now it gained international legitimacy, joining the United Nations together with West Germany in 1973. Moreover, this growing international legitimacy was initially a substitute for weak domestic legitimacy. From Moscow's vantage point, this was welcome. But equally important was Bonn's recognition that the key to improved intra-German ties lay in Moscow and that it was necessary to nurture cooperative ties with the Kremlin if intra-German détente were to flourish.

The Soviet Union's policy toward the intra-German relationship always involved a delicate calculus of costs and benefits.[29] It had to ensure that any intra-German rapprochement did not develop a momentum that it could not control, and it had to be careful to ensure that closer ties between the two Germanies did not undermine socialism in East Germany. Ulbricht had warned Moscow of the dangers to the stability of his society from increased penetration by West Germany. In the light of the events of 1989, he was entirely correct.

The Schmidt Era

Schmidt's Ostpolitik

Helmut Schmidt did not have the same emotional commitment to Ostpolitik as his predecessor. However, since he was chancellor almost twice as long as Brandt, he developed a broader-based relationship with the Soviet Union. During Schmidt's tenure, the United States became increasingly disillusioned with détente, finally pronouncing it dead after the Soviets invaded Afghanistan. The Federal Republic came under pressure to chill relations with Moscow that it to some extent resisted, particularly on the economic front. The resulting transatlantic tensions presented the Kremlin with potential opportunities for dividing the alliance. But a

number of factors militated against major Soviet gains, the most significant of which was Schmidt's commitment to containing the Soviet military buildup and remaining firmly in the Western camp, despite his increasing estrangement from the Carter administration.

Another reason for the lack of Soviet progress on improving ties with
Germany was Brezhnev's increasing incapacity in his last few years in
office. All the former Soviet officials who have written their memoirs
claim that after 1974, Brezhnev was only nominally in charge and was for
long periods too ill to function properly. He showed signs of decline
during his 1978 visit to Bonn, and on his last state visit, in 1981 he was
accompanied everywhere by a team of doctors and was only able to concentrate for a few hours a day. Brezhnev's long illness raises questions
about who was running the country and making foreign policy decisions
in the early 1980s. It appears that an increasingly gerontocratic Politburo
governed by consensus. There was, needless to say, little room for initiative in this period.

Schmidt continued the FRG's active relationship with the Soviet
Union. As he said after he retired, "For many long centuries, they [the
Russians] have been our neighbors, and because they will continue to be
so, we Germans want to have normal relations and live in peace with
them."[30] In the 1970s, there were two major bilateral issues—emigration
and trade. At that time there were about 1.9 million ethnic Germans in
the USSR, most of whom lived on collective farms in Central Asia. Like
the Jews, they had the distinction of being one of the two major Soviet
nationalities without their own national republics in the USSR and were,
therefore, technically eligible for emigration. In the 1970s and 1980s,
Bonn offered economic incentives to Moscow to promote emigration to
West Germany. The Soviets were willing to cooperate because the ethnic
Germans were not as highly educated as some other groups seeking to
emigrate. Initially, the number of German emigrants rose in the 1970s,
roughly in the same proportion as the number of Jews permitted to emigrate. After 1977, when ten thousand people emigrated, the numbers
declined, sinking to 460 in 1985; in all, during the 1970s sixty thousand
Germans were allowed to leave for the FRG, while sixteen hundred emigrated to the GDR.

Economic relations, in contrast to emigration, were a success story. In
1978, the USSR and FRG signed a twenty-five-year cooperation agreement, which sounded more grandiose than the reality, because it was a
framework agreement the concrete details of which remained to be implemented.[31] Nevertheless, in certain areas, particularly gas pipeline
deals, economic ties flourished. After the invasion of Afghanistan, the
Germans, along with the rest of the European Community, refused to

follow the U.S. in imposing sanctions on the Soviets; they also defied U.S. extraterritorial attempts to stop the construction of the Urengoi natural gas pipeline. Nevertheless, Moscow complained that economic ties were hindered by German export restrictions imposed under U.S. pressure.[32]

Aside from these areas of direct bilateral interest, the Soviet Union wielded important indirect influence over the FRG because of its presence in Berlin and because of the considerable influence it exercised over the development of intra-German ties. Disagreements over the interpretation of the 1971 four-power Berlin agreement persisted.[33] Nevertheless, Moscow chose to make West Berlin an "oasis of détente" in a desert of deteriorating superpower relations, as a salutary reminder to Bonn of how dependent it was on Soviet goodwill for undisturbed ties with West Berlin.

Although the Soviets interpreted Schmidt's Ostpolitik favorably, they became increasingly critical of his policy on missile deployments. Schmidt first called attention publicly to the problem of Soviet SS-20 intermediate-range missiles targeted against Western Europe in a 1977 speech to the Institute of Strategic Studies in London, when he argued that measures must be taken to counter the Soviet military buildup.[34] Schmidt's speech was in part a reaction to a more widespread anxiety in Europe that the U.S.–Soviet strategic arms limitation agreements represented a superpower condominium that neglected European security concerns, but it was also a genuine reflection of unease about the military asymmetry in Europe. The 1979 NATO two-track decision to deploy American Pershing and cruise missiles in Western Europe if arms control talks failed was a direct outcome of West German pressure. Schmidt's concern about Soviet military might and its political implications was a major setback for Soviet strategy in Western Europe, which sought to use military power both to control Eastern Europe and to intimidate the West.

As U.S.–Soviet détente began to wane, some sectors of the West German public began to express anxiety about the possibility of a nuclear conflagration in Europe—an anxiety that was reinforced by the anti-Soviet rhetoric of the first Reagan administration. Certain sectors of the German population, particularly the youth, became critical of America, and the USSR's peace propaganda found receptive ears among them. By the end of the 1970s, the antinuclear movement's ranks had grown, supported by the Lutheran Church and the new ecological political party, the Greens. For these groups, the United States was a greater danger to world peace than was the Soviet Union. They expressed understanding for Soviet insecurities and agnosticism about the nature of Soviet military aims which, in general, were considered benign and defensive.

The Soviets responded to the sometimes harsh rhetoric emanating from Bonn and Washington by increasing their peace propaganda and reiterating that they, unlike the United States, were genuinely interested in disarmament. The Kremlin regarded the peace movement as investment capital for the future: today's youth leaders would be tomorrow's political elite. However, the Kremlin's policies in this area also revealed the conflicting pressures of Westpolitik and Blokpolitik. The West German peace movement rapidly spread to the GDR, via the Lutheran Church which was active in both countries, and its members criticized both the American and the Soviet nuclear arms buildup. The antinuclear movement in East Germany formed the nucleus of a dissident movement that, a decade later, helped bring down the GDR.

Schmidt's Deutschlandpolitik *and Soviet-GDR Relations*

For Brandt and Bahr, the long-term purpose of the Eastern treaties was to attenuate the division of Germany.[35] But Schmidt had a somewhat more sober attitude toward reunification. He talked in terms of centuries, not decades. By the end of his period in office, however, *Deutschlandpolitik* had become far more important because the international situation had changed. As U.S.–Soviet relations deteriorated after the invasion of Afghanistan, the FRG and GDR sought to sustain their rapprochement, displeasing both of their superpower protectors. Of course, Moscow was reassured by the FRG's commitment to intra-German détente at a time when the United States was denouncing détente in general. From the point of view of Soviet Westpolitik, the West German interest in *Deutschlandpolitik* was welcome. From the point of view of Blokpolitik, however, the GDR's determination to pursue détente had potentially adverse consequences for Soviet power in Eastern Europe.

Under Schmidt, intra-German economic ties intensified. These ties included not only trade, but substantial credits from the FRG to the GDR, including a DM 800 million interest-free "swing" credit and many other visible and invisible financial flows, amounting to DM 2 billion per year.[36] Besides the obvious benefits to the GDR, the Soviets gained from these economic ties in three ways. The FRG's willingness to supply the GDR with hard currency via personal financial transfers, and with oil, eased the GDR's dependence on Soviet financial and material resources. Second, through intra-German trade Moscow gained access to West German technology, either directly or embodied in East German manufactures. Third, the USSR benefited politically from intra-German economic ties. Goods and money from the FRG helped raise the East German standard of living far above that in any other CMEA nation. This material well-being appeared to help stabilize the GDR. Consumer communism was to some extent a substitute for political legitimacy.[37]

The political impact of the intra-German relationship was more mixed. The Kremlin's problems with Honecker and his determination to carve out his own relationship with the FRG began shortly after he came into office. Although the Kremlin had supported Honecker in 1971, it became clear that the GDR leadership resented the Soviet-FRG rapprochement and was becoming increasingly jealous of what it considered to be Brezhnev's favoring of Bonn over East Berlin. The relationship between Honecker and Brezhnev deteriorated as the decade wore on.[38] The Soviets had their "own information sources" in the East German Politburo and became increasingly irritated by reports of Honecker criticizing Brezhnev and the Soviet Union. There was also a growing realization in Moscow that the East German leadership, not West Germany, was most likely to undermine socialism in the GDR.[39]

Under Helmut Schmidt, human contacts between the two Germanies increased. Before détente, 2.5 million West Germans and West Berliners used to visit the GDR every year. In 1979, the figure was 8 million, to a country with a population of 17 million, with 1.6 million East Germans (mainly senior citizens) visiting the West. These human ties were the main reason for the FRG's pursuit of intra-German détente, the political reward for economic largesse; and on the other hand, allowing these human contacts was the political price that the GDR had to pay for the undoubted economic benefits of the relationship. During these years, the pursuit of *Abgrenzung* (differentiation) intensified, with the East German government attempting to prevent contacts between West Germans and East Germans in sensitive positions, particularly in the army.

As the 1970s progressed, however, East German society was increasingly penetrated by West Germany. As much as 85 percent of the population watched West German television every night, emigrating in their living rooms. Not only could they view American soap operas; they could also see how well West Germans lived and how freely they could criticize their government. East Germans began to appreciate the contrast between the real quality of life in the Federal Republic and the way in which it was depicted in their official media. Since the construction of the Berlin Wall, the population had become fairly realistic about the limits of government toleration of diversity, and it had come to terms with a somewhat schizophrenic life in East Germany, pervaded by constant influences and images from West German television.

The most intractable problem facing the East German leadership was its inability to develop a separate socialist German national identity. West Germany acted as a strong magnet for the GDR population. West Germans were also Germans, and the idea of a socialist German identity propagated by the SED before 1989 never took root in the GDR. Ironically, after unification, it transpired in retrospect that East Germans did indeed have a separate identity—derived from years of political socialization and isolation from the outside world—that was different from that of West Germans and expressed itself after 1989 largely in opposition to what was perceived as West German condescension toward their provincial country cousins, the *Ossis*.

The reaction in both German states to the Soviet invasion of Afghanistan altered the Soviet view of the costs and benefits of the relationship.[40] The FRG, echoing other West European nations, stressed that the invasion was an East-South affair, not an East-West affair, in hopes of maintaining its dialogue with both the Soviet Union and East Germany.[41] And although the GDR officially supported the Soviet invasion, privately the East German leadership expressed its discontent over the lack of prior consultation. (Documents from the Russian archives reveal that few even in the Soviet hierarchy, let alone in Eastern Europe, were consulted about the invasion). The GDR leadership was determined to insulate its relations with the FRG from the harmful effects of the Soviet invasion. As both German states sought to maintain their dialogue, one high Soviet official complained to a high West German official that the pace of intra-German ties was "zu viel, zu schnell" (too much, too quickly).[42]

If Afghanistan and the NATO decision to deploy INF in Europe should arms control talks fail heightened Soviet concerns, then events in Poland in 1980–81 reinforced GDR dependence on the Soviets because of the SED's doubts about East German society's ability to withstand the Polish "bacillus." This led to a retrenchment in intra-German ties. From August 1980 to December 1981—from the founding of the Solidarity trade union to the imposition of martial law—Honecker was the upholder of Soviet orthodoxy. Shortly after the birth of Solidarity, he instigated a series of actions designed to set back intra-German ties. He doubled the minimum currency exchange fee for visitors from West to East Germany in order to discourage visits, and demanded that the FRG recognize East German citizenship for refugees from the GDR.[43] These moves to some extent assuaged Soviet concerns about the pace of intra-German ties.

However, these restrictive moves were partly offset by the GDR's policies aimed at continuing the intra-German dialogue. Indeed, in 1981, Honecker suddenly raised the specter of reunification. "Be careful," he warned the West Germans, "socialism will one day also knock on your door—and then the question of the unification of both German states will be posed completely anew." This remark may have been as much a warning to Moscow as an offer to Bonn. In 1977, Gromyko had said to Falin, "We certainly don't need a united Germany, not even a socialist one. A united socialist China is enough for us."[44]

The Kohl Era

In October 1982, the SPD-FDP coalition government fell, exhausted, divided, and without any clear direction. Helmut Kohl, a Catholic Rhinelander from Ludwigshafen, son of a tax official, who liked to refer to himself as "Adenauer's grandson," took over the chancellorship. Born in 1930, and therefore too young to have fought in the war, he joined the CDU as a young man and rose rapidly to power. A shrewd politician who was constantly underestimated both at home and abroad, he had opposed the Ostpolitik treaties a decade earlier. However, he was a centrist in his own party and was eventually willing to accept the fait accompli of the new Ostpolitik.

Soviet policy toward the Kohl administration went through various cycles, but its main thrust was a hardening toward Bonn and a visible downgrading of West Germany in the Kremlin's West European strategy until Kohl's reelection in 1987. It was natural that Moscow would look askance at a CDU-CSU government. After all, the CDU-CSU had vigorously opposed the SPD's Ostpolitik a decade earlier.[45] Yet Kohl made it clear from the outset that he favored continuity in West German foreign policy, while Foreign Minister Hans-Dietrich Genscher was a strong supporter of Ostpolitik. What irked the Soviets was not Kohl's Ostpolitik, but his Westpolitik, his determination to carry out the 1979 NATO two-track decision on deploying Pershing and cruise missiles to counter the effects of the Soviet SS-20 missiles.

Soviet ties with the FRG were also hampered by the intermittent paralysis of the Kremlin, with two infirm leaders following in quick succession. In fact, Yuri Andropov's policy toward the FRG, designed to prevent the deployment of missiles, was one of the few active—and ultimately ineffective—areas of Soviet foreign policy in these years, the other being a series of arms control proposals directed at the United States. After Andropov died and was succeeded by Chernenko, there was stagnation in many areas of Soviet foreign policy, including relations with the FRG.

Kohl's Ostpolitik

The Soviets were understandably wary when Kohl became chancellor. Nevertheless, they emphasized the need for continued good relations between the two countries, especially after the 1983 elections. It was unlikely that the new conservative coalition would dismantle the elaborate treaty system of détente that had evolved over the past decade, nor would it disturb the profitable business ties between the two nations.

According to Soviet spokesmen, the Kohl administration was a negative force for two reasons—its active support of the deployment of American missiles and of the U.S. Strategic Defense Initiative, and its endorsement of the revanchist claims of expellee organizations that refused to accept the loss of former German territories to the East. Before the missile deployments began in December 1983, the major thrust of Soviet policy was to appeal to the West German population to reject them. The Kremlin argued that the deployments were a breach of the 1970 Renunciation of Force Treaty and that Germany would now become a launching pad for an attack on the Soviet Union. Sometimes the Soviets stressed that the Kohl government itself had taken initiatives in this direction and at other times they emphasized American pressure.[46]

In reviewing the barrage of Soviet propaganda directed at the FRG, it is questionable how much the Soviets really feared the deployments and how much their campaign was rhetoric aimed at dividing an increasingly nervous West German public. Both factors probably played a role in the development of their policy. During the 1970s, the Soviets had deployed SS-20s targeted at Western Europe, which raised serious concerns about the European balance of force. In overall nuclear terms, the USSR was at least equal to the United States. Although American Pershings could reach Soviet soil from West Germany in six minutes, the United States had made it clear that the missiles were essential not for their own security, but for that of Europe. The real issue was minimizing Western Europe's vulnerability to the Soviet use of military might for political purposes. Some Western specialists stressed that the Soviets really feared the cruise missiles because of their great accuracy. But if the Soviets were so concerned about the Pershing deployments, surely they would have pressed harder for an arms control agreement. According to Georgi Arbatov's memoirs, the Soviet leadership was divided about the decision to deploy SS-20 missiles, but the Politburo went along with it because it was part of a continuous process of force modernization.[47]

The Soviet messages aimed at the German public invoked powerful historical symbols and stressed that Moscow had legitimate security fears, arising out of the Russia's experiences at the hands of the Germans in two twentieth-century world wars. Moscow claimed that since Germany had attacked Russia in 1941, it must be particularly careful not to threaten the USSR again. It also pointed out that the SS-20s were defensive missiles, aimed at countering a Western buildup. The West German Communist Party, supported by the Soviets, sponsored the Krefeld Appeal, which collected four million signatures against deployment. But despite all these Soviet moves, the missiles were deployed.

Having lost the Pershing battle, Moscow launched a new campaign against the Kohl administration: it accused the CDU-CSU of being revanchist and warned of the dangers of a new right-wing renaissance in Germany. The USSR was switching from a mixed relationship of partnership and confrontation to one of outright conflict. The Kremlin overemphasized the influence of neo-Nazi elements in West Germany. These groups did, of course, exist, as well as various expellee organizations whose members vowed to regain all the German territories lost in 1945 so that they could return to their homelands. After the 1970 treaty, however, Soviet rhetoric about revanchism had subsided. To some extent, the Kohl administration itself fueled the new Soviet campaign. Whereas the SPD had avoided giving any support to the expellee organizations, Kohl and some of his cabinet members attended their meetings. Of course, the expellees supported the CDU-CSU and not the SPD, so Kohl's actions were motivated by internal politics. The expellee associations contained some extremists who wanted to take back territories in Czechoslovakia, Poland, the USSR, and the GDR by force. The Soviets, of course, highlighted and exaggerated the influence of the radicals and the extent of government support for them.

The timing of the Soviet attacks was significant: the campaign against revanchism began just prior to the year devoted to celebrating the fortieth anniversary of victory in Europe. In order to recall and justify the sacrifices made by the Soviet population—sacrifices that continued to affect the Soviet population—the German bogey was resurrected. Marshal Ogarkov, then chief of the Soviet General Staff, led off the campaign, asserting that "revanchist, neofascist organizations . . . are galvanizing their activity . . . with the obvious connivance and even direct participation of the authorities."[48] A few months later, Lev Bezymensky, a major political commentator, drew the analogy further, linking the private groups to the FRG government and to Washington.[49] Yet, in private, Soviet officials admitted that the expellee groups were essentially isolated and that the majority of the population was not revanchist.[50]

Although the Kremlin downgraded its ties with the FRG to punish Kohl for his support of U.S. military policy, some cooperative links between the two countries continued. Kohl visited Moscow in 1983 and was the first—and as it turned out the only—Western statesman to meet with Yuri Andropov during his brief tenure in office, apart from brief conversations at Brezhnev's funeral. Foreign Ministers Genscher and Gromyko met several times, as did Genscher and Konstantin Chernenko, though these meetings were relatively unproductive. Moreover, Soviet behavior in Berlin indicated that the Kremlin still wished to preserve this island of détente: even at the height of the anti-revanchism campaign, Berlin remained quiet. In this case, actions spoke louder than words. A *Pravda* article early in 1986, while admitting that there were differences of opinion about the interpretation of the Berlin agreement, stressed the importance of maintaining the improved status of West Berlin.[51]

Kohl's Deutschlandpolitik and Soviet-GDR Relations

Prior to the Kohl administration, the SPD was more active than the CDU-CSU in pursuing *Deutschlandpolitik* and stressing the importance of eventual reunification. During the 1970s, as intra-German ties improved, parts of the CDU-CSU continued to criticize what they considered an illegal state and the conservative daily newspapers *Die Welt* and *Bild Zeitung* continued to refer to the GDR in quotation marks. When Kohl came into office, therefore, neither the Soviet Union nor the GDR anticipated that the pursuit of intra-German ties would become such an important part of West German policy. Indeed, the CDU-CSU arguably pursued a more vigorous *Deutschlandpolitik* than did the SPD. To some extent, this was in the Soviet interest, since it maintained the FRG's commitment to détente during a period of increasingly hostile U.S.–Soviet relations. But there were limits to the Soviet support of intra-German ties. These were reached when it became clear that East Berlin was more interested in intra-German détente than was deemed "healthy" by Moscow, particularly since Kohl's pursuit of *Deutschlandpolitik* had not led to any distancing of Bonn from Washington.

The Kohl administration pursued intra-German ties on a number of levels, the most visible of which was a series of new credits to East Germany. In October 1981, the Soviets announced a major cutback in their oil deliveries to the GDR, forcing East Berlin to spend $640 million to make up the shortfall on Western markets. Although Honecker entreated the Kremlin to reconsider its decision, warning that the GDR's growing hard currency debt burden could destabilize its society, Brezhnev answered that he could not reverse his decision because of the USSR's series of bad harvests, which necessitated selling more oil for hard currency instead of exporting it for soft currency to Eastern Europe.[52] Honecker's realization that he could no longer count on Soviet economic assistance by invoking political instability led him to deal with a man who had, until then, been a staunch anticommunist, long reviled in the East German media—Bavarian Prime Minister Franz Joseph Strauss. A conservative rival of Kohl's and an arch critic of Ostpolitik, Strauss put together the first of a series of West German credits from Bavarian banks,[53] a DM 1 billion loan that was followed by a second DM 950 million loan. Shortly after the first loan, the GDR government waived the minimum currency exchange fee for children and senior citizens and in 1984 allowed forty thousand people to emigrate legally to the West, the largest outflow of emigrants since the construction of the Berlin Wall. A number of cultural and scientific agreements, long stalled over the question of West Berlin's inclusion, were also signed.

Foreign Minister Genscher suggested part of the reason for this more vigorous *Deutschlandpolitik*: "The two governments [of Germany] do not want the differences over the missile question to lead to a deterioration of the general situation between East and West. . . . a return to the Cold War would have particularly serious repercussions for the two German states."[54] West Germany was determined to maintain the momentum of the intra-German rapprochement despite tensions between the superpowers. The invigorated *Deutschlandpolitik* was also the reverse side of a more active West German Westpolitik. One might even use a Bismarckian analogy to describe it as a form of reinsurance policy, to ensure continued dialogue with the GDR even if relations with the USSR deteriorated because of missile deployments.

West German political commentators linked the renewed emphasis on ties with the GDR to changes taking place in the Federal Republic, particularly the questioning of West Germany's postwar identity and a new search for historical roots. As Richard Löwenthal, one of the intellectual architects of Brandt's Ostpolitik, put it, the new intra-German relationship was a result of "first, the revival of a sense of German nationhood during the period of détente, and second, the rising sense that they face a common threat as détente has given way to confrontation between the two superpowers."[55]

Paradoxically, Kohl's *Deutschlandpolitik* made the German question less open, at least in the short run. The increased intra-German ties under Kohl and the repeated invitations to Honecker to visit the Federal Republic appeared to increase the legitimacy and stability of the GDR and reinforce its separateness from the FRG. This cannot have been the original intention of the West German government. But there seemed to be no way out of this paradox. A West German policy of intensifying ties with East Germany, undertaken partly to mitigate the effects of the deployment of American missiles, was bound in some ways to increase the standing of the GDR and to make it appear that unification was less likely.[56]

The East Germans had to make political concessions in order to enjoy the economic benefits of the intra-German relationship. One unwanted byproduct of these ties was the influence of the West German peace movement in East Germany, encouraged by the close links between the Protestant churches in both Germanies, links which were part of the East German quid pro quo in return for economic largesse. The church links brought financial gains to the GDR via the West German funding of social services—hospitals, kindergartens, old age homes—for East German Christians, but they were in other ways unwelcome. East German Christian antinuclear activists criticized both Western and Soviet policies, which particularly irked the USSR.

Had the East German government been well attuned to Soviet cues on the development of intra-German ties during the missile deployment era, then the Kremlin might have regarded Kohl's *Deutschlandpolitik* as unequivocally positive. However, Moscow began to realize that his policy was not serving its interests when the GDR stubbornly clung to the policy of intra-German détente. After all, Erich Honecker had received Soviet support in his bid to oust Ulbricht a mere decade earlier because he had endorsed the Soviet rapprochement with the FRG and the Berlin agreement. What had changed was Soviet policy, not East German policy. Although the GDR continued to be a loyal ally of the Soviet Union, it was unwilling to forgo the economic or political gains of intra-German détente. It was also displeased by the deployment of new Soviet SS-21, 22, and 23 missiles.

The high point of the thinly veiled Soviet polemics over the nature of détente was the cancellation in September 1984 of Honecker's projected visit to the FRG, to be the first ever by a GDR head of state. Honecker, who was born in the Saarland, would have visited his birthplace and the summit would have enhanced his prestige. The ostensible reason for the cancellation were some highly critical remarks made by a few CDU politicians. But it is clear that Honecker was forced to give in to Soviet pressure not to go, and that the so-called insulting remarks were merely a pretext for the cancellation. Newly released documents show that Chernenko's staff vetoed a German-German joint declaration that would have resulted from the visit. Chernenko asked Honecker, "Are you sure that your visit will not be used as an impetus to a stronger all-German mood and for more discoveries of differences between the Soviet Union and the GDR regarding the FRG and the Kohl government's policy after the missile deployments?" Honecker pleaded to be permitted to go the FRG until the last moment, but not only Chernenko but also Gorbachev criticized the state of GDR-Soviet ties, until Honecker was forced to cancel his visit.[57] Shortly thereafter, when Gromyko met with Reagan and the U.S.–Soviet dialogue resumed, the prohibition on intra-German ties was eased. But Moscow had made its point. However useful the Westpolitik effects of the intra-German relationship, the key Soviet goal had shifted back to Blokpolitik, to control over Eastern Europe, and if the intra-German nexus threatened that, then it must be sacrificed.

The fluctuations in Soviet attitudes toward the intra-German relationship under Kohl illustrate Moscow's ambivalence about ties between the two Germanies. At first, Kohl's intensification of the dialogue was beneficial for Moscow. The new credits not only boosted the GDR economy in a time of growing indebtedness, but also indirectly benefited the Soviet economy. Politically, Kohl's policy enhanced the GDR's prestige and perhaps convinced Moscow that despite the chancellor's active support of U.S. military policy, the intra-German lever might be productive in dividing the allies. However, when it became clear that the latter objective would not be realized, the Soviets began to reassess the intra-German dialogue's political utility. The GDR's unexpectedly positive response to Kohl, despite divisions within the country over the missile question, influenced Moscow to retrench its support of the dialogue. Ultimately however, the economic utility of the relationship was such that there were also limits to the degree to which Moscow would permit a retrenchment of the dialogue. As the Soviet economy went further into decline, intra-German economic relations were increasingly necessary for Moscow. This, in the end, hastened the downfall of the GDR regime.

The USSR, the FRG, and the GDR in the Mid-1980s

Looking back over fifteen years of Soviet-West German détente, a Soviet leader might well have been satisfied that many of Moscow's objectives had been realized. Bonn recognized the boundaries of Eastern Europe and the GDR. It committed itself to a long-term dialogue with the USSR and to a continuing economic relationship. Thus, the postwar period of West German–Soviet antagonism was over, and West Germany and the USSR began to return to more familiar historical patterns of cooperation. The postwar enemy image of the USSR had been softened by the Kremlin's willingness to sign the Renunciation of Force Treaty and other treaties. Key parts of the population—in particular the youth— became increasingly critical of American policy and some began to espouse openly neutralist views. Even if the government remained staunchly Atlanticist, there were enough currents of discontent within the alliance and interest in overcoming the division of Europe by finding a "third way" that there were possibilities for future change in German-Soviet relations.

Was West Germany equally satisfied with the fruits of détente with the Soviet Union? Naturally, the response to Ostpolitik depended on where on the political spectrum people were located. Generally, there was a consensus that détente had brought positive results. It had stabilized the situation in Europe and had reduced the consciousness of danger emanating from the East. It had led to closer ties with Eastern Europe, especially with the GDR. It had brought economic benefits and had increased the FRG's international prestige. Berlin, in contrast to the pre-détente era, was calm and relatively secure, after two decades of turbulence and uncertainty. Relations with Moscow were more predictable. Nevertheless, détente had not lessened the Soviet military presence in Europe—indeed, Soviet military might increased during the 1970s—and it had not removed the political challenge from the East.

Moscow's German problem changed after 1969. The German question was no longer one of boundaries or Bonn's rejection of postwar geographic and political realities. A German problem, however, remained. Berlin was a potential point of conflict with the Western powers. It was a powerful tool for Moscow, but West Berlin also represented one of the most visible outposts of Western values, culture, and prosperity in central Europe, always a potential challenge to Soviet control over Eastern Europe. Moreover, Berlin played a role in Moscow's other German problem, namely the relationship with the GDR, which became more strained after détente.

One could argue that the Soviets profited from the intra-German relationship in the 1970s. It prevented a worsening of the economic situation within CMEA by shoring up the GDR economy. Politically, it ensured West German recognition of the need to heed Moscow on ties with the GDR. But the disagreements with Honecker were a reminder of the difficulties of managing the intra-German dialogue. The archives reveal that the Soviet-GDR relationship came under increasing strain as the intra-German relationship developed its own momentum, and as Honecker felt more secure in asserting East Germany's own interests. In this sense, détente with Western Europe—especially with West Germany—was instrumental in undermining Soviet control over Eastern Europe, especially the GDR. But the seeds of this dilemma were already laid shortly after Stalin's death. The heyday of Soviet control had been from 1949 to 1953, the "nasty, brutish, and short" (to quote Hobbes) period of high Stalinism. As soon as Khrushchev began to de-Stalinize, Soviet control began to erode. In 1970, when Brezhnev decided to pursue both Westpolitik and Blokpolitik in Europe, he unwittingly set in motion a dynamic process that culminated in the fall of the Berlin Wall. Perhaps if there had been significant domestic political and economic reform under Brezhnev, and similar reforms in Eastern Europe, détente would not have undermined Soviet rule. But dynamism in Westpolitik combined with domestic immobilism proved to be a fateful combination.

The Soviet-German relationship during the waxing and waning of détente was central to the definition of Soviet foreign policy interests in both parts of Europe and a major factor in Soviet-American relations. What began as a process promising the Kremlin success on two fronts— the resumption of cooperative relations with West Germany and the international recognition of East Germany which would enhance its legitimacy—became derailed by the beginning of the 1980s. The double dé-tente (Soviet–West German and West German–East German) in many ways undermined the stability of the GDR which had been based on Stalinism and isolation. Thus was détente's fatal flaw from the Kremlin's point of view. It ultimately proved impossible to calibrate a triangular Soviet German policy in a less confrontational era.

Détente also led to a reexamination of national identity in both German states. During the 1970s, as East-West tensions eased, some West Germans began to distance themselves from their postwar pro-American views and reopen questions about their links to the East. Similarly, the East Germans, as they became more familiar with West German society during the 1970s, began to change their attitudes toward the West. Even before the fall of communism, therefore, a rethinking of national identity had begun in the FRG and the GDR.

The détente era reflected four major historical currents of Russian-German relations—a return to traditional complementary bilateral economic ties, whose interruption had been an aberration of the early Cold War years and which were a product of bilateral resource complementarity; benign Soviet–West German cooperation to reduce tensions in Europe; close, but strained and less benign Soviet-GDR cooperation to maintain the orthodox communist system in the Warsaw Pact states; and Soviet–West German antagonism over missile deployments.

When Gorbachev came into office, there was little reason to believe that the nature of the German problem would change. The West remained concerned that Moscow might play its "German card" and offer the West Germans a much closer relationship with the GDR that would necessitate a distancing between Bonn and Washington. For its part, the USSR worried about the stability of its most important Warsaw Pact ally. But Moscow was seriously out of touch with the real domestic situation in the GDR. With hindsight, one can indeed ask how the division of Germany served Soviet interests by 1985; but that was not the perception at the time. The division of Germany was considered the sine qua non of Soviet security.

Three

Rethinking the German Question: Gorbachev and the Two Germanies, 1985–1988

> Of all the countries in Eastern Europe, the German Democratic Republic was most dependent on Moscow's will. It was, so to speak "the jewel in the crown of the Russian Empire."
> (*Georgi Shakhnazarov, Gorbachev's advisor on Eastern Europe*)[1]

> I did not in principle exclude the reunification of the German nation, but I considered the discussion about this question on the political level premature and harmful.
> (*Mikhail Gorbachev, on his discussions with President Richard von Weizsäcker, 1987*)[2]

THE GORBACHEV revolution and German unification, both of which precipitated the collapse of the communist system in Europe, were arguably the most dramatic developments of the second half of the twentieth century, both of which caught the world by surprise. Given the human mind's natural tendency to infuse historical turning points with logic and coherence, it is difficult to accept the idea that momentous changes can occur as a result of confusion, an unanticipated conjunction of circumstances and non-decisions. Yet a close examination of the evolution of Soviet policy prior to and during 1989–90 reveals that German unification, although an outcome of Gorbachev's policies, was indeed an unintended consequence, and that none of Gorbachev's close advisors ever dreamed that it would occur during their political lifetimes even though some may have recognized that in the long run the division of Germany was untenable. The process of unification both invoked earlier patterns of German-Russian relations and represented a major break with the past. Thus, the issue of how Soviet perceptions about the German question changed during the first Gorbachev years is key to understanding both how and why unification took place so rapidly.

Gorbachev wanted to reform Soviet communism, not to destroy it. He wanted to create a stronger, more viable Soviet Union. Helmut Kohl wanted to improve ties with the GDR and encourage the reform of its repressive regime; despite his rhetorical commitment to unification, he never anticipated it nor, some might argue, did his party or any other mainstream West German political party seriously desire it. And Erich Honecker certainly opposed it. Yet, developments in the Soviet Union after 1985 set in motion a train of events that led to the disintegration of the postwar international system and the rise of new countries—a non-communist, postimperial Russia, a united Germany, the Newly Independent States of the former Soviet Union and postcommunist Eastern Europe. It should be emphasized that neither of these developments was inevitable. There were so many "mights." Gorbachev might have been able to salvage the Soviet Union had he moved more decisively on reforms and recognized earlier the depth of discontent of the non-Russian nationalities. Unification might also not have occurred had the people of the German Democratic Republic not taken to the streets to defy their leaders. The GDR might not have erupted in 1989 had Honecker retired earlier and his successors reformed the repressive system. Moreover, German unification might never have occurred had Gorbachev not managed to prevail over his opponents during a short window of opportunity in 1990. Russians and Germans today agree that that period was brief, and Kohl was able to take full advantage of it.

During Gorbachev's first three years in office, there were few hints of the revolutions to come. The Soviet Union's foreign policy was largely a continuation of previous policies. New Political Thinking only made itself fully felt in 1988. Soviet European policy sought to maximize political and economic contacts with Western Europe while at the same time trying to stabilize Eastern Europe through the encouragement of Gorbachev-style reforms there. This balancing act was, of course, ultimately unsuccessful because Gorbachev's domestic reforms and his new détente with Western Europe contributed toward the unraveling of communism in Eastern Europe. But it is important to remember that Gorbachev genuinely believed until 1989 that socialism in Eastern Europe, as well as the Soviet Union, could be reformed. Gorbachev set out to strengthen the Soviet Union domestically and internationally through liberalization and reform, but he did not realize the far-reaching consequences of his policies. There were a few in his immediate circle who understood the vulnerability of communism in Eastern Europe. These included Foreign Minister Eduard Shevardnadze, East European expert Georgi Shakhnazarov, and foreign policy advisor Aleksandr Yakovlev.[3] After 1989, Gorbachev's policies toward Western and Eastern Europe underwent major revisions because the environment had changed so dramatically. The pace of change accelerated beyond what any advisors had envisaged. But, by then, the USSR was largely reacting to events over which it had little control.

This chapter chronicles the USSR's struggles to bring New Political Thinking to bear on the German question and on its relations with its allies and with the West. It discusses the evolution of New Political Thinking toward Europe and examines the development of Soviet policy toward East Germany and West Germany, comparing the major bilateral issues between the two countries, the extent to which policy toward the two German states changed over the first three years, and Gorbachev's own shifting and uncertain German priorities. Germany remained central for Soviet policy, yet the definitions of Soviet security themselves were changing. Above all, coherent rethinking of European priorities became increasingly difficult against a background of growing domestic ferment within the Soviet Union, which consumed the energies of Gorbachev and his closest advisors. Thus, a preoccupation with internal exigencies created a more fluid and laissez-faire environment in Eastern Europe that encouraged change as the hitherto vigilant eyes of the Kremlin became less focused.

New Political Thinking

The Meaning of Ideology

Was there a conceptual basis for the policies that produced German unification? Or was New Political Thinking a purely rhetorical device that had little influence on policy? New Political Thinking was a series of maxims articulated by Gorbachev and Shevardnadze after 1986 that sought to apply the message of domestic restructuring to the realm of foreign policy. It became a group of ideas associated with the belief that the dialectical international system of the Cold War years was now a thing of the past and had been replaced by a new, interdependent world. Throughout the Soviet period, Western scholars and policymakers disagreed about the importance of ideology in Soviet foreign policy. Was the Soviet Union just like any other great power, pursuing its national interests? Or was it essentially different because it was a communist power? Did its official ideology commit it to a profoundly different view of the world, one that was fundamentally incompatible with that of the West? As George F. Kennan wrote in his landmark "Mr. X" article in 1947, "ideology . . . taught [the Russians] that the outside world was hostile and that it was their duty eventually to overthrow the political forces beyond their borders. The powerful hands of Russian history and tradition reached up to sustain them in this feeling."[4] In the West, conservatives stressed the uniqueness of Soviet foreign policy which resided in the fact that communist ideology was a major determinant of foreign policy and viewed any accommodation with the West as essentially tactical. Those who were more centrist or to the left of center believed that Soviet foreign policy was determined more by realpolitik than ideology, implying that it was possible for the West to make durable agreements with Moscow. While most observers concurred that by the Brezhnev era, ideology was used mostly as a rationalization for policies motivated by realpolitik concerns, there was still the question about how much Marxist-Leninist ideology shaped the Soviet leadership's view of the world even if it did not determine their actions.

These questions became much more pressing after the end of the "period of stagnation," as the Soviets called the Brezhnev era, when Gorbachev announced his commitment to New Political Thinking in foreign policy as a complement to perestroika and glasnost domestically. Many outside observers greeted with skepticism a series of initial pronouncements from the Kremlin that the basis of Soviet foreign policy had radically changed and that it would henceforth be "deideologized." With hindsight, one might argue that although Gorbachev announced these changes in ideology as a rationalization for a pragmatically driven, less confrontational foreign policy, there was a demonstrable connection between the espousal of New Political Thinking and subsequent changes in Soviet foreign policy.

After the collapse of the Soviet Union when a series of documents on Soviet foreign policy was made available, it did indeed appear as if ideology had played a more important role under Brezhnev than was previously believed. Politburo documents dealing with major foreign policy issues—for instance, the invasion of Afghanistan—stressed the ideological justifications for actions. Considering that these documents were not intended for public consumption, the perceived necessity to rationalize among comrades in ideological terms suggests that ideology, at least as a common language and a dialectical way of interpreting the outside world, were of considerable importance under Brezhnev. The Soviet Union indeed was not just like any other traditional great power.[5]

New Political Thinking, therefore, was an important break with the past inasmuch as it criticized many of the premises of Brezhnev's foreign policy and explicitly rejected ideology and the international class struggle as determinants of foreign policy. Without this fundamental change, it is doubtful that Gorbachev would have been able to adopt the laissez-faire attitude toward his fraternal socialist allies that he did after 1985. The conceptual revolution preceded the behavioral revolution, and New Political Thinking involved both tactical and strategic changes.[6] However,

Gorbachev continued to justify his policies by explaining that they would create a better socialist world, not by rejecting the premises of socialism. Many of Gorbachev's close advisors, in their memoirs and articles, stress how seriously they took New Political Thinking, because it renounced the previous class-based analysis of international affairs and allowed for much greater flexibility. But the rejection of the old rules of the game and the absence of new ones meant that improvisation in Soviet foreign policy became the norm, facilitating the events that led to German unification.

When Gorbachev became secretary general of the CPSU in March 1985, there was little reason to anticipate how revolutionary his domestic or foreign policies would be. A former law student from Stavropol, he had risen in the party ranks as a functionary responsible for ideological issues and was a protégé of the former head of the KGB, Yuri Andropov. He was an apparatchik, but a man of ideas rather than an engineer as Brezhnev had been. He first began to question the Soviet system after his comrades in the local party organization criticized Khrushchev's secret speech at the Twentieth Party Congress in which he denounced Stalin. Gorbachev's comrades, to his dismay, refused to support the attack on the "cult of personality." The next defining moment of disillusion was the Soviet invasion of Czechoslovakia. "How," he asked, "could we invade our fellow Slavs, who were not anti-Russian, and destroy 'Socialism with a human face'?" Despite these doubts, however, he continued to rise in the system.[7]

As party secretary responsible for agriculture in the early 1980s, his career had weathered a series of bad harvests, indicating that he must have possessed considerable political acumen. Since one did not become head of the CPSU by criticizing the party, it was assumed that although he was only in his midfifties and was of a new generation, his policies would not be radically different from those of his predecessors. Yet, with remarkable speed compared to the immobilism of the past twenty years, he announced his intention to introduce far-reaching changes in the Soviet system with two new slogans: glasnost, or greater openness in political life, and perestroika, the restructuring of the political and economic system.

Gorbachev's New Political Thinking in foreign policy was a response to domestic exigencies and flowed directly from them. Under his leadership, foreign policy was driven much more overtly by internal necessity than at any other time since Stalin's death in 1953. On his accession, Gorbachev was forced to acknowledge the unwelcome truth that the Soviet Union in 1985 owed its superpower status to only one factor—its military might. But even its military power was increasingly threatened by its growing technological backwardness and failure to progress to the Third Industrial Revolution, in contrast to the West and to the Pacific

Rim. The economic success of Japan, an overcrowded island nation with virtually no indigenous natural resources, was a particularly humbling example to the Soviets. Gorbachev and his colleagues acknowledged that if the Soviet Union did not become a technologically advanced country by the twenty-first century, it would no longer be a superpower. Since the new Soviet leader did not take over the Kremlin in order to preside over the demise of his empire, the most pressing need was to transform the economy technologically. This required an opening up of society domestically but also a transfer of resources from the military to the civilian sector and greater economic interaction with the West. A less confrontational and less militarized foreign policy was a prerequisite for these goals.

The essence of New Political Thinking, according to Gorbachev, "is very simple: nuclear war cannot be a means of achieving political, economic, ideological or any other goals. . . . Clausewitz's dictum that war is the continuation of policy only by different means, which was classical in his time, has grown hopelessly out of date."[8] Between 1985 and 1988, Gorbachev and Shevardnadze, furthermore, explicitly renounced the international class struggle. The Marxist-Leninist view of the international political system as a struggle to the death between imperialism and socialism was a thing of the past. International problems could no longer be solved militarily, and definitions of security must be broadened. Security must be mutual and international politics could no longer be a zero-sum game. One state could not enhance its security by increasing another's insecurity. The world had become interdependent and nations could no longer isolate themselves from each other.[9] Shevardnadze further stressed the need to overhaul the Soviet Foreign Ministry, ossified by decades of bureaucracy and lack of innovation and honest debate. Glasnost and perestroika must also come to the ministry, he declared.[10]

"Europe, Our Common Home"

Gorbachev stressed that his new thinking was particularly important for relations with Europe. The major slogan was a phrase that Gorbachev took from Brezhnev, "Europe, our common home" (*nash obshchii dom*).[11] The Soviet Union, he declared, was indeed a European power with historical and cultural roots in both halves of the continent. (Gorbachev also talked about "Our common Asian home," but never developed the concept as fully as that of the European home.) If Europe was a common home, then there could be a variety of connections between the Eastern and Western halves of the house, implying that the division of Europe could at least be mitigated, if not overcome. The common home theme lent itself to an impressive amount of linguistic ingenuity that enlivened Soviet writings on Europe. The metaphorical possibilities—the house itself, the apartments, their interconnections, the hallways, and the views—were endless. During the first three years, some basic questions preoccupied proponents of this theme. What should be the connections between the Eastern and Western parts of the house? How would the most complex part of the house—the divided German apartment—be constructed? Would the United States lease a room as a permanent lodger in one of the Western apartments or could it be only a temporary tenant?

Most commentators, while suggesting that the Eastern and Western apartments should build more connecting rooms, stressed that they would still remain separate. Seasoned political commentator Yuri Zhukov, for instance, wrote, "It was willed by history that Europe should stay divided for centuries although the peoples inhabiting it have always had much in common. Realists are aware that frontiers resulting from war, particularly a world war, can only be altered by a new war which in the nuclear age would be suicidal for humanity."[12] Two Foreign Ministry officials predicted that "the system of security in Europe will evidently still long be based on the existence of two military blocs. Greater security will be achieved by adjusting their relations rather than disbanding them."[13] One writer went further, saying that the real importance of the common European home would be that Western Europe would stabilize Eastern Europe economically.[14]

There were few clues, prior to 1989, about the architecture of the German apartments. In what was to be one of the more tantalizing comments on this theme, veteran German expert and Central Committee advisor, Nikolai Portugalov, made a prescient prediction: "One can well imagine that the owners of two sovereign and independent German flats, each living his own lifestyle, would maintain close relations, all the more so as when both speak the same language, it is easier to reach agreement. And then there would come a time when the obnoxious alien military presence would be removed from the flats in the central part of the house."[15]

The issue on which there was considerable movement during the first three Gorbachev years was America's place in the common home. At the beginning, Soviet commentators suggested that the United States would not be a full-time resident. However, by 1987 most officials had accepted that the United States would remain a European power. In May 1987, Gorbachev said, "The historical relationship between Western Europe and the United States, or, say, between the Soviet Union and the European socialist countries, is a political reality. It may not be ignored if one pursues a realistic policy. A different attitude would upset the existing equilibrium in Europe."[16] In retrospect, the willingness to admit that the

United States had a legitimate role in Western Europe may have been motivated by the desire to affirm that the Soviet Union had a legitimate role in Eastern Europe, as the East European populations increasingly questioned this foundation of postwar Soviet policy.

When Gorbachev came to power, he was aware that the situation in Eastern Europe was serious. But he diagnosed the problem as one of performance rather than a crisis of the entire system. His initial message to Eastern Europe was, therefore, to emulate the Soviet Union and introduce reforms that would rejuvenate socialism. In the eyes of the majority of East Europeans, socialism had lost whatever attraction it had once had as a system that delivered basic economic well-being and social justice. Whereas many East Europeans welcomed Gorbachev's domestic reforms and viewed him as an antidote to their repressive leaders, the majority of them did not favor the reform of socialism—they wanted to get rid of it. But, Eastern Europe was still viewed as essential to the USSR's security—in all its dimensions. It was inconceivable that the Soviet Union could survive and prosper without its fraternal allies, with whom it was so closely linked politically, economically, militarily, and ideologically.

Gorbachev's early pronouncements on Eastern Europe sounded positively Brezhnevite. Relations with socialist allies were, he said, "based on the full equality and comradely mutual assistance of sovereign states" who uphold "the principle of socialist internationalism."[17] Subsequent pronouncements by high-level officials claimed that "imperialists" were slandering the concept of proletarian internationalism and that the relationship between fraternal allies was not changing. The Warsaw Pact was renewed for twenty years in April 1985 with no modification in its organization or purpose.

However, other, more moderate voices were beginning to emerge.[18] At the Twenty-seventh Party Congress, the first to be held since Brezhnev's death, Gorbachev's speech on foreign policy contained the seeds of change. Declaring that "radical reform is necessary," he catalogued the sins of Soviet leaders from Stalin to Brezhnev, who had stifled socialism with bureaucracy and personality cults.[19] The implication was that what had gone wrong in the Soviet Union had also gone awry in Eastern Europe. But if Gorbachev was criticizing socialism within the USSR and Eastern Europe, he was not yet prepared to reject the principle of Soviet hegemony in Eastern Europe. "We have significantly strengthened the position . . . of world socialism in the international arena," he declared, adding, "We believe that the diversity of our movement is not synonymous with disunity."

The Twenty-seventh Party Congress bore certain similarities to the Twentieth Party Congress, when Khrushchev shocked the world by denouncing Stalin and committed himself to a new course in the Soviet Union. Like Khrushchev, Gorbachev believed that the Soviet system had to change, and realized that Eastern Europe would have to reform too. But, like Khrushchev, he did not think through the implications of change in the Soviet Union for Eastern Europe. Indeed, one of Gorbachev's weaknesses was that he failed to give the East Europeans clear guidelines about the degree to which they could deviate from the Soviet Union in their societal organization. If Stalin and Brezhnev had committed major sins, then how could one confine one's criticisms to domestic policy or policy toward the West? Surely their policies toward Eastern Europe were equally open to criticism? Both Khrushchev and Gorbachev sought to insulate their domestic reforms from change in their relations with their satellites. In Khrushchev's case, Soviet troops had to put down uprisings in East Germany and Hungary as a result of the Kremlin's failure to appreciate the consequences of demanding radical change at home. But Gorbachev would eventually make the political decision not to use force—with very different consequences. Yet it was inevitable that, when East Europeans heard Gorbachev stress the need for reform and reject Brezhnev's policies, they should assume that these remarks also applied to their relations with Moscow.

Gorbachev's policy toward Eastern Europe in his first few years was contradictory, combining orthodoxy with a few tantalizing hints of change. One of these came from Aleksandr Yakovlev who said early on in 1989 that it was conceivable that some of the Eastern European apartments in the common European home might have "Finnish furnishings," implying more autonomy from Moscow.[20] This lack of imagination about the Eastern apartments reflected a basic problem with New Political Thinking. While Gorbachev stressed the need for glasnost and perestroika in Eastern Europe, his policies toward his Warsaw Pact allies right from the beginning were reactive, not proactive. The stakes involved in Eastern Europe were much higher than those in Western Europe, yet the room for maneuver was narrower and the problems both within Eastern Europe and between Eastern Europe and the Soviet Union more intractable. They could not be fixed by arms control agreements or high-level summits. The Soviet empire had lost its legitimacy, but Gorbachev and his advisors were not ready to recognize this reality in the first few years.[21] Thus, Gorbachev confined himself to criticizing Brezhnev's policies in the region, intimating that Eastern European countries should emulate glasnost and perestroika and solve their economic and political problems in their own way. This policy was dubbed in 1989 by Gorbachev's sardonic press spokesman, Gennadi Gerasimov, the "Sinatra Doctrine," as in "I Did It My Way." However, the "Sinatra

Doctrine" in fact became the Gorbachev Doctrine, as the Soviet leader urged his fraternal partners to adopt Soviet-style reforms. Eastern Europe should, in fact, do it "their way," in the Soviet mold.[22]

The other theme in New Political Thinking on Eastern Europe was the gradual renunciation of the Brezhnev Doctrine. Slowly, Gorbachev and his advisers admitted that the Soviet Union would no longer use military force to impose stability on its partners. During a trip to Yugoslavia, Gorbachev apologized for past Soviet mistakes and reiterated that every socialist state had the right to determine its own future without interference, acknowledging that "no one has a monopoly on the truth." He made similar remarks on a visit to Prague in 1987. When asked what the difference was between Dubček and Gorbachev, Gerasimov replied simply, "Nineteen years."

Until 1988, Gorbachev's team advising him on Eastern Europe was concentrated in the CPSU Central Committee's International Department, headed by longtime ambassador to the United States Anatoly Dobrynin, and its Information and Propaganda Department, led by Aleksandr Yakovlev, whose deputy, Nikolai Shishlin, was an East European expert. The Central Committee secretary in charge of relations with the Socialist countries was Vadim Medvedev, whose large staff worked for the Central Committee's Department for Liaison with the Communist and Workers' Parties of Socialist Countries. These top policymakers belonged to the CPSU's reformist wing. In April 1988, presaging a change in his view of Eastern Europe, Gorbachev abolished the Department for Liaison, which had always coordinated Soviet policy in Eastern Europe, and created a Politburo Commission on International Policy, headed by Yakovlev, whose task was to coordinate policy toward Eastern Europe and the rest of the world. In September 1988, the International Department was reorganized, reduced in size and given a new head—Valentin Falin, a German specialist, who was to play a largely obstructionist role in 1989–90. His first deputy chief, Rafael P. Fyodorov, also a hardliner on German issues, was responsible for Eastern Europe. The tenor of his views was suggested by a conversation in Moscow in September 1989 where he declared that there were "too many Jews in the Hungarian Communist leadership," warned about the dangers from Germany, and suggested joint U.S.–Soviet action to combat their mutual German enemy.[23]

As the debate over policy toward Eastern Europe intensified, it became increasingly clear that if Gorbachev and his colleagues truly believed in freedom of choice, then this had to apply to countries other than the Soviet Union. As he himself had written, "every nation is entitled to choose its own way of development, to dispose of its fate, its territory and its human and natural resources."[24] With hindsight, Gorbachev stresses that it was his commitment to freedom of choice that ultimately affected his decisions on Eastern Europe and East Germany.[25] Moreover, East Europeans drew their own conclusions about the far-reaching implications of Gorbachev's military policy. By the end of 1988, Gorbachev had signed the INF agreement, had agreed to conventional force reductions in Europe, and had announced a unilateral withdrawal of 50,000 Soviet troops (out of 565,000) and 5,000 tanks from Eastern Europe. If, in fact, the USSR and Western Europe were to enjoy more cooperative military relations and the Soviet Union stressed the defensive nature of its doctrine and posture, then it became increasingly unlikely that the Kremlin could engage in a secret military buildup similar to that preceding the invasion of Czechoslovakia in 1968 without seriously endangering its new détente with the West.

Throughout these first three years, the dual debate, over domestic East European reform and over Soviet relations with Eastern Europe, continued. More liberal Soviet commentators began to admit that relations between the Kremlin and its allies would have to change radically. Gorbachev was more cautious, suggesting, in his 1987 visit to Prague and in other gatherings, that the Soviet Union did not have the right to interfere in the internal affairs of its allies. The Aesopian language about Eastern Europe remained, with few clear guidelines for the relationship. This ambiguity was a deliberate part of the Khrushchev/Brezhnev strategy. Gorbachev and most of his advisors found it difficult to envisage a more equal relationship with allies that would nevertheless preserve Soviet hegemony in the area. And while many were ready to accept reforms and change within the socialist fraternity, no one was prepared to renounce hegemony altogether. Additionally, many of the old guard in Eastern Europe, who had come to power under Brezhnev, increasingly resented Gorbachev's pressure to reform and became more determined to distance themselves from the Soviet leader in order to hang on to power. The most passionate and stubborn of all was Erich Honecker of East Germany.

Gorbachev and East Germany, 1985–1988

"Es war eine Intimfeindschaft" (they were intimate enemies) declares Günter Schabowski, the last party boss of East Berlin, of the Honecker-Gorbachev relationship.[26] After all, Honecker, as a loyal Communist of the old school trained in Moscow, believed that Moscow held the key to the ultimate socialist truth. He once said that he grew up among people "whose relationship to the Soviet Union was . . . a holy principle . . . and the measure of whether they were really Communists."[27] But his reverence for the motherland of socialism was increasingly tempered by his discomfort at the new leader. Soviet-GDR relations were already tense when Gorbachev came to power, but they deteriorated rapidly as he pursued his reform course. In the beginning, Gorbachev viewed East Germany as the bulwark of Soviet security in Eastern Europe, admired its economic achievements, and believed that he could improve ties with the Honecker government after the tensions of the preceding years. After the 1987 West German elections and the beginning of the new rapprochement with the FRG, relations with East Germany became more antagonistic, largely because of Honecker's growing resistance to implementing Gorbachev's reforms domestically. As the West German threat receded, the potential danger to the Soviet Union from the GDR began to grow.

There were three major issues in the Soviet-GDR relationship: foreign policy, domestic economic reform (perestroika), and domestic political reform (glasnost). Whereas the GDR mostly supported Soviet foreign policy, it felt increasingly threatened by Moscow's pressure to introduce domestic reforms.

Foreign Policy

When Gorbachev first came to power and enunciated the principles of New Political Thinking in foreign policy, the GDR leadership was elated. After five years of Soviet opposition to the inter-German dialogue and to Honecker's insistence on maintaining détente in Europe, Gorbachev criticized the Brezhnev-era policies and suggested major arms control measures. Honecker felt vindicated. According to Schabowski, he "considered himself the number one expert on the FRG in the Warsaw Pact" and expected Gorbachev to listen to his wisdom on this subject.[28] Honecker had first met Gorbachev in 1966, when the latter had visited the GDR as a provincial party secretary to study East German economic reforms. The young Soviet politician was impressed by what the GDR had achieved after the devastation of the war.[29] Their first really substantive meeting was in May 1985, and their joint communiqué said that both leaders rejected "all concepts . . . that proceed from the postulate of an unresolved German question."[30]

Gorbachev underscored the renewed importance of the GDR by attending the Eleventh (and last) SED Party Congress in East Berlin in April 1986, the first time in fifteen years that a Soviet general secretary had attended an SED Congress.[31] Declaring "complete agreement on all basic questions," the two leaders criticized the FRG for its "revanchist" policy on the German question, but agreed that the dialogue with Bonn must continue because of the necessity of preserving peace in Europe. Yet when Honecker raised with Gorbachev the subject of visiting the Federal Republic, the Soviet leader, citing the danger from Pershing missiles, asked "What should I tell my people, Erich, if you visit the Federal Republic in this situation?" "And," retorted Honecker, "what can we tell our people who are very worried about peace and want me to make this trip?"[32] Honecker's resentment at having to obey his master who was also his junior was obvious to his SED colleagues, who had to endure frequent tirades against Gorbachev during Politburo meetings.[33] Gorbachev, who met six times with Honecker between 1986 and 1989, contrasts his relationship with the GDR leader to that of his predecessor: "Brezhnev and Erich Honecker over the years developed a great sympathy for each other, they liked each other a great deal. Erich and I soon switched to "ty" [the familiar form in Russian]. Despite that, we never developed a really open and trusting relationship."[34]

Honecker apparently made his delayed visit to the FRG without Gorbachev's blessing. The Soviet general secretary wanted to make his state visit to Bonn before the GDR leader did, but Honecker preempted him. The 1987 Honecker visit to Bonn, in many ways the triumph of his career and his long search for international acceptance and equal treatment from the FRG, was replete with irony. When Honecker arrived at the Chancellery, the Bundeswehr band struck up the two German national anthems, as the frail, unsmiling Honecker stood stiffly to attention next to the hearty and self-confident Kohl, a living metaphor for the difference between the two Germanies. Honecker visited his birthplace in the Saarland, highlighting the many ways in which Germans in two states were united by personal ties and a common sense of nationhood.[35] This high point of his political life was to be his last hurrah, because he was unable to utilize it to strengthen his position either at home or in Moscow. Moreover, by this time, Honecker had already realized that the closer the ties between the two Germanies, the less vital East Germany would be as the bulwark of Soviet security. On the other hand, the FRG, which had for thirty-eight years scrupulously avoided recognizing the GDR as a separate state, came the closest it had ever been to doing precisely that—three years before the country disappeared. Although Bonn was careful to define Honecker's trip only as "a working visit" and not a "state visit" this was the nearest the two countries ever came to dealing with each other on a normal international basis. Indeed, Honecker would later on use precisely this argument when the West Germans sought to try him on charges of treason.

The visit produced no startling results, but West Germans spent some time analyzing Honecker's tantalizing remark, "the day will come on which borders will no longer separate but unite us, as the border between the German Democratic Republic and the Polish People's Republic unites us."[36] The West Germans took this to mean that the two German states could only have a satisfactory relationship when the FRG was

willing to give full international recognition to the GDR. Indeed, a veteran Soviet commentator claimed that this visit "has confirmed the existence of the two German states. Erich Honecker was given a reception
befitting his status as a head of a foreign state."[37]

The area on which there was perhaps the most agreement between
East Berlin and Moscow was arms control. After all, Honecker was well
aware of the popular opposition within the GDR to the stationing of
Soviet SS-24 missiles in East Germany in retaliation for the INF deployments in West Germany. From the beginning, therefore, Gorbachev's
proposals on reducing and eventually eliminating all long-range ballistic
missiles, his agreement to destroy all INF weapons in 1987, and his conventional arms control proposals all received enthusiastic GDR support,
as did his constant criticism of the U.S. Strategic Defense Initiative and
West Germany's possible participation in it. Like the USSR, the GDR
viewed arms control agreements not only as a means of pacifying its own
nervous population, but as a way of advancing East-West cooperation,
particularly in trade and technology, thereby improving the GDR's own
technological position. Thus, any reduction in defense spending would
benefit the civilian economy in the GDR's constant search to approach
FRG economic levels.

The SED party archives support this view of general GDR satisfaction
with the international aspects of Gorbachev's policies prior to 1989.
However, they also reveal some snide comments made by GDR leaders
who felt they understood better than the upstart Soviet leader the true
nature of international politics.[38] There was also constant nervousness
about the Soviet Union's tendency to downplay the fundamental antagonism between communism and capitalism. As Honecker told his hosts in
Bonn during his 1987 visit, the two systems were as irreconcilable as "fire
and water." The GDR leadership rejected the basic assumption of New
Political Thinking that "universal human values" had replaced the class
struggle.[39] But Gorbachev's deeds in foreign policy, as opposed to his
words, served GDR interests and seemed to validate positions that Honecker had been arguing for some years.

An analysis of the Honecker-Gorbachev correspondence between 1985
and 1989 reveals, however, that as early as October 1986, the East German leader became increasingly concerned about Gorbachev's pursuit of
the common European home and of improved ties with West Germany.
After all, the GDR was a child of the Cold War and its special importance
on the frontier between socialism and capitalism would be diminished by
a new rapprochement between the two. Moreover, a new Soviet–West
German détente would call into question the special status that the GDR
had acquired in the 1980s as the security bulwark against West German
missiles. Despite Honecker's own desire for closer inter-German ties,

therefore, he felt threatened by the prospect of warmer Soviet–West German relations.

Perestroika

The Honecker government proved increasingly impervious to Soviet suggestions that the GDR restructure its economy. After all, did the GDR not have the highest standard of living in the communist bloc? Did it not produce technology of a significantly higher quality than the Soviet Union? If so, why the need to restructure the economy? It was in the economic debate that the GDR leaders' sense of superiority over their more backward Soviet masters emerged most clearly. Honecker at one point smugly presented Gorbachev with a microchip that the GDR produced that was not available in the Soviet Union. His response to Gorbachev's suggestion that the GDR might profit from economic perestroika was thus one of ill-disguised contempt: "The young man has been making policy for only a year, and already he wants to take on more than he can chew." Or, in the words of Politburo ideologue Kurt Hager, answering a question about the need to follow the Soviets, "Would you, by the way, feel obliged to redo the wallpaper in your apartment just because your neighbor has put up new wallpaper?"[40] As Gorbachev wryly recounted, "Honecker told me that the GDR had introduced perestroika seventeen years before."[41]

The GDR economy during the Gorbachev era was considered to be stable and inherently viable, even though it had problems.[42] East Germany's special economic relationship with West Germany gave it financial benefits and access to goods that no other CMEA country enjoyed. Yet it also had some of the most restrictive laws on foreign participation in its economy. After the fall of the GDR and the discovery of the low level of production standards, the absence of a work ethic (the adage that "only Germans can make communism work" was, in fact, untrue), environmental disasters, and other problems common to socialist economies, many questioned why the West had so readily accepted the superficial appearance of a reasonably well-functioning GDR economy. At the time, however, most outsiders believed GDR statistics. It was the GDR population that realized they were false.

Inasmuch as the Gorbachev revolution was driven by the Kremlin's consciousness of the USSR's economic decline, the GDR assumed an increasingly important role in Soviet economic plans. Gorbachev singled out the GDR as the key country that would determine the ultimate success or failure of Soviet reform efforts. In this sense, Gorbachev retained an almost naive belief in the GDR's economic prowess. Moreover, the

Soviets believed that in order to maximize the gains from Soviet-GDR ties, Honecker had to introduce economic reforms similar to those in the USSR so as to improve East German productivity. The 1986–90 Five Year Plan trade agreement foresaw an increase in bilateral trade "without precedent in the world."[43] But Gorbachev's attempts to tighten economic integration with the GDR, especially on the technological level (he believed that the GDR could produce microchips equal to those used in SDI research) met with an unenthusiastic response.[44] From the GDR's standpoint, tighter integration with the USSR threatened its ability to advance technologically. It saw its trade future with the West and the Pacific Rim, not with states that were less developed economically than itself. The Soviet-GDR economic relationship, however, was not purely bilateral: inter-German trade also affected it. By 1987, Soviet ambassador to the GDR Vyacheslav Kochemasov was criticizing the GDR for not being more forthcoming with information about its foreign trade, particularly with the FRG, and he was admitting that the USSR and GDR were rivals in the pursuit of trade with West Germany.[45] It was becoming increasingly difficult for either the Soviet Union or East Germany to insulate their relationship from the influence of the Federal Republic. The more Bonn intruded both politically and economically, the more suspicious Moscow and East Berlin became of each other.

Glasnost

Gorbachev's domestic policies complicated East Germany's ability to develop a separate national identity and hastened the downfall of the GDR. It was the fear that glasnost would ultimately undermine the SED regime that drove Honecker to dig in his heels and become increasingly estranged from reality. After all, the GDR was different from all other members of the socialist fraternity because it lacked one major prerequisite for a viable nation-state: a national identity. All attempts at *Abgrenzung* or at developing a socialist national identity had failed. Most East Germans identified with their Western brothers and sisters and had little that was specifically East German that gave them a sense of national cohesion. Gorbachev's advisor Georgi Shakhnazarov criticizes the GDR for insisting that the two Germanies were not only two states but also two different nations, since this idea appeared ridiculous to every second East German who had relatives in West Germany. Perhaps, he muses, "if the GDR had survived three hundred years, a special nation would have developed there."[46]

In the absence of a viable national identity, the SED leadership, by 1985 one of the most repressive in the bloc, believed that any domestic liberalization would threaten its power and would begin to unravel the "first socialist German state." Honecker, like most of his East European colleagues, had come to power at the height of the Brezhnev era, and still clung to the beliefs that had forged the Soviet–East German relationship at that time. Unlike Gorbachev, he did not believe that there was anything fundamentally wrong with East Germany's society or economy, and he was determined to resist Soviet pressures to change. If Gorbachev truly believed in "freedom of choice" for his fraternal allies, then why should the GDR not choose to stay as it had been for fifteen years?

Honecker's initial response to glasnost was to argue essentially as Ulbricht had done when he resisted Soviet pressures toward inter-German détente in 1969–71. He stressed that the GDR had long since made its own distinctive contribution to socialism, that its economy was more successful than that of the Soviet Union, and that given its strategic location on the boundary between socialism and capitalism and the constant danger from West Germany, it was entitled to pursue a more restrictive media and information policy.[47] As Honecker wrote to Gorbachev, "It is important for us to fight on one and not two fronts."[48]

In this struggle to create and sustain a legitimate national identity in an era of change, the past cast an increasingly menacing shadow over the embattled Honecker regime. The most threatening aspect of glasnost was the attempt to fill in the "blank spots" of history and to confront the Stalinist past in all its manifestations more openly. Gorbachev calculated that exposing the real horrors of the Stalinist past would strengthen his legitimacy at home. Honecker knew that exactly the opposite applied to his own regime: challenging orthodox interpretations of history, the myths on which the GDR had been constructed, would further undermine the GDR's legitimacy. The increasingly open debates about history had a major impact on Soviet society and on their opponents; but Honecker and his colleagues believed that such debates in the GDR would seriously destabilize the country. Early on, Gorbachev's speeches were censored; offending passages were not published in East German papers. But since most East Germans watched West German television, they knew all about glasnost and perestroika, so the censorship was in vain. By challenging the old communist orthodoxy, Gorbachev became a hero to young and dissident East Germans, representing for them the hope of a less repressive, more honest socialism. Indeed, the deputy chief of mission in the Soviet embassy in East Berlin first realized that the situation in the GDR was becoming untenable in June 1987, when young East Germans thronged into the street near the Wall to listen to a rock concert taking place on the other side. "Gorby, Gorby," they shouted as the Volkspolizei began to arrest them.[49]

The most egregious example of the Soviet-GDR rift came in 1988, when Honecker, without consulting with a number of his Politburo colleagues, banned the distribution of *Sputnik*, a German-language digest of

Soviet articles with a circulation of 130,000. The offending article dealt with the origins of the Hitler-Stalin Pact, suggesting that there had been considerable collusion between the two prior to the outbreak of the Second World War and that the Soviets had not been forced into the pact because of British and French prevarication. These revelations struck at the heart of GDR (and Soviet) orthodoxy, implying that Stalin had indeed actively sought a relationship with Nazi Germany. They were more threatening to the GDR than to the Soviet Union, because they called into question the GDR's antifascist credentials and its more favorable view of Stalin than that prevalent in the USSR. Honecker declared that *Sputnik* was no longer making a "contribution to the consolidation of German-Soviet friendship" and was instead "providing distorted depictions of history." In a subsequent Central Committee meeting, Honecker accused the Soviet Union of tolerating historical revisionism by "bourgeois types gone wild." As his wife, the dour education minister, had previously declared, "Those who flirt with the banner of freedom under the motto of more openness will be shown the limits." Many of Honecker's colleagues, however, were greatly taken aback by the banning of *Sputnik*. This incident provoked into more open opposition those in the hierarchy who until then had kept their misgivings about Honecker to themselves. As Politburo member Günter Schabowski says of the *Sputnik* incident, "Honecker could not and would not understand that Gorbachev, as an instrument of history, had set in motion necessary processes that could not bypass the GDR."[50]

The SED's exasperation with the Soviet leadership was expressed in an evaluation of Gorbachev's speech to the Soviet Nineteenth Party Conference in July 1988. The review was mixed, with the SED focusing on anything that strengthened socialism and criticized imperialism. But, at the end of the detailed report, the author wrote: "As is well known, today many historical publications in the Soviet Union do not serve the interests of the Party and political responsibility because they concentrate onesidedly on mistakes. One must also bear in mind that the CPSU in the past has opened up a wasteland in the investigation of its history."[51] Given the increasing Soviet irritation with East Berlin, it is notable that Gorbachev did not try to remove Honecker by 1988, replacing him with a more perestroika-minded leader. Those who participated in the events claim that Gorbachev was indecisive, but also admit that there were few reform-minded candidates to choose from.[52]

Gorbachev and West Germany, 1985–1988

Gorbachev's official views about West Germany from 1985 to 1988 reflected the conventional communist wisdom: the FRG's decision to deploy U.S. intermediate-range missiles had made it an increased threat to Soviet security; the close cooperation between Kohl and Reagan proved that "revanchist" forces in Bonn were still powerful; but, despite these political problems, the FRG was still a desirable trading partner. In 1985, Soviet–West German relations were at their lowest ebb since the Adenauer era, a fact that disturbed the Germans more than the Soviets. Gorbachev's own experience with West Germany was very limited. He had visited in 1975, while he was the Stavropol party boss, to mark the celebrations of the thirtieth anniversary of the end of World War II. He later described the visit as "interesting though difficult": he was struck by how underdeveloped the Soviet Union was compared to the countries of Western Europe. He later recalled arguing with Germans that it was not the Soviet Union's fault that Germany was divided at the end of the war;[53] but, as he constantly reiterated, this was now a fact of international life and could not be changed.

Gorbachev's main advisors on Germany, the so-called *Germanisty*, were, of course, also part of the old school of thinking, known to their detractors as the "Berlin Wall." Shakhnazarov recalls that it was much harder to work with Soviet Germanists than with the Germans themselves. "They were a special breed of people, who, as a rule, were distinguished by their high professionalism and extreme distrust—one might even say suspiciousness—in relation to the object of their study—the Germans and Germany. The basis of their worldview, formed during World War II, had remained unchanged since then . . . they could not let go their experience in the struggle against fascism."[54] Two of the most important Germanists, Valentin Falin and Yuli Kvitsinsky, had served in West Germany. Falin, a former ambassador to Bonn and head of the Novosti Press Agency, became the head of the International Department of the Central Committee in 1988. Kvitsinsky became ambassador to Bonn in 1986. Although both of them understood West Germany well and received considerable media attention there, there is little evidence that either of them were prepared to think innovatively about the future of Germany. Nikolai Portugalov, who worked for the Central Committee, was also not a "new thinker" on Germany. Well after unification, Portugalov insisted that the *Germanisty* had always favored a united, neutral Germany.[55] A fourth advisor, Daniil Melnikov, who had directed the USSR's propaganda effort against Nazi Germany, played a lesser role because of his age and health. When Gorbachev first came into office, the Third European Department of the Ministry of Foreign Affairs was responsible for policy toward West Germany and, as guardians of Soviet orthodoxy on Berlin and the German question, had a privileged status within the ministry. Shevardnadze began to bypass the German group in his search for more innovative approaches to East-West tensions, and this led to considerable bureaucratic infighting.

The initial West German reaction to Gorbachev was cautious. Since the USSR had increasingly distanced itself from the FRG after Kohl's election and the 1983 deployment of the INF missiles, the ruling coalition's expectations were low. Kohl and Genscher were concerned about the tense state of Soviet—West German relations because of the heightened fears of East-West conflict among their own population. Moreover, the Kohl government hoped for improved relations with Moscow to maintain the momentum of closer ties with East Berlin. The CDU-CSU actively sought to cultivate ties with the Kremlin. Perhaps the most surprising convert was the leader of the CSU, Franz-Josef Strauss, inveterate anticommunist and *bête noire* of the Soviets. His conversion had begun in 1983, when he had helped arrange the GDR loans, and he subsequently developed close contacts with Alexander Schalck-Golodkowski, the wealthy and infamous GDR middleman who arranged many secret German-German deals. In December 1987, not long before his death the following year, Strauss piloted his own airplane to Moscow, met with Gorbachev and other leaders, and returned claiming that it was no longer necessary to fear an "offensive, aggressive intention on the part of the Soviet Union." Gorbachev later expressed regret that the Soviet Union had not responded earlier to the Bavarian leader's feelers and described him as "an unusually fascinating man."[56]

Genscher committed himself early on to improving ties with Gorbachev. During his July 1986 visit to Moscow, he was struck by Gorbachev's stress on domestic exigencies that were driving his foreign policy.[57] In February 1987, at a time when most Western observers remained skeptical, Genscher gave a major speech at the Davos World Economic Forum urging the world to "take Gorbachev at his word" and respond to Soviet initiatives. Later on that year, he presented Czech leader Gustav Husák—no fan of perestroika—with an "I like Gorby" button. Comrade Husák was not amused. Genscher had previously been criticized by conservatives inside and outside the Reagan administration for being too conciliatory toward the USSR, but this new form of "Genscherism" foreshadowed a general Western warming toward Gorbachev. Slowly, the German public became more positively inclined toward the Soviet Union, unlike, for instance, the far more skeptical French.

The INF Agreement

"Why, they ask," wrote Portugalov in 1986 of his conversations with leading West Germans, "does the Soviet Union, while pursuing a more active European policy, supposedly persist in 'ignoring' the FRG, although only recently Bonn . . . enjoyed the reputation of being Moscow's 'privileged' partner?" The answer was simple: "The Pershing 2s in the FRG . . . represent for the Soviet Union an immediate threat to its security emanating from German soil."[58] Until the signing of the INF agreement, this was a major reason for Soviet reluctance to improve ties with the FRG. Although the United States, and not the FRG was the USSR's major interlocutor on arms control, Moscow continued to punish West Germany for its acceptance of American missiles.

During his first year in office, Gorbachev largely reiterated the Andropov line on INF, offering to reduce the number of Soviet medium-range missiles in Europe to the level of the combined total of analogous French and British weapons if the United States removed all of its Euromissiles and if it halted its SDI program. At the Geneva summit in 1985, Gorbachev and Reagan clashed so vehemently over SDI that little progress was made on INF. At Reykjavik, in 1986, Gorbachev dropped the long-standing Soviet insistence on counting French and British missiles in the negotiations, and he and Reagan agreed in principle to accept America's "zero option" to eliminate all intermediate-range missiles in Europe. But SDI proved such a stumbling block that the summiteers went home empty-handed.

In 1987, Gorbachev gradually backed down from his previous positions—linking INF and SDI, refusing the U.S. demand for on-site inspections, and keeping one hundred Soviet SS-20 warheads in Asia—and by the end of the year had essentially accepted the American agenda. In February 1987, he publicly announced his support for the zero option— that is, destroying all Soviet and American intermediate-range missiles. In April, he offered to withdraw Soviet shorter-range missiles that had been deployed in Europe and in July demanded that the warheads for seventy-two West German Pershing 1A missiles (short-range warheads controlled by the United States and deployed years earlier) also be included in the agreement. This demand was aimed primarily at the Germans and caused problems both within Kohl's cabinet and between Bonn and Washington. Ironically, most Western observers had assumed that Gorbachev would try and drive a wedge between Washington and Bonn by offering a deal—the elimination of INF tied to a renunciation of SDI—that the West Germans would accept but the United States could refuse. Instead, he offered a deal that was more palatable to the Americans than to the Germans.

In 1987, a potentially nightmarish scenario emerged for the West German government. It faced the specter of the withdrawal of INF missiles combined, at Washington's insistence, with the modernization of the Lance missiles, a less than five hundred-kilometer-range missile whose future was now elevated to a litmus test of German-American relations. From the point of view of the German government, "The shorter the range, the deader the Germans": that is, Germany would now be stuck with a group of battlefield weapons that, in a potential nuclear exchange, would explode in and around Germany without involving the United States, conjuring up the specter of nuclear singularization and decoupling from the United States. The INF controversy, therefore, became not only one between the German peace movement and the Reagan administration, but between the latter and the Kohl-Genscher government.[59] By August 1987, after some hard bargaining, Kohl pledged that West Germany would destroy its Pershing 1A missiles after the INF treaty was implemented and the United States agreed to postpone the modernization of Lance missiles until a later date.

In the aftermath of the December 1987 INF treaty, it appeared that the Soviet Union had made considerable gains, in relations both with the United States and with the FRG. Soviet policy had undergone a complete change in a mere four years. From an economic point of view, the INF treaty did not involve the transfer of significant resources from the civilian to the military economy. Politically, however, it was a brilliant example of Gorbachev's public diplomacy, which enhanced his popularity in Western Europe, cemented his image as a sincere proponent of peace and disarmament, and reinforced his campaign for the denuclearization of Europe. He had largely undone the damage of the Brezhnev era and reversed the image of the Soviet Union inexorably bent on an endless military buildup.

Economic Ties

When Gorbachev came to power, West Germany was the USSR's most important capitalist trading partner. The new Soviet leader assumed that he could continue his predecessors' policies of decoupling politics and economics, and promoting trade with West Germany (while receiving additional credits) irrespective of political ties. Gorbachev's agenda envisaged more intense East-West economic cooperation than did that of his predecessors. Since Germany had traditionally been the Soviet Union's major supplier of advanced technology, Gorbachev sought to accelerate and broaden economic links with the FRG. This was, however, problematic as long as Moscow continued to shun Bonn politically.

Gorbachev tackled the foreign aspects of perestroika by introducing legislation that was designed to make Soviet goods more competitive internationally. For the first time since 1917, foreign trade was given legal status as an important component of Soviet economic activity. The September 1986 Foreign Trade Law provided broader rights for Soviet enterprises to engage in cooperation with other CMEA countries and in joint ventures with the West. The Ministry of Foreign Trade lost its long-standing monopoly over the conduct of foreign trade, and export-import decision making was decentralized.[60] However, the state monopoly over foreign currency remained, and the issues of pricing and convertibility raised many questions about how effective these reforms would be, even as the USSR applied to join the GATT and the IMF.

The legalization of joint ventures with Western firms was another major Gorbachev innovation, to produce both consumer goods and technology. Initially, it was decreed that the Soviet share of any joint venture must be at least 51 percent. By 1990, foreign firms were allowed to own up to 100 percent of their ventures. But joint ventures ran into problems from the beginning. The Soviets preferred to use these deals to produce goods for export to the West to earn hard currency, but the European firms were more interested in producing for the Soviet market. Since no Soviet foreign trade organization had been allowed to negotiate independently for sixty years, there was some confusion about what their powers were and this complicated all the joint-venture projects. Otto Wolff von Amerongen, head of the Ostausschuss der deutschen Wirtschaft, the major West German East-West trade lobbying group, was cautiously positive about joint ventures, but pointed out that the most successful ones were small-scale. Generally, the larger, more industrial joint ventures rarely advanced beyond the phase of signing papers.[61]

Gorbachev took other steps to increase trade with the Federal Republic. Reversing three decades of Soviet policy, he praised the European Community and gave new impetus to the stalled EC-CMEA talks. The debate among Soviet experts mirrored this move away from the traditional view that the EC was weak, doomed to fail, riddled with contradictions, and under the thumb of the United States.[62] There were pragmatic reasons for this change: Gorbachev realized that the commitment to create a single European market would result in a stronger, vital community of 250 million people from which the Soviet Union would be excluded unless it established relations with the EC. In September 1985, the EC-CMEA talks, broken off under Brezhnev, resumed, and in 1988 a framework agreement was signed. In 1989, the USSR completed its own bilateral agreement with the EC.

Gorbachev's attempts to revive trade with West Germany and other countries and his pursuit of international economic perestroika were hampered not only by domestic resistance but also by the international economic situation. The Soviet Union was essentially a one-crop economy in international terms, with energy exports to Western Europe providing 80 percent of Soviet hard currency earnings, and oil alone 60 percent. Nine months after Gorbachev took power, oil prices began to fall, going from $28 per barrel to below $10 in 1986, then rising again but remaining quite volatile. Moreover, shortly before the price collapse, the dollar had begun to fall against Western currencies. The Soviets sold their oil and gas in dollar-denominated currencies and purchased machinery primarily from the FRG, France, and Japan, whose currencies rose against the dollar. They were, therefore, doubly affected by the falling dollar. By some estimates, Moscow lost up to $60 billion in hydrocarbon revenues between 1985 and 1989 because of failing oil prices.[63] It also took more oil to pay for machinery imports than previously. Thus, Gorbachev's plan for large-scale German technology imports that would improve Soviet economic performance was undermined by the USSR's lack of hard currency to pay for the German technology. Credits were the answer; but given the cool state of political relations, they were not forthcoming in Gorbachev's first years.

It became clear by 1988 that Gorbachev's economic reforms had improved neither Soviet domestic performance nor the USSR's international economic position.[64] Although Gorbachev's advisors continued to argue that perestroika increased the chances for more East-West trade, the truth was that apart from energy, the Soviets had little that the West wanted to purchase, and the domestic situation was so uncertain that Western partners were wary of investing.[65] Otto Wolff argues that the FRG had initially expected a significant increase in trade with the USSR after the 1986 Five Year Modernization Plan. But exactly the opposite happened, much to the dismay of Yakovlev and Shevardnadze, among others.[66]

A number of factors contributed to the improvement in West German–Soviet relations after 1988, but the economic impetus was clearly one of the most important. If the USSR could not secure the economic benefits it desired through economic reforms, then it must offer the Germans other incentives. Historically, West Germany had responded positively to Soviet political inducements that were designed to increase German economic largesse.

After Gorbachev had signed the INF treaty and sent conciliatory signals to Bonn, this strategy succeeded. Baden-Württenberg Prime Minister Lothar Späth took a high-level high-technology delegation to Moscow to discuss increased business in February 1988. Since Späth was the leader of the German Land with the highest technological level, his visit was symbolically important. But this ostensibly economic summit had a concrete political agenda: Späth brought a message from the chancellor, saying that he wanted urgently to meet with Gorbachev. This time, assured that the economic relationship would improve, the Soviet leader relented.[67] When Kohl finally visited Moscow in October 1988, economic and scientific matters were high on his agenda, including plans to train Soviet managers. As Leonid Abalkin, one of Gorbachev's economic advisors, said, when asked what was most important for perestroika to succeed, "The most important thing . . . came during Chancellor Kohl's visit to Moscow, when he promised to train annually a thousand young Soviet industrial cadres in Germany in the techniques of Western management. . . . Germany will benefit from this; but we [will benefit] much more."[68]

Political Relations

Despite the rhetoric of New Political Thinking and the common European home, Soviet-FRG relations were very slow to improve after Gorbachev came into office. When Yuli Kvitsinsky met with the Politburo, prior to his departure for Bonn as the new ambassador in March 1986, Gorbachev summarized Soviet policy toward West Germany—a reserved attitude toward political dialogue, and continuation of the economic relationship. Falin, who also attended the meeting, predicted that the CDU would lose the next election but suggested that the USSR support the CDU to lessen its chances of victory. They agreed that at some point in the future bilateral relations must improve, but Gorbachev made it clear that there could be no talk of a summit for the foreseeable future. Kvitsinky, not surprisingly, left the meeting confused about what the policy should be and what concrete steps should be taken to implement it.[69]

The West German government, from the beginning, was interested in improving ties with Moscow, but soon realized that the Kremlin was rejecting its feelers. In July 1986, it appeared that Gorbachev was softening his policy toward the FRG. Genscher visited Moscow, bringing with him a message from the chancellor that Bonn would like to improve bilateral ties. Genscher argued that the Federal Republic could not be excluded from the common European home; indeed the character of the house would largely be determined by the German-Soviet relationship. Gorbachev claimed that the USSR had no interest in separating the United States from West Germany, but reiterated his criticism of the FRG's security policy.[70]

However, the new momentum ended abruptly in October 1986, when Chancellor Kohl, in an interview with *Newsweek* magazine, said: "I don't consider [Gorbachev] to be a liberal. He is a modern Communist leader who understands public relations. Goebbels, who was one of those responsible for the crimes of the Hitler era, was an expert in public relations too."[71] Seizing on this unfortunate remark (it was, of course, sacrilege to mention Gorbachev and Goebbels in one breath), the Soviets abruptly canceled a planned visit to Moscow by Minister of Technology Heinz Riesenhuber.[72] Kohl issued a statement claiming that he had been misinterpreted and apologized for any false impression that was created, but it was too late. *Pravda* lambasted Kohl, without mentioning the Goebbels quote, for a number of international sins, including a visit of his to the United States.[73] For the next six months, Soviet–West German relations returned to the deep freeze. However, the Kremlin continued to court the SPD, hoping that they would win the election. Former Chancellor Willy Brandt led a delegation to Moscow in May 1985, met with Gorbachev, and condemned the SDI program jointly with the new Soviet leader. Contacts with the SPD, particularly over arms control issues, increased.

As it turned out, Kohl was reelected. He put out several feelers, to no avail. After a few months, however, the Kremlin realized that it had nothing to gain by isolating the FRG. The CDU-CSU/FDP coalition would be in power for another four years, and if Gorbachev were truly interested in pursuing a more dynamic policy toward Western Europe, West Germany was the key country politically and economically. Moreover, with the softening of American policy toward the USSR and prospects for an INF agreement in sight, this was the time to respond to Kohl's overtures. Genscher, who emerged from the 1987 election with increased power, had also made it clear that he favored new initiatives toward Moscow.

Finally, in July 1987, President Richard von Weizsäcker traveled to Moscow, Leningrad, and Novosibirsk, emphasizing scientific and technological ties. Gorbachev admonished him, "We do not want to hear any more translations from English into German. We want serious relations with the Federal Republic and would like to know when the time for those relations will come." But the most publicized part of the meeting came when the subject of German unification was raised. "Churchill and the Americans," declared Gorbachev, were responsible for the division of Germany, "And history will decide what will be in a hundred years."[74]

It appeared that improved ties were there to stay when Chancellor Kohl visited Moscow in October. The summit—the first meeting between the Soviet leader and the West German chancellor since 1985 and the first time ever that the West German defense minister was part of such a delegation—covered a wide range of issues: economic relations, the German question, Berlin, Soviet Germans, arms control, and East-West relations. Although there were disagreements on the future of a divided Germany, the general tone of the meeting was cordial and optimistic. "The ice has been broken," declared Gorbachev. As a result of his visit, Kohl responded, a new chapter, as opposed to a new page, in German-Soviet relations had begun.[75] A DM 3 billion credit, raised by a Deutsche Bank–led consortium contributed to the successful summit outcome, and Kohl took 50 businessmen with him to Moscow to discuss a variety of joint ventures. In assessing the meeting, *Pravda* highlighted Genscher's statement that the COCOM export controls must be reassessed, a constant theme in Soviet criticisms of West Germany, but this time legitimized by Genscher's own pronouncements.[76]

A West Berlin Door?

West German officials had initially hoped that New Political Thinking might dissipate the tensions surrounding West Berlin, but on this issue there was no compromise from Moscow. The rhetoric of new thinking was grandiose and optimistic. The reality, especially in Berlin, was more sober. Beginning in 1985, Soviet pronouncements reiterated the traditional view on a matter that the 1971 four-power agreement had never resolved—that West Berlin was not a component part of West Germany and never would be. The Kremlin accused the West of "provocative" acts in trying to change the status of West Berlin; commemorating the twenty-fifth anniversary of the erection of the "normal frontier control" (i.e., the Wall), *New Times* reminded its readers that "This frontier lies between two worlds with two opposing ideologies and world outlooks, between human mentalities and habits and ways of life."[77] When a Soviet diplomat suggested in 1987 that the Wall might soon disappear, he was roundly reprimanded by the Kremlin, which reiterated that West Berlin was "a special political entity," whose status could not be changed.[78]

The most tangible proof that Soviet views on Berlin were ossified was that several major Soviet–West German scientific and technical agreements that would have greatly benefited the Soviet economy were held up because the Soviets refused to include West Berlin in them. In view of the fact that even in the Brezhnev era, the Kremlin had agreed to Berlin clauses, this rigidity, which was counterproductive to Soviet domestic interests, is noteworthy. It can perhaps be explained by the general lack of clear planning in the Foreign Ministry and the inability to think through consistently the consequences of Soviet actions for Soviet interests. The CMEA-EC talks were held up until 1988 because of Moscow's refusal to recognize West Berlin's links to the FRG as an integral part of the EC. When Shevardnadze visited Bonn in 1988, he refused to proceed with negotiations fleshing out a 1986 scientific and technological framework agreement because institutions based in West Berlin would be involved. A Soviet-FRG cultural agreement was similarly stalled when Shevardnadze said that West Berlin artists and singers could not participate.[79] Moreover, in October 1988 the Soviets responded to President Reagan's

1987 Berlin initiative aimed at expanding air links to the divided city and promoting more international events there by declaring there was "no practical need whatsoever" to increase air links.[80]

Just before Kohl's 1988 visit, however, Gorbachev began to make some concessions—in particular, recognition of West Berlin's right to take part in Soviet-FRG cultural activities—in order to ensure that bilateral agreements could be signed. During the visit he went further, and said that the USSR had no objection to West Berlin's participation in European and international relations, but reiterated the city's "special status." Asked whether the common European home would have a door in West Berlin, he replied, "Without such a door its design would look incomplete."[81] Reluctantly, the Soviets accepted the West German proposition that West Berliners or West Berlin–based organizations be identified in FRG–Soviet cultural and scientific exchanges on the same list as West Germans, instead of on separate lists. Nevertheless, Gorbachev for three years forfeited significant scientific and technical benefits by his intransigence on West Berlin.

Emigration was another area where new political rhetoric was not matched by action for a number of years, another holdover from the Brezhnev era that took too long to discard. In principle, Gorbachev supported liberalized emigration from the Soviet Union; but it took until almost the end of the USSR to alter Soviet laws. In the early Gorbachev period, the West German government continued to press the Kremlin to allow more ethnic Germans to emigrate. At that point, Moscow's stance on emigration was a significant measure of its willingness to improve ties with Bonn. In 1986, less than 1,000 emigrated; in 1987, the numbers rose to 14,000 and in 1988 to 45,000. There was a clear correlation between the state of Soviet–West German relations and the numbers of emigrants. Gorbachev realized that more financial incentives would be forthcoming from Bonn if ethnic Germans were permitted to leave. Glasnost did have an early impact on the ethnic Germans, inasmuch as it facilitated an open debate about their deportation under Stalin, and the need for their full rehabilitation and return to the territory of the former Volga republic. To some extent, this debate encouraged emigration by revealing the callous way in which the Soviet government had treated ethnic Germans after 1941, but it also led to the formation of groups of ethnic Germans who lobbied for the restoration of their republic in the USSR, instead of emigration. The emigration issue was, as in the Brezhnev era, linked to both domestic and foreign policy, which ensured that there would be no swift action in changing the Soviet attitude.

Inter-German Relations

Although the more traditional Soviet foreign policy specialists were wary of improving inter-German ties that might undermine Soviet interests, there was a growing realization that the GDR's instability resulted from domestic problems and the alienation of the population from its regime rather than from any "provocations" by the West German government. Yet, with the exception of the Honecker visit, the Soviets reacted to developments between the two Germanies, rather than determining them. Moscow still had veto power over relations between the FRG and GDR, but little influence beyond that, and no coherent strategy.

Moscow watched very carefully the emerging dialogue between the West German SPD and the SED. As part of the second phase of its Ostpolitik, the SPD in opposition began a series of talks with theorists in the SED on common problems. The first major achievement of this cooperation was the 1985 SED-SPD agreement on a chemical weapons–free zone in Europe. Hailed by the Kremlin (although Soviet accounts rarely mentioned that this was a joint, as opposed to an SED, product) and denounced by the CDU/CSU and other nonsocialist groups in the West, the accord amounted to SPD recognition of the SED's legitimacy.[82]

There followed more sensitive talks, on common "ideological problems," such as issues of war and peace—the first such dialogue since the split in the German Left in 1918–19. Eventually the talks produced a paper drawn up jointly by the SPD Commission on Fundamental Human Values and the Academy of Social Sciences of the Central Committee of the SED, although there were many disagreements during the discussions.[83] Discussions on fundamental ideological questions were a much more delicate matter than talks on chemical weapons for the Soviet Union and the GDR because they called into question the very nature of socialism and communism and contradicted fundamental Leninist principles. After all, Lenin had many times vilified the Second International and the European socialist parties for their support of World War I and their lack of a revolutionary consciousness, and had decreed that socialists and communists were ideologically opposed to each other; and in line with this tradition, there was practically no discussion of the talks in the Soviet press. Nevertheless, the joint paper, while outlining areas of disagreement, represented a breakthrough both in communist-socialist relations and in inter-German ties.[84] The paper argued that capitalism and socialism could find a common approach to problems of peace, among other issues. It was rejected by hardliners within the SED and by the right wing of the SPD, but it was in line with Gorbachev's New Political Thinking.

Another event that also had an important though indirect effect on German-German relations was the Chernobyl disaster. Chernobyl was a seminal event in the development of the Gorbachev revolution, because it forced a reluctant Soviet leadership, for the first time ever, to admit the truth about a nuclear disaster, even if that admission came too late for those whose health was destroyed by the accident. But Chernobyl also affected Soviet foreign policy, forcing Gorbachev not only to be more open with Western governments but to reassess the meaning of the international ecological movement.

After Chernobyl, when the USSR could no longer maintain the fiction that its nuclear power plants were much safer than those in the West when they were in fact much more dangerous, the Kremlin pursued a more cooperative policy toward ecological and antinuclear groups. Moreover, the West German Greens were highly supportive of Gorbachev's efforts to rid the world of nuclear weapons.[85] However, by legitimizing the Green Party, the Kremlin had at last removed all official obstacles to contacts between the West and East German ecological movements, a development not welcomed by Erich Honecker. After all, the East German Lutheran Church, itself heavily involved in the antinuclear movement, had become the major haven for dissidents, many of whom expressed their opposition to SED rule by agitating against nuclear power plants. Gorbachev changed Soviet policy toward new social movements because it enhanced his popularity in West Germany and because it was necessary after Chernobyl to bolster his credibility domestically. But what may have shored him up at home and in the West contributed toward the further questioning of the East German system.

The German Question

Early in 1987, West German government spokesmen, acting on information provided by their intelligence services, announced that Gorbachev had asked four top German experts—Falin, Portugalov, Daniil Melnikov of the Institute for World Economy and International Relations, and Georgi Arbatov, Director of the Institute of the USA and Canada—to produce a study on Germany with a view to "resolving" the German question. Rumor had it that two solutions were being considered: a German-German confederation; or the removal of U.S. and Soviet troops from both parts of Germany. Although this study never materialized, the rumors surrounding it raised German hopes. Moreover, in February 1987, Portugalov published an article in which he claimed that East and

West Germans belonged to the same nation, directly contradicting Honecker's pronouncements and those of previous Soviet leaders.[86] Portugalov, like other leading Germanists at the beginning of the Gorbachev era, was considered to be well connected to the Soviet intelligence apparatus. His writings, therefore, reflected the official views of at least some of the political class.

There was at least one individual who was willing to go beyond conventional wisdom and advocate a more radical solution to the German question. This was Vyacheslav I. Dashichev, a military historian, German expert, and deputy director of the Academy of Sciences' Institute for the World Socialist Economic System. Although Dashichev was well known to Western scholars who dealt with German-Soviet issues and remarkably open in his views, he was an outsider in terms of the inner party decision-making circles and somewhat of a maverick. Nevertheless, April 1987 he became head of a consultative group for the Foreign Ministry dealing with Eastern Europe. Since he was already known for his critical views and was unpopular in the International Department of the Central Committee, he assumed that this appointment was a result of Shevardnadze's intervention. He chose as the group's first project a discussion of the German question. At a seminar on November 27, 1987, he presented a paper to the study group entitled "Some Aspects of the 'German Problem.'"

The paper reached some sensational conclusions. Dashichev praised past Soviet policy on Germany but argued that the current situation had become counterproductive to Soviet interests and that new ways of dealing with Germany should be pursued. Dashichev suggested six possible solutions: continuation of the status quo; a unified, neutral Germany; a unified Germany integrated into the Western alliance; departure of East and West Germany from the Warsaw Pact and NATO and their continued existence as two neutral states; a confederation between the two neutral German states; and conclusion of a peace treaty with both German states, maintaining them in the two alliance systems. Dashichev argued that the status quo solution was, in the long run, not in Soviet interests. He rejected the third option, a united Germany in NATO, as against the interests of East and West because it would lead to a Germany "dominating economically and militarily." He argued that the second option, a unified, neutral Germany, would best serve the national interests of the USSR. At the end of his paper, he declared that the Soviet Union must expect that, as a result of internal developments in the GDR and FRG, "unexpected changes" might happen.[87]

Dashichev's paper was provocative even though he did not come out in favor of a united capitalist Germany in NATO. He was roundly denounced at the seminar and accused of "defeatism." A year later, in November 1988, at a Central Committee meeting attended by officials from the Foreign and Defense ministries, the KGB, and research institutes, Dashichev argued that it was impossible to build a common European home as long as Europe was divided. He was attacked by Falin, who said that the European status quo was untouchable.[88] He was declared *persona non grata* in the GDR and was unable to obtain a visa for travel there. The subject of a change in East Germany's status was so sensitive that any hint was heresy to both the Soviet Foreign Ministry and the Central Committee. And yet, two years later, Germany was united.

New Political Thinking had produced major changes in Soviet political doctrine about relations with the West and minor changes in discussions about relations with Eastern Europe during Gorbachev's first three years. But is there any evidence that either Gorbachev or Shevardnadze or any of their close advisors had begun in any systematic way to rethink the German question, other than vague pronouncements such as "history will decide" the issue? Soon after Gorbachev came into power and cautiously began to criticize Brezhnev's foreign policy, Western experts—particularly those in the Federal Republic—started to examine carefully every statement that high-level Soviet officials made that dealt with Germany and the German question. Articles were periodically written after carefully perusing Soviet statements that revealed nuances in the discussion of Berlin, the German nation, or the future of Germany. But if one goes back and reviews all the evidence, one must conclude that prior to 1989, there was little innovative thinking in the USSR on the future of Germany. Despite what Soviet politicians have said with hindsight, and recognizing that there is a difference between public and private pronouncements, the fact is that until the situation in the GDR began to deteriorate rapidly, the Kremlin did not give any serious thought to revising the status of East Germany or to bringing down the Berlin wall. Gorbachev could talk of "a hundred years" with President von Weizsäcker; but few Soviets even thought about changing the status of Germany in decades as opposed to centuries.

However, Gorbachev's words had a major impact on Germany. Spurred on by his theoretical pronouncements, the issue of German identity became increasingly important, especially in East Germany. The more the USSR encouraged inter-German ties, the less viable the concept of two nations became, and, despite the Kremlin's misgivings about some aspects of these ties, it had to accept them because they served broader Soviet interests in Europe. Moreover, Gorbachev had explicitly said that Eastern European countries should pursue their own destinies. The perceived diminution of the Soviet threat also led some West Germans to question aspects of their postwar identity, even if they did not take the possibility of unification seriously. Whereas the French had said of the Alsace-Lorraine after losing the territory to Germany in 1871, "Pensons-y toujours, n'en parlons jamais" (think about it always, but don't ever talk about it) the West German attitude toward unification was the inverse: "Parlons-y toujours, mais n'en pensons jamais (talk about it always, but don't ever think about it).

By the beginning of 1989, the Kremlin was a prisoner of its own rhetoric, which constantly reiterated the success of the socialist fraternity, while Gorbachev and his advisors became increasingly aware that the situation in Eastern Europe, especially in East Germany, was increasingly untenable. But major changes in Soviet policy could not be internally generated, given the opposition that Gorbachev had already encountered. Only when East Germans took to the streets was the Kremlin finally forced to react. By that time, as Gorbachev realized, it was already "five minutes to midnight."[89]

Four _____

Wir Sind Ein Volk: Germany Unites

Question. Will you yourself experience
   unification?
Chancellor Helmut Kohl. No, probably I will
   not live to see it.
   (Interview with Helmut Kohl, 1988)[1]

[The Wall] will be standing in fifty or a
hundred years. That is quite necessary to
protect our republic from thieves, not to
mention those who are prepared to disturb
stability and peace in Europe.
   (Erich Honecker, January 1989)[2]

BETWEEN 1949 AND 1989, the division of Germany, upon which the division of Europe was predicated, was the nonnegotiable bedrock of Soviet
security in Europe. A united Germany in NATO was depicted as the
Soviet Union's greatest nightmare. Close partnership with the GDR and
rapprochement with the FRG were the official goals of Soviet foreign
policy from Khrushchev to Gorbachev. But within one year, from 1989
to 1990, the Soviet Union went from being the leader of the Warsaw
Pact, whose linchpin was the German Democratic Republic, to accepting
not only the end of communism in Eastern Europe but also the disappearance of the GDR and a united Germany's full membership in
NATO. As two participants noted, by the end of the 1980s Gorbachev
had neither a strategy nor tactics in his German policy. "A system that
was unsustainable internally could not in the long run be effective exter-
nally."[3] Yet the reality was much more complex. When one recalls the
central, existential importance of the German question in Soviet foreign
policy, it is astounding that Moscow could have allowed East Germany to
vanish so quickly, with so little violence and with only modest compensation from the West.

The way in which Germany was dramatically and speedily united after
forty years of division reveals much about the impact of the Gorbachev
revolution not only on the implementation of Soviet foreign policy but
also on the decision-making process. Gorbachev's European policies cre-

ated the environment that facilitated German unification. He accepted that Eastern Europe had the right to pursue its own policies without Soviet interference; he stressed self-determination; eschewed force as a means of resolving international disputes; and encouraged debates within communist societies. The Soviet Union played only a limited role in the events that led to Honecker's ouster, the fall of the Berlin Wall, and the upheavals in the East German party and government. The USSR was the enabler, but not a major actor in the events themselves. Once Gorbachev had agreed to the principle of unification, the Kremlin did play a more significant role in negotiations on the external aspects of how it was to be accomplished. But even in these talks, the USSR's major leverage was its veto power. The agenda was set by the Western Powers, and Moscow reacted, rather than initiated policies.

The story of the internal German unification is largely one of the Soviet Union and the other three occupying powers responding to dramatic and rapid changes, encouraged by Gorbachev's declaratory and operational policies, that soon moved beyond their control. Often, it looked as if Gorbachev and his colleagues did not, in fact, have choices. And yet, throughout this period, the Soviet Union remained a military super-power. It retained a large number of troops and weapons in Eastern Europe, especially the 500,000-strong presence in East Germany. It could have used these troops to prevent the collapse of the GDR. But it did not do so, nor did the East German regime ever ask for Soviet military assistance. Moreover, with hindsight it is clear that a very specific set of circumstances between October 1989 and October 1990 enabled the Soviet Union to take actions which would have been unthinkable a year earlier or later. These circumstances included Gorbachev's domestic position, which was reasonably strong during the crucial period of negotiations; the demise of communism in Poland, Hungary and Czechoslovakia; the improving Soviet relationship with the West; and the East German population's courageous, nonviolent revolution.

The way in which unification was negotiated continues to affect German-Russian relations, in terms both of agreements and of expectations and mutual perceptions. The impact of the unification process has outlasted the collapse of the Soviet Union. The details of the negotiations on German unification have been ably and extensively chronicled by many of the key participants who were directly involved in the process.[4] This chapter will, therefore, highlight the key aspects of the collapse of the GDR and the move toward German unification, as well as Soviet and German expectations and perceptions of each other during the negotiations that continue to affect their bilateral relations today.

This chapter focuses on the following questions about the Soviet assent to unification:

How had Soviet policies toward the Federal Republic evolved by the time of
Gorbachev's visit to Bonn in June 1989? To what extent did they facilitate
German unification?

How had Soviet policy toward Eastern Europe and the GDR evolved by the
fall of 1989? What was the Soviet role in Honecker's fall and what were
Soviet expectations of his successor's ability to implement real reforms?

How and why did the Soviet Union change its position on German unification
between November 1989 and February 1990?

Despite Moscow's attempts to brake the rush toward unification, it
was virtually impotent in face of a resolute East German population and a
Western side that, despite its internal divisions, was able to develop consistent positions on promoting unification as peacefully as possible.
Moreover, it became increasingly clear that Gorbachev, like his predecessors, had not developed a coherent all-German policy. The bifurcation
in German policy was reflected institutionally. The Foreign Ministry took
charge of relations with capitalist West Germany, whereas the CPSU
Central Committee was largely responsible for ties with the GDR and its
ruling party as a "fraternal" state. This highlights a major problem in the
making of German policy. Below the level of Gorbachev and Shevardnadze, there was little coordination between officials who dealt with
East and West Germany. The bureaucratic consequences of not dealing
with Germany as a whole reinforced Gorbachev's inability to seize the
initiative once the East German revolution had begun.

Moscow and Bonn before Honecker's Fall

In the first half of 1989, the central preoccupation in the Kremlin's policy
toward West Germany was planning Gorbachev's visit to the Federal Republic, which was to be an important symbol of the Soviet leader's commitment to closer ties with the whole of Western Europe. Prior to Gorbachev's visit to Bonn in June 1989, the USSR continued to improve
relations with the Western European countries. In February 1989 the
Presidium of the Academy of Sciences held a special meeting to discuss
the common European home which was attended by Foreign Ministry
officials. The conference called for a second, Helsinki-type CSCE meeting to reassess security relations in Europe. The following week, the Ministry of Foreign Affairs and the Central Committee held a similar meeting
stressing closer all-European economic ties and the withdrawal of foreign
troops from European states—on both sides of the Iron Curtain.[5]
Clearly, a major debate among the various branches of the Soviet party
and government hierarchy was underway, seeking to incorporate Gorbachev's arms control proposals into a viable new strategy.

Negotiations between the European Community and CMEA moved toward their successful conclusion in the summer of 1989, the Berlin problem having been finally satisfactorily dealt with. Meanwhile, perestroika had done little to improve Soviet economic performance, which was indeed deteriorating. Despite Gorbachev's commitment to economic reform, he never moved beyond tinkering with the command economy, instead of attacking the system's basic structural problems. Like Brezhnev, he somewhat naively believed that Western technology and trade would enable the USSR to become a technologically advanced country. The economic imperative behind a more conciliatory Westpolitik was, therefore, as strong as ever.

The Western alliance recognized that events in the eastern part of Europe were moving at a hitherto undreamed-of pace and it wanted to encourage these changes. At the Brussels summit in May 1989 celebrating NATO's fortieth anniversary, President Bush and his allies agreed to substantial cuts in NATO forces to match Soviet proposals. They also agreed to postpone debate on the controversial issue of modernizing short-range weapons in Germany, including the Lance missiles which the Germans did not want modernized. As a result of the summit, the new American secretary of state, James Baker, developed a close relationship with Genscher, which was to become crucial during the negotiations on the external aspects of German unification. Indeed, Baker told President Bush before the summit that German unification would soon be back on the agenda.[6] The NATO summit also backed Bonn's efforts to improve ties with the Soviet Union. Following the summit, President Bush visited Germany and addressed the Federal Republic as a "partner in leadership," acknowledging its "key role," as well as explicitly calling for the Berlin Wall to come down. The United States was signaling both that it wanted to respond to Gorbachev's moves and that it approved of closer Soviet-German ties.[7]

Gorbachev made his first official visit to Bonn after two important experiences. The first was his May 1989 visit to Beijing, signaling the end of the Sino-Soviet cold war. He was hailed as a hero by the dissident students in Tienanmin Square who, shortly after he left, were massacred by the Chinese government. This was a chilling reminder to most of the outside world that communist governments could still deal with their opponents in the old violent way and a tonic for those East European leaders (like Erich Honecker) resisting Gorbachev's reforms. The second experience was the first session of the newly elected, raucous and pluralistic Congress of Peoples' Deputies, chosen in the first free competitive elections since 1917. The congress—initially largely pro-Gorbachev but subsequently increasingly critical of his policies—reconfirmed his election as president, a post he had assumed following Gromyko's "retirement" in

October 1988. Gorbachev's trip to Germany had to be shortened because of his internal problems, particularly the growing conflict in Uzbekistan. It was obviously a relief for him to visit a country where he received unabashed adulation, after the mounting criticism at home, but domestic pressures, particularly the growing ethnic conflicts in the non-Russian republics, diverted his attention from foreign policy issues.

Gorbachev's visit to Bonn was a turning point in Soviet-German relations, not only because of the concrete results it yielded but because it highlighted the contrast between the warming Moscow-Bonn ties and the increasingly chilly Moscow–East Berlin relationship. Gorbachev visited West Germany from June 12 to 15, at the height of his international popularity, and saw for himself the adoring crowds with their endless adulation. "Gorbymania" was born.[8] When the Soviet leader who had aroused such hope and admiration arrived in Bonn—the last major West European capital that he visited, four years after coming into office—he elicited only superlatives from the press, who compared him to John F. Kennedy.

Prior to Gorbachev's visit, German and Soviet public opinion polls showed both how the image of Russians had changed in Germany and how the image of Germans had changed in Russia. West Germans rated Gorbachev far above both their own chancellor and all the other major Western leaders. Ninety-five percent of CDU-CSU voters considered Gorbachev farsighted, 94 percent felt he was full of ideas, and 95 percent believed he was hardworking. The corresponding values for Kohl were 58, 46, and 81 percent. Gorbachev was better known in West Germany than was Johannes Rau, the SPD leader. Moreover, whereas in 1981 there was a significant gap between West German perception of Americans being friendly and trustworthy and Russians being unfriendly and untrustworthy, this contrast was virtually absent from the 1989 opinion poll, where Russians and Americans were almost on an equal footing.[9] A *Moscow News* survey of Muscovites at the same time found considerable ignorance about the details of West German politics and society (only 63 percent, for instance, knew that Kohl was the chancellor), but also an overwhelming belief that Soviet–West German relations had improved since the beginning of perestroika (78 percent) and a slight majority arguing that the Soviet Union, rather than the FRG, was responsible for these improvements. Although 97 percent of the respondents had never visited West Germany, 85 percent of those under thirty said they would like to work there for some time.[10]

The image of West Germany as a prosperous, desirable place to work, as opposed to a breeding-ground of neo-Nazis, was very much in evidence on Soviet television during Gorbachev's visit. Soviet viewers were shown young West Germans in their affluent homes and hard at work in factories and offices. The message was clear—if you want to live like West Germans, you must work like them. Gorbachev himself was greatly impressed by the workers whom he met at the Hoesch factory in Dortmund and threw away his prepared text to engage them in a lively, open discussion.[11] This was a far cry from the traditional Soviet media coverage of the revanchist West German state that oppressed its workers and had legions of unemployed.

A major focus of Gorbachev's visit was economic, reinforcing the impression that his reforms were not succeeding and that he believed that he needed more Western assistance. But as in the past, Soviet expectations of West Germany's willingness and ability to turn around the inefficient Soviet economy were highly unrealistic. Between 1984 and 1988, there had been a steady decline in Soviet–West German trade. It had risen since Chancellor Kohl's visit, with West German imports from Russia rising 17 percent to $1.25 billion, and exports climbing 30 percent to $1.75 billion. But this was still only 2 percent of total West German trade.[12] Gorbachev and his advisors continued to place their hopes in joint ventures. arguing that Germany had not been bold enough in pursuing them. But in his speech welcoming Gorbachev to the Ostausschuss der deutschen Wirtschaft, its president, Otto Wolff von Amerongen, warned his Soviet guest that "joint ventures are the highest and most difficult form of economic cooperation. We must not exaggerate them." He reiterated that bilateral trade would continue to be the most important form of economic interaction.[13] Moreover, Gorbachev admitted that the USSR had only used 15 percent of the Deutsche Bank credits extended in July 1988 because it did not want to add to its already large debt-service payments.[14] Gorbachev visited Stuttgart, capital of Baden-Württemburg to drum up support for more high-technology projects in the USSR and to criticize remaining American-inspired technology transfer controls that his German hosts also disliked.

Altogether, twenty-three separate agreements were signed during the visit, including ones on environmental, cultural, and scientific-technical cooperation, on exchange of information about nuclear power plant accidents, and on educational and other types of exchanges. One agreement provided protection for German investments in the Soviet Union and another created a German training and development program for Soviet managers, a project discussed during Kohl's trip to Moscow. A couple of agreements could not be signed because of continuing differences over Berlin, but still the concrete results of the summit were considerable.[15] The negotiations involved a concrete German commitment to support perestroika, but fell short of more grandiose Soviet schemes—echoing both past West German–Soviet meetings and future Russo-German summits, where the German business community remained reticent.

The most notable outcome of the summit, and one that suggested how far Soviet thinking on Eastern Europe and Soviet foreign policy had come, was the Joint Declaration, which had been in the making for a year.[16] Intended as a sequel to the 1970 Moscow Treaty, it spelled out basic principles of European politics and Soviet–West German relations. The major significance of the Bonn Declaration, as it came to be known, was its implications for Soviet policy in Eastern Europe. The document stated that "The Federal Republic and the Soviet Union consider it a paramount objective of their policy to continue Europe's historical traditions and thus to contribute to overcoming the division of Europe. They are determined to work together on concepts of achieving this goal through the building of European peace and cooperation—in which the U.S.A. and Canada also have a place."[17] If Europe's division was to be overcome, then surely so must Germany's division, especially since the declaration emphasized the importance of Soviet-FRG relations in securing a peaceful order in Europe. The other major signal was the statement about the need to guarantee "the right of all peoples and states to determine their fate freely and to base their relations with each other on legal, sovereign norms." Gorbachev had spoken about freedom of choice previously, including in his December speech at the United Nations, but in a major document on Soviet–West German relations, this assumed added significance. Surely freedom of choice had to apply to everyone, including citizens of the GDR. Indeed, a careful perusal of the language in the declaration, and its references to the right of peoples to self-determination, shows that it reflected decades-old West German legal language on the right of the GDR population to free elections.[18]

Despite these portents of radical new thinking on Germany, however, the old Soviet ambiguity remained. The subject of the GDR barely came up in Gorbachev's discussions, and when asked about the Berlin Wall in his press conference, Gorbachev sounded a little like Erich Honecker. "There is nothing eternal under the sun. . . . The Wall appeared in a specific situation and was not dictated by some evil design. . . . The Wall can only disappear when the preconditions that gave rise to it vanish."[19] Shevardnadze, however, sounded a different note in his discussions with Genscher. Responding to President Bush's call to tear down the Wall, Shevardnadze said that the Wall would fall when the conditions were right, but that this required a certain degree of trust and respect among all sides. Genscher believed that at this point, Moscow had a good idea of the real state of affairs in the GDR. Shevardnadze admitted that, unlike the USSR, the GDR would not allow "any fresh air in."[20] The signals from the Soviet visitors seemed to be strong, but they were mixed. Gorbachev, like the adoring German media, however, considered his visit a great success. "Everything went very well," he told Ambassador Kvit-sinsky, "Perhaps too well. Let's think about how we can move further forward with this."[21]

Shortly after Gorbachev's departure, however, the German public received a sober reminder that despite his foreign policy successes, the Soviet leader faced mounting domestic problems. In a discussion on West German television, representatives from the Congress of People's Deputies said that Soviet public opinion was not particularly impressed by Gorbachev's success in Germany. The situation in the USSR, they said, was getting worse all the time. Gorbachev was promising things that he could not deliver. The growing domestic crisis was, of course, one of the major reasons for Gorbachev's desire to improve ties with the West for the sake of bolstering his economic program. It ultimately led him to make far more radical decisions regarding Eastern Europe than he initially wanted to.

Was Gorbachev's trip to West Germany a prelude to rethinking relations with East Germany? The evidence is conflicting. As Anatoly Cherniaev, Gorbachev's chief foreign policy advisor, and Gorbachev himself pointed out, the visit to the FRG in June 1989 had a profound effect on his understanding both of the differences between Soviet propaganda and the reality of West German society and of the differences between East and West Germany. In a general way, it may have reinforced his belief that the division of Germany was not forever. In a private conversation with Kohl, he discussed the future of Europe in overall terms; but there is little evidence to support rumors that a deal on German unification was struck then, which included economic concessions involving large sums of money.[22] In his memoirs, Kohl recalls that, as he and Gorbachev sat watching the Rhine, he told his Soviet guest: "Look at the river flowing past. It symbolizes history, it is not static. You could dam the river; it is technically possible. But it would overflow the banks and find its way to the sea. So it is with German unity."[23] The chancellor believed that his words had a profound impact on Gorbachev's thinking about Germany. Gorbachev's warm reception in the FRG enabled him a few months later to begin negotiating with Bonn on German unification on a foundation of friendly ties that had been laid during his June summit. In this sense, one should not exaggerate the importance of statements from some Soviet politicians in early 1989 about the German question being "open." At this point, whatever he may have believed about the longer term, Gorbachev had not accepted the possibility either of the GDR's imminent demise or of unification within a short time. He and his advisors knew that the situation in the GDR had to change, but none of them were in favor of rapid unification.

"But Erich, Who Will Be Left to Turn Out the Lights?"

Meanwhile, events in Eastern Europe were unfolding at a dizzying pace. The East German revolution was part of a wider drama that began peacefully in Poland in January 1989 and ended violently in Rumania in December. Within one year, forty years of communist rule in all six Central and East European countries were overthrown. The domino effect—as one communist regime fell, the next began to crumble—was remarkable. In each successive country, communism collapsed more quickly than in the previous one, just as between 1945 and 1949, each communist regime was imposed more quickly than the previous one. By barely interfering with the fall of the first domino, Poland, Gorbachev set in motion a chain reaction that generated its own momentum, accelerated the fall of communism in each successive country, and finally exploded (and imploded) in the streets of Bucharest on Christmas Day. The fall of Honecker and of the GDR can be fully understood only in this context.

Gorbachev's moves toward conventional force reductions in Central Europe had affected domestic developments in the Warsaw Pact states. In the summer of 1987, Gorbachev advisor Aleksandr Yakovlev had visited the GDR for a "vacation." His real mission was to assess the situation in the country. "What do you think, isn't the Group of Soviet Forces in Germany too big? What will happen if we announce a unilateral reduction in our forces?" he asked Ambassador Kochemasov.[24] Gorbachev's December 1988 speech to the United Nations announced the beginning of a significant unilateral withdrawal of Soviet forces from Eastern Europe. In addition to reducing the Soviet armed forces by 500,000 officers and enlisted men, Gorbachev promised to withdraw from the GDR, Czechoslovakia, and Hungary six tank divisions—5,000 tanks and 50,000 troops—which would then be disbanded. Gorbachev announced these cuts partly for economic reasons, but also to reinforce the message that he was indeed serious about New Political Thinking and about modifying the Soviet role in Eastern Europe. These cuts amounted to a far more significant reduction of Soviet forces in Europe than did the INF agreement. Moreover, Soviet forces in Eastern Europe had not only been directed against the West, whether in their official role of defending the Warsaw Pact from NATO aggression or their actual one of intimidating it by an offensive threat; their function had also been to enforce Soviet control over Eastern Europe. The force reductions, together with a number of statements hinting that the Brezhnev Doctrine was for all intents and purposes dead, signaled that a new policy was emerging: Soviet troops and tanks were unlikely to keep unpopular leaders in power. Gorbachev was sending a chilling message to leaders in Eastern Europe who opposed him, and a message of hope to their peoples. Moreover, in January 1989, Shevardnadze had told Genscher that the USSR ultimately intended "to withdraw all of its military forces from the territories of other countries": the majority of these forces were stationed in East Germany. The Soviet foreign minister also said that the mere withdrawal of weapons was less important than overcoming the division of Europe—a remark that Genscher took as a "revolutionary signal."[25]

Poland had been preparing for its revolution since August 1980 when the independent Solidarity trade union won its first victory—legal recognition of its right to exist. Outlawed after Polish leader Wojciech Jaruzelski's declaration of martial law in December 1981, it had thrived underground (with a little help from the West). Jaruzelski, who had the best relationship with Gorbachev of all the East European leaders, finally lifted the ban on Solidarity in January 1989, allowing it to enter into roundtable discussions with the Communist Party, opposition parties, and the Catholic Church on constructive political change in Poland. Initially, Gorbachev played a facilitating, as opposed to a proactive, role in the Polish revolution. He did not challenge Jaruzelski's decision, but allowed Poland to exercise its freedom of choice. Six months later, however, Gorbachev played a decisive role in ending Communist rule in Poland. After the first postwar free elections, held in in June, Solidarity won a stunning ninety-nine out of a hundred seats in the new Senate. In the lower house, the Sejm, all but two of the thirty-five top party and government officials, who had run unopposed, lost their seats when more than half of the voters crossed out their names on the ballot. By August 1989, Jaruzelski had to name a prime minister and, despite the unambiguous results of the elections, was hesitant to appoint a non-Communist. Moreover, some of his fraternal allies were very nervous about the implications of the Communist Party renouncing its monopoly on state power. A furious Nicolae Ceauşescu, the Rumanian dictator, summoned Shevardnadze to the telephone while he was on vacation at the Black Sea, and demanded that the Warsaw Pact take "decisive military action" against Poland. Ironically, at the eleventh hour, Ceauşescu was trying to resuscitate the Brezhnev Doctrine, which he had vigorously opposed in 1968. Shevardnadze and his aides discussed the situation and decided against intervention, fully realizing that this might spell the beginning of the end of Soviet power in Eastern Europe.[26] Shortly thereafter, Gorbachev made a critical phone call to Mieczysław Rakowski, the Polish Communist Party leader, in which he told his fraternal colleague that the Soviet Union would accept a government with a Communist minority and a non-Communist prime minister. This indeed was the end of the Brezhnev Doctrine. At the decisive moment, Gorbachev intervened to ensure that the Polish Communists accepted the results of the peoples' free choice. Tadeusz Mazowiecki, a prominent Catholic intellectual associated with Solidarity, became prime minister.[27]

The next domino was Hungary, where liberalizing domestic reforms had also begun in January. But the decisive foreign policy decision was taken on May 2, when the government began to dismantle the Iron Curtain—literally, by removing the barbed wire and pulling out the electronic devices along its border with Austria. From now on, anyone was free to leave Hungary. The USSR voiced no objections. Yet Hungarian participants in these decisions subsequently admitted that they knew very well what the broader implications of this move might be. Since East Germans could still travel to Hungary without visas, what was to prevent them from leaving for Austria and other points in the West, in the absence of strict border controls? The Berlin Wall really began to come down when the Austro-Hungarian border was opened: this was the true beginning of the end of the GDR. The Hungarian move recalled the old East German joke about allowing free travel out of the GDR. Honecker discusses with his Politburo colleagues whether they should allow East Germans to travel to the West, and his colleagues ask plaintively, "But Erich, who will be left to turn out the lights in East Germany?"

By the summer of 1989, the situation within the GDR had become very tense, and Soviet-GDR relations frostier. The Soviet leadership was aware of the mounting societal unrest, but unable to convince the Honecker leadership of the need for reform. Honecker and his increasingly isolated comrades felt threatened every time one of their fraternal allies took steps in the direction of liberalization, and they redoubled their efforts at controlling their restive population. When Gorbachev visited Bonn, *Neues Deutschland* commented rather tersely on the visit and omitted all of his references to self-determination.[28] When Honecker visited Moscow in late June, to be briefed by Gorbachev on his trip to West Germany, *Pravda* reported that the interlocutors "united by traditional friendship and relying on common views on fundamental socialist construction" had enjoyed warm, friendly discussions. They even talked about preparations for the Twelfth SED Congress to be held in May 1990.[29] The Soviet Foreign Ministry described the atmosphere as one of "mutual understanding and warmth," but details of the talks suggested a dialogue of the deaf, with Gorbachev emphasizing the importance of perestroika and Honecker praising the GDR's achievements.[30] Indeed, on his last official visit to the USSR, Honecker went out of his way to emphasize his devotion to the Soviet past. He visited Magnitogorsk, where he had worked as a young man in a brigade that stamped the city's steel mills out of frozen earth.[31] But those "heroic" days of Soviet communism were forever gone.

According to Kochemasov, Honecker came to Moscow greatly concerned about the impact of events in Hungary and Poland on the GDR and determined to try and mend fences with Moscow. He even assured Gorbachev, at this eleventh hour, that East Germany supported perestroika and would introduce its own reforms. He was particularly concerned about Bonn's influence on events on Poland and Hungary, voicing fears that the FRG was trying to destabilize the GDR. Gorbachev assured Honecker that he had discussed this with Kohl, and that Kohl had categorically denied that the FRG was trying to utilize the GDR's problems to its own advantage. Honecker returned in an upbeat mood from his visit to the USSR. "We understood each other clearly on all questions," he told Kochemasov of his talks with Gorbachev. "Now we will think about what this means for developments in our country and for our future cooperation."[32]

But it was indeed "five minutes to midnight." The time for reform in the GDR had already passed. Faced with change in Poland, Hungary, and the USSR, the hitherto rather passive East Germans began to demand their own perestroika more actively. Demonstrations and marches emanating from Protestant church gatherings grew. In Leipzig, there were regular Monday night demonstrations. Opposition parties began to form, encouraged by the realization that the results of the May local elections had been falsified.[33] Within the highest echelons of the SED, there was growing concern about Honecker's intransigence and isolation from reality. His illness in July (he was rushed back from a Warsaw Pact meeting in Bucharest to have an operation) removed him from many of the day-to-day discussions. Soviet observers were becoming increasingly alarmed. In July, Dashichev, from whom Soviet officials had distanced themselves, described the division of Germany as "abnormal," and in September warned those in the USSR and GDR resisting change that "It is dangerous and unreasonable to forget the past. But it is equally unreasonable and . . . dangerous . . . to live by the past alone, to be guided by what had historical bases half a century ago but is senseless now."[34]

Valentin Falin, no fan of Dashichev's, realized that the situation in the GDR was almost beyond repair. In a memorandum to the Soviet leadership, he warned that popular dissatisfaction with the regime could lead to "mass demonstrations that would be difficult to control"; that Honecker no longer enjoyed the full support of the party but was unlikely to retire; and that given the tense state of relations between the CPSU and the SED, Moscow had little leverage over East Berlin, which had rejected a reform course.[35] However, Falin's main objective, and that of most of the Soviet leadership, was that reform communists should take power in East Germany and create a more humane socialist government there, one that would not have to be maintained by the presence of Soviet troops. At this point, it was inconceivable to most Soviet officials that the GDR population would not welcome a reformed socialism, especially since that was what many of the new opposition groups, particularly New Forum, were demanding.

While both the Soviet and East German governments struggled to devise a viable strategy for dealing with the East German situation, the Hungarian government made a momentous decision that was "the catalyst for the collapse of the SED's power."[36] Throughout the summer, thousands of disaffected East Germans had gone to Hungary; many had taken up residence in the West German embassy in Budapest. Since the West German government automatically recognized GDR citizens as FRG citizens, their hope was to be allowed to leave for West Germany. With conditions in the embassy becoming intolerable, and with 10,000 East Germans wanting to emigrate having to be housed in temporary camps, Hungarian Foreign Minister Gyula Horn decided that this situation could not continue. Hungary and the GDR had signed a treaty obliging Hungary to repatriate any East German citizens who were trying to flee to the West. Horn decided that Hungary could no longer honor this treaty. West Germany had become Hungary's major Western economic partner, had given it substantial credits, and had encouraged its reformist government. In a series of intense discussions between Hungarian and West German officials, especially Horn and Genscher, the two sides worked out an agreement whereby the Hungarians, in a move that was unprecedented in the history of the Warsaw Pact, would break their treaty with the GDR and allow the East Germans to leave for West Germany, with financial and transportation assistance from Bonn.[37]

The Hungarians had sounded out the Soviet reaction before making their final decision, and had heard no clear objection. Shevardnadze had asked Horn how many East Germans, in his opinion, wanted to leave the GDR. When Horn replied, "perhaps one or two million," Shevardnadze said that he thought they should be allowed to leave because they could not be kept there by force.[38] The Soviets were officially informed one day before the decision was taken. Kohl also sounded Gorbachev out, asking him whether he would support the Hungarian move. The Soviet leader replied: "The Hungarians are good people."[39] Although the Soviets were presented with a fait accompli, they could still have attempted to veto the deal. Gorbachev did not do so, because the price of intervention would have been far too high in terms of his relationship with the West. But the opening of the border, he must have realized, might mean more than a flood of new East German refugees. After all, if East Germans could go freely to West Germany via Hungary, what use was the Berlin Wall?

Although the initial Soviet official reaction to the opening of the border on September 11 was neutral and made no mention of the East German government's protests against the action, the next day TASS denounced the "illegal departure abroad" of East Germans to West Germany and defended the East German government. Gennadi Gerasimov also criticized the West Germans for accepting these illegal East Germans, but fell short of criticizing Hungary.[40] Clearly, there was much internal Soviet dissension about their course of action. The East German leadership, of course, had no such inhibitions. After his ouster, Honecker blamed the demise of socialist solidarity for his fall, saying that the Warsaw Pact should have disciplined Hungary for its actions. Honecker in fact tried to summon a meeting of Warsaw Pact foreign ministers to censure Hungary, but the Soviet leadership demurred.[41]

The final push toward revolt came from the as yet unreformed Czech government, albeit for different reasons than those of the Hungarian government. As more and more East Germans crowded into the West German embassy in Prague, the Czechoslovak government began to fear that its population would become infected with the East German virus of discontent. It implored its East German comrades to do something and persuade its citizens to return, but to no avail. The East German government, contemplating the upcoming celebration of the forieth anniversary of the founding of the GDR, wanted to avoid trouble at all costs. As Genscher and his aides negotiated an agreement with the Czechs, Shevardnadze intervened to make sure that the East Germans went along.[42] At the same time, the Soviets were warning the Federal Republic not to take advantage of the refugee situation.

This was the last straw for Honecker. The embittered East German leader fumed when he saw the pictures of Genscher standing on the balcony of the FRG embassy in Prague, telling the East Germans they could leave and receiving rapturous applause. But Honecker's quintessentially apparatchik response only hastened his downfall. In his typical East German legalistic way Honecker insisted that all the emigrants travel to the West by train through East Germany, which made no geographical sense. They were then to give up their identity papers, so that they could technically leave the GDR as "irresponsible antisocial traitors and criminals," as opposed to refugees. But this particular piece of communist legal pedantry had unexpected results. As the "freedom trains" passed through the GDR, carrying tens of thousands of emigrants, thousands more would-be emigrants crowded station platforms along the route, hoping the trains would stop and desperately trying to jump aboard. Local officials were barely able to control the crowds thirsting for even a brief taste of freedom. Local farmers not trying to leave also waved enthusiastically to the trains as they passed through the countryside—the first time that people

in the more remote rural parts of the GDR had been mobilized to pro-
test. The refugees from Czechoslovakia thus emboldened their fellow-
citizens in the GDR to contemplate leaving forever, and the whole country was in an uproar.

Honecker's Last Hurrah

What could the USSR do to prevent the further disintegration of the
GDR? As more and more refugees left for West Germany, and as disgruntled members of the GDR *nomenklatura* became more frustrated, the
approaching forieth anniversary of the founding of the GDR posed a
major problem for the Soviets. The GDR leadership was intransigent, the
mood within the country turbulent, thousands of people were demonstrating in every major city, and thousands continued to leave for West
Germany. Gorbachev did not want to attend the anniversary celebrations.[43]
But the Soviet leadership decided that he had to attend the ceremonies,
because he needed to meet with the whole SED leadership, as opposed
to Honecker and his few remaining loyal aides, in order to evaluate for
himself what future chances for the GDR there really were.[44] The Soviet
Union and the GDR had become so estranged that leading Soviet officials no longer had a clear sense of the possibilities for reform. Although
some East Germans later claimed that there had for some time been
secret contacts between East German and Soviet reformers aimed at oust-
ing Honecker, there is no evidence that any concerted Soviet-GDR coordination on this issue took place. The Soviets were too preoccupied with
their own domestic economic and political problems, and they had already served notice that their East European allies were free to choose
their own governments. Within the SED Politburo, a group of younger
members—notably the heir apparent Egon Krenz and Günter Schabowski, secretary of the Berlin party organization—had begun to meet in
secret to discuss how to get rid of Honecker.

   Gorbachev, as might have been expected, received a hero's welcome
when he arrived in East Berlin on October 6, to celebrate the glorious
fortieth anniversary of the "First German Workers' and Peasants' State."
The East Germans, like the West Germans, greeted "Gorby" with enthusiasm, even adulation—but for them, unlike the West Germans, it was
almost a matter of life and death, facing as they were an increasingly
menacing party leadership. "Gorbachev, help us, save us!" they shouted,
as he rose to address them from the podium.[45] As Mieczisław Rakowski,
the Polish party secretary, translated this for Gorbachev, he said, "These
are party activists! This is the end!"[46] Gorbachev's speech was moderate
and statesmanlike, but its message was clear: he quoted President Rea-

gan's 1987 appeal to tear down the Berlin Wall without explicitly rejecting it; he spoke about the "sovereignty" of the people; and he stressed
how interested the East German people were in perestroika (obviously
annoying the man standing next to him on the dais).[47] In his private talks
with Honecker, Gorbachev spoke mostly about the situation within the
Soviet Union and the difficulties of implementing perestroika. His fa-
mous warning, "Life punishes those who come too late," was in fact a
description of the Soviet situation,[48] but its implication for the GDR was
unmistakable. Honecker, in contrast to Gorbachev, gave an utterly unrealistic portrayal of the situation within the GDR, failing to mention demonstrations, emigrants, or the faltering economy. Gorbachev—like most
of Honecker's colleagues—was obviously stunned by Honecker's lack of
a grasp on reality. After the East German leader had finished his upbeat
talk, Gorbachev turned to his colleagues and let out an audible hissing
sound, indicating his dissatisfaction. Schabowski claims that Gorbachev
did not explicitly encourage him and Krenz to oust Honecker; Krenz
claims that he did, by pronouncing, as his parting words, "Deistvuite!"
(act).[49] Thus, at this crucial juncture, the Soviet leadership intervened at
least indirectly to influence the outcome of the GDR crisis. According to
Falin, he, Gorbachev, and Georgi Shakhnazarov had wrongly assumed
that the SED, unlike the Polish or Hungarian party, had an efficient and
effective group of younger party functionaries who would be able to
implement perestroika in the GDR and salvage socialism. They all
knew Honecker's days were numbered. Krenz's parting words to Falin
were, "Your side said everything that had to be said. Our side understood
nothing."[50]

Honecker's political life was to last a mere eleven days longer. While
Krenz, Schabowski, and others plotted the details of his removal from
power, Honecker contemplated the use of Chinese-style tactics against
the increasingly vocal demonstrators. The message of the Tienanmin
massacre lay in the eye of the beholder, and in Honecker's shortsighted
view, this was the only effective way to deal with his disloyal population.
Indeed, Honecker met with the Chinese deputy prime minister on Monday, October 9, the day for which a huge demonstration was planned in
Leipzig, just in case anyone had missed the point. It was known that
about 100,000 demonstrators would take part in the march, and rumors
were rife that a "Tienanmin" scenario might occur. The people of
Leipzig had themselves seen police in riot gear and with equipment that
they had never seen before, and feared a possible bloodbath; yet they
were determined not to be cowed.[51]

There are differing versions of exactly what happened at the demonstration. Egon Krenz claims that Honecker was so far removed from reality that he had no plan to deal with any major crisis that might erupt, and

that it was the people on the ground who prevented violence. He strongly denies that the Soviet government ordered its troops to remain in their barracks, because this implies that someone had seriously considered using the Soviet army to crush the demonstration, which he claims was not the case.[52] Viacheslav Kochemasov says that Krenz called him the night before the demonstration and that they both agreed that no blood should flow. Kochemasov claims that he ordered the commander in chief of the Western Group of Soviet Forces (those stationed in the GDR), Boris Snetkov, to ensure that the troops remained in their barracks.[53] Other reports have Soviet tanks actually blocking the entrances to East German military compounds near Leipzig to prevent the National People's Army from moving out.[54] The truth is probably somewhat less dramatic. Certainly, the Soviet forces did nothing to prevent the Leipzig demonstrators from marching and thus enabled the East German revolution to begin. Beyond this enabling role, however, it is not clear that Honecker had ever actually planned to unleash a bloodbath or that Krenz stopped it.[55] Certainly, Leipzig was an armed camp on October 9 and riot-equipped police reinforcements were sent in to intimidate the population. But the evidence suggests that the East German people, through their own restraint, avoided a bloodbath. They, and not the Soviet or East German authorities, deserve the ultimate credit for the peaceful outcome.[56]

What happened in Leipzig was that the resolve and discipline of the demonstrators, assisted by entreaties from a group of prominent Leipzig cultural and political figures, ensured that the riot police did not have to use their weapons. The demonstrators marched peacefully, amazed that they were not greeted with bullets. From their midst rose the cry that was to become the first mantra of the revolution, "Wir sind das Volk" (we are the people), until it was later changed to "Wir sind ein Volk" (we are one people, that is, Germany is one country). The revolution had begun. On October 16, at a discussion at the Soviet Embassy in East Berlin, most diplomats agreed that since the GDR was an "artificial" state, unification was inevitable. The Soviet task now was to ensure that a unified Germany remained neutral. But none of this discussion was reported to Moscow.[57]

That week, Honecker's opponents in the Politburo were finally ready to move. Krenz and Schabowski sent Harry Tisch, the trade union leader, to Moscow to inform Gorbachev of what was to happen. As Schabowski said "We did not want any advice from Gorbachev that he anyway could not have given us. We just wanted him to know that we wished to make up for our historic delays." Gorbachev received Tisch's news with little comment, wishing Tisch and his colleagues good luck in their endeavors. Schabowski also recruited the Soviet ambassador, Kochemasov, to assist the cause by using his influence with Prime Minister Willi Stoph.[58] The actual Politburo meeting at which Honecker was fired was, like any event long in the making and full of intrigue and tension, an anticlimax. Willi Stoph proposed the motion to relieve Comrade Honecker of his functions as general secretary and Honecker, after some argument, submitted, even voting for his own ouster. As he told Kochemasov after the meeting, "I did not have any choice. The situation itself dictated this decision, as you well know."[59] Honecker's ouster, therefore, was not planned by the Soviet Union. Even though Honecker later accused the Soviets of betraying him, this is probably because he could not accept that his own colleagues would, of their own free will, have conspired against him. But he had to face the unpleasant truth: as Brezhnev had warned him twenty years earlier, without Soviet troops to come to his assistance he was ultimately powerless.

In the broader sense, however, Gorbachev and his colleagues enabled the plot against Honecker to succeed because of their explicit message that Eastern Europe should exercise freedom of choice in its political and economic decisions and because they also committed the USSR not to intervene militarily in Eastern Europe. In other words, they exercised influence by not interfering and refusing to support the status quo. At the crucial point, Gorbachev did nothing to prevent Honecker's ouster (it is unclear what he could have done, short of using troops). If the Soviet Union had really had the power to select the leaders of East European states, as it certainly had when Ulbricht was forced out in favor of Honecker, then surely it could have replaced Honecker with a reformer a few years earlier, when it became clear that Honecker was resisting Gorbachev-type reforms to the detriment of the GDR's stability and of the USSR's prestige abroad. By October 1989, the Soviet Union was reduced to hoping—although Gorbachev and Shevardnadze may no longer fully have believed—that the new leader, Egon Krenz, might be able to salvage socialism in the GDR.

The Fall of the Berlin Wall

There is some evidence that when Krenz came to power Gorbachev believed in the remote possibility that the GDR could still be saved. But Krenz's few weeks in office convinced the Kremlin that the SED was rapidly losing control of the country. As Shakhnazarov writes, "The change of party leaders could alter very little."[60] Moscow's preferred candidate was in all likelihood Dresden party chief Hans Modrow, known to be a supporter of Gorbachev-type reforms. But the Kremlin could only sit by and observe as the number of people demonstrating in East Germany, as well as the number of East Germans fleeing to West Germany, increased exponentially. Krenz was a supreme example of "too little, too late." He was unacceptable both to those who wanted reform socialism in the GDR and to the growing numbers who demanded an end to socialism. After all, he had long been Honecker's "crown prince," his handpicked successor, responsible for security matters, and was seen to have been as culpable in perpetrating the repressive regime as his mentor.

Krenz's first and last visit to Moscow as head of the SED on October 31 elicited a more activist Soviet policy. It produced an agreement that the GDR should take all the necessary measures to introduce reforms and ensure that unification did not become a real option. Gorbachev warned Krenz that his difficulties were just beginning. Krenz assured him of his commitment to reform and to close GDR-Soviet relations and was relieved when Gorbachev promised that the USSR would uphold its economic commitments to East Germany. Indeed, Gorbachev expressed shock when Krenz revealed to him how precarious the GDR's economic situation was. Gorbachev recited all the reasons why German unification would be against the interests of both the GDR and the FRG. He suggested to Krenz a calculated triple plan of action: closer coordination between Soviet and GDR policy toward the FRG, closer Soviet–West German relations to weaken U.S.–FRG links, and broader contacts between the GDR and other Western countries. In essence, this was a restatement of the old agenda, although for once Soviet policy toward both German states seems to have been better coordinated. For his part, Krenz promised to handle demonstrations without violence and, ironically in view of what happened ten days later, swore that no mass demonstration would end with a rush on the Berlin Wall.[61] Krenz also claims that Gorbachev believed that reform socialism could succeed in the GDR, but that this would require cooperation not only with Moscow but also with Bonn. Krenz left feeling that he had renewed support from the Kremlin.[62] But the Soviet Union could do little to help the GDR. It had too many of its own problems.

Ten days after Gorbachev and Krenz had agreed that unification was not on the agenda the Wall came down.[63] Both the Soviets and the East Germans have taken the credit for the opening of the Wall. At various points, different actors in this drama took decisions, but during the tense and chaotic night of November 9–10, no one was in a position to have full information or oversee everything. What is clear, however, is that the Berlin Wall was opened because of a fundamental misunderstanding between the East German government and the people over a hastily written piece of travel legislation, and because neither the Soviets nor the East German leadership were ultimately willing to use force.

Five months earlier, Yakovlev had asked Kvitsinsky in Bonn whether the Berlin Wall was really necessary anymore. Kvitsinsky answered that if the wall came down, so would the GDR. The Kremlin should decide whether or not it still needed the GDR.[64] Markus Wolf, former head of the Stasi's Hauptverwaltung Aufklärung (counterintelligence) and subsequent critic of Honecker and Krenz, claims that in July 1989 his friends in the KGB were asking about the West German view of reunification and the removal of the Wall.[65] But in a telephone call to Kochemasov on November 7, Gorbachev said presciently, "The Soviet people will never forgive us if we lose the GDR."[66] Amidst a growing debate within the Soviet Union about the future of Germany, one issue elicited consensus. If the GDR wanted to stem the hemorrhage of its people, it had to liberalize travel, as had the Soviet Union and other socialist countries. After all, many East Germans believed that they would return, if only they had the chance to see West Germany. Moreover, the Czechoslovak authorities, themselves under pressure from growing domestic unrest, issued an ultimatum to the GDR government to do something to stop the swelling tide of East Germans seeking refuge in the West German embassy in Prague—thirteen hundred of them by November 3. Most participants—or at any rate those close to the main actors—concur that the Soviets had agreed, in principle, that the GDR should allow its citizens to travel abroad freely.[67] There is little evidence, however, that the Kremlin expected the Berlin Wall to be breached literally a few hours after the new regulations were announced.

The way in which the new travel regulations were debated was typical of the disarray in which the SED Politburo—once feared as a highly efficient, Prussian-style bureaucratic organization—found itself in early November. In all of the discussions, some of which were public, little distinction was made between temporary departure and permanent emigration. For a communist government hitherto paranoid on the subject of disloyalty and the lure of the lurid West, this lack of differentiation between wanting to see West Germany for a week and wanting to abandon the Socialist Fatherland is unsurprising. But this confusion helped open the Berlin Wall. On November 6, it was announced that a draft of a new travel law was in the making. At this point, 100,000 people had left the GDR since the opening of the Hungarian border in September, and Gregor Gysi, a prominent SED reformer, demanded on television that every citizen receive a passport and be allowed to travel without having to apply for a visa. Meanwhile, Krenz and his colleagues were preoccupied with a three-day Central Committee meeting, during which half the Politburo was ousted and Hans Modrow and other new faces finally joined. Their attention was not on travel laws, but on political maneuvering.

The Council of Ministers was given the task of rewriting the new travel laws, and submitted various drafts to Krenz, which he read only perfunctorily, immersed as he was in his own political struggles. On November 7, GDR Foreign Minister Oskar Fischer telephoned Kochemasov to inform him of the Czechoslovak ultimatum and the need for the GDR to formulate a travel law. Krenz himself had not raised the subject with Kochemasov, much to the latter's later discomfort, although issues of four-power control over Berlin were clearly involved.[68] Igor Maximychev, deputy chief of mission in the Soviet embassy, recounts that Shevardnadze phoned Kochemasov on a secure line on November 7 to say that if "our friends" want this law, we should not oppose it. On November 8, during a discussion at the Soviet embassy in East Berlin, it was agreed that the USSR would have to accept whatever happened, even though some of the participants believed that Krenz was about to open the border altogether and criticized him for not taking into account the need to consult with the four occupying powers. According to Maximychev, despite Soviet concerns, there was no alternative but to endorse whatever Krenz and his colleagues decided, and Krenz was told that the Soviet side would not interfere. In the absence of any objections from the 213 members and candidate members of the SED Central Committee, "The decision to end the Berlin Wall, under conditions which made the speedy demise of the GDR practically inevitable, was taken almost accidentally, in essence, without anyone noticing it."[69]

And so, when a harried and distracted Krenz handed Günter Schabowski two sheets of paper outlining the new legislation that had not yet been endorsed by the Cabinet on the evening of November 9, neither he nor Schabowski had fully digested what this travel law really meant. Indeed, Schabowski was out of the room for much of the time while the legislation was discussed. Schabowski then gave a live press conference on the recent changes in the Politburo; as TASS pointed out, this was the first time that the SED had told its population who held what positions in the new Secretariat and Poltiburo.[70] Schabowski read one sheet of paper outlining the new travel law and said that he would not answer any questions about it. But five minutes before the end of his press conference, in response to an Italian journalist's question, Schabowski pulled a second, crumpled sheet from his pocket with more instructions, and announced that a decision had been made "that makes it possible for every citizen of the GDR to travel abroad via the border crossing points of the GDR." Despite his nonchalant announcement of the new law, journalists immediately seized on his statements and began asking for more precise details. Schabowski became flustered, since he himself was not familiar with the law. When someone asked whether people would need a passport, his answer was negative; and responding to a question about when the new law was to go into effect, he declared that it would do so "immediately." This momentous news was a product of misunderstanding. In fact, the law was to go into effect at four o'clock the next morning but, according to Schabowksi, that was not on the sheets that Krenz had handed him. The governing mayor of West Berlin, Walter Momper, by contrast, fully understood what Schabowski had said. He immediately went on television and announced, "The day that we have awaited for twenty-eight years has come."[71]

While Schabowski went home to Wandlitz, the nouveau riche *nomenklatura* enclave, stunned East Berliners began to take in what they had just seen on television. Slowly and peacefully, thousands began to converge on the crossing points from East to West Berlin. It was the fifty-first anniversary of the *Kristallnacht*, when the Nazis had burned and looted Jewish businesses and synagogues and deported thousands. History was again reaching a turning point. The East Berliners, some in their pajamas, stood at the border, and their cry became louder and louder: "Open the Wall! Open the Wall!" Meanwhile, West Berliners, by now glued to the television, realized that something momentous was about to happen and they, too, took to the streets. Suddenly, to the utter surprise of the East Berliners, and contrary to what Krenz had promised Gorbachev, the border guards opened the gates. The East Berliners walked into the welcoming arms of the West Berliners, and they drank champagne and began to dance on the wall. The party lasted all night. When it was over, East Germany, the only country that had built a wall to keep its own citizens in rather than to keep foreign enemies out, had for all intents and purposes ceased to exist. When the West German Bundestag, meeting in a late-night session, heard the news that the Wall was open, its members rose spontaneously to sing the national anthem. The national question was, once again, truly open.

Who was responsible for opening the Berlin Wall? Schabowski recounts that when he received a phone call that evening describing to him what was happening, he spoke to Krenz, who seemed unperturbed. Krenz recounts in his memoirs that Erich Mielke, the head of the Stasi, had called to ask him what to do and Krenz, who above all wanted to avoid violence, had told him to let the people through.[72] But even before this conversation, some local border guards, after consulting with their Stasi colleagues, had begun to open the crossing points.

Indeed, most people who participated in the decision making during the night of November 9 agree that the immediate decision to open the Wall came not from the East German or Soviet hierarchy, but from frustrated East German border guards who were not given clear instructions. Harald Jaeger, the former deputy commander of the border crossing on the Bornholmerstrasse, recounts that he and his colleagues laughed incredulously as they watched Schabowski's press conference. But as the evening wore on, thousands of East Berliners gathered at the crossing, demanding to be let into West Berlin. The situation became critical. Jaeger kept calling his superior in the Stasi for instructions, but received none. He and his colleagues were armed, but had been told not to use their weapons. They tried unsuccessfully to persuade their fellow citizens to turn back. Ironically, in a testimony to the Stasi's view of its citizens, the guards had instructions about what to do if people tried to break through the border violently, but not if they did so peacefully. Finally, at 10:30 P.M., when 20,000 people had gathered at the gate, Jaeger called his superior and said, "We can't stop them. We must open the border. I shall open the border and let the people out." His Stasi boss merely replied, "OK." Then Jaeger wrote in his log for November 9: "Controls lifted: can do nothing more. Period."[73]

A few days later, Gennadi Gerasimov said that the decision to open the Wall came solely from the GDR and that the East Germans had not asked Gorbachev to give the green light, although the Kremlin supported the decision.[74] Gerasimov stressed that the Soviet authorities had been informed neither in Berlin nor in Moscow ahead of time. Falin claims that Kochemasov consulted with the Soviets about the new travel law, and that he was told that border regulations and travel were "the GDR's internal matter."[75] However, when Kochemasov tried to reach Shevardnadze and Shakhnazarov on November 9, neither of them were available. Maximychev recalls that he decided not to awaken his boss on the night of the ninth, because he doubted that Kochemasov would want to inform Moscow about what had happened unless Kochemasov was convinced that his superiors in Moscow really wanted to receive this news.[76] When the call from Moscow finally came on the morning of November 10, the question from the head of the GDR desk in the Foreign Ministry was, "Did we agree to this?" The answer from the Soviet embassy in East Berlin was that the Foreign Ministry should check this out with the Kremlin, but nothing could have been done to prevent the fall of the Wall. By the end of the day on November 10, Gorbachev had sent a verbal message to Krenz telling him, "Everything was done completely correctly."[77]

After he resigned, Shevardnadze claimed that opponents of the new Soviet policy toward Germany had demanded "the deployment of intervention and blocking divisions along the borders," which he, of course, opposed.[78] For a few hours on November 10, some of the hardline members of the SED leadership tried to reverse the course of events of the previous night and considered using the East German army to close the borders. But the National People's Army, whose morale had sunk greatly as the regime became increasingly repressive, was disinclined to obey. Moreover, Shevardnadze specifically told Kochemasov that the Soviet troops were "not to undertake any action." There were, therefore, explicit Soviet instructions not to engage in any repressive measures against the population.[79]

Thus, the Soviet Union was not directly involved with the decision to open the Wall on the night of November 9–10.[80] It was made by local border guards and eventually sanctioned by higher-ups. Indeed, the Soviets were probably as surprised by the fall of the Wall as were the East Germans. By this time, the KGB and GRU were not supplying Moscow with good intelligence because the situation was in such flux. But in a broader sense, of course, the Soviet Union did open the Wall, because it had already decided not to use its forces to keep the East German population imprisoned.

Soviet and East German participants in the drama, even though they diverge on many issues, agree on these crucial points.[81] Krenz has stressed that the major goal, shared by the Soviet and East German leaderships, was to avoid violence at all costs. Gorbachev had said to him in Moscow, "You must not view the people as an enemy. If the people rise up against policies, then you must think about how to change the policies." Krenz suggests that there may have been a misunderstanding between him and the Soviets on the crucial question of Berlin, because Berlin involved four-power rights, but it would have been surprising if Gorbachev and his colleagues believed that travel liberalization would not be applied to Berlin.[82] As Shakhnazarov writes, "The fall of the Berlin Wall was without doubt the key event which ushered in a new era in international relations. On the other hand, it was one of the most important consequences of the Gorbachev reform, which we can rightly call the reform of the international system."[83] Gorbachev himself says that this all happened because of Soviet initiatives.[84]

The Crucial Three Months: Gorbachev Accepts Unification

Although the Soviets had allowed the Wall to fall, they were by no means ready to accept publicly that unification would be the next step. Gorbachev now faced a threefold challenge: to limit the damage to the prospects for socialist renewal in the GDR; to negotiate with the three other occupying powers in Berlin; and to utilize improved ties with the Federal Republic to slow down the momentum toward unification. His leverage over the GDR was limited and he was torn between negotiating with the weak GDR regime and the strong FRG government. As far as four-power rights were concerned, both British Prime Minister Margaret Thatcher and French President François Mitterrand were unenthusiastic about unification, and it was difficult to tell what the real, as opposed to the rhetorical, American position on unification was. From November to January, therefore, Gorbachev was trying to balance and integrate these contradictory aspects of his policy toward Germany.

After the world had recovered from the scenes of Germans dancing on the Wall, the morning after brought a series of new and hitherto unthinkable questions. Reaction in the West was cautiously optimistic. President Bush's response to the Berlin Wall scenes on television was prescient: "If the Soviets are going to let communism fall in East Germany, they've got to be serious—more serious than I realized."[85] No one in the Kremlin, however, would openly admit this for some time. Yet the day after the Wall came down, Gorbachev entreated Kohl, who had returned from a visit Poland to address a mass meeting in Berlin, to calm the population down, and avoid anything that might further threaten the GDR's existence. Gorbachev stressed that changes mean instability, and that it was important to maintain stability. This, after all, was the essence of Soviet Westpolitik and German Ostpolitik. Kohl assured him he valued his relationship with Gorbachev very highly and that together they would attack the current problems.[86] At the time, Kohl and his aides pondered the deeper meaning of this request: already one day after the Wall was opened, the USSR was appealing to West Germany not to further destabilize East Germany. How the tables had turned![87] Meanwhile, Gorbachev sent alarmist messages to Washington, London, and Paris about the danger of West German designs on the GDR.[88]

The West Germans themselves were amazed by the turn of events. Horst Teltschik, Kohl's national security advisor and himself a Sovietologist, recounts how stunned they were by the fall of the Wall and the sheer dimensions of the surge toward freedom. Kohl, who one year earlier had given an interview in which he had predicted that German unification would not come in his lifetime, was now faced with irrefutable proof to the contrary. Politicians from the mainstream parties in West Germany had by this time grown quite accustomed to the division of Germany and had no drive to move beyond rhetoric on the issue of unification. Indeed, Kohl's immediate reaction was to try to prevent a radicalization of the situation and to seek to work together with Krenz and his successor Hans Modrow. Kohl also told President Bush that it would be an economic disaster if unification occurred within two years.[89] Yet the sheer pressure of numbers, with thousands of East Germans leaving for West Germany, forced him to act. But Kohl's policy was a two-track one. It is to his great credit that he recognized reality when it confronted him, and, being an astute politician, grasped that unification was now inevitable, even though it might be possible to delay it. But how to move toward unification and still placate the nervous Russians?

Unlike the Soviets, the West Germans began to develop a plan of action once the Wall fell. There was a flurry of diplomatic activity during November, as Kohl tried to devise a strategy for dealing with the new reality. He initially focused on self-determination for the GDR, a position which Gorbachev could not but endorse. But East and West German and Soviet definitions of self-determination differed considerably. Meanwhile, Mitterrand and Thatcher hardened their positions on German self-determination, insisting that German unification would hinder further progress on European unity.[90] By the end of November, Kohl realized that he had to seize the initiative. He presented a ten-point plan to the Bundestag on November 28, one that envisaged constructing a network of closer ties between the two German states. The plan proposed the formation of various joint GDR-FRG commissions on ecology, culture, and economic and political issues. Eventually, after an unspecified time, the commissions would lead to vaguely defined confederal structures. In other words, Kohl was promising a gradual rapprochement between the two Germanies, but did not promise unification in one state; rather, his plan still envisaged two German states for the foreseeable future.[91] Kohl had a pressing reason for presenting this plan when he did. Now that there were no border controls between the two Germanies, East Germans continued to emigrate to West Germany at very high levels—130,000 in November alone—raising serious concerns about how West Germany could absorb them. The GDR economy was in free fall, and the population's confidence in their "reformed" government very low.[92] Kohl sought to persuade them to stay in the GDR by promising eventual confederal relations. He consulted neither with his allies nor with his coalition partner, the FDP, before giving this speech, causing considerable anxiety in some NATO capitals and irritation on the part of his foreign minister.[93] Kohl's reasons were the product of sound politics: he wanted to take the initiative ahead of the SPD, traditionally the party that had stressed German unity, and as Teltschik later wrote, "We achieved our goal. The chancellor seized the leadership role in the German question."[94]

Gorbachev reacted angrily to Kohl's ten-point plan. Meeting with Genscher in Moscow on December 5, he complained that Kohl had promised to consult with him during their November 11 telephone conversation, but had betrayed his trust by forcing the question of unification. And, continued Gorbachev, a confederation would have a single foreign policy. Where would the FRG be? In NATO? The Warsaw Pact? Or neutral? Genscher was clearly uncomfortable during this discussion, but Gorbachev himself put forward no new suggestions.[95] Genscher describes this meeting as the most difficult that he ever had with Gorbachev, attributing the Soviet leader's ire to the fact that "Gorbachev did not want to give the impression that he was being overtaken by events. He wanted to remain an actor and an organizer, to control developments and not be put on the defensive. But he also knew that the German question demanded an answer after the events in the GDR."[96]

But Gorbachev had passed up the opportunity to take the initiative on Germany at his Malta summit with Bush a few days before he met Genscher. He expressed his irritation with Kohl's plan and said of the German problem, "History created this problem and history will have to solve it." Responding to reporters' questions after the summit, he said, "Any artificial acceleration of the process would only exacerbate and make it more difficult to change."[97] But he also said, in passing, that a united Germany should remain neutral, implying that he accepted the possibility of such a state.[98] Indeed, the U.S. side emerged from Malta convinced that Gorbachev was malleable on the German issue.[99]

By December, therefore, the signals on Germany emanating from the Kremlin were mixed. Although Portugalov had privately indicated to Teltschik that the Soviet leadership was considering a variety of options in the German question, publicly the Soviets rejected the idea that unification was an immediate issue. However, events in Eastern Europe were moving much faster than they had ever imagined, and as every communist government in Eastern Europe collapsed, this influenced their policies toward the GDR. The Czech domino began to topple with remarkable speed. On November 24, General Secretary Miloš Jakeš resigned. By December 10, Václav Havel, the dissident playwright who had been imprisoned for much of 1989, was the new president of Czechoslovakia. As the joke went, Poland took ten years, Hungary ten months, East Germany ten weeks, Czechoslovakia ten days and Rumania ten hours. By the end of December, the GDR and the USSR were the only Warsaw Pact states that still had Communist governments. Gorbachev could accept that communism's days were numbered in the GDR, but he could not yet digest the fact that the GDR state itself was truly on the point of collapse. Egon Krenz finally resigned on December 6, and Prime Minister Modrow now was fully in charge, but, by this time, it was too late to make a difference. Demonstrations continued, only now the banners read "Ein deutsches Volk, Ein deutsches Land" (One German People, One German Land). The people had spoken clearly.

Throughout December, the Soviets became increasingly critical of Western policy on Germany and both Gorbachev and Shevardnadze became more uncompromising rhetorically. Nevertheless, Shevardnadze was also thinking ahead. Pavel Palazchenko, who interpreted for Gorbachev and Shevardnadze, recalls a conversation with the Soviet foreign minister as they flew to Brussels in December for Shevardnadze's pathbreaking visit to NATO headquarters—the first time that a high Soviet official had set foot in "enemy" territory. Shevardnadze, he recalls, real-ized that unification was inevitable, all the more so because as a Georgian operating in the Soviet system, he was particularly sensitive to issues of national self-determination and identity. But the pace of German unifica-tion alarmed him and he feared that if it came too soon, Gorbachev's whole domestic program would be endangered: "We could perhaps slow it down but we could not stop it. The big question was how this would be received in the Soviet Union. Could it become the straw that would break the back of Gorbachev's perestroika?"[100] Shevardnadze's speech to the Political Committee of the European Parliament in Strasbourg on December 19 typified this duality—the recognition that unification was in the long run inevitable but the fear that if it came too soon, it would endanger the Gorbachev revolution. He stressed that the world had to respect the sacrifices of the Second World War, and that Europe had to overcome its own division before one could talk of German unity. But he also discussed the possible international ramifications of German unifica-tion, raising issues that came to dominate the agenda in the first six months of 1990.[101]

Gorbachev's critics on both the left and the right have accused him of failing to devise any strategies to deal with different options as the GDR began to unravel. "After 9 November 1989 there was a complete lack of concepts in Soviet policy toward Germany," writes Dashichev, "There was no clarity vis à vis German unification, the political and military status of Germany, or the rights of the former Allies."[102] Kochemasov argues that Gorbachev could have done much more to influence not only the situation in the GDR but also Kohl's policies, but did not do so. "The reasons for such passivity," he concludes, "are hard to understand."[103] Gorbachev also continually sent mixed signals. After the lawyer Gregor Gysi had been elected head of the newly created successor party to the SED in mid-December, Gorbachev called him and promised to do every-thing in his power to stabilize the GDR and pursue a more active policy on the German question. Gorbachev ended the conversation by saying: "Rest assured, Mr. Gysi, the Soviet Union, in its own interests, can't let the GDR down."[104] It is remarkable that the German problem, which had dominated Moscow's foreign policy for so long, elicited only reactions, and no proactive policies, from the Kremlin. Between November 9, 1989 and July 16, 1990, when Gorbachev agreed to the external aspects of unification, there seemed to be no consistent Soviet plan of action nor a conceptual basis for discussions with the West.

Finding a rational answer to the question of why Gorbachev and his colleagues had no strategy presents a challenge to those who assume that states pursue their national interests in some reasonably consistent way. But in the case of Gorbachev and German unification, several factors militated against devising a coherent strategy. First, Gorbachev was primarily preoccupied with constant internal crises and challenges to his authority; the exigencies of domestic politics distracted him from focusing squarely on foreign policy. Second, the group that did focus on Germany and did have strong views, the *Germanisty,* were largely opposed to the flexible policies of Shevardnadze and Gorbachev, and their ideas were, therefore, regarded with considerable skepticism by the Soviet leadership. Third, Gorbachev faced a serious dilemma: events in Germany were rapidly moving toward an outcome which he did not want—unification—but which he felt that he could not stop. The Soviet reluctance to accept publicly that Germany would be unified was deeply rooted in Soviet political culture. The USSR had lost 27 million people in World War II, and the division of Germany was the price the Germans had to pay for this devastation. To reunite Germany would call into question why so many Soviet citizens had sacrificed their lives in the Great Patriotic War. But it was also very difficult to devise a strategy that could slow down the rush to unification without shedding any blood or antagonizing the West. In other words, there were few alternatives other than accepting unification or preventing it with violence.

The one area in which Gorbachev and Shevardnadze sought to take the initiative and brake the momentum toward unification was when they tried to resuscitate four-power rights in Berlin. After all, Berlin was still officially under four-power jurisdiction and, some Soviets argued, the GDR technically had no right to open the borders on November 9. But the real purpose of raising the four-power issue was to remind Germans in both Germanies that they were not masters of their own fate and to reinforce French and British opposition to unification. The Soviet Union called a four-power meeting of ambassadors in the Berlin Allied Control Council building (the first in eighteen years) in order to deliberate on "the control mechanisms created by the former allies of the anti-Hitler coalition."[105] Although the United States was hesitant about attending this meeting because of concerns about Germany's reaction to this sudden assertion of victors' prerogatives forty-five years after the war, the British and French were more receptive. But the Western side insisted on discussing only issues involved with the Allied Berlin initiatives proposed by Reagan and renewed by Bush. These dealt with raising Berlin's international profile, but not with the German question per se. The meeting yielded few results; but the very fact that it was held and that it produced a photo opportunity of the four ambassadors representing occupation forces standing in front of the old Allied command headquarters infuriated the Germans. "What was this supposed to mean? An admonition to the Germans?" recalls Genscher.[106] Soviet critics, however, especially those at the East Berlin embassy, argue that the USSR could have done more to influence what happened had it invoked four-power rights more consistently.[107] In fact, Moscow subsequently sought to use the four-power mechanism a number of times, but the three Western powers resisted. The issue of four-power rights contains another clue as to how Germany was unified: even when Moscow had a coherent plan, firm and consistent West German and American policies rebuffed Soviet overtures that went counter to the Western agenda.

By late December, the Kremlin's message was that it accepted in principle that the status of the two Germanies would change, but that it wanted the pace of change to slow down. During these weeks, Gorbachev and Shevardnadze were also keenly aware of the opposition in the USSR to the collapse of communism in Eastern Europe and particularly in the GDR. The opposition came from the military and many party functionaries.[108] It appeared that the entire basis of postwar Soviet power and influence was being eroded. Under these circumstances, the public face of Soviet diplomacy on German unification was very cautious. Yet, when all was said and done, there was little that Moscow could do to stop the process of unification as more and more East Germans began to vote with their feet. Those remaining had lost their fear and would not submit to a government that they considered illegitimate. Nevertheless, there were enough rebels in the GDR who favored a "third way" between old-style communism and capitalism to give those similarly inclined in the Soviet Union hope that the GDR might remain in some improved form.

Throughout December and January, a pattern of Soviet behavior was to emerge that was all too reminiscent of the days before New Political Thinking. On the one hand, a variety of advisors and old German hands would drop hints indicating Soviet flexibility on the German question. On the other hand, both Shevardnadze and Gorbachev would make hardline statements reminding the world that the results of World War II could not be undone. Of course, they were not alone in their concerns about Germany. French President François Mitterrand stunned his allies by taking the unprecedented (and, in retrospect, ill-advised) step of making a state visit to the teetering GDR on December 20, apparently to shore up its legitimacy and serve notice to his friend Helmut Kohl that Germany's neighbors were concerned about the pace of events and did not welcome the prospect of reunification.

Although the Soviets were unable to develop a systematic bargaining strategy, they had begun to devise means of optimizing their limited leverage in this chaotic situation. In the middle of December, the West German ambassador in Moscow told Teltschik that the Soviet leadership was complaining that the promised Soviet-FRG economic cooperation had not developed as they had hoped. Three weeks later, Ambassador

Kvitsinsky told Teltschik that the situation in the Soviet agricultural sector was deteriorating and that Moscow urgently needed food assistance. The implied message, coming before Kohl's visit to Moscow, was that it was in Bonn's political interest to offer some more economic carrots to Moscow. Money was not irrelevant in the dance toward German unification. Indeed, when Kohl went to Moscow in February, he pledged DM 220 million in food aid. During this period, West German politicians were frustrated by these conflicting Soviet signals, wondering which ones to take seriously. But their primary focus was to ensure that their Western allies stood behind them as unification became inevitable.

While the Soviet side prevaricated, Kohl and his advisors realized that in order to prevent the economic collapse of East Germany, monetary union would have to come swiftly. By the end of December they were beginning to work out the details of a currency union between the two Germanies as another means of stabilizing the GDR economy so as to persuade East Germans to remain there.[109] The SED, meanwhile, continued to live in a fairy-tale world. At its last party congress, during which it changed its name to SED-PDS (Party of Democratic Socialism), German unification was barely discussed, as the leadership spoke about reinvigorating reformed socialism and dialogue with other parties. "A unification of the GDR and FRG is not a current political question," declared Hans Modrow, "and no one who sincerely desires a healthy and peaceful development should artificially speed it up or include it in an election campaign."[110] Yet, despite these Soviet and East German attempts to deny the reality of what was happening, Moscow slowly began to realize that it would have to accept reality in order to fashion a credible response. On December 19, Kohl and Modrow had fleshed out Kohl's idea of a *Vertragsgemeinschaft* (treaty community) although their respective interpretations of what this meant were very different.

As the West German government moved toward working out the details of currency union, the Soviet leadership finally confronted the reality of unification—even though it continued to speak with a forked tongue after assenting to the principle of German unification, reflecting the enormous domestic controversy surrounding the issue.

On January 26, 1990, Gorbachev summoned his closest group of advisors for a tough four-hour session on Germany—the first such meeting dealing with the issue in a systematic way since the fall of the Wall. Prime Minister Nikolai Ryzhkov, Aleksandr Yakovlev, Shevardnadze, KGB chief Vladimir Kriuchkov, Falin, Cherniaev, Rafael Fyodorov from the International Department, former Chief of the General Staff Sergei Akhromeyev, Gorbachev advisor Sergei Tarasenko, and Shakhnazarov took part. The assembled Soviet German experts disagreed on whether the CDU-CSU or SPD view (favoring a much longer timetable for unification) would prevail. There was a general consensus that Soviet German policy should focus on West, as opposed to East, Germany, and all the participants recognized, however reluctantly, that Germany would be united. But Gorbachev said that the USSR must defend its interests, that the FRG should leave NATO, and that a united Germany should be demilitarized. The participants also agreed to coordinate Soviet policy more closely with that of France and Britain, since neither country was enthusiastic about unification. Thus, by the end of January, Gorbachev and his advisors had accepted the inevitability of German unification, even though in early February, at a Central Committee plenum, Yegor Ligachev, by now Gorbachev's nemesis, lashed out against the attempt to "force the unification of Germany."[111] The external details, however, remained to be discussed.[112]

On January 28, Modrow and the other party leaders in the East German coalition decided that, in view of the instability in the GDR, the first democratic elections should be moved up from June to March. The following day, when Modrow was in Moscow to present his ideas for confederal structures rather than unification, Gorbachev told journalists that "no one ever casts doubt in principle on the unification of the Germans," though he insisted that German neutrality be a precondition for negotiation.[113] In this way, Gorbachev "pulled the rug out from under the feet of his ally." It was too late for confederal structures.[114] Indeed, Kohl speculates that, had Gorbachev at this point offered rapid unification in return for Germany leaving NATO and becoming neutral, his plan would have been popular in both German states and the course of history might have been much different from what eventually emerged in July.[115] In a conversation with U.S. Secretary of State James Baker on February 9, Gorbachev was assured that the United States would not take advantage of the situation to undermine Soviet security and would do everything it could to make sure that German unification proceeded smoothly. Baker and Gorbachev agreed that German unification was an issue for the Germans themselves to decide.[116]

The Soviet assent to unification became official when Kohl visited Moscow on February 10. Kohl stressed that the internal and external aspects of German unification must be dealt with together. United Germany could not be neutral, but he was sure that an arrangement could be worked out whereby NATO would not extend into GDR territory. Gorbachev listened and then uttered words that surprised and delighted his hosts: there was no difference of opinion between the Soviet Union, the Federal Republic, and the GDR about the right of the Germans to find their own path toward unification. "I said long ago that a solution to the German question would be a matter for history to decide. And history has gone to work with surprising speed. We must weigh our actions very carefully, taking truly historic criteria into account."[117]

Inwardly jubilant, Kohl and his aides reacted in a restrained way. They knew that the decisive breakthrough had come. Gorbachev had managed to prevail over opponents of unification. Moreover, the Germans promised that they would assume all the economic and financial obligations that the GDR had to the USSR, an issue that was of considerable concern to the Soviets. During this meeting, Gorbachev uttered another sensational sentence: he realized that German neutrality was unacceptable to many countries, including the Germans. He did not know what Germany's ultimate status would be, but this remained to be determined. Falin turned to another veteran Central Committee apparatchik, Vadim Zagladin, and acidly declared that since the German problem had been solved, they could now retire.[118] The formal communiqué did not discuss questions of Germany's international status, but stressed the agreement over the principle of unification.[119] The Soviet endorsement of unification had come just in time. Five weeks later, on March 18, the East German electorate, in its first free vote and contrary to most predictions, gave an overwhelming endorsement to the CDU and its allied parties, and thus to rapid unification. The conservative coalition won 49.8 percent of the votes, while the Social Democrats, who favored a slower path to unification and were traditionally strong in the eastern part of Germany, garnered only 21.2 percent of the votes.[120]

In a mere three months Gorbachev moved from vague statements about history deciding Germany's fate to a full, direct endorsement of unification. Despite the sometimes harsh rhetoric from Shevardnadze and others, Gorbachev and his close aides were eventually able to accept reality. The old German hands, however, were not. The *Germanisty* had a far greater stake in opposing German unity. After all, their entire careers had been built on ensuring that the two German states remained separate and did not threaten Soviet interests.[121]

What in the end decided the issue for Gorbachev was the national question. He realized that the Modrow government would no longer be in power after the March elections; and if East Germany could no longer be socialist, how could there be an East German state? After all, the Poles, Hungarians, and Czechs and Slovaks retained a strong national consciousness, separate from communism; when communism fell, the Polish, Hungarian, Slovak and Czech nations remained. But East Germany had never developed a separate national identity. Its only justification for existence had been that it was a better, socialist Germany. With socialism rejected, nothing was left. It became, in the words of the dissident writer Stefan Heym, "a footnote to history."[122]

Once the Soviets bowed to the inevitable, they sought to maximize the gains from West Germany. Early in 1990, this meant increased assistance—a DM 220 million package of humanitarian assistance on February 9—and promises of greater economic involvement. It also meant West German assurances that a future united Germany would not be hostile to Soviet interests. But this was indeed modest compensation for losing what had once been regarded as the jewel in the crown of the Soviet empire. Now that Moscow had ceded the internal aspects of unification, Gorbachev only had one trump card left—Germany's international status. Yet, in reality, his options were few. The question of neutrality versus NATO membership was, with hindsight, less open than many at the time believed. By the end of the intense six-month period of negotiating the external aspects of German unity, Gorbachev might well have recalled the advice he gave to students in Treptow Park (site of the massive war memorial to Soviet soldiers) during his October visit to the GDR: "Don't be afraid of life. Even though it may bring you surprises, don't be afraid of it."[123]

Reflections

The way in which the Soviet assent to German unity was arrived at— almost serendipitously, with few clear decision-making landmarks and the Soviet Union conceding in the face of determined Western policy—has affected the way in which Russians and Germans view each other today. The USSR watched the fall of Honecker almost from the sidelines. The Soviets were marginal players in the fall of the Berlin Wall and in the events that led to the collapse of East German socialism and of the GDR. Even the Soviet ambassador to East Berlin and the Soviet intelligence apparatus were poorly informed about the real state of affairs in East Germany, and were told of developments after, and not before, they took place.

Moscow did, however, retain some influence over East German policies, and was consulted by the East German leadership after Honecker's fall. But the Kremlin's responses were fragmented, unfocused, and essentially reactive. Preoccupied as he was with his domestic problems, Gorbachev paid only partial attention to what was happening in the GDR. After the Wall, came down, he had no concept of what should happen in East Germany although he wanted to avoid unification. But by the time he convened his brain trust on Germany in January 1990, the USSR had already de facto conceded unification, despite its protests against Kohl's ten-point plan and the Allied response.

The East German party and government officials were also unable to act in a concerted way. After Honecker's fall, and under pressure from increasing demonstrations, the *nomenklatura* was mainly concerned with holding on to power and had no systematic reform plans. When Modrow finally took over in December, the East German population had already lost confidence in the possibility of reformed socialism succeeding.

West Germany played the most important enabling role of any outside power because of its negotiations with the Hungarian and Czechoslovak governments on allowing East German refugees to leave for the FRG. However, West Germany was no more in favor of rapid German unification than was the USSR. Kohl's ten-point plan was both a response to the pressure from refugees flooding West Germany and to the outcome of his desire to preempt his political competitors. But Bonn, unlike Moscow, seized the initiative and began to try to shape developments in the GDR in consultation with its allies. Kohl had a greater role in setting the agenda than did his Soviet partner. The United States also played a pivotal role in supporting West German policies and persuading Gorbachev to accept them.

Could the Soviet Union have prevented German unification? Theoretically yes. But if the Soviets had used force to keep the GDR in existence, East-West cooperation, an essential component of Gorbachev's revolution, would have ended. Domestic perestroika would also have disappeared because Gorbachev would have lost his credibility as a reformer. Thus, though force was a theoretical option, it was not a practical one, especially after the Soviet Union formally renounced the Brezhnev Doctrine at a Warsaw Pact meeting in December 1989. Gorbachev had unwittingly hastened the downfall of the GDR by his policies. History had decided that the German nation would unite not in a hundred years, as Gorbachev had predicted in 1987, but a mere five years after he came to power.

What lessons did the Western side learn from these three whirlwind months? They realized that, although the Kremlin opposed unification, it would only employ only words, not deeds, to counter the inter-German momentum. Faced with a united Western front, Gorbachev gave in. Apart from sporadic attempts to revive four-power rights, there were no Soviet initiatives. Despite what Gorbachev, Shevardnadze, and their colleagues have written *ex post facto*, there is no evidence that in 1989 they were seriously contemplating German unification in the near future. It was thrust upon them. Thus, as the second—and more difficult—phase of negotiations on German unification began, West Germany and its allies anticipated only sporadic opposition from the Soviet Union. Nevertheless, there were nagging doubts during the first half of 1990. Might Gorbachev and Shevardnadze suddenly change their modus operandi and present the West with a tough, coherent strategy?

Adenauer in Moscow, 1955. Nikita Khrushchev, with back to camera, talks with (*left to right*) Nikolai Bulganin, Georgi Malenkov, and Adenauer; in the shadow behind Malenkov is Vyacheslav Molotov. When Molotov denounced the sins of Hitler and the German people, Adenauer retorted, "Who actually concluded the agreement with Hitler, you or I?" (Courtesy German Information Center)

Berlin is divided, August 13–14, 1961 West Berliners (*right*) talk to East Berliners as the Berlin Wall goes up. It would be the last of such conversations until 1989. (Courtesy German Information Center)

The no-man's land. By October 1961, the historic Brandenburg Gate, once the symbol of Prussian glory, stood in the middle of a bleak and heavily-mined death zone. (Courtesy German Information Center)

Ostpolitik at its peak, September 1971. Chancellor Willy Brandt (*right*) and Soviet General Secretary Leonid Brezhnev enjoy the scenery on a boat off the Crimean peninsula. Three years later Brandt would be forced to resign, betrayed by an East German spy. (Courtesy German Information Center)

The thaw. Chancellor Helmut Schmidt (*left*) and East German leader Erich Honecker confer near Berlin, on Schmidt's first official visit to the GDR, December 13, 1981. That night, martial law was declared in Poland. "I am sure Mr. Honecker is as surprised by this as I am," commented Schmidt to the consternation of many. (Courtesy German Information Center)

"Reagan go home!" Demonstrators in West Berlin march against President Ronald Reagan's visit and the deployment of Pershing missiles, November 1982. Despite their opposition, the missiles were deployed, a major setback for the Soviet Union. (Courtesy German Information Center)

Honecker's last hurrah. Chancellor Helmut Kohl (*right*) greets East German leader Erich Honecker on his first (and last) state visit to Bonn, September 1987. After visiting his birthplace in the Saarland, he told Kohl that the two German systems were as irreconcilable as "fire and water." (Courtesy German Information Center)

The final kiss. Erich Honecker (*right*) greets his nemesis Mikhail Gorbachev on his arrival in East Berlin to celebrate the fortieth anniversary of the founding of the GDR on October 6, 1989. Raisa Gorbachev looks on. Twelve days later, after Gorbachev had warned him that "Life punishes those who come too late," Honecker was ousted. (Courtesy Reuters/Corbis-Bettmann Archive)

"Wir sind ein Volk!"
(We are one people).
A West German border
guard (*left*) and his
East German coun-
terpart stand by
impassively as
Germans begin to
tear down the Wall,
twenty-eight years
after its construction,
on November 9, 1989.
(Courtesy German
Information Center)

Meeting in the Caucasus. A smiling Helmut Kohl (*left*) reacts to Gorbachev's assent to a united Germany's membership in NATO, July 15, 1990. Gorbachev was heavily criticized by his Soviet opponents for making this concession. (Courtesy German Information Center)

Day of triumph. On October 4, 1990, leading German politicians celebrate unification in Berlin, forty-one years after Germany was divided. *Left to right:* SPD leader Oskar Lafontaine, Minister of Technology Heinz Riesenhuber, former Chancellor Willy Brandt, Foreign Minister Hans-Dietrich Genscher, Chancellor Helmut and Mrs. Hennelore Kohl, German President Richard von Weizsäcker, former GDR Prime Minister Lothar de Maizière, Finance Minister Theodor Waigel. (Courtesy German Information Center)

The new partners. Chancellor Helmut Kohl and President Boris Yeltsin enjoy the sights of the Siberian Lake Baikal, July 1993. Their personal relationship was to become crucial to the new American-Russian-German strategic triangle. (Courtesy German Information Center)

Five

United Germany and NATO: The Kremlin Decides

We have a problem with NATO. It's an
imagery problem. It would look as if you had
won and we had lost. The short-term problem
is, how can explain this domestically? The
long-term problem is, how do you know that
what we'll see ten years from now is going to
be what we want? . . . The lessons of history
suggest that we cannot be relaxed about the
Germans.
  (Shevardnadze to Baker, 1990)[1]

We were very lucky that the Soviets never got
their act together.
  *(Western participant in the Two Plus Four
  negotiations)*[2]

The acceptance of a united Germany in NATO
was one of the most hated developments in
Soviet foreign policy, and it will remain so for
decades.
  *(Soviet Foreign Minister Aleksandr
  Bessmertnykh)*[3]

NOW THAT Gorbachev had in principle assented to German unification,
the central question was what a united Germany's role in Europe would
be. Soviet views on this issue were shaped by forty years of Cold War
realities and by communist propaganda that had demonized NATO as
the imperialist alliance par excellence, devoted to the destruction of socialist countries. Gorbachev had announced the de-ideologization of Soviet foreign policy, but the ghosts of foreign policies past continued to
haunt the Kremlin's visions of European futures. The Soviet leadership
remained a prisoner of its past pronouncements and there was a visceral
aversion to NATO among the foreign policy elite. Moreover, as the communist empire collapsed, Gorbachev and his colleagues became increas-

ingly concerned about appearing to be humiliated by the West, fearing that their domestic opponents would use that against them. The West was also in an uncomfortable position. While it was determined to secure Soviet concessions, it did not want these concessions to lead to Gorbachev's overthrow.[4] Thus, the negotiations required a delicate mix of firmness and flexibility.

Moscow played a more important role in the negotiations determining Germany's external fate between February and September 1990 than it did in the question of Germany's internal unification. But, as in 1989, its main leverage was negative. It had veto power, but was ultimately unable or unwilling to suggest a consistent, coherent agenda of its own, one that might have produced an outcome other than united Germany's full integration in NATO. There were three related issues to be determined: whether a united Germany should remain part of NATO or eschew all alliances and become neutral; whether foreign troops should remain on German soil; and how and when Germany should become a fully sovereign nation.

This chapter discusses three aspects of the external unification process:

What were the major factors that influenced Soviet decisionmaking? How and why did the Kremlin change its policies on Germany's inclusion in NATO?

What was the West German government's agenda during this process? How did it go about trying to influence Moscow to change its policies?

What was the role of the United States in supporting Germany's agenda and brokering German unification?

Once Gorbachev told Kohl that the Soviet Union would not block German unification, the USSR renounced any influence over the internal aspects of unification, although it continued to argue intermittently about the legal ramifications of the process. After all, Gorbachev had stressed that this was an issue for the two German states themselves to regulate. Nevertheless, the legal aspects of internal unification affected the external aspects. West Germany's constitution permitted unification to take place in two different ways. The first choice was the procedure provided for in Article 23 of the FRG's Basic Law—essentially an *Anschluss* whereby the GDR would join the FRG on the day of unification and accept Bonn's constitution as its own, as had the Saarland in 1957. Article 23 was essentially a takeover of East Germany by West Germany, not a merger. The other possibility was to follow Article 146, which would have meant that the two German states would have drafted a completely new constitution for a reunified German state that would have reflected the interests of the GDR, as opposed to East Germany accepting the West German constitution lock, stock, and barrel. Within East Germany, those who had made the revolution—those who still believed that reformed socialism could make a contribution to the new Germany and who did not want to give up this last act of GDR sovereignty— backed article 146. Those on the left in West Germany were of the same opinion. Within the Soviet Union, the *Germanisty*, who showed their colors as hardliners during this last, intense phase of unification negotiations, also opposed Article 23[5]—partly because that article made it easier for a united Germany to remain in NATO, whereas Article 146 would have reopened the entire question of Germany's international status.[6]

Until the March 18 election in the GDR, the USSR continued to exercise some influence over East Berlin via the relationship between Modrow and Gorbachev. The election, however, put an end to this cooperation. The CDU-CSU, which had campaigned on a platform of rapid unification under Article 23, became the predominant power in the GDR, winning 49 percent of the votes. The SPD, which favored a much slower timetable for unification and had been predicted to win, garnered only 21 percent, and the PDS (successor to the SED) 17 percent. After the March election, moreover, Gorbachev dealt almost exclusively with West, as opposed to East, Germany. The new noncommunist East German government under CDU Premier Lothar de Mazière was largely excluded both by Moscow and Bonn from all major foreign policy decisions.

Between February and September 1990, in a mere seven months, the entire postwar map of Europe was redrawn and the results of World War II were revised. It was a period of frantic negotiations on a variety of levels, but the Western powers realized that their window of opportunity was small. Gorbachev was under growing pressure domestically, denounced both by hardliners who accused him of dismantling socialism, and by reformers who accused him of moving too slowly. Boris Yeltsin was Russia's rising star, and after his election as president of the Russian Federation by the newly elected Russian Congress of People's Deputies, he and his colleagues began to challenge Gorbachev's authority as head of the CPSU and of the USSR. At the same time, the Baltic states and Ukraine had also elected their own legislatures and were demanding independence.

During the seven months of negotiations on German unity, therefore, the Soviet president was under siege from both the communists and the reformers. But the flight of East Germans to West Germany continued, placing increasing pressure on Bonn to complete the unification process and persuade nervous East Germans to stay at home. The United States and the Federal Republic hoped that by pushing for the fastest possible completion of the internal unification they could keep Moscow off balance, facing an array of unwelcome choices but ultimately accepting Western terms.[7] Since the Soviets had no particular reason to accelerate the process of unification, they responded to a Western agenda, although their negotiating partners were sensitive to the need not to make it appear as if the West had forced concessions on them. The Germans in particular were concerned not to take actions that might so undermine Gorbachev's own power that he might be removed from office. It is important to remember, from the hindsight of the mid-1990s, that the major concern in 1990 on the part of many of Germany's neighbors, in particular France and Britain, was that Germany was poised to become a great power again once unification was completed. Prime Minister Thatcher recounts a conversation she had with President Mitterrand: "Germany has veered unpredictably between aggression and self-doubt. [Mitterrand] was more concerned than I was. He observed that in history, the Germans were a people in constant movement and flux. At this, I produced from my handbag a map showing the various configurations of Germany in the past, which were not altogether reassuring about the future."[8]

Given the magnitude of the issues involved, it is hardly surprising that there was much dissension in the Soviet Union over German unification. Indeed, it is remarkable how rapidly the entire negotiating process was concluded. However, the internal Soviet debates over whether Germany could remain in NATO and, if so, under what conditions, inevitably spilled over into the negotiating arena. For much of the period, Shevardnadze sounded more hardline than Gorbachev, especially over the question of Germany's membership of NATO. The foreign minister privately told his Western negotiating partners that he had to adopt intransigent positions because he felt particularly vulnerable to conservative domestic criticism.[9] This, together with the fact that Gorbachev believed that some Western countries—most notably France and the United Kingdom—did not want unification, explains the confusing array of proposals made by Moscow during these five months. Moreover, the Germans were by no means certain that they would achieve their ultimate goal of a united Germany fully integrated into NATO. Some German officials would have accepted less than full integration, and were several times amazed by the concessions that the Soviets made and the ease with which their goals were achieved.[10] Given the variety of Soviet views, and their continuing criticism of NATO membership, which lasted until and after the day the final treaty was signed, it is all the more surprising that the Western side was able to achieve all of its objectives without making any major concessions. Central to the successful outcome of these negotiations were Soviet divisions, disorganization, and distraction because of domestic problems, and Western coordination and resolve, despite significant differences among the allies. But the successful conclusion was not foreordained. It was a product of both luck and statecraft.

After Germany was divided into two states in 1949, the core of all Soviet proposals on Germany included a provision that a future united Germany must be neutral. Stalin's 1952 proposal stipulated this, albeit permitting Germany some indigenous armed forces. In addition, there was always a minority in West Germany that supported the idea of Geman neutrality.[11] Moreover, the constant Soviet criticism of NATO was echoed by the peace movements in both Germanies, so that by 1990 a significant number of East Germans, including those who opposed communism such as the postcommunist Defense Minister Rainer Eppelmann and Foreign Minister Markus Meckel (both pastors), also initially opposed a united Germany within NATO.

Closely tied to the question of neutrality was the broader issue of NATO's future role. Although many Western observers believed that one of the Kremlin's prime goals during the Cold War was to create fissures within NATO and to eliminate the U.S. military presence in Europe, the Soviet Union's policy toward NATO was always ambivalent. At certain key points, Soviet leaders took actions suggesting that, while they wanted to weaken U.S.–German ties, they did not want to remove entirely the American presence from Europe because America acted as a stabilizing force that could contain West Germany. The Soviets realized that a Europe without America and in the absence of total Soviet control would mean a Europe in which Germany could become too powerful.[12]

These same issues faced Gorbachev and Shevardnadze in 1990. If German neutrality was unacceptable to the West, what were the alternatives? One was to demand that a peace conference of all those countries involved in World War II be convened. Since there had never been a peace treaty to end the war, there was some legal justification to this proposal. However, the Germans wanted to avoid such a conference at all costs, because it raised the specter of many countries demanding reparations from Germany. Stalin had never received the reparations from the Western zones of Germany that had been promised him at Yalta, and this issue was bound to come up.[13]

If united Germany were indeed to remain within NATO, how could one justify this to the Soviet people, barely able to digest the quick fall of Eastern Europe? U.S. Secretary of State James Baker had provided the answer to Gorbachev, meeting with him in February two days before he gave Kohl the green light on unification. He asked the Soviet general secretary if he would prefer to see a united Germany outside of NATO and with no U.S. forces stationed there, which might acquire its own nuclear weapons, or a unified Germany tied to NATO, with assurances that NATO's jurisdiction would not shift one inch eastward from its present position. Gorbachev agreed that "an extension of the zone of NATO is unacceptable."[14] At this point, Baker was referring to an extension of NATO jurisdiction to the territory of the GDR, not to the broader question of future NATO enlargement. After all, the Warsaw Pact still existed and the discussion was solely about Germany. But the Soviets faced an old dilemma. NATO had, after all, been created for the purposes of dual containment of the Soviet Union and Germany. The second aspect of containment was normally discussed only in scholarly Soviet publications and was not part of the public debate. Despite their revulsion at the idea of permitting a united Germany in NATO, the alternative—a large, powerful, free-floating, potentially nuclear Germany—was equally, if not more worrying. NATO was the devil they knew; a united neutral Germany was the devil they did not know and could not predict.[15]

Once they decided to accept Germany's full integration in NATO, the Soviets focused on the size of a united Germany's armed forces and on economic compensation for their major concessions—a belated form of reparations. If one examines the process of negotiations, therefore, the central decision was about NATO, but several other sets of discussions combined to influence Soviet willingness to compromise. Of course, Gorbachev could have refused the NATO solution or dragged the negotiations on for much longer; but it became increasingly clear that, if he wanted continued Western support for his reforms so as to strengthen his domestic position, there was no reason to hold up the talks and every incentive to speed them up.[16] In theory, the Soviet Union had choices; in practice, its room for maneuver was narrowing throughout 1990.

The Origins of Two Plus Four

There is some disagreement about the paternity of the idea for the Two Plus Four talks—the negotiations between the two German states and the four occupying powers in Germany—that handled the external aspects of unification. After February 10, the first issue to be resolved was how the negotiations on Germany's external unification were to be conducted. Although the Kremlin had initially insisted either on a peace conference involving all the parties to World War II or on the four-power mechanism, it became clear that the Germans must be included in these discussions. Indeed, some Germans argued that the two Germanies alone should negotiate their international role, but the other powers resisted them. It was an unprecedented situation that demanded unusual compromises. What mechanism could satisfy the Soviets, the Germans, and the other Western powers?

According to Cherniaev, he proposed the idea of talks involving the four occupying powers and the two German states—which he termed

"Four Plus Two"—at the January 26 meeting in Moscow. Gorbachev immediately supported him, and Akhromeyev agreed to supervise the withdrawal of Soviet troops from East Germany. The participants also agreed that the USSR should maintain closer contact with Britain and France, realizing that they were more skeptical about unification than were the United States or the two German states.[17]

Gorbachev claimed that "the idea for such a procedure [Two Plus Four] was conceived in Moscow and in Western capitals at the same time and independently of one another."[18] His statement is an accurate reflection of what transpired. In January, the U.S. State Department's policy planning staff had agreed that four-power talks were not appropriate for deciding Germany's future. The Two Plus Four forum would be the most effective. Genscher had made it clear to Bush that the Germans did not want to be relegated to the *Katzentisch* (side table) in these negotiations, as they had been during the four-power talks on Germany in the 1950s and 1960s.[19] The Americans presented the plan to the British and the French, and then secured Genscher's assent. Genscher insisted, however, that the forum be named "Two Plus Four," not "Four Plus Two" as the Soviets suggested. He wanted to underline that the two German states, and not the victor powers, were the main actors in these negotiations.[20] The idea for Two Plus Four was thus the product of synergy between Western and Soviet ideas. At the end of January in a speech in Tutzing, Genscher had begun to develop what became known as the Genscher Plan, designed to ensure Germany's continued membership of NATO but also to reassure the Soviet Union. He stressed the role of the Conference on Security and Cooperation in Europe (CSCE) and other European structures, and then gave a promise to the Soviets: "What NATO must do is state unequivocally that whatever happens in the Warsaw Pact there will be no expansion of NATO territory eastward, that is to say closer to the borders of the Soviet Union."[21] At this point, Genscher believed that unless a special NATO status for the GDR were offered, the Soviets might block German unification.

Of all the four victor powers, the United States was the only one that had no serious reservations about German unity and did much more than the other three to promote it. America had neither been invaded nor occupied by the Nazis as France and the USSR had been, nor had it suffered from their bombing, as had the British. Moreover, given its leading role as the superpower guarantor of West German security, Washington had more clout with Bonn than did its allies as members of the European Community. Thus, the United States took the lead in the Two Plus Four process. The State Department realized that the CSCE, with its thirty-five members, would be too unwieldy a body to negotiate German unity. A conference of the four victor powers alone, on the other hand, would deny Germany its self-determination. Thus, the best solution was to have the four victor powers plus the two German states negotiate. This forum had the major advantage of avoiding a large peace conference and allowing Germany a full say in negotiating its future while not victimizing the Russians. There were potential drawbacks, however. This forum would give prominence to the legal Soviet veto through the USSR's four-power rights, creating a structure through which the USSR could prevent Germany's NATO membership. The Soviets could also use this arena to demand concessions on the size of the future German army, and the presence and role of allied forces in Germany.[22] The United States and Germany decided, however, that this was the best forum in which to negotiate unification's external aspects.

Baker then flew to Moscow to discuss the issue. Gorbachev responded, "Four Plus Two, Two Plus Four, assuming it relies on an international legal basis, is suitable for the situation." He made it clear that the USSR still preferred Four Plus Zero or Four Plus Two, that is, that Germany should not have equal rights with the four occupying powers, but he did not object to the process. Baker was struck by Gorbachev's willingness to accept the formula, but noted that Gorbachev was denying the reality of the decline of the USSR as a superpower.[23] By agreeing to the Two Plus Four mechanism, Moscow had conceded that the two German states had as much right as did the four powers to determine how the external aspects of German unity should be decided. Indeed, the formula implied that Germany's interests came before those of the four powers. This is why it aroused considerable opposition in Moscow.

In his memoirs, the embittered Valentin Falin, after berating the Soviet leadership for having no concept of what it wanted from a united Germany, blames Shevardnadze for overruling Gorbachev. According to Falin, Shevardnadze defied Gorbachev's orders to speak of "Four Plus Two" and instead spoke of "Two Plus Four."[24] Even though one should interpret Falin's remarks with some skepticism, he is correct in arguing that the Soviet side continuously gave mixed signals.

The Two Plus Four mechanism was officially launched at the "Open Skies" foreign ministers' conference in Ottawa on February 12, 1990. The discussions were difficult. As Shevardnadze writes, "It would be an offense against the truth for me to say that 'the Six' had a smooth path from the first step."[25] Genscher and Shevardnadze had a particularly tense and long negotiation over both the form and content of the negotiations.[26] Not only was the Soviet side reluctant, but Chancellor Kohl's advisors were wary about the Foreign Ministry taking on too much control over the process of German unity.[27] At the end of January, Kohl's chief of staff, Rudolf Seiters, had therefore convened a working group on unification that was to meet regularly.[28] Nonetheless, throughout the next few months there was constant bureaucratic infighting between the Chancellery and the Foreign Ministry, which was not untypical for Germany but caused concern among the other negotiating partners. Sometimes, the United States negotiators bypassed the Foreign Ministry in favor of the Chancellery which, they felt, held positions more compatible with those of the United States than did Genscher and his colleagues. It must be remembered, however, that all of the participants were groping their way into uncharted territory. The Western side had no idea how much the Soviets would be willing to concede, and the Soviet side was deeply divided. Eventually, the Two Plus Four process took on a life of its own and produced dynamics that neither the Western nor the Soviet side had ever envisioned.

There were four plenary Two Plus Four meetings—in Bonn on May 5, Berlin on June 22, Paris on July 17, and Moscow on September 12. In between these plenary sessions at the ministerial level, lower-ranking political, military, and legal officials met constantly to work out the complicated details. The central issue of whether a united Germany could remain in NATO and if so, in what kind of NATO, was eventually resolved bilaterally between Gorbachev and Kohl, and the major military question, the size of a future German army, was officially resolved in the Vienna talks on Conventional Forces in Europe. But these agreements were all incorporated into Two Plus Four.

At the same time, the West and East Germans were negotiating the internal aspects of unification, especially the monetary union, which went into effect on July 1. Monetary union was and remains a subject of great controversy because of the favorable exchange rate given the East German mark for political reasons. For some transactions the rate was one East German to one West German mark, out of all proportion to the real relationship between the strong West German and the failing East German currency. But Kohl overrode the chairman of the Bundesbank on this issue, claiming that the favorable exchange rate was the only way to prevent more East Germans from migrating to West Germany.[29]

Chancellor Kohl's summit with President Bush shortly after the Ottawa meeting was important for both the agreement and disagreement between Bonn and Washington. At the Camp David summit both leaders agreed that a united Germany must remain "a full member of NATO, including participation in its military structure." The current territory of the GDR was to have a "special military status" which took into account the security interests of neighboring states, including the Soviet Union. This represented a compromise between different points of view on the German side. Defense Minister Gerhard Stoltenberg had rejected the Genscher Plan formula that there would be no extension of NATO's jurisdiction to the former GDR territory. How, asked Stoltenberg, could

NATO defend the eastern part of Germany once Germany was united? He stated publicly that the Bundeswehr could be deployed in the East after unification if the need arose. Genscher, however, was willing to promise that neither NATO troops nor Bundeswehr units would be allowed on East German territory after unification, a position that worried the other three Western powers; and at this point Kohl intervened, concerned that Germany not antagonize the Soviets, to support the Genscher position. James Baker, however, made it clear to Kohl that unless a united Germany were a full NATO member, the United States would withdraw its troops from Europe.[30] Eventually, it was agreed that Bundeswehr units not assigned to NATO should be allowed on East German territory.[31]

While the Two Plus Four negotiations progressed, the question of Poland's borders suddenly became a major crisis, although in reality it was a nonissue. But the crisis reflected the growing nervousness among Germany's neighbors about the speed with which unification was taking place, preventing the negotiating parties from fully thinking through the implications of what they were doing. The FRG had recognized the Oder-Neisse boundary between Poland and the GDR in December 1970, and had reasserted this pledge by signing the CSCE Final Act in 1975. Only a few nationalist groups within West Germany were calling for a return to Germany's 1937 boundaries, that is, the recovery of Pomerania, Silesia, and most of East Prussia, which it lost to Poland in 1945. The *Vertriebene* (those expelled from those regions) were well organized, but few seriously believed that they could return to the lands from which they were expelled after World War II. However, for domestic reasons, Kohl needed the support of the expellee groups and did not want to go out of his way to alienate them. Moreover, the far-right Republikaner party had done very well in local elections that year, making the CDU/CSU especially concerned about the nationalists' ability to attract expellee votes.

The question now arose whether a united Germany would recognize Poland's borders, given that the Yalta and Potsdam conferences, which had provisionally decided on Poland's boundaries, had not produced a final peace treaty. Kohl refused to commit a united Germany to recognizing Poland's borders, claiming that this could only legally be done after German unification had been achieved, when a newly and freely elected all-German parliament could vote on the issue. Although most of the U.S. government understood the domestic reasons for Kohl's refusal to commit himself at this point, President Bush sought to persuade Kohl that it was important for Germany's international credibility at such a delicate time to make a firm commitment on Poland. Kohl, after initially refusing to budge, changed his position by mid-March. After the March 18 election, the East and West German parliaments separately passed resolutions recognizing Poland's Western borders as final. Subsequently, at the July 17 Two Plus Four meeting, the Poles signed an agreement with both German states that required a united Germany to remove from its laws all language referring to the Polish-German border as provisional. Thus, the issue was settled to both sides' satisfaction, but not before West Germany managed to reinforce suspicions in the minds of neighbors who were anyway inclined to wonder whether a united Germany might begin a new *Drang nach Osten*.

Divisions among the Soviets

While the Western powers were more or less agreed on their goals, despite bureaucratic infighting over strategy and tactics, there was no consensus within the Soviet leadership about what it wanted from the Two Plus Four talks. Indeed, the USSR went into the talks with no agreed-upon agenda. A working group on Germany, led by Deputy Foreign Minister Anatoly Adamishin and European Department head Aleksandr Bondarenko, had been formed in the Foreign Ministry, but its influence was limited because Gorbachev himself played an active role in decision making. Broadly put, Gorbachev and Shevardnadze sought to obtain the best settlement possible—one that maximized the USSR's remaining role as a world power—under less than optimal circumstances. The need not to lose more power and prestige and further undermine their positions domestically was ultimately more important than the details of Two Plus Four. Their leverage was diminishing by the week as the internal process of German unification accelerated. Although some Soviet spokesmen continued to speak of a neutral Germany, it is doubtful that either Gorbachev or Shevardnadze considered this a realistic option by February. Nevertheless, until the March 18 GDR election, they may have hoped that German unification would mean confederal structures, rather than *Anschluss* under Article 23. They were not reconciled to full NATO membership for a united Germany. As Shevardnadze said in early March, "the forecast of a united Germany's membership in NATO is not in accordance with our ideas about our own national interests."[32] Gorbachev recounts that at a contentious May 3 Politburo meeting before the first plenary Two Plus Four session, Shevardnadze was instructed to insist on military neutrality for Germany, or at least on German membership in both NATO and the Warsaw Pact.[33] Until at least the end of May, neither

Gorbachev nor Shevardnadze were willing to consent to full German NATO membership.

There was general Soviet agreement that the armed forces of a united Germany must be reduced to much less than what the combined Bundeswehr and NVA (National People's Army) would be, and that Germany must remain nonnuclear. The Soviets initially asked for a ceiling of 200,000 men in the armed forces. The Kremlin was willing to concede that, eventually, all Soviet troops would be withdrawn from German soil. There was, of course, an economic dimension too. The Soviets wanted to ensure that a united Germany would assume all of the GDR's economic obligations and that Germany would intensify its economic contacts with the USSR, especially on the technological level, which would require a drastic reduction of the COCOM lists.

How did Soviet thinking on NATO membership evolve? Between February and June, a confusing and sometimes contradictory set of proposals emanated from different officials in the Foreign Ministry, the Kremlin and other institutions, underlining the serious domestic challenges Gorbachev faced. The proposals included supporting full German membership of NATO (only Dashichev said this publicly); membership of Germany in both NATO and the Warsaw Pact; the neutralization and demilitarization of Germany; a military-political status in NATO for Germany similar to that of France, that is, Germany would withdraw from NATO's integrated military command but remain within its political structures; membership of the western part of Germany in NATO, with "associate" status for the eastern part; and various permutations and combinations of these. Those who believe that the Soviet Union was run with an iron hand from the Kremlin, one that deliberately produced a cacophony of well-coordinated proposals in order to confuse the West and seduce its more left-leaning populations, might interpret these mixed signals as deliberate. It is far more likely that the contradictory signals were a genuine reflection of serious disagreement in the Kremlin, the Foreign Ministry, and the Ministry of Defense, and of the need to placate the opposition.

Pavel Palazchenko, who interpreted for both Gorbachev and Shevardnadze, argues that "the two-plus-four process was basically a front and it was rather skillfully played by both sides—both Gorbachev and Shevardnadze understood pretty well that any kind of slowdown [of unification] would be at our expense. It would be *us* slowing the process down and *them* basically looking on and it would not slow the train." Aleksandr Bessmertnykh, who became foreign minister after Shevardnadze's resignation in December 1990, reaffirms the view common among most Soviet Foreign Ministry and Central Committee officials that "an event of this magnitude [German unification] just happened without a strategy, without joint efforts by some, without planning. . . . There was no strategy, there were only tactics." Sergei Tarasenko, Shevardnadze's chief aide, recalls that Shevardnadze deliberately chose officials like Aleksandr Bondarenko, a hardline World War II veteran, to be included in the group discussing the terms of unification, because he was trying to coopt his opponents. But these attempts at inclusivity also led to sharper rhetoric. Those in Russia who took part in this process remain divided over whether there was a plan or a strategy. Their views often depend on where they were in the bureaucratic process and on their personal views of Gorbachev and Shevardnadze.[34]

Even though Gorbachev and Shevardnadze eventually realized that full German NATO membership was inevitable, there is also considerable evidence that they were constantly improvising and testing the West. For instance, at a Warsaw Pact foreign ministers' meeting, Shevardnadze gave a tough speech against German membership in NATO. The Czechoslovak, Hungarian, and Polish foreign ministers spoke up in favor of German membership, and Shevardnadze then thanked them privately for their speeches, explaining that he and Gorbachev were under growing pressure from the military at home and welcomed the support by Warsaw Pact colleagues for Germany's NATO membership.[35]

Given the Kremlin's ambivalence on NATO membership, it is remarkable that Moscow did nothing to make the Germans "an offer they couldn't refuse" that might have fallen short of full NATO membership, a scenario which some in the West initially feared. Nor did Moscow consistenly play its British and French cards. Indeed, many Germans were amazed that the Soviets did not try harder on a consistent basis to persuade them to abandon the full NATO solution, especially since there were some in the German foreign policy establishment who were receptive to such a proposal. Nor did Moscow try concertedly to drive wedges between the Western negotiating partners, although it did so episodically. The Soviets proposed the French option (political but no military integration) as one possibility, but they never argued it systematically and consistently.[36] Some of their Western negotiating partners agree that had the Kremlin decided on this option as the only one they would espouse, Moscow might well have been able to persuade the Germans that a French solution was in their interests and was the maximum that Moscow could tolerate. But, instead, the Soviets misplayed their hand, failing to settle on one plan and throwing out a series of uncoordinated proposals.[37]

On the face of it, it seems extraordinary that the USSR was unable to come up with a coherent negotiating strategy for what was, after all, the most important series of talks about its future security since 1945. The answer lies in the deep divisions within the Soviet elite, making it impossible to arrive at the prior consensus that was a prerequisite for a concerted negotiating strategy. Gorbachev and Shevardnadze were constantly maneuvering to keep their opponents, including the *Germanisty*, at bay. They were fighting a two-front battle with their domestic opponents and with the West. Former CIA chief Robert Gates recalls that during his February visit to Moscow, KGB head Kriuchkov complained that the Soviet people were "dizzy with change." He himself had concluded that perestroika had been a terrible mistake. It was time to slow down.[38] Falin claims that the International Department of the Central Committee proposed three preconditions before the German status quo could be changed: reunification did not mean annexation (Article 146 instead of 23); NATO membership with the presence of nuclear weapons was excluded; and the final treaty had to deal with issues related to the redeployment and rehousing of Soviet troops. Gorbachev, in the end, only accepted the third precondition. He paid little attention to the briefing notes and documents prepared for him by Falin and others, presumably because these advisors did not share his views.[39]

Former German Defense Minister Stoltenberg recounts that the Germans had the sense that the Soviet side was constantly improvising, and also hoping that Germany would reward their concessions with vast economic payoffs.[40] Former Soviet ambassador to Washington and head of the Central Committee's International Department Anatoly Dobrynin has another interpretation. Gorbachev, he writes, "began to emerge as a virtual monarch . . . increasingly making important decisions by himself. At that critical, final moment of the Cold War, Gorbachev and Shevardnadze had no coherent, balanced, and firm foreign policy to end it in a fitting and dignified way on the basis of equality."[41] As time wore on, and Gorbachev and Shevardnadze were unable to placate their domestic opponents or achieve consensus. They took major decisions together with only a few loyal colleagues, because otherwise negotiations on German unity would have been completely stalled.

Indeed, the key to understanding the lack of a coherent negotiating strategy on the Soviet side during the first seven months of 1990 is the growing domestic crisis within the Soviet Union. By this time, Gorbachev had alienated many of the reformers who had initially supported his programs. They felt that he had betrayed his promises and remained too wedded to the domination of the Communist Party and to "old" thinking. Many of Gorbachev's leading reformist critics had opted for political careers within the Russian Federation, whose newly elected legislature had in March chosen Boris Yeltsin, former colleague and now Gorbachev nemesis, as their president. Gorbachev's reformist critics focused on the national question—the desire of the constituent republics of the USSR, Russian and non-Russian, for independence—to argue their case against the Soviet leader. Eventually, at the Twenty-eighth

Party Congress in July, Yeltsin and his allies left the Communist Party, declaring open warfare on Gorbachev.

Even more disconcerting, however, were the hardline critics who accused Gorbachev of having gone too far in his reforms and giving up both the Soviet empire and the Communist Party's monopoly of power without having improved the USSR's economic performance.[42] The hardline critics, unlike the reformists, came from institutions such as the Communist Party, the KGB, and the military, which had coercive resources not available to the reformers, and were thus more threatening for Gorbachev. As he tried to placate critics from the left and right, the Baltic states became increasingly assertive about their right to independence, posing new challenges to Gorbachev and intensifying his dilemma: if he responded with force, he would appease his conservative critics, but he would alienate both the domestic reformers and the West. If he allowed the Baltic states to become independent, he risked a possible hardline coup. Gorbachev was now confronting the initial stages of the crisis that would eventually lead to the 1991 putsch and his subsequent ouster. Thus, he was constantly distracted and unable to concentrate his full attention on negotiations over Germany. The speed with which the negotiations were conducted also militated against developing a more coherent policy.

As Kohl's aide Horst Teltschik wrote in his diary, "We regularly ask ourselves whether part of our problem lies in the fact that with Bondarenko, Falin, Zagladin, Portugalov, and Kvitsinsky, a 'German mafia' is advising Gorbachev and Shevardnadze, people who were already important in Gromyko's time, whereas today others are noticeably more flexible and open than before."[43] The irony is that the participation of a united Germany in NATO represented the ultimate defeat by Gorbachev, Shevardnadze, and their supporters of the party's *Germanisty* who had made their careers on and thus developed a considerable stake in the German status quo.

Irrespective of the domestic crisis, however, there was the issue of what bargaining levers the USSR possessed, had it wanted to influence the outcome against German membership in NATO. On the face of it, the negotiating assets were quite formidable: 380,000 Soviet troops and their dependents on GDR soil; four-power rights over Berlin and Germany; and the possibility of stalling arms control talks, both nuclear and conventional, that the West was anxious to conclude. Yet levers are only credible in negotiations if all parties involved believe that they might actually be used. Given everything that Gorbachev and Shevardnadze had said and done, it was highly unlikely that the Soviets would use their troops for political pressure now, if they had not done so in November 1989. Moreover, their four-power rights were dependent on the other three powers agreeing with them, otherwise they would have to exercise a veto and alienate their partners. And if they stalled arms control talks, they would forfeit other benefits promised to them by the West, and their newly gained image in the West would be seriously challenged. In short, their bargaining assets were, on paper, formidable but in reality of questionable efficacy. The issue of what incentives they had to offer the Germans to eschew the full NATO option was also complicated. Given the USSR's weak economic and political situation, Gorbachev possessed few positive bargaining levers to tempt the Germans as an alternative to the use of the veto.

Strategy of the Germans

Despite disagreements between the Chancellery and the Foreign Ministry, there was general consensus after February on Germany's goals in the complicated negotiating process.[44] Although some officials found it hard to believe that the USSR would permit a united Germany to remain a full NATO member, that was the official German position.[45] Germany was also pushing for the end of four-power rights and the regaining of full sovereignty—including the total withdrawal of Soviet troops from German soil within a reasonable time—as soon as unification was achieved, although, at the beginning of 1990 the German government did not believe that unification would come as quickly as it did. Having prevented the convening of a multilateral peace conference to decide its fate, Germany also insisted that no other countries play a major role in the Two Plus Four negotiations.[46] Genscher wanted to link these issues to redesigning a new European security system, whereas the Chancellery was more focused on links between internal and external unification and the NATO question. But both Kohl and Genscher realized that it was vital to keep engaging the Soviets and to offer them whatever incentives were available.

Germany could, in fact, offer considerable political and economic incentives to influence Soviet decision making. Among Germany's key assets were its economic strength and its ability to offer Moscow a special relationship after unification, one that would create the structure for a long-term political partnership and would thus enhance the USSR's prestige after its loss of Eastern Europe. On the political front, Boris Meissner, a veteran, well-respected Sovietologist who advised the Kohl government, suggested to Teltschik that, to sweeten the pill, Germany should propose a comprehensive bilateral treaty to be signed upon unification, committing a united Germany to renunciation of force and to long-term cooperation with the USSR. These negotiations should begin before unification. Kohl quickly signed on to this idea, and, according to Teltschik, when he informed Kvitsinsky of this plan, the departing Soviet ambassador replied that it had always been his dream "to achieve for Germany and the Soviet Union something similar to what Bismarck had accomplished."[47] Kvitsinsky recalls that Gorbachev also responded positively to the idea of a comprehensive bilateral treaty.[48]

Kohl and his advisors also used a strategy analogous to that of Brandt and Bahr in 1969–70, offering economic incentives to influence Soviet decisions.[49] There were two major issues: the GDR's debts to the USSR, as well as other economic obligations which were spelled out in no less than 360 different treaties; and the USSR's acute need for both short-term humanitarian and longer-term assistance, as well as credits. Kohl had already assured Gorbachev that united Germany would assume all of the GDR's economic obligations, a promise that greatly alarmed Economics Ministry officials. They questioned how (and at what price) a market economy could take over the contractual obligations of a centrally planned economy. The task was indeed enormous: the GDR was, after all, the Soviet Union's largest trading partner. 35 percent of the GDR work force was employed in enterprises that exported there, and deliveries to the USSR formed 40 percent of GDR exports, employing about 500,000 people and accounting for about 10 percent of Soviet imports. The Soviets supplied the GDR mainly with raw materials in exchange for manufactured goods, on the same pattern as that of trade with West Germany. The FRG supplied about 6 percent of Soviet imports and it was expected that a united Germany would eventually supply more than one-fourth of all imports, because of new German bank loans and uncertainties about future Soviet suppliers in Eastern Europe. The Soviets faced a possible loss of seven billion GDR marks in trade revenues after unification, since the eastern part of Germany would redirect its trade westward. Moreover, the GDR was the USSR's major supplier of high technology, including sensitive military technology. Was a united Germany to continue to sell military goods and spare parts to the Soviet Union?

When Economics Minister Haussmann visited Moscow in late May, Prime Minister Ryzhkov told him that the USSR expected Germany to compensate it for all the economic disadvantages it would suffer from German unification. Deputy Prime Minister Ivan Silaev went further: Bonn should guarantee that in the future, trade between a united Germany and the USSR would increase. He provided Haussmann with a letter detailing all of the products and industries involved in Soviet-GDR trade and other economic relations, from fuel for nuclear power plants to the considerable Soviet property rights in the GDR.[50] The German side thus accepted a considerable (and at that point still unknown) economic burden—including the promise to continue purchasing from the USSR the products it had sold to the GDR, which would hardly sell on a capitalist German market. These included some manufactured goods and military hardware.

The issue of aid to the Soviet Union was also problematic, since its economic needs were enormous and incalculable. But Kohl and his advisors recognized how important it was to offer the USSR assistance in such a way that it did not look like "an Ethiopian relief program," as one official said. In a discussion with Kohl on May 4, Shevardnadze raised the question of financial assistance, assuring him that the USSR was a good credit risk, given its massive resources. A few days later, Kvitsinksy, by now back in Moscow in the Foreign Ministry, submitted a request for a DM 20 billion credit with a five-to-seven year payback term. Kohl immediately decided to give a forthcoming response. He asked the heads of the Deutsche and Dresdner banks, Hilmar Kopper and Wolfgang Roeller, to work out the details.

On May 13, Teltschik flew with the two men to Moscow, on a mission so secret that Teltschik refused to reveal the names of his fellow passengers even to the government pilot. After intense discussion with their Soviet partners on the state of the economy, they reiterated the government's willingness to take over the GDR's economic obligations and to give new credits, which Gorbachev described as "oxygen" for perestroika. A few days later, in a discussion with President Bush, Kohl said that Germany was willing to give a DM 5 billion ($3 billion) credit to the Soviets as part of the overall German settlement.[51] On May 22, Kohl made this offer to Gorbachev and promised to talk to his partners in the G-7 and G-24 about further, long-term credits. The DM 5 billion credit was the largest single loan ever granted the Soviets and the conditions were much better than usual for a country with proven repayment problems. The Deutsche Bank was to manage the credit, which would be guaranteed by the Hermes credit insurance company, at market interest rates. The Soviets would have more than fifteen years to repay.

The issue of linking German economic incentives to Soviet political concessions raises similar questions to those connected with the USSR's and Germany's broader negotiating stance. Despite numerous attempts to link economic and political issues, there was no concerted Soviet strategy at the beginning of the negotiations detailing the German economic concessions that were to be a prerequisite to Soviet assent on the NATO issue. At different points the Kremlin raised a variety of economic demands but with no consistent plan. In June 1989 at the summit in Bonn, when Kohl raised the subject of unification, Gorbachev had asked the chancellor if he could rely on West German economic assistance if it were urgently needed.[52] Gorbachev may well have operated on the basis of a tacit linkage, assuming that West Germany realized that unification carried with it a substantial price tag. It is also possible that the same domestic constraints that prevented the USSR from offering a credible alternative plan for German membership in NATO also made it impossible to pursue a consistent, as opposed to an ad hoc, linkage strategy.[53]

During the negotiations, the Soviet side sporadically used its economic plight and its loss of GDR trade to pressure the Germans. Gorbachev and Shevardnadze bargained from a position of weakness but they still held the trump card in the Two Plus Four talks—NATO membership. The German side was well aware of the potential linkage, and although the economic burdens Germany incurred were considerable, the political stakes involving its future security and sovereignty were so high that it was willing to respond positively and expeditiously. Moreover, in the end, Germany made few political concessions in the pursuit of its goals. The recognition of the Polish border was forced on Germany earlier than the Kohl administration wanted, but the principle of recognition was never in doubt. The major problem, according to a leading German expert on the USSR, was that "there is a growing contradiction between growing political interests of cooperation with the Soviets and the escalating economic difficulties of doing so."[54]

The U.S. Strategy

United States long-term goals after January 1990 were almost identical to those of Germany, although they sometimes disagreed over tactics: a united Germany should remain a full member of NATO, whose jurisdiction would immediately extend to the territory of the former GDR.[55] Washington also played a major role as broker between Germany and the Soviet Union. In addition, the United States used its considerable political assets—primarily the commitment to continue treating Gorbachev as the leader of a major world power—to offer the Soviets incentives to agree to NATO membership for Germany.[56] But the U.S. had always adopted a very different attitude toward East-West economic relations and the use of economic incentives and sanctions than had its NATO partners.[57] It considered trade a privilege and was unwilling to use it as a carrot, although it did use it as a political stick. By early 1989, however, the United States faced a dilemma. It was willing to offer economic assistance tied to a promise of further economic reform; but growing problems in the Baltics, caused by the Soviet imposition of sanctions against Lithuania after it declared its independence, made it difficult for domestic reasons—particularly Congressional condemnation of Soviet actions—to offer substantial economic incentives. At the Washington summit at the end of May, the U.S. signed a trade agreement with the USSR; but only after Shevardnadze had made it quite clear that, having made major concessions on Germany's NATO membership, "The Soviet Union could not return to Moscow empty-handed."[58]

On the other hand, Washington used its political clout to intervene several times in the negotiations both bilaterally and multilaterally, through NATO, to influence Soviet decisions. After all, from the Soviet point of view, the United States was still the country from which it sought recognition as an equal, especially as it became visibly weakened through the loss of its East European empire. It was very important for Gorbachev and Shevardnadze to be seen to be taken seriously by Washington. Moreover, America had a significant role to play in assuaging Soviet fears about the rise of a united Germany. With the GDR about to disappear from history, only America could offer guarantees about the structures in which a future Germany would be embedded.

The United States also had to be mindful of residual German fears that Washington and Moscow might conclude a separate deal over Germany's head, a traditional concern in Bonn. Thus, the small group of people within Washington who negotiated the details of German unity had to achieve a delicate balance between assuaging Soviet and German fears and acting in the interests of the Western alliance. Cognizant of the fissures within the Soviet leadership and the need to support Gorbachev against his opponents, President Bush also had to listen to his own domestic constituency, particularly Baltic interest groups who were quite powerful within the Congress.

The United States played a decisive role in influencing Soviet policy at two junctures. The first was during Gorbachev's summit with Bush at the end of May. Gorbachev arrived in Washington in a weakened domestic position. Boris Yeltsin—with whom Gorbachev's relations were very frosty since it was the latter who had fired him from the Politburo in 1988 and had publicly humiliated him—had just been elected president of the Russian Federation. Economic conditions were not improving, and criticism of Gorbachev's foreign policy was growing. Bush and his advisors took the lead in offering the Soviet Union formally what had previously been informally discussed in Moscow: "nine assurances" on German unification. These were:

1. A reaffirmation that a united Germany would renounce nuclear, biological, and chemical weapons.

2. Agreement to pursue talks on conventional forces in Europe (CFE) and make sustantial cuts in the Bundeswehr.

3. Assurances of NATO's willingness to negotiate on short-range nuclear forces (SNF).

4. A promise to redefine NATO strategy in light of the end of the Cold War.

5. A renunciation of German claims to Polish and Soviet territory. The territory of the united Germany would comprise the FRG, GDR, and Berlin.

6. A pledge not to station NATO troops in the former GDR for a transition period.

7. Agreement that Soviet troops would remain in eastern Germany for a transitional period at German expense.

8. A proposal to institutionalize the CSCE and make it a pan-European organization in which the Soviets would play a leading role.

9. Extensive German economic assistance to the USSR.[59]

Gorbachev's reply, when first presented with these assurances, was contradictory. He said that a united Germany in NATO would mean "the end of perestroika." He talked vaguely about a "nonaligned" Germany but also suggested that the USSR itself might join NATO. Bush then asked him jokingly whether he could imagine Marshal Akhromeyev serving under NATO General Galvin.[60] The Washington summit, although decisive in terms of the NATO issue, was tense and difficult. Gorbachev reiterated one of the array of Soviet demands at that time, namely that Germany should belong to both NATO and the Warsaw Pact or to neither. "You are a sailor," he told Bush (referring to the American president's navy background, not to their unfortunate seafaring experiences during the December 1989 summit on a ship off the coast of Malta, when the weather was very rough). "You will understand that if one anchor is good, two anchors are better." Bush rejoined that he did not understand "how two anchors would work."[61]

"The train has already overtaken us," said Gorbachev of German unification, and Bush, agreeing, pointed out that there were fundamental differences between American and Soviet views on this issue. The Soviet leader stressed how much the legacy of World War II still affected his people. Bush told Gorbachev that he understood the Soviet people's fears about Germany, given their experiences during the war, but, he added that one should not ignore fifty years of German democracy since 1949. Gorbachev was convinced that Washington feared that if Germany were not in NATO, then the alliance might collapse and the U.S. would withdraw from Europe. He reassured Bush that the USSR had no interest in such an American withdrawal.[62]

Later on, however, when Bush said that, consistent with CSCE principles, each nation should be allowed to choose its alliance relationship, Gorbachev, to the surprise of his advisors (and the horror at least of Falin), replied "I agree with your formulation."[63] Bush continued, "The USA is unequivocally advocating united Germany's membership in NATO. But, should Germany prefer to make a different choice, the USA will respect it." Gorbachev countered, "The U.S. and the USSR are in favor of Germany deciding herself in which alliance she would like to participate." Thus, at the same meeting, Gorbachev had made two important statements about NATO: he did not want a united Germany only in NATO but he respected the right of the Germans to self-determination. Indeed, he and Shevardnadze had openly disagreed on this question at the summit. Moreover, when Thatcher visited Moscow around the same time, Gorbachev did not say that a united Germany in NATO was unacceptable, but Defense Minister Yazov insisted that it was impossible.[64] This indicated the great ambivalence that the top Soviet leadership felt. Gorbachev's assent on the question of alliance membership was reflected in the Washington summit press statement indicating that the two leaders agreed that alliance membership was a matter for Germany to decide.[65] The United States had taken an important step toward showing the Soviets its good faith and indicating that it took seriously Soviet concerns about Germany and would be willing to guarantee that these fears would never materialize. This bilateral negotiation was also intended to show Gorbachev that he was highly regarded in the White House, at a time when he felt domestically besieged.

Nevertheless, after this summit, the West was again reminded of the instability of Soviet positions. At a Two Plus Four session, Shevardnadze undercut almost everything that had been decided in Washington when he called for the retention of four-power rights after unification, a five-year transition period in which united Germany would remain both in NATO and in the Warsaw Pact, and ceilings on the Bundeswehr.[66] This more intransigent stand was a reflection of domestic disagreements—in this case, a Politburo document that could not be disregarded—but it highlighted another problem in these negotiations: even though Moscow might agree to something in principle, there was always the question of a timetable. The West expected agreements to be implemented within a reasonable period of time; but the Soviets dealt with their internal dissent by backtracking on agreements and then justifying their reversals by claiming that they had a five-, or ten-year, as opposed to a one-year period in mind.

The other major American contribution involved NATO's mission. The Americans working on German unification had understood that they must "de-demonize" NATO for the Russians. For some time, the U.S. had been working on a plan to revamp NATO goals and strategy to present a more benign NATO, one dedicated to cooperation as opposed to confrontation as communism collapsed in Eastern Europe. President Bush felt that Moscow was more likely to compromise if NATO redefined itself. He encountered resistance from the French, who felt removed from much of the decision making, opposed the downgrading of

NATO's nuclear component, and were concerned about the rapidity of German unification—especially after Kohl announced in the middle of May that the first all-German elections would be held in December. Nevertheless, the U.S. and its other NATO partners were able to push through a consensus and prevail.[67]

At the July summit in London, NATO issued a declaration outlining its new mission. Baker had sent an advance copy of the declaration to Shevardnadze, in an attempt to secure Soviet assent. The document said that NATO's main activities would henceforth be as much political as military; stressed that the Soviets were no longer adversaries; proposed close cooperation between NATO and the Warsaw Pact; relegated nuclear weapons to weapons of last resort; and pledged to transform the character of NATO's conventional defense and to limit NATO forces' offensive capabilities.[68] Foreign Ministry spokesman Gennadi Gerasimov's reaction to the declaration was that it would help Gorbachev win over opponents of German unification: "Now we can show them they are wrong." Later on, Gorbachev confirmed this view: "We have received a very important impulse from the conference in London . . . which brought very positive steps. . . . If the step of London had not been made, then it would have been difficult to make headway at our meeting [with Kohl in the Caucasus]."[69]

Arkhyz or "Stavrapallo"? Gorbachev Concedes

By the beginning of July, both Germany and the United States had offered the USSR political and economic incentives to make German membership in NATO more palatable. But the Soviets continued to insist that they could not accept the exclusive NATO option. Meanwhile, American negotiators still feared that the Soviet Union might offer the Germans partial membership in NATO or some other combination of neutrality, demilitarization, and no nuclear weapons on German soil that would be acceptable to the Germans, but not to the Americans, British, or French. The multilateral and bilateral aspects of unification diplomacy were now becoming more intense and coordinated from the Western side. But the major question remained: When and how would the Soviets come to closure on the NATO issue?

The first Two Plus Four ministerial meetings had achieved a considerable amount. But the ministerial meeting that convened in Bonn on May 5, three months after the mechanism was created, indicated the difficulty of establishing an agenda acceptable to both sides and achieving a consensus among the Western participants. There was a wide gulf between the four Western powers, on the one hand, and the USSR and GDR on the other. There were four major topics of discussion: the border issue, the Berlin problem, the termination of four-power rights, and the question of future European security structures.[70] Shevardnadze made his negotiating partners quite nervous when he proposed a "package approach . . . that nothing has been agreed until all aspects of a settlement have been agreed and a total balance of interests . . . has been found." Although his interlocutors realized that some of this was for domestic consumption, the idea of one grand treaty settling everything was not to their taste. Shevardnadze went on to "reaffirm our negative attitude toward Germany's membership of NATO, for such a decision would very substantially affect our security interests, would mean a sudden breakdown in the correlation of forces in Europe, and would create a dangerous military-strategic situation for us."[71]

The second Two Plus Four ministerial meeting in Berlin on June 22 yielded no further progress on NATO. Baker made it clear to his Soviet and East German interlocutors that Germany must become fully sovereign on the day of its unity and must not be "singularized" through any special arrangements such as those suggested by the Soviet and East German sides.[72]

The debate about NATO was, of course, related to the question of the future of the Warsaw Pact. As part of the ongoing debate within the Soviet elite, General Batenin, one of the military reformers, wrote an article saying that it made no sense for Germany to be in both NATO and the Warsaw Pact, since the latter was already collapsing.[73] This point was brought home when the Political Consultative Committee of the Warsaw Pact met on June 7, the first time that this highest pact organ had come together since the fall of communism. The GDR delegation contained West German advisors, while Poland, Czechoslovakia, Hungary, Rumania, and Bulgaria were by now mainly interested in Western assistance and finding a graceful exit from the unpopular alliance. The Soviet side came prepared to discuss reforms in the organization, but not its abolition. Kvitsinsky describes the meeting as "the most unpleasant negotiating session that I ever remember having to endure. A haze of insincerity lay over the negotiations; people were afraid to name things by their proper names and escaped by wording the document in ambiguous formulas. I felt as if I were participating in a meal where the guests were stealing silver spoons while the host was not looking."[74]

By this time, Gorbachev and Shevardnadze realized they would have to defeat their opponents if they were ever to find common ground with the West on the NATO question. The opportunity to do this presented itself shortly thereafter, during the Twenty-Eighth—and last—Communist Party Congress. Shevardnadze had just returned from a series of meetings with Genscher, including in Brest-Litovsk and Münster. These two locations carried a great deal of historical symbolism for him. Shevardnadze's brother had been killed by the Germans at Brest at the beginning of the war, Münster was the place where the Peace of Westphalia had been signed in 1648, ending the Thirty Years War and the 1918 Treaty of Brest-Litovsk had removed Russia from World War I. The meetings had strengthened his desire to resolve the German issue, but he had to deal carefully with his opponents. Indeed, at these meetings, Shevardnadze had been more conciliatory with Genscher over the question of Germany's external ties than he was with the United States.[75] Bilateral talks with Germany were what remained of any Soviet strategy.[76]

Gorbachev and Shevardnadze went into the Congress under siege from their opponents on every front, especially foreign policy. Not only was there criticism from the right, but Yeltsin, Gavriil Popov, the mayor of Moscow and Anatoly Sobchak, mayor of Leningrad, dramatically announced that they were quitting the Communist Party, challenging Gorbachev from the left. The Right accused Gorbachev of betraying communism and the Soviet Union because of his reforms and because he had renounced the Soviet empire; the Left claimed that he had backtracked on his reforms and was too beholden to the Communists.

After answering attacks from his critics on his domestic policy, Gorbachev rose to defend his foreign policy, stressing the importance of freedom of choice for Eastern Europe. But it was Shevardnadze who, without mentioning the NATO issue, vigorously defended Soviet foreign policy toward Germany, after Falin had said that German NATO membership was impossible and others had accused Gorbachev of undoing the gains of the Great Patriotic War. Shevardnadze later wrote that his "personal fate was on the line" and that he was delighted when the news of the London NATO summit arrived, showing that the West had responded to Soviet concerns, because that helped him in his struggles with the Congress.[77] In his speech he denied that "the collapse of socialism in Eastern Europe [is] a grave defeat for Soviet diplomacy." It would have been, he continued, "had our diplomacy aspired to prevent changes in neighboring countries, had they resulted in a deterioration or exacerbation of relations with them." And he stressed that a united Germany would pose no threat to the Soviet Union: "In the future 'Greater Germany,' the army will be smaller than the army of today's FRG army. What could be better for us? . . . I am convinced that with German unification, the Soviet Union will cooperate intensively and on a mutually beneficial basis politically, economically, and in all other areas. I tell you openly, comrades, it is not in our interests to drag out the resolution of the external aspects of German unity. . . . "[78] In a subsequent interview, Shevardnadze revealed that of the hundreds of questions he had received from deputies to the Congress, over half were about German unity, and the majority of those highly critical.[79] After a hard fight, Gorbachev and Shevardnadze emerged victorious. Gorbachev's major nemesis, Yegor Ligachev, had been defeated and a new Central Committee elected, many of whom were committed reformers. Gorbachev was now stronger than he would ever be again. The window of opportunity had opened. It was time to act on German unity.

As Kohl, Genscher, and their aides prepared to depart for a summit in Moscow, they received news that the USSR was rapidly using up the DM 5 billion credit that they had arranged only two months before, a sign of the continuing Soviet economic difficulties. Gorbachev had invited Kohl to visit his home town of Stavropol in the Caucasus, and this augured well for the upcoming summit. In the previous weeks, there had been considerable debate within Germany and between Genscher and Shevardnadze about the size of a future united German Bundeswehr. All sides agreed that it would not be the sum total of the NVA and Bundeswehr, which would have amounted to 667,000 men, but something much smaller. The question was how small. Initially, the CDU had proposed a ceiling of 400,000, and the SPD (and the Soviets) 240,000. The West had agreed that this issue would be decided in the second round of CFE talks in Vienna, to avoid the impression of singularizing Germany by imposing limits on it alone. But the talks were dragging on, and Kohl wanted a resolution of the question. Genscher argued for a reduction of the Bundeswehr to 350,000, and the abolition of the NVA. Kohl and Stoltenberg favored a figure of 400,000. At this point, the Soviets also had not come up with any firm figure, and this was a topic of discussion as Kohl and Genscher flew to Moscow. They continued to haggle over the last 50,000 troops.[80]

From the German perspective, there were two remaining hurdles that had to be overcome: the total abolition of four-power rights over Germany and the full membership of a united Germany in NATO. The German leaders knew that this was perhaps the most important summit of all; yet they were not sure how Gorbachev would react following the Party Congress. When Kohl arrived in Moscow, he and Gorbachev began their bilateral talks. After some pleasantries, the Soviet leader got right to the point: He assumed that a united Germany would remain within the borders of the GDR, FRG, and Berlin and that NATO military structures could not be on East German territory after unification. When asked by Kohl whether a united Germany would recover full sovereignty, Gorbachev said that of course it would. Then, continued the Soviet leader, the question of Germany's membership in NATO was clear: of course Germany would belong to NATO, but there had to be a transitional period during which NATO's jurisdiction did not extend to eastern Germany. That was it. Gorbachev had said yes to full sovereignty and to membership in NATO. Kohl sat there, outwardly showing little reaction, as Gorbachev added that four-power rights would be terminated immediately after unification, with no transition period. As Teltschik recalls, the Germans had not expected such an unambiguous endorsement from Gorbachev, particularly so early on in the talks, and he and Kohl had trouble hiding their amazement and joy.

After this first round of talks, they all flew to Stavropol, to which no other foreign leader had yet been invited, and then took a helicopter to Arkhyz, a picturesque North Caucasian mountain retreat. There, in spectacular surroundings, the two sides hammered out the rest of the details. The question of the Bundeswehr size was still contentious, and Shevardnadze and Gorbachev were not in full agreement on this point. Shevardnadze insisted on 350,000; Genscher countered with 370,000. Gorbachev asked Kohl for less than 370,000, but Kohl brought him round. After discussing economic assistance and the position of ethnic Germans in Russia, Gorbachev dropped the final bomb: he agreed that as soon as Germany was unified, Bundeswehr units could be stationed in the former GDR and Berlin and these could be integrated in NATO after the last Soviet troops had withdrawn. Also, from the day of unity, NATO would be responsible for the whole of Germany. As Teltschik points out, these were positions that had been given up by the Germans months before because they never expected the Soviets to agree to them. Gorbachev had gone beyond their wildest expectations. All of the pieces of the German unity puzzle were now in place: there were no more questions about Germany's sovereignty or its future military status.[81] Gorbachev had, in Falin's embittered words, waved his magic wand.

In his memoirs, Shevardnadze muses: "We could not stop the reunification of Germany, except by force. And that would have meant disaster."[82] Gorbachev stresses that German unification was not an isolated event, "but part of our common commitment to a new Europe."[83] The *Germanisty* were outraged by the Arkhyz meeting and furious that they were excluded from it. Valentin Falin describes the Caucasus agreement as an act of "political masochism," claiming that Kohl and Genscher looked at Gorbachev in total disbelief when he agreed to the NATO option. Falin claims that he wrote a briefing paper for Gorbachev just before the summit in which he warned him that American intentions were "not altruistic" and that this was their last chance to look after Soviet interests. He argued vigorously against the "*Anschluss*" between West and East Germany; insisted that united Germany not become a member of NATO, or, at a minimum, not belong to its integrated military command; and warned Gorbachev against accepting any agreement on the questions of the USSR's property rights in the GDR or the ecological damage done to the GDR by Soviet troops until Soviet experts had looked into this as thoroughly as had the Americans. According to Falin, on reading his memo and speaking with him the night before his meeting with Kohl, Gorbachev said, "I will do what I can. But I fear that the train has already departed." Falin later commented, "On the side of the Soviet Union there were no statesmen, but only petit bourgeois in the highest positions who forgot everything that had existed in the past."[84]

Falin recalls that Brandt told him that when Kohl asked Gorbachev in Arkhyz to give him a list of prominent East Germans who should not be prosecuted after unification, Gorbachev refused, saying that the Germans must work this out themselves. Claiming that Gorbachev does not have a "clean conscience," Falin thus comes close to accusing both Gorbachev and Shevardnadze of committing treason against communism by betraying their comrades in the GDR. He suggests that Shevardnadze had received "some kind of secret financial payoff" from West German industrialists. This charge is reminiscent of those who accused Beria in 1953 of wanting to "sell" the GDR, and of chief ideologist Suslov's attacks on Khrushchev when he was ousted in 1964, reminding him that the GDR was not for sale "for all the gold in the world."[85] In any case, it is clear that dissension within the Soviet leadership continued until the moment of Gorbachev's compromise, and that the decision to meet Western conditions was made by a very small circle of people, namely Gorbachev, Shevardnadze and a few close and trusted aides.

Cherniaev, who was part of this small circle, refutes Falin's accusations. "Imagine if Gorbachev had listened to the advice of the Politburo and such experts as V. M. Falin. What would the result have been? They could have stalled everything, but Germany would anyway have been united—without us and against us. And we would not have received the compensation that the Germans gave us—material and political." He describes the intense discussions in the Caucasus that had already moved beyond the NATO question: "The discussion was no longer about how unification would proceed, but about what our relations would be like afterwards, and what [Germany's and Russia's] role would be separately and together in Europe and in the world."[86] Anatoly Dobrynin, on the other hand, concurs with the hardline view: "Gorbachev missed his great opportunity and missed it badly. The magic wand didn't work. His Western partners played their own realpolitik."[87]

To the outside world, the press conference following the Arkhyz meeting, held at nearby Zheleznovodsk, was nothing short of sensational. Kohl, describing the meeting as "a new pinnacle in the history of German-Soviet relations," announced eight main points:

　　1. German unification embraces the FRG, the GDR, and Berlin.
　　2. When unification takes place, all four-power rights will be completely abrogated.

3. A united and fully sovereign Germany will be able to decide which alliance it joins.

4. Germany will negotiate with the Soviet Union a treaty on troop withdrawals, which must be completed in three or four years.

5. NATO structures will not extend to the former GDR as long as Soviet troops are still there. Bundeswehr units that are not part of NATO can immediately be stationed in the former GDR.

6. For as long as Soviet troops remain on the territory of the former GDR, troops from the three Western powers will remain in Berlin.

7. The FRG will make a statement during the Vienna talks committing it to reduce a united Germany's armed forces to 370,000.

8. A united Germany will renounce the production, possession, and siting of nuclear, biological, and chemical weapons and will remain a member of the nuclear nonproliferation regime.

Kohl also spoke about future economic and financial cooperation. In the question-and-answer period, both Kohl and Gorbachev denied that there were any analogies to Rapallo.[88]

The international media reaction to the Zheleznovodsk press conference was varied, depending on the countries' position. *Pravda* spoke of "Realism and Trust"; the London *Economist* referred to "Stavrapallo," invoking the ever-present ghost of Rapallo. Some complained that this was a bilateral German-Soviet deal that had been concocted by excluding the other powers involved in the negotiations. And yet this bilateral deal was the product of an intense five months of meetings and bargaining, in which the United States had played a major role.[89] As Teltschik recalls, "In the first half of the year [1990] the energies of the world powers were almost exclusively focused on Germany. It was our good fortune that no other decisive events diverted the attention of our American partners."[90]

The nine assurances offered Gorbachev in Washington in May represented an important milestone on the path to unification by assuaging Soviet fears about a united Germany's future role. The question of the size of the Bundeswehr was also the product of multilateral, as well as bilateral, diplomacy. In other words, the groundwork for this summit had been laid by the four Western powers involved in the negotiations. Gorbachev chose to announce his decision at a bilateral meeting, because he did indeed want to develop a "special relationship" with Germany, one that would offer substantial economic and political benefits after unification. But the Germans themselves only negotiated what were by then agreed-upon Western positions. The significance of Arkhyz was that it cemented a personal relationship between Kohl and Gorbachev, as well as between Genscher and Shevardnadze, and committed both sides to partnership after unification. But it was not the beginning of a sinister bilateral axis against the interests of Europe or the United States.

The major breakthrough had been achieved in the Caucasus, but two months of intense negotiation followed, during which the details of the agreements were laboriously worked out. Although Gorbachev had agreed to everything that the West suggested, the Soviets tried at various points to obtain more money from the Germans, indicating both their economic plight and continuing dissension among the top decision makers. Immediately after the Caucasus meeting, the third ministerial Two Plus Four meeting was held in Paris. At this meeting, Shevardnadze and Genscher informed their surprised and generally supportive colleagues about the outcome of the Caucasus talks. The major achievement in Paris was the ratification of the agreement on the Polish border, in the presence of the Polish foreign minister. The treaty that was to emerge from this session would guarantee the Oder-Neisse line as Poland's western border following unification.

The future of German-Soviet economic cooperation remained high on the Kremlin's agenda, and during the next two months it tried to strike the best deal possible. At this point, the German leadership was beginning to realize how expensive German unification might be, and although they were very cognizant of the need to continue to offer the USSR financial incentives, they were also keenly aware of their own financial limitations. Moreover, as the USSR's largest Western trading partner, the FRG was particularly affected by the Soviets' inability to repay credits. Indeed, part of the DM 5 billion credit had gone toward the repayment of old debts. By the end of 1990, the USSR was DM 2 billion in arrears in credit repayments, mainly to medium-sized German firms.[91] As Wilhelm Christians, head of the Deutsche Bank, said, the major reason for the reluctance of German firms to expand business ties was because "The Soviet Union has stopped paying its bills. . . . The Soviet Union must acquire a reputation as a reliable debtor."[92] Coming from a long-term supporter of German-Soviet economic ties, this reflected the general German wariness about extending more credits. Bonn winced at comments such as those made by Portugalov, when he announced: "We hope that we will be saved from looming catastrophe by the German economy and German private investment."[93]

While the Soviets continued to bargain over the timetable and structures for withdrawing their troops, in late August Deputy Prime Minister Sitaryan began discussions with Finance Minister Waigel on compensation for troop withdrawal. At the same time, Kvitsinsky was trying to secure more comprehensive and detailed clauses in the proposed German-Soviet treaty than his German partners were willing to offer.[94] On September 5, the Soviet ambassador in Bonn, Vladislav Terekhov, presented a new DM 36 billion bill to the German government, all of which was related to the stationing in and withdrawal from East Germany of

Soviet troops. This was five times more than the Germans were willing to pay, and bargaining between the Soviets and Germans continued. On September 7, five days before the final Two Plus Four meeting was to take place, Gorbachev and Kohl had their first telephone conversation since Arkhyz—the most expensive of the unification process. Kohl offered Gorbachev a total package of DM 8 billion, most of which would go toward building houses and providing training for Soviet soldiers returning from the GDR. The Germans did not want to pay for the costs of continued troop stationing in Germany, as the Kremlin had demanded. Gorbachev, who spoke as if he were under great pressure, reacted frostily: by Soviet calculations, at least DM 11 billion was needed for housing construction alone. If one added transportation and stationing costs, therefore, the sum would be much higher. He implied, in this last-minute attempt at linkage, that the success of Two Plus Four talks would be jeopardized if Bonn were not more generous. Kohl and his advisors were surprised by the harshness of Gorbachev's tone. Two days later, Kohl told Gorbachev that he could not offer what Sitaryan had most recently proposed, namely DM 16–18 billion, but that Germany was willing to give 12 billion. Gorbachev continued to bargain hard, implying that German unification might still be in question if more assistance was not forthcoming. "That was a clear message," writes Kohl, "I realized I was obliged to offer the Soviet Union an additional 3 billion interest-free credit." (He had discussed this option with his advisors prior to the phone call.) Thus, after extremely difficult telephone negotiations, Germany went a large way toward meeting Soviet economic demands, because Bonn was determined to gain its sovereignty and to complete unification the next week.[95]

Indeed, the question of whether Two Plus Four would be successfully completed was unanswered right until the very last moment before the treaty was signed. The speed with which German unification was negotiated was largely responsible for this uncertainty. In August, Shevardnadze was still arguing that four-power rights could only end when the unification treaties had been ratified by their respective parliaments. Another source of friction was the details of the withdrawal of Soviet troops and the role of the Bundeswehr in the eastern part of the country. Shevardnadze also tried to lengthen the time frame for the withdrawal of Soviet troops. Other contentious issues were exactly what weapons could be deployed on former GDR territory and what kind of NATO exercises might take place there. At the eleventh hour, compromises were made on all of these issues, but during a particularly tense moment, Bondarenko, when asked what options Moscow might consider, replied, "None at all"; he had no instructions from Moscow. Indeed, participants in the hectic last hours of the last Two Plus Four were amazed by how the high-level

Soviet negotiators seemed to be improvising.[96] They had not brought competent legal experts with them, and at the last moment, Germany was able to secure concessions in some of the legal language because the Soviets were inadequately prepared. Moreover, the British nearly prevented the document from being signed because of disagreements with Germany over military maneuvers in East Germany. Foreign Minister Douglas Hurd argued that it was premature to sign the Two Plus Four treaty, because no one knew how long Gorbachev would be in power and thus it was important to have the freedom to conduct NATO maneuvers in eastern Germany when NATO so chose. Hurd's unexpected statement prompted an angry midnight call by Genscher to Baker, who was already asleep, to iron out this last glitch.[97] Finally, by September 12, the West had succeeded in winning Soviet agreement to full suspension of four-power rights, unrestricted deployment of German conventional forces within the entire country, and Germany's being allowed to exercise its sovereign rights to determine how or when to apply the treaty's stricture against allied troops being deployed in the former GDR.

On September 12, the Treaty on the Final Settlement with Respect to Germany was signed, ratifying much of what had already been agreed upon between Germany and the Soviet Union and between the United States, its allies, and the USSR, including Germany's borders; its renunciation of atomic, biological, and chemical weapons; the reduction of the Bundeswehr; the withdrawal of Soviet troops by the end of 1994; and no permanent stationing in eastern Germany of Bundeswehr units integrated into NATO until all Soviet troops had withdrawn. Four-power rights were terminated and Germany was fully sovereign and free to choose its alliance.[98] On September 13, the bilateral Soviet-German Treaty of Good Neighborliness was initialed by the two foreign ministers. On October 3, Germany was united and became fully sovereign.

After the fall of the Soviet Union, when the issue of NATO enlargement arose, Gorbachev and many of his former colleagues—including those who had broken with him—argued that promises had been made during the negotiations on German unity that NATO would not be enlarged. In his memoirs and in private conversations, Gorbachev is adamant that the West assured him to this effect. Permitting a united Germany to remain in NATO was difficult enough for Moscow; it was understood that, as a quid pro quo, NATO would not expand to Russia's borders. The Western allies have always denied that such a promise was made. What is the truth? What was promised? Did the West renege on its commitments? As with so much that was involved in German unification, ambiguity and misperceptions abound. The record shows that no explicit promises on NATO expansion were made, but what was implied during the negotiations ultimately lies in the eyes of the beholder. Nevertheless, the broader context must be kept in mind. In 1990, the Warsaw Pact still existed. Few people were thinking ahead beyond unification to what Europe would look like after the collapse of the USSR and the Warsaw Pact, because, in September 1990, Gorbachev still appeared to be holding on to power.

In February 1990, during Baker's visit to Moscow, he discussed with Gorbachev Genscher's Tutzing proposal not to extend NATO "jurisdiction" to the territory of the GDR. At this point, Baker was talking solely about this territory, not about any further extension of NATO. After this statement, however, the White House, which had not fully apppreciated the legal significance of this formula, reworked it to argue that eastern Germany would have a "special military status" within NATO. Participants in the negotiations who have seen the relevant documents deny that any commitment not to expand NATO was made to Gorbachev, because no one at that point was thinking in these terms.[99] Nevertheless, it is undeniable that Genscher's longer-term vision was of an all-European security system that had moved beyond military blocs. Moreover, one can also argue that the Two Plus Four agreement was negotiated in a spirit of East-West understanding that foresaw future cooperation between the USSR and the West. For the Russians, therefore, the expansion of NATO violates the spirit, if not the letter, of the Two Plus Four Treaty, a treaty that symbolized a new era of East-West accord after the Soviets had made so many concessions.

The final act in the German-Soviet drama came on November 9, the first anniversary of the fall of the Berlin Wall. During Gorbachev's visit to Bonn, a united Germany signed its first foreign treaty, the Treaty on Good Neighborliness, Partnership, and Cooperation with the USSR. This is quite a remarkable document, given the state of Soviet–West German relations prior to 1988. The treaty, which was to be in force for twenty years, foresaw a close partnership between the two states and the emergence of a peaceful Europe in which both countries would play a major role. It anticipated cooperation on a wide range of governmental and nongovernmental levels in which people-to-people contacts would be stressed, and consultation on all international crises. Reading this treaty, it is difficult to imagine that, a year earlier, the parties had been on opposite sides of the Cold War.[100] A second treaty, on Developing Comprehensive Cooperation on the Economy, Industry, Science, and Technology, envisaging close cooperation on all these levels and committing both sides to intensify their bilateral trade, was also signed.[101] Both leaders praised each other lavishly in their speeches, pointing to the contribution of both sides to the peaceful achievement of German unity.

Repercussions

Even after the treaties were signed, opposition to German unification and to the Two Plus Four treaties persisted in the Soviet Union. The treaties faced a tough fight in the Supreme Soviet and especially in its foreign relations committee. Here was a new legislative body eager to break with Soviet traditions and flex its muscle against entrenched bureaucracies, and determined not to submit to pressure from the executive. But the fight over the German treaties was also a personal vendetta by the old communist *nomenklatura* against Shevardnadze, whose policies were seen by many as having sold out Soviet interests.

The two major antagonists in the fight for ratification, Kvitsinsky and Falin, were both communist apparatchiki who had a vested interest in the status quo. But Kvitsinsky, despite his prior opposition to unification and the NATO solution, was a loyal bureaucrat who saw it as his duty to defend his foreign minister. Falin, on the other hand, was the head of an organization that had recently lost power to the Foreign Ministry. Shevardnadze's stature and influence with Gorbachev had grown considerably since 1985, and his ministry had eclipsed the International Department.[102] The key decisions on German unity had been made by a small ad hoc group of close advisors to Gorbachev and Shevardnadze. Thus, the struggle over ratification was not only about the single most important development in Gorbachev's foreign policy, but was also a fight between the old and the new, between the parliament and the executive, between the Communist Party and a more pluralist Russia, between those who had been overtaken by history and those who still wanted to make history.

As soon as the Two Plus Four treaties were signed, opposition to them within the Supreme Soviet became more vocal, as did the criticism from the military and other institutions. The opponents found a relatively trivial issue around which to rally: how the GDR was to end its 1975 Treaty on Friendship and Cooperation with the Soviet Union. Soviet jurists decided that since the treaty had originally been ratified by the Supreme Soviet, it would have to be repealed in the same way. Although this was legally questionable, a session of the Foreign Policy Committee of the Supreme Soviet was called, and sparks began to fly. Falin, by then a deputy in the Congress of People's Deputies, likened the Arkhyz agreement to Beria's alleged plan to give up the GDR. According to Kvitsinsky, who was horrified by the discussion, Falin criticized the Foreign Ministry, saying that it had totally neglected the question of the USSR's treaty obligations to the GDR. After the stormy session, Gorbachev called Falin and berated him for his conduct. But Falin claimed that he had done this deliberately, to ease the way for the ratification of the Two Plus Four treaties, by taking a hard line early on.[103] The question of the GDR-Soviet treaty was subsequently dropped.

By the time the treaties came up for ratification on March 4, 1991, Shevardnadze was no longer foreign minister. He had resigned in December, against Gorbachev's wish, warning that a coup against reform was imminent (it was, in fact, eight months away). He was replaced by Alexander Bessmertnykh, a career diplomat and America expert who never enjoyed the same stature as his predecessor. Prior to ratification, the opponents tried to play one more trump card. They claimed that if the treaties were not ratified, the USSR would have the right to demand up to DM 1,900 billion in reparations from Germany, since it would still be able to exercise rights as a victor power. Although this suggestion—the product of research by a German professor—was in the realm of fantasy, it did raise the question of German reparations for Soviet victims of Nazism. West Germany had paid reparations to Jews and others persecuted by the Nazis as well as to Israel, and there was some legal basis for doing the same for Soviet citizens, since nothing had ever been paid by the GDR. In late February, therefore, Germany declared its willingness in principle to pay reparations to Soviet victims of Nazism. This influenced the ratification debate, and showed that the Soviets were still trying to haggle over the price of unification, after it had already taken place.[104]

When the treaties were eventually ratified, Kvitsinsky gave a tough speech defending them, emphasizing that they were in the USSR's best interests because the process that had begun in the GDR in the fall of 1989 could not be stopped. The Soviet Union must not repeat its historical mistakes in its policies toward Germany. He stressed the economic advantages for the Soviet Union of the DM 12 billion to go toward building housing for Soviet soldiers. Now was the time to begin a new chapter in German-Soviet relations. Kvitsinsky relates that the deputies decided not to have an open debate because some of the opponents of ratification wanted to remain anonymous so that they could in the future go to Germany and conduct business there.[105] A week later, Erich Honecker was spirited away at night in a Soviet plane from the Soviet military hospital in East Berlin to Moscow, eliciting loud protests from Bonn, which had not been consulted. This was the last act of Soviet-GDR solidarity and the last time that the USSR exercised powers in Germany, although in fact the pacts were ratified and the USSR no longer had any legal rights there.

The treaties on troop stationing and withdrawals remained to be ratified. Here, again, the Soviets sought, and gained, more money from the Germans before the vote took place. One day after Two Plus Four was ratified, General Burlakov, who was in command of Soviet troops in Germany, demanded an extra DM 10.5 billion compensation for Soviet immovable property remaining in Germany and another DM 4.2 billion for the construction of housing for returning soldiers. The German government promised to look into the matter and did indeed eventually give some more money after the ratification.[106]

The Soviet Bargain

After all the memoirs and analyses that have been written about German unification, the most puzzling question remains: why did Gorbachev, in a mere 392 days, agree to the renunciation of most of the Soviet Union's gains from the Second World War, in which 27 million Soviet citizens had died? As we have seen, Gorbachev did have more options in 1989 than later on, when his reforms and foreign policy were blocked domestically. Short of the use of the Soviet Union's considerable military force, Gorbachev and Shevardnadze could still have used delaying tactics, or they could have tried in a far more concerted way to pressure the Germans into accepting a settlement well short of full membership in NATO.

Part of the answer to these questions lies in the ambivalence that Gorbachev and Shevardnadze had toward the whole issue. On the one hand, the creation of the Soviet empire in Eastern Europe was the basis of Soviet global influence, a source of pride and status, and a legitimization of the great international socialist fraternity. On the other hand, Gorbachev and Shevardnadze had become acutely aware of the growing costs of maintaining the empire and the detrimental effect that these costs had on their own attempts to preserve and reform the Soviet system. There was the growing realization that socialism in Eastern Europe enjoyed little popular legitimacy, and it was becoming an increasing burden for Moscow to sustain unpopular leaders. Without renouncing its control over the region, the Soviet Union would never be able to reform itself and escape from the international censure that its domination there had imposed. Moreover, having committed himself to New Political Thinking and to freedom of choice for all countries, Gorbachev had to pursue operational policies consistent with his declared policies if he were to remain a credible world leader. Certainly, by the fall of 1989, Gorbachev's desire to bring the Soviet Union into the world community and his belief that without significant Western involvement, the USSR would never solve its economic problems, had modified his views on the necessity of holding on to Eastern Europe or the GDR. If the only way to retain the East European empire was to use force—which would have made it impossible to increase and diversify Soviet economic ties with the

West and be accepted as part of the "civilized" international community—then it was not worth holding on to it.

But that does not mean that Gorbachev had a coherent strategy. Neither he nor Shevardnadze went into the discussions on German unity with a clear set of priorities that represented a consensus among different factions. Unlike their Western counterparts, who worked hard to develop a clear set of plans and negotiating strategies in the face of domestic differences, the Soviet Union did not have such a consistent strategy, because of the tremendous domestic differences over the subject and also because of the decline of the Communist Party, which in former times would have coordinated this process more effectively. On the one side Shevardnadze appeared to be reconciled to German unification in NATO, but then vacillated between a conciliatory and a hard line, to placate his critics. Then there was Gorbachev, who seemed to be less convinced than Shevardnadze of the wisdom of this course, but nevertheless inclined toward change, although at a much later date than the Western side envisaged. Arrayed against them were the *Germanisty* in the party apparatus and the Foreign Ministry, who fought hard to keep the status quo or secure a united Germany's neutrality even after unification had been agreed on. If Soviet diplomacy gave the impression of improvising or of trial and error, that was because Moscow had to respond to rapidly developing events within Germany at a time when Soviet domestic turmoil was increasing.

German unification was achieved during the brief window of opportunity during which Gorbachev was able to keep his opponents on the right and left at bay, and during which the United States was able to turn its full attention to the negotiations. If the GDR had fallen six months later and negotiations had begun in the fall of 1990, then Gorbachev would have been far more beholden to his hardline critics and the United States and its allies would have been diverted by the Gulf War. Timing, in this case, was of the essence.

The resoluteness of the West was an important factor influencing Soviet negotiating strategy. It would have been difficult, although not impossible, to drive wedges between the Western powers, but this strategy was never consistently tried. Personal diplomacy was also very important.[107] The contacts between Shevardnadze and Genscher, Genscher and Baker and Shevardnadze and Baker, played a crucial role. So did the contacts between Gorbachev and Kohl, Gorbachev and Bush, and Kohl and Bush. Precisely because there was no overall Soviet strategy and no clear institutional division of labor, frequent personal contacts were very important in assuring the USSR that its interests would not be detrimentally affected. Moreover, the United States and West Germany both negotiated in a highly capable fashion. The other players, France and Britain, were important but less central. The GDR was only marginally involved, and was never allowed to put forward its own plans. As the main advisor to the East German foreign minister said, "The GDR, with the greatest stake in unification, lost the most in the process. That is the congenital defect of unification." This sense that the GDR's interests had been ignored (for instance, in June 1990, 65 percent of the GDR population was against NATO membership) was one of the many psychological burdens that were inherited by the new Germany.[108]

Economic factors, though not decisive, certainly influenced Gorbachev and Shevardnadze. The traditional belief in the priority of Russo-German economic relations affected the Soviet leaders' thinking. West Germany used economic statecraft skillfully and was forthcoming every time the Soviets asked for new assistance and credits during these negotiations, because Bonn realized that this was the major concrete gain it had to offer the Soviets in return for renouncing East Germany. The other major factor influencing Soviet decision making was West German willingness to cut the armed forces of a united Germany by 45 percent of what the total NVA and Bundeswehr would have been. This helped to convince the Soviets that forty-five years after the end of World War II, there was a new Germany that did not harbor aggressive military intentions.[109] This was only plausible within the context of the NATO London summit and the pledge to redefine NATO's mission and goals, deemphasizing the element of East-West confrontation.

Moreover, it appears that at least by July if not before, Gorbachev had come to believe what Baker and Bush had pointed out to him earlier: namely that a united Germany firmly embedded in NATO, with the United States and others guaranteeing its future peaceful course, would reinforce Soviet security much more than a neutral Germany that might be tempted to acquire nuclear weapons or expand *à tous azimuths* if unchecked. As Gorbachev writes in his memoirs:

> The following considerations were decisive in influencing the Soviet Union and its former partners in the anti-Hitler coalition not to oppose German unity: a democratic, politically stable, and economically healthy Germany, which accepts its borders and is content with its political system as well as its role in Europe and the world will become one of the most important positive factors in European and international developments. . . . That was one side of the problem. But the second side is overcoming the discrepancy between the quality of life in Eastern and Western Europe. Germany—and the West—will not be able to avoid involvement in this issue.[110]

Since Germany emphasized the importance of multilateral assistance, Gorbachev also viewed Kohl as his main supporter among the G-7 group, facilitating the USSR's entrance into the international economic club. He also hoped that Germany would take the lead, after unification, in devising a new European security structure in which the Soviet-German partnership would play a major role.[111] At least, that was the best interpretation one could offer for what were major Soviet concessions.[112]

On October 3, 1990, unity day, the participants in the negotiations were euphoric and exhausted. By this time, Gorbachev's domestic troubles were making him more beholden to his critics on the right, the United States was caught up in preparations for the Gulf War, and the atmosphere had changed. But it is important to understand the expectations that both the Soviet and the Germans had after unification. Neither side at this point had begun to digest the foreign policy consequences of unification for their respective countries. The USSR had now lost its empire and Germany had become a fully sovereign, major European power. Bonn had spent so much time reassuring the French, British, Poles, Israelis, and others that a reunified Germany would not become the Fourth Reich that it had not begun to deal with what its new foreign policy role should be, nor with what other countries' expectations might be.

The intense negotiations on the internal and external aspects of unification resulted in a seismic change in the European security system. The Warsaw Pact and CMEA were dead; in their place emerged a group of new postcommunist states struggling to make the transition to a more prosperous, more democratic system. Soviet policy toward Europe was no longer bifurcated. Moscow looked increasingly to Western Europe and to Germany as its relations with Eastern Europe quickly atrophied. German unification would have been impossible without the prior changes in Eastern Europe, and both the Soviets and Germans had had to react to events in the GDR over which they had increasingly little control. Now they had to come to terms with the consequences of these actions. The negotiations had been focused on details, but the sum of all the parts had implications which no one could possibly have foreseen. Soviet expectations of the impact of German unification on the bilateral relationship were initially higher than those of Germany. Perhaps because the Soviets had conceded so much, they expected a greater payoff. Indeed, Dobrynin, echoing other Soviet critics, writes that "Gorbachev's dream of a new Europe, with a new security system encompassing all states, including Russia, did not come true. . . . In exchange for the generous Soviet concessions Gorbachev and his devoted lieutenant Shevardnadze offered the West, they could and should have obtained a more important role for the Soviet Union in European affairs, but they did not." Maximychev echoes this, adding, "Gorbachev was unable to realize the historic chance that was presented him. As a result, we stand today before the threat of a new division of our continent."[113]

The Legacy of 1989–1990

One major legacy of unification was that a united Germany was as central to Soviet foreign policy as a divided Germany had been, for many of the same reasons. United Germany was the USSR's major economic partner, key to its economic health. Whereas the GDR had strengthened the Soviet military and West Germany had been considered a potential military danger, a united Germany no longer threatened Soviet security because the unification of Germany had ended the Cold War. Germany would continue to be the USSR's most important European partner and ties between the new Germany and the Soviet Union could be far more congenial than Soviet ties with either German state had previously been.

The way in which Gorbachev and Shevardnadze negotiated German unification had an impact both on Soviet domestic politics and on Soviet-German relations that outlived the Soviet Union itself. Unification was not negotiated through the normal Soviet channels—the Politburo, the Central Committee, and the various state bureaucracies. Instead, the party per se became increasingly irrelevant, and decisions were made by a small ad hoc group, often improvising and with no clear guidelines. There was no broad consensus on German unification—it was the product of decisionmaking by a small group of people. The party's power was fast fading during 1990 and the total reversal of Soviet postwar German policy was achieved by bypassing the party's International Department.

By the same token, Gorbachev's vacillation and the contradictory speeches made by the major Soviet participants also laid the groundwork for a backlash against Gorbachev and his advisors by those who believed that East Germany had been sold too cheaply. Moreover, criticism of Gorbachev for not insisting on more concrete promises for the USSR's future role in Europe resurfaced soon after the collapse of the USSR. This, in turn, has influenced the post-Soviet debate about whether Moscow was too compliant a partner of the West and strengthened the position of those arguing for a tougher Russian policy. Anatoly Dobrynin also makes a charge about the way in which unification was negotiated that still resonates today. Initially, Gorbachev and his advisors had agreed that German unification would be the last act in a gradual process of the overcoming of Europe's division during which both NATO and the Warsaw Pact would be dissolved. "But then there was a metamorphosis in Gorbachev's behavior. Under Western pressure which came through confidential channels, he began to uncouple German unification from the general problem of European security."[114] The failure to resolve questions about future European security structures left unanswered questions about the future role and size of NATO and about Russia's place in Europe.

German unification created a new agenda in Soviet-German relations. It was not lost on Germany that in the end the USSR conceded most of Germany's demands. In the long run, this has fundamentally altered the nature of the bilateral relationship by placing Germany in the role of the agenda setter. In the short run, the withdrawal of the 380,000 Soviet troops and their dependents became the paramount bilateral issue. The onus was on the Germans to fulfill their economic and political obligations, which became increasingly costly as the price of integrating the two German states rose astronomically. But the new agenda had one major drawback for the Soviets and later the Russians. Beyond commitments on aid and trade, and vague promises of creating a new system of European security, there was nothing to ensure continued German involvement after the Soviet troops had withdrawn. The Soviets retained some leverage over Germany as long as their troops were there; after their departure, Germany would eventually have to redefine its interests in Russia.

During the negotiations on German unity, the United States played an extraordinary role, both as initiator of policies and broker between the parties. France and Britain were also important players. This was, however, the last time that Washington, as an occupying power, would exercise such influence. Once four-power rights were terminated and Germany achieved full sovereignty, the United States' relations with both Germany and the Soviet Union changed. America's ability to influence German policies declined, as did that of the USSR. Without the division of Germany, the nature of ties among the Western powers and between them and the USSR was irrevocably altered.

The process of German unification also raised questions of national identity for both the USSR and the FRG. Yes, East Germans had overwhelmingly supported the idea that Germans were indeed one nation. But the way in which both the internal and external aspects of unification were negotiated excluded the East Germans and left a legacy of bitterness in the GDR. The Two Plus Four process only nominally gave postcommunist East German officials any say in questions involving troops and NATO membership. The fact that East Germans were largely irrelevant in the negotiations on unification, a process that they had made possible through their courageous actions, contributed to the difficulties that East and West Germans have had in forging a new national identity.

German unification, combined with the slow disintegration of the Communist Party and the USSR itself, also deeply affected Soviet national identity. Along with the independence of Eastern Europe, it encouraged non-Russian groups within the Soviet Union to pursue their own independence. Unification brought to a head the identity crisis: after all, what was the Soviet Union without its fraternal allies in Eastern Europe? The loss of East Germany and Eastern Europe raised uncomfortable questions about what communism and all its accompanying sacrifices had actually accomplished. Eastern Europe's rejection of both Brezhnevite and Gorbachev-style communism further delegitimized Gorbachev domestically. Georgi Shakhnazarov admitted that things did not turn out the way Gorbachev and his advisors wanted in the process of German unification; but, he added, Gorbachev achieved as much as he could given the circumstances.[115] The inability to affect developments in Eastern Europe was one of the most difficult aspects of German unification for the Gorbachev team. Hence Gorbachev's frequent use of railroad imagery—his references to German unification as a speeding train over which the Soviet driver had lost control.

Six

Implementing Unification:
Russia and Germany, 1992–1997

> Russians and Germans are the two largest
> nations in Europe. Their relationship is
> decisive for the fate of the entire continent.
> (*Boris Yeltsin, April 1994*)[1]

> Relations between Russia and Germany are
> today tension-free, trusting, and friendly. This
> is Boris Yeltsin's achievement. We want to
> build on these relations in both sides' interest
> and confidently proceed from the hope that a
> free, democratic, and market-oriented Russia
> will remain a peaceful, predictable and stable
> partner for Germany and our neighbors.
> (*Helmut Kohl, March 1993*)[2]

> For Bonn, Moscow is a Janus-faced partner.
> Should it look to the future? Or should it look
> back in anger? It is going in both directions at
> the same time.
> (Süddeutsche Zeitung, *March 1994*)[3]

ALTHOUGH German unification was the most dramatic event in the collapse of the international communist system, it was by no means the final act. One year later came the collapse of the USSR, the breakup of Yugoslavia, and the outbreak of war in the Balkans. There was to be no encore to the intense, heady days of Soviet-German negotiations on unification, and both sides' initial expectations were never fulfilled. Moscow and Bonn were not to enjoy the luxury of reconstructing ties during a calm period after the turmoil produced by the demise of communism in Eastern Europe. As post-Soviet Russia began its long and difficult march toward democracy and capitalism, neither Moscow nor Bonn had a clear vision of what Russo-German relations could or should become. Russia was no longer Germany's enemy; but it had yet to become a true partner.

After the collapse of the Soviet Union, Germany and Russia remained preoccupied with the "old" Cold War agenda—implementing the unification treaties. In the final year of the Soviet Union, the dramatic events that united Germany were receding into the past, and the mundane and time-consuming task of implementation, rather than the excitement of negotiation and redrawing the map of Europe, preoccupied both sides. The major German objectives were ensuring that Soviet troops withdrew from the former GDR as soon as possible and promoting stability in the chaotic and potentially dangerous post-Soviet situation. Russian goals were to secure as much economic assistance as possible from Germany and to gain its political support for the struggling new Yeltsin government. During the immediate post-Soviet period, Germany had a larger stake in the outcome of the Russian transition than did any other country, because of the troop withdrawal issue. After the Soviet troops had left eastern Germany, the bilateral relationship remained tenuous, reflecting the uneasy post-Soviet transition. New issues began to emerge, far less amenable to classical diplomatic solution than those during the Cold War.

After 1991, two new countries faced each other—Germany and Russia had never before existed within the borders that they acquired in 1990 and 1991—and their preoccupation with their respective domestic challenges limited their capacity and enthusiasm for developing active new foreign policies. Both countries' historic struggles to establish viable national identities within uncertain boundaries had in the past led to instability and war in Europe. Thus, two countries that were politically and geographically new but searching for their benign, as opposed to aggressive, historical roots had to transform the legacy of Soviet–West German and Soviet–East German ties into a workable postcommunist modus vivendi without alarming either the newly emerging democracies of Eastern Europe or the European Community as it moved toward closer integration.

Despite the superficial similarities of the problems that both countries faced, the challenges and stakes were in fact widely divergent. Although it had to cope with the economic challenge of rebuilding eastern Germany, the new Federal Republic emerged strengthened in 1991, aware that its problems were soluble within a reasonable time horizon, even though the Kohl government had greatly underestimated not only the economic but also the political and psychological costs of unification. The situation in Russia was far more fragile and uncertain. Centuries of autocracy and seventy-four years of communism had left a legacy of economic and political ruin, and an enormous amount of fear about an unknown and unpredictable future. Russia had to build a democracy and a market society simultaneously from scratch—something never attempted before—and at the same time cope with the dual shock of losing its external empire in Eastern Europe and its internal empire, the fourteen other republics of the Soviet Union. Dire predictions of large-scale violence, instability, and collapse were rife inside and outside Russia. Yet Russia remained a nuclear superpower with a large standing army even as it renounced its ideological struggle with the West.

Russia's major external challenge after December 1991 was to define and conceptualize a new foreign policy, debating how to divide its priorities between the "near abroad"—the states of the former Soviet Union—and the rest of the world. As relations with the former Soviet states took priority, ties with the outside world were relegated to second place. Moreover, postcommunist Russia faced the challenge that Bolshevik Russia had faced after 1917—bringing new cadres into the foreign policymaking process, who had sufficient knowledge and expertise to formulate effective policies but were not too attached to the previous system.

Germany, too, had to embark on the search for a new foreign policy identity, largely because its neighbors and allies expected it to assume new responsibilities with its increased size. The greatest challenge was how to reconceptualize priorities for the development of ties with Eastern Europe, on the one hand, and Russia and the post-Soviet successor states on the other. As German priorities changed, east-central Europe—Germany's own "near abroad"—began to assume a new importance. A further issue was balancing economic and political interests in the East and bilateral, as opposed to multilateral, policies. There was more overt discussion of future foreign policy options in Germany than in Russia; but these rarely went beyond generalized statements about the importance of all-European security. Most of the more alarmist forecasts about a possible new Berlin-Moscow axis—from intimations of a "new Rapallo" to predictions that Germany might abandon Russia after the troops were withdrawn—were minority views. But the overriding fact in all these debates was uncertainty. Both Germany and Russia were moving into uncharted territory with no accepted rules of the game, in contrast to the comfortable predictability of the Cold War years.

The Putsch

The major challenge for Bonn and Moscow after unification was to insulate Soviet-German relations from the turmoil in the USSR and ensure that the agreements concluded between the two sides in 1990 survived the Soviet upheavals. The Germans were especially preoccupied with the impact of Soviet disintegration on their relations with the USSR, because Bonn stood to lose more than did Moscow. It was far more important for

Bonn than for Moscow that the Soviet troops leave the former GDR as expeditiously as possible.

Throughout 1991, both sides were able to protect the implementation of the unification agreements from the political roller-coaster in the USSR, but their ability to broaden the bilateral agenda was limited by Gorbachev's fragile domestic position. The first major shock—to the Germans as well as Gorbachev—was the unexpected resignation of Eduard Shevardnadze. This was an unwelcome surprise not only to Gorbachev, who lost one of his increasingly scarce reformist allies, but to the USSR's Western partners, who feared that Gorbachev's moves to the right domestically would be mirrored by a return to more hardline diplomacy. Shevardnadze's policies were continued by his successor, Aleksandr Bessmertnykh. But, neither Germany nor the United States developed a rapport with Bessmertnykh similar to that which they had with Shevardnadze.

In 1991, Gorbachev confronted the issue that ultimately brought down the Soviet Union: the desire of the non-Russian Soviet republics to emulate Eastern Europe and break free from Moscow. German unification had emboldened the non-Russian republics. After all, if Moscow could give up the GDR, why not let Estonia go? Repeating the patterns of previous Soviet leaders in less enlightened times, Gorbachev used the period during which much of the world was distracted by the Gulf crisis to crack down on the Baltic republics, whose parliaments were demanding independence. Soviet troops killed Lithuanians and Latvians, provoking outcries not only in the West but among the reformers in the Soviet Union. As the struggle between the reformers and antireformers continued, Boris Yeltsin's star was rising. In June 1991, he was elected by popular vote to the newly created presidency of Russia, thus gaining a base from which to pursue his struggle against Gorbachev. The key issue became the future relationship between the republics of the Soviet Union and the drafting of a new Union Treaty that would give the republics more autonomy.

While the reformers favored such a treaty, those opposed to Gorbachev denounced the very idea of negotiating with the republics. As the September date for the signing of the treaty approached, the conservative opposition decided to move. Shevardnadze's dire predictions nearly came true in August, when a group of Gorbachev's opponents staged a coup, put Gorbachev under house arrest and tried to turn back the clock to the pre-perestroika era. The inebriated, disorganized plotters' inept attempts to bring back communism showed how far the Soviet Union had come since 1985. Generals and party members alike were unable to bring off a successful coup, in the face of popular resistance and worldwide media coverage.

During the tense three days of the coup, Genscher was in constant touch with Shevardnadze (now out of power but still politically active), as was Kohl with both Gorbachev and Yeltsin.[4] Germany's support for Gorbachev during the coup was as strong as that of any other Western government, given the uncertainties about what was actually happening in the first twenty-four hours and the perceived need not to alienate completely the State Emergency Committee that purported to be running the county, in case they remained in power.[5] Yeltsin's defiance of the putschists enhanced his domestic popularity and forced Germany and other countries to take him more seriously than they had before. It was no longer possible to maintain the conventional Western Gorbachev-centric view that Yeltsin was an unpredictable provincial politician who liked to make life difficult for the courageous Soviet leader.

There were some major irritants in the relationship as the USSR disintegrated, particularly Erich Honecker's midnight escape to Moscow. Foreign Minister Aleksandr Bessmertnykh claimed that the German government had been informed about his departure before the fact. Despite German protests, Honecker's flight was convenient, inasmuch as it removed the difficult question of whether and how to prosecute the former head of state. There were a number of ironies in the "Honecker affair," not the least of which was the fact that Gorbachev, the man who had supported the ouster of Honecker, ultimately came to Honecker's assistance. According to Boris Pankin, who was foreign minister from August to November 1991, during one of his first talks with the Soviet leader "Gorbachev told me frankly that he did not know what to do with Honecker." Pankin was charged with negotiating with both Gorbachev and Yeltsin over Honecker's fate, but concluded that "Honecker was a hot potato that [the Germans] were actually anxious not to handle."[6] As the Soviet Union was collapsing, Honecker took refuge in the home of the Chilean ambassador in Moscow, asking to be sent to Chile, where his daughter lived. Yeltsin subsequently told Honecker that the Russian state would not protect him and eventually extradited him to Germany, where his trial was cut short on grounds of ill health. He died in Chile in 1994.

After the putsch, and the USSR's recognition of Baltic independence in September, the German government began to digest the unpalatable fact that Gorbachev's days in office were numbered: yet, like other Western governments, it hoped against hope that Gorbachev would be able somehow to keep what was left of the Soviet Union intact. All Western leaders admired Gorbachev for what he had done to permit communism to collapse in Eastern Europe, improve East-West relations, and reduce the military threat emanating from the Soviet Union. They feared that a breakup of the USSR would unleash military and political forces and refugees that would destabilize Europe. As Genscher explains, Germany did all it could to support Gorbachev in his attempt to devise a new Union Treaty: "This was not only an expression of our personal ties, but also because we were concerned about the political, military, and economic consequences that the collapse of the Soviet Union could bring in its wake. We were particularly interested in the question of nuclear weapons: there could be no proliferation."[7]

The West opposed Soviet communism; but it also understood the Soviet mentality and had developed a modus vivendi with the USSR. Gorbachev had come to represent a favorite German concept: he was *berechenbar*, "predictable"; in other words, you knew what to expect of him. The end of Gorbachev meant the resurgence of powerful nationalist forces in parts of the Soviet Union barely known to or understood by the West, with unpredictable consequences. The breakup of the USSR would make whatever followed Gorbachev "unpredictable." Germany, which had spent four decades fighting its own nationalist demons and downplaying the relevance of nationalism, was particularly disturbed by the Soviet breakup. After all, was not the twentieth century the ultimate testimony to the evils of nationalism? What did its resurgence in the East portend for the next millennium?

After the Fall: Yeltsin's Russia

After Gorbachev's resignation, the German-Russian relationship developed cautiously, embodying elements of both continuity and change. The continuity was provided by the implementation of the unification agreements. The change was a product of Yeltsin's evolving political position, of Kohl's difficulties with integrating the new Eastern Länder (states) into a united Germany, and of developments in Eastern Europe and the Balkans. Although the agenda from 1990 had to be addressed, that did not guarantee that a new relationship could easily be constructed. It would require careful nurturing. If their neighbors worried out loud about the rise of a "new axis," or Rapallo revisited, Bonn and Moscow were more concerned with maintaining the momentum of their ties than with exorcising the ghosts of decades past. Germany's major concerns focused on the destabilizing consequences of Russia's weakness. Moreover, Germany consciously sought to share the burdens of reconstructing Russia. Germany was wary of "going it alone," for both economic and political reasons. It could not cope with the cost and it did not want to arouse its neighbors' historical suspicions of Germany's aims in the East.

The Russian view of Germany after the breakup of the Soviet Union mirrored broader debates over Russia's role in the world. Many neocommunists continued to criticize Shevardnadze and Gorbachev for selling German unity too cheaply, against the interests of the Soviet people. The majority of Russians, however, looked to Germany as both a model and a source of assistance for Russia's transition. They realized that Germans had finally achieved their postwar goal of unity, but that Germany, too, was a country in transition, integrating a communist into a democratic state. Thus, some Russian politicians felt that Germany had more understanding for Russia's problems than did any other Western country. But Russians were also sobered by the realization that even with Germany pouring $100 billion a year into the Eastern Länder, with a population of 16 million, there were serious economic and political problems in East Germany. How could 150 million Russians, without a rich Western relative, possibly expect their transition to proceed smoothly? Russians also tried to take comfort from the example of postwar West Germany, which had arisen from the desolation of *Stunde Null* (zero hour) in 1945 to become a democratic, prosperous, capitalist country. But they also appreciated that Germany, because it had been defeated in a war, had then been occupied and received massive institutional and financial support from the United States and its allies, because of their fear of the spread of communism. The USSR had been defeated in peace, not war. It had died of self-inflicted wounds and could not expect a Marshall Plan, since there no longer was a communist enemy to fight.

Russia's major fear was not of German assertiveness, but of German disinterest. As one analyst noted:

> We must not exaggerate the chances for a speedy rapprochement between Russia and Germany. It is very clear that the FRG is far less prepared to cooperate with today's Russia than it was with the former Soviet Union. The goal of German unity . . . has been achieved. Its political magnetism, which had provided a specific economic and political interest in cooperation with the former USSR, has become a historic achievement. The most negative influence on the development of our bilateral relations is the situation of political instability and severe, protracted economic crisis in Russia.[8]

Germany's evolving view of Russia was shaped by two contradictory imperatives: the desire to concentrate resources on integrating eastern Germany and ensuring that East-Central Europe progressed toward a democratic market society; and the recognition that Germany would have to expend more resources than initially envisioned on stabilizing Russia. Recognizing that it had a special responsibility toward Moscow because of German unification, and was therefore bound to spend more government money than was any other Western country, Bonn nevertheless shied away from developing an assertive new bilateral relationship. Its great fear was the possible advent of an authoritarian government in

Moscow which might, before August 1994, reconsider troop with-drawals, or that the outbreak of ethnic conflict within both Russia and the CIS would spill over into central Europe and threaten Germany's own stability. Hordes of refugees fleeing upheaval would place unbear-able strains on the newly unified German polity as it struggled with its own antiforeigner violence.

The Russia that emerged from the ruins of communism was led by a man who both impressed the West and made it uneasy. Initially, Bonn had tended to disregard Yeltsin, viewing him as an uneducated *muzhik*, bent on undermining the erudite, sophisticated Gorbachev. Having cap-tured the world's attention as an opponent of Gorbachev and the hero of the August putsch, Yeltsin unsettled his Western interlocutors, who were strong supporters of Gorbachev with whom, in the words of a French politician, "we feel more reassured."[9]

But, by September 1991, the German government realized that if its relationship with Russia was to continue smoothly, it would have to deal with Yeltsin. At the end of November, Yeltsin made his first state visit as president of Russia to Germany. Although Kohl's discomfort at welcom-ing him was evident at the arrival ceremonies, the meeting produced a joint declaration dealing with political, economic, and military questions. Yeltsin received a positive press, with some commentators echoing Prime Minister Margaret Thatcher's remark about the unknown Gorbachev in December 1984. Yeltsin, they said, is a "politician with whom we can do business."[10]

German policy toward Russia quickly evolved into economic and polit-ical support for Yeltsin, as the politician most likely to pursue democratic reforms and stabilize the country. During the struggle over economic reform between Yeltsin and the Congress of People's Deputies in Decem-ber 1992, at a previously scheduled meeting with Yeltsin Chancellor Kohl demonstratively declared: "We in Germany unequivocally support Presi-dent Yeltsin's reforms for democracy and market economy."[11] Similar statements were forthcoming in the period before the April 1993 referen-dum, when Yeltsin asked and won approval for his reforms.[12] As the con-flict with the Congress deepened, Kohl made it clear in his discussions with President Clinton and other Western leaders that the Russian presi-dent might have to use undemocratic means in order to ensure the suc-cessful outcome of his program. Germany, like the United States, ap-proved of Yeltsin's assault on the Congress of Peoples' Deputies in October 1993, and saw itself as one of the major movers in coordinating support for Yeltsin.[13] The results of the December Duma election, in which extreme nationalists and neo-communist parties did much better than expected, further strengthened Germany's resolve to orchestrate a greater multilateral assistance effort for Russia. German government support for Yeltsin, like that of other Western countries, continued through the 1996 presidential elections, despite the military intervention in Chechnya and increasingly authoritarian moves by some members of Yeltsin's government.[14] Kohl and Yeltsin developed such a close personal relationship that Kohl was more explicit in his support of Yeltsin in the 1996 presidential election than was any other major Western statesman, precisely because of his desire for continuity and stability and fear of the unknown.[15] Kohl was also the first Western visitor to meet with Yeltsin after his prolonged absence from the Kremlin and his heart surgery, in January 1997. Bonn praised Yeltsin's decision to shake up his cabinet and elevate economic reformers Anatoly Chubais and Boris Nemtsov to first deputy prime ministers. When Yeltsin visited Baden-Baden in April 1997 to receive the German Media Prize, he brought with him microfilms of the archives of the SED and of Walther Rathenau, the German foreign minister who negotiated the Rapallo Agreement and whose papers were confiscated by the Nazis and subsequently taken by the Soviets. The German media found this piece of historical symbolism tantalizing.[16]

There was, of course, a major asymmetry in the German and Russian attitudes toward and influence over the bilateral relationship. Germany had as much impact as any outside country on Russia's domestic situation, since it was by far the largest aid donor. Even though an outside power could have only a limited influence, Germany's was certainly greater than that of any other country except the United States. Russia had no similar influence on Germany. Its major cards were German gratitude for unification and its weakness: it had the potential to disrupt European security and German society, if it reneged on the troop withdrawals; but Germany did not need Russia in order to complete its postunification transition in the same way as Russia needed Germany in order to complete its postcommunist transition. The asymmetrical interdependence of the Cold War years—German dependence on the USSR for continued inter-German links and the Soviet Union's lesser dependence on Germany for economic benefits—had been replaced by an even less symmetrical interdependence, with the balance now favoring Germany.

After the Soviet collapse, the Russian-German relationship was dominated by four bilateral issues: troop withdrawals, ethnic Germans, the future of Kaliningrad, and economic ties. By 1997, with all the troops withdrawn, new issues, much more difficult to resolve than the old agenda, became increasingly more important. Moreover, throughout this period, Germany constantly sought to multilateralize its ties with Russia in order to relieve the material burden on its own resources and to allay suspicions that it sought to revive Rapallo.

Troop Withdrawals

The successful withdrawal of Soviet troops was Germany's top priority for the first four years after reunification. It was the major achievement of the post-Soviet period, an enormous task, unprecedented in Soviet history, and potentially a logistical nightmare. But Bonn realized that as long as there were Soviet troops on German territory, Germany would not feel fully sovereign. The Soviets had agreed to troop withdrawals in four years as part of the Two Plus Four negotiations and the bilateral Soviet-FRG agreements; but as in other aspects of these negotiations, they had bargained from weakness and without fully thinking through the implications of such a rapid withdrawal. When it was all over, Defense Minister Pavel Grachev described the decision by Gorbachev and Shevardnadze to repatriate the Western Group of Forces from Germany in only four years as "the crudest political blunder." The return had caused "extraordinary difficulties," chiefly connected with providing accommodation for returning professional soldiers. "It's simply not that easy to bring back a machinery as huge as this within four years." But, once given the order, "We did not run from Germany, but left it in the scheduled time with a proudly raised head."[17] The reasons for the remarkably smooth withdrawal were efficient German organization, Russian realization that little could be gained and much lost from disrupting the process, and German willingness to "sweep some issues under the rug."[18]

Under the 1957 stationing agreement with the GDR, Soviet forces enjoyed extensive rights stemming from their status as an occupation force. There were 380,000 troops and dependents in 1990, still on a high state of alert. Despite the countless Soviet–East German "friendship meetings," and the annual "Week of Brotherhood in Arms," contacts between Soviet and East German soldiers had always been restricted. Soviet soldiers mainly stayed in their barracks and had limited contact with the inhabitants of the country they occupied. This was partly to isolate them and hide the fact that East Germans lived much better than Soviets, a reality that nevertheless became increasingly known to the soldiers. Thus, relations between East Germans and Soviet forces were never particularly cordial.[19]

Bonn had two major concerns about troop withdrawals. As the situation within the USSR became increasingly chaotic, Bonn tried its best to insulate the troop withdrawal schedule from the vagaries of Kremlin infighting. Its major fear was that a change of government in Moscow might cause a reevaluation of and possible end to the withdrawals. The other concern was that with unemployment and homelessness facing re-

turning soldiers, there might be massive desertions or requests for political asylum in Germany.

The troop withdrawals were under the command of Colonel General
Matvei Burlakov and his liaison, Major General Hartmut Foertsch, who
developed a cooperative relationship.[20] According to the October 9,
1990, agreement between Germany and the USSR, the Germans were to
provide DM 7 billion for stationing and withdrawal costs, and DM 7.8
billion for housing construction. The immovable property left behind by
Soviet troops was to be sold at market value, and compensation for damage was to be deducted from the proceeds.

Troop withdrawals did proceed more or less on schedule, although the
Soviets threatened at various points to renege on their side of the bargain, seeking to use post facto linkages. Burlakov proved to be a tough
bargainer and effective spokesman for Soviet—and later Russian—interests. One major Soviet complaint was that the housing, for which the
Germans were paying, was not being constructed quickly enough in the
Soviet Union, thus delaying the withdrawal of troops. The German answer was that the money had been disbursed, but local bureaucrats in the
USSR were delaying construction projects. The housing issue was a constant source of irritation throughout the entire process.

Given the disorderly political scene during the USSR's last year, what
is surprising is not that the Soviets at various points sought to up the ante
on troop withdrawals, but that the withdrawals went so smoothly. The
Germans spent considerable time and energy making sure that this would
happen; but the Soviets could still have halted the withdrawals had they
been willing to bargain hard for more German concessions. What deterred them was the possibility that the Germans might retaliate economically if Moscow did not stick to its side of the agreement. But it is also
likely that just as with the Two Plus Four negotiations, the general disorganization of Soviet politics and uncertain chain of command made it
more difficult to pursue an effective, coherent strategy.

Former West German Defense Minister Gerhard Stoltenberg recalls
two meetings he held with Soviet officers that vividly demonstrated the
rapid disintegration of the Soviet chain of command. The first meeting,
in March 1991, held in the main Soviet base at Wünsdorf, was a stiff,
orderly affair, with prepared questions for the German defense minister,
little real discussion, and great Soviet reluctance to speak up. The second,
held after the putsch and in the presence of officials from the Defense
Ministry in Moscow, was completely different. There were no prepared
questions, the session was very lively, and the entire discussion focused on
the Soviet officials, with sharp challenges to them from the Soviet officers. An officer from the Moldavian republic asked where he would re-

turn to if the USSR broke up. "What is my country?" he wanted the Moscow officials to answer. The wife of an officer wanted to know whether there would be any food in the Soviet Union when they returned. The officers expressed open skepticism and hostility toward representatives from the Soviet Ministry of Defense and were dissatisfied with their answers. What a difference six months had made![21]

Once the Soviet Union broke up, parts of the troop withdrawal agreement were called into question. Would the non-Russian soldiers still take orders from a Russian, as opposed to Soviet, army? The "Western Group of Forces of the Russian Federation" was as ethnically mixed as other branches of the Soviet military, with a high number of Central Asians among the rank and file and up to 30 percent Ukrainians in the officer corps. German (and Russian) fears about non-Russians deciding that they no longer owed allegiance to the Russian army proved to be largely groundless. But questions about where the officers would return—and where housing should be built—were more problematic. It turned out that strictly enforced discipline and comparatively high professional standards acted as stabilizing forces within the military, and the Western Group of Forces successfully survived the breakup of the USSR.

As soon as the USSR collapsed, the Russian government asked for an extra DM 7 billion to cover the costs of extra housing, higher transit fees, and the value of the real estate left behind in Germany.[22] During Chancellor Kohl's December 1992 visit to Russia, Germany promised Russia an extra DM 550 million to cover housing costs in return for a Russian agreement to withdraw all the troops by August 31, 1994, instead of December 31 as had initially been agreed in 1990. Kohl and Yeltsin also resolved many of the issues involved with mutual property claims, declaring all claims null and void. Germany waived its right to demand compensation for damage done by the Russians, and Russia agreed not to press for payment for immovables left behind.[23]

A major German fear was that instability in Russia might affect the troop withdrawals, especially given the state of the Russian military—humiliated by their loss of status and growing impoverishment, confused by their loss of ideological mission, and searching for a new role in a chaotic state. During the 1993 struggle between Yeltsin and the parliament, Ruslan Khasbulatov, Yeltsin's opponent, attacked the Russian agreement to accelerate the withdrawal of troops from Germany, using as his argument the lack of housing.[24] Burlakov himself, although less critical, also said that the major problem was the lack of quarters for the returning soldiers in Russia; but he blamed Gorbachev and Shevardnadze for this.[25] The assault on the parliament in October 1993 had no visible impact on the troops' willingness to withdraw. Neither did the unexpected success of Vladimir Zhirinovsky's ultranationalist Liberal Democratic Party in the December 1993 Duma elections. Zhirinovsky appealed to the disgruntled military, promising them that he would restore their status and mission, and Burlakov announced that Zhirinovsky had received 24 percent of the votes of the Western Group of Forces.[26]

The Germans also became increasingly concerned about the conduct of the troops that left—and of those that stayed. Stories of departing soldiers taking everything possibly movable with them—including washbasins, wall fixtures, and furniture—abounded. More serious was the fact that organized crime had spread from Russia to Germany, and that soldiers were engaged in a variety of illegal activities. By 1994, Russian officers had admitted that the black market was thriving on the remaining bases.[27] The German government complained that these illegal activities had cost it millions of marks between 1992 and 1994, asserting that Russian weapons had been sold to German criminals and neo-Nazi groups.[28] After Burlakov returned to Moscow, he was suspended as deputy defense minister in October 1994 and charged with massive corruption. His opponents claimed that he had actively been involved on a large scale weapons trade, bribery, and other criminal activities. A Russian reporter who specialized in exposing corruption among troops in Germany was killed in October 1994 by a bomb that exploded in his briefcase, leading some to claim that Grachev himself was behind the assassination.

The fall of the USSR, plus problems with the construction firms and local officials, necessitated new building plans and caused delays. By the time the last troops had left, 40 percent of the returning officers and warrant officers lacked housing.[29] Troop departures had major domestic repercussions in Russia. Homeless, unemployed officers symbolized the dramatic humiliation of the once great Soviet armed forces and were potentially a major source of support for right-wing groups. Yeltsin tried to placate the officers with pay raises and promises of homes in the near future. But General Aleksandr Lebed, commander of the Fourteenth Army in Moldova, whose political ambitions and opposition to Yeltsin grew in 1994, claimed that there would be a "rebellion of the discontented" if the returning troops were not better treated. He did not blame the Germans for the situation, however. Kohl was "a wise person both as a theoretician and as a man of action: in our country only Lenin was as capable as Kohl."[30] In his 1996 presidential election campaign, Lebed appealed to disgruntled military officers who had returned from Eastern Europe and the Baltics.

As the last brigades began to leave, Germans and Russians confronted the question of how to agree on an appropriate send off for the troops. The last American troops were scheduled to withdraw from Berlin at the end of August 1994, although 100,000 remained in other parts of Germany. But inevitably questions of equivalence, and whether one should

commemorate troop withdrawals by focusing on the past or on the future, arose in both countries. Burlakov had asked for a joint military ceremony to commemorate the departure of Russian and Allied troops, as
had the Berlin parliament. Those arguing for joint ceremonies pointed
out that while the Russian troops had been occupiers in the GDR, they
had arrived in Germany as liberators from Fascism, and could no longer
be regarded as occupiers. It was very important, moreover, not to insult
the Russians at this symbolically important juncture.[31] Others pointed to
a basic asymmetry: once the Russian troops withdrew, only a treaty of
friendship would bind the two countries; but when the allied troops
withdrew, Germany would remain closely tied to them in NATO. All the
more reason, therefore, to be generous to the departing Russians.[32] Germans who did not favor joint ceremonies reiterated that it was wrong to
create false symmetry: the western troops had built up Berlin and West
Germany and helped it become a prosperous democracy, while the Soviet
troops had occupied and oppressed the GDR.

During Yeltsin's visit to Bonn in May 1994, Germany and Russia had
agreed to hold a ceremony in Berlin at the end of August, to bid farewell
to the Russian troops. The last Russian military parade in Berlin in June
drew an unexpectedly large and enthusiastic crowd of 40,000 people. By
August 31, 22 divisions, 49 brigades, and 42 independent regiments
numbering 546,200 troops had been withdrawn from Germany to Russia
in three years and eight months.[33] At the final ceremony, Yeltsin, in one
of his more erratic moves, and apparently inebriated, seized the baton
from the conductor of the military band, conducted the band himself,
and sang along, to the embarrassment of his hosts and colleagues. Both
German and Russian officials sought to portray the troop withdrawals in
the most positive light. Quoting Bismarck, Yeltsin reminded the Germans
that "a powerful Russia will bring [Germany] greater friendship, that
friendship with her is essential" for Germany.[34]

The German government tried to make the withdrawal more palatable
by offering various forms of military partnership to the Russians. On a
visit to Moscow in April 1993, defense ministers Rühe and Grachev
signed an agreement on military cooperation, similar to those that Germany had signed with Poland and Hungary. It envisaged exchanges of
information on a variety of subjects and joint training sessions. Later on
Rühe proposed joint maneuvers with the Bundeswehr, and General Klaus
Naumann, Bundeswehr Inspector General and the highest-ranking German soldier was allowed to go to Volgograd and honor the German dead
in a joint Russian-German ceremony marking the Battle of Stalingrad—
the first time such an event had taken place. The extent to which the
German-Russian military relationship had radically changed was evident
when Deputy Defense Minister Andrei Kokoshin expressed concern

about cutbacks in the German defense budget, because Russia was eager to sell high-technology weapons to Germany. He gave Naumann a catalogue detailing all the weapons that Germany could purchase from Russia.[35] The major compensation for the withdrawal of troops was, therefore, financial assistance and the promise of future cooperation. By September 1994 the single most important part of the unification agreements had been completed.

Ethnic Germans

Another Cold War legacy that had both domestic and international implications for both countries was the situation of ethnic Germans in the Soviet Union. These were the descendants of eighteenth-century settlers who had been attracted to Russia under Catherine the Great with promises of unlimited farmland to cultivate. In 1764, she issued what a later historian termed "a masterpiece of immigration propaganda," a decree extending impressive privileges—including free transportation to Russia, freedom to practice any trade, interest-free loans, and exemption from military service—to persuade Germans to colonize parts of southern Russia. Between 1764 and 1768, 30,000 Germans came to Russia. The next wave of immigration came at the end of the eighteenth century, this time Mennonites from Prussia fleeing religious intolerance. They had become prosperous farmers, largely in the Volga region, although some had eventually settled in Ukraine. After two centuries of living in Russia, their German language had become archaic and filled with Russian words, and they themselves had become Russified and had lost contact with Germany and Germans. Thus, although they considered themselves German and did not assimilate into Russian society, their "Germanness" was out of date by two hundred years. After the Revolution, Stalin created a Volga Autonomous Soviet Socialist Republic in 1924, in which Germans enjoyed the "advantages" of his nationalities policy, including instruction in the German language and the eradication of illiteracy—until the Nazi attack on the USSR. An August 1941 decree accused Germans in the Volga Republic of being "diversionists and spies, who on a signal being given from Germany are to carry out sabotage in the areas inhabited by the Germans of the Volga." About 800,000 of them were deported to Siberia and Central Asia, primarily the Kazakh republic, in 1941, like the Chechen, Ingush and Crimean Tartars. Although officially rehabilitated in 1964, they were not permitted to return to their traditional homes along the Volga because Stalin had abolished the Volga ASSR.[36]

Prior to 1990, the West German government had offered financial incentives to the Soviets to induce them to allow ethnic Germans to emigrate. Mass emigration began under Gorbachev in 1987. The next year 47,000 left, and in 1989, 150,000. In that year, encouraged by the climate created by perestroika, ethnic Germans founded lobbying groups seeking to advance their interests. Their leaders presented various demands—restoration of the Volga republic, emigration to Germany, possible settlement of the Kaliningrad area—and were divided among themselves whether to press for better conditions within the USSR or to emigrate. By 1991, however, the German government completely reversed its position on emigration, and began to offer financial incentives to keep the Germans in Russia. With the financial and social burdens of unification and growing manifestations in both parts of Germany of hostility toward foreigners, the German government decided that it could no longer absorb up to two million new immigrants. It put State Secretary Horst Waffenschmidt from the Interior Ministry in charge of finding a solution to the problem. He suggested a restoration of the Volga Republic with German financial assistance; but Gorbachev was lukewarm to this idea because he feared that it would provoke ethnic tensions at a time when he was finding it increasingly difficult to deal with nationalities issues.

After the fall of the USSR, the German and Russian governments shared the same goal: as foreign ministers Klaus Kinkel and Andrei Kozyrev said in a joint statement, both governments were concerned about the emigration of Russian Germans and both wanted them to stay in Russia.[37] Given the dislocation and discrimination that ethnic Germans had experienced in the Soviet Union since 1941, it was not surprising that they were ambivalent about remaining in Russia. In addition to their past sufferings, the Germans in Kazakhstan, who had meanwhile grown to a million people, faced Kazakh nationalism and assertive Islam, and those leaving for Russia had to confront the suspicions and prejudices of Russians and other ethnic groups. The German government wanted to stem the flow of immigrants and the Russian government wanted to retain what it considered to be a productive ethnic group for whose resettlement it had also been promised considerable sums of money.

During Yeltsin's November 1991 visit to Germany, both sides agreed to establish a German-Russian Intergovernmental Commission that would deal with the ethnic Germans. In March 1992, a presidential decree concerning the rehabilitation of the Russian-Germans was published. The commission held its first meeting in April 1992. Russian Minister of Nationalities Valery Tishkov and State Secretary Waffenschmidt signed an agreement about the gradual re-creation of the Volga Republic, beginning with the establishment of self-governing German *raioni* (districts) in the Saratov and Volgograd regions. However, this agreement had to be ratified by the Supreme Soviet and became a hostage of the struggle between Yeltsin and the parliament. By early 1993, Waffenschmidt admitted that, realistically, the Volga Republic would not be restored soon; the best solution was to create German districts, both in the Volga region and the Omsk and Altai in West Siberia, where Germans would have their own representative body and some self-rule.[38] Sergei Shakhrai, then Minister of Nationalities, promised that the 500,000 Germans in West Siberia would have increased autonomy, expressed the hope that this would attract ethnic Germans from neighboring Kazakhstan, and in general advocated the "national-cultural rebirth" of Germans in Russia. However, he played down the reestablishment of the Volga Republic.[39] In 1994, Germany promised a further DM 65 million and Shakhrai reiterated that Russia was "interested in keeping all Russian Germans in Russia." But on a visit to Bonn, Shakhrai admitted that the restoration of German autonomy in Russia would have to be a movement "from below," and that the Russian-Germans could only do this if they moved in large enough numbers to certain areas. He had already told the State Duma that the only way that the Russian-Germans' statehood could be restored would be to pass a new federal law creating territorial units based on ethnicity. This would not only take several years, but would also go against the current Russian policy of phasing out such units.[40]

It proved to be very difficult for ethnic Germans to migrate in large numbers to the Volga area, to which most of them would have opted to move, because of Russian resistance. The Saratov population, for example, made its views clear, both in a referendum and at a session of the local Soviet. Fearing that an influx of ethnic Germans and money from Germany might endanger the position of the Russians and that they might lose their homes to returning Germans, the local Soviet in June 1992 voted against creating an autonomous German administration in Saratov. "We will not permit a restoration of the Third Reich on the banks of the Volga," said one enraged deputy.[41] But the Soviet agreed to "create conditions to resettle citizens of German origin and other nationalities on the territory of the *raion*, without encroaching on the interests of the indigenous population."[42]

By 1996, Bonn realized that the attempt to keep ethnic Germans in Russia might well fail.[43] It was also unable to secure an agreement with Ukraine to resettle ethnic Germans in areas from which they had been expelled in 1941. Germany's Law of Return grants automatic citizenship to anyone who can prove that they are of German ethnicity. The War-Related Compensation Act, which came into operation in 1993, now permits 225,000 Germans from the former Soviet Union and Eastern Europe to enter Germany every year, but only those born before 1993 qualify. There has also been tension between the German Foreign Ministry, which opposes putting too much pressure on Yeltsin on the Volga

Republic issue, and the Interior Ministry, which has ultimate responsibility for the Russian-Germans, and which favors a tougher policy.[44] During his September 1997 visit to Russia, German President Roman Herzog appealed to ethnic Germans to remain in Russia, but conceded that "the gate to Germany remains open for them."[45]

The ethnic German question, although of lesser importance when compared to the major German concerns about Russian stability and European security, nevertheless remains a major reason for continued German involvement in Russia. It also illustrates that although the German and Russian governments agree on this issue, the outcome may not be to either side's liking, because most ethnic Germans will leave Russia. The resistance to restoring the Volga Republic on the part of the local population illustrates not only the continuing importance of the Second World War in shaping peoples' attitudes toward Germans, but also the inability of the Yeltsin government to impose its will on the regions. In addition, it reveals ambivalence on Moscow's part about how to deal with ethnic self-assertion as its tries to keep the Russian Federation together. The German government has offered economic incentives to the Russian government to restore the Volga Republic, but in the postcommunist era, a more democratic Russian government cannot deliver on its promises because it has to take into account local sentiments and listen to its electorate. As the German government rethinks its own policies on nationality and citizenship, the Russian-Germans, who are linguistically and culturally very different from the Germans of Germany, represent a problem that has broader political and social implications. Russian-Germans are disliked in Russia for being German. But there is some hostility to them in parts of Germany because they are seen as "too Russian." Catherine the Great's immigration coup has created a minority that is accepted neither by Russians nor fully by Germans.

Kaliningrad

The ethnic German question is linked to the Kaliningrad problem, which is potentially an explosive security issue between Russia and Germany for two reasons: Germany's special interest and future activities in this region; and the broader question of the area's role in European security, especially after Poland joins NATO, bringing the alliance's territory to the border of this Russian exclave. The region centering on the former Königsberg, founded in 1302 and once the home of Immanuel Kant, is a graphic example of the damage that the Soviet communist system inflicted on the peoples and lands it ruled. Prior to World War II, this northern district of what was then East Prussia was the granary, dairy, and meat supplier to the rest of Germany. After the Soviet takeover in 1945, its 1.2 million Germans were deported, and the territory served the Red Army as a garrison area, maneuver terrain, and missile depot. It also became a center for the fish processing industry and for the supply of 90 percent of the world's production of amber, but agriculture and cattle farming went into decline, necessitating large-scale imports of food. And Kaliningrad—probably the most highly militarized area in the USSR—became one of its environmental disaster areas.

The strategic importance of Kaliningrad has grown as a result of the general weakening of the Russian position in the Baltic region after the Soviet collapse, both because it is no longer contiguous with the rest of Russia and because it is now the country's only warm-water Baltic port.[46] At the same time, the area has become a subject of considerable interest to German businesspeople who originally came from the Köenigsberg area, as well as others. East Prussia was the home of many of Germany's former Junker families, who were delighted to be able to visit their ancestral estates after forty-five years of exile, and talk openly about reinvigorating the desolate area.[47]

Both the German government and private groups were sensitive to Russian concerns about possible German designs on Kaliningrad. Ethnic German groups in Russia proposed early in 1992 that Bonn designate Kaliningrad an area of resettlement. The German government, reiterating that the Two Plus Four Agreements had stated unequivocally that Germany had no outstanding territorial claims, reacted very cautiously. It did not designate the area as one of resettlement, but announced several aid packages for all the inhabitants of the region. Despite the German government's caution, however, a steady stream of ethnic German migrants has come to Kaliningrad since 1990. Officially, there are 5,000 ethnic Germans there, but the actual total might be as high as 15,000—as against 200 in 1989—out of a population of 500,000 in the city of Kaliningrad.[48] In view of the polarized domestic situation in Russia, however, any issue that touches Russia's sovereignty or suggests interference by outside powers remains a political liability for reformers. In March 1994, when the Germans reiterated their desire to open a consulate in Kaliningrad—in return for a Russian consulate in Frankfurt—Kozyrev, echoing Yeltsin's Security Council, reacted sharply. This question, he insisted, must be put off indefinitely because it smacked of "a relapse into the German urge to the East." Legally, the establishment of a German consulate there would imply Germany's recognition of the borders of the oblast, but Kaliningrad Governor Yuri Matochkin did not accept this logic.[49] He described as "pure impudence" a suggestion in the European Parliament that the EU develop a "special relationship" with the Kaliningrad area.[50]

But the real issue in Kaliningrad is the Russian military buildup there, and here the German government has unambiguously stated its case. In January 1994, a CDU-CSU statement claimed that "It must be made clear to the Russians that their behavior in the region is viewed as a test case for Russian policy in general," and warned Russia against turning the region into a "military bridgehead."[51] The Germans were not the only ones concerned by the buildup in the area, as returning Soviet troops from Germany, Poland, and the Baltics arrived in Kaliningrad—and did not leave. In April 1994, Polish President Lech Wałęsa called the presence of 100,000 Russian troops in Kaliningrad an "alarming phenomenon." Indeed, the Poles are suspicious of both Russian and German activities in Kaliningrad, considering it a Polish city. Lithuania also has historic claims in Kaliningrad, and the Lithuanian government expressed similar fears, suggesting that a large concentration of Russian troops there might violate the CFE Treaty.[52] By the autumn of 1994, Kaliningrad had the largest concentration of troops in Europe.

Defense Minister Pavel Grachev fueled European fears during a visit to Kaliningrad in March 1994. His stated purpose was to review the future of the Baltic fleet, following the naval withdrawals from Poland and the Baltic states. Reductions in the military budget had promoted a debate about whether Russia could still afford to maintain its Baltic fleet. Between 1991 and 1994 the fleet was reduced by 40 percent in both ships and personnel, and by 1997 3,770 retired officers were on the waiting list for housing.[53] During his visit, Grachev criticized budget cuts, reaffirmed that the Baltic fleet would continue to exist, and said that a Kaliningrad Oblast Special Defense Area was to be created, consisting of ground forces, military aviation, air defense forces, and naval units, under the jurisdiction of the defense minister and the General Staff. In response to criticisms of this plan, Matochkin claimed that after the defense region had been set up, there would only be 26,000 troops in the region.[54] Nevertheless, there are serious questions about whether Russia has violated the CFE Treaty by concentrating so many forces there.

Given the security concerns, Germany sought to defuse tensions by focusing on economic development. It responded favorably to Matochkin's calls for the creation of a free economic zone with customs and tax breaks in which several countries would be involved. However, the legal structure necessary for promoting investment was never provided. The major task, as Germany saw it, was to build a viable administrative and economic structure that would enable the region to survive in the post-Soviet era. The Germans became the main advocates for multilateral involvement in Kaliningrad, using their influence with the G-24 and the EU to introduce proposals for the region and hoping that by building up the economy, they might influence Russia to stress the region's economic, as opposed to its military, potential.

Despite the German government's cautious stance vis-à-vis Kaliningrad, Russian officials and observers continue to impute more devious motives to German policies there, given the strategic vulnerability of the entire region. In particular, they equate suggestions by Bundestag members or journalists with government policy.[55] Various proposals have been put forward by a variety of Germans: the integration of Kaliningrad into the Baltic region; its transformation into the "Luxemburg of the Baltic Sea"; the creation of a "Russian-German Republic of Königsberg"; and the demilitarization of Kaliningrad and its integration into the European Union.[56]

It is doubtful that any of these proposals will seriously be considered as long as Russia regards Kaliningrad as vital to its strategic position. On a visit to Kaliningrad during the 1996 election campaign, Yeltsin, after receiving a dagger from the sailors, declared: "Kaliningrad Oblast is Russian soil. Nobody should have any doubts about that." And, in October 1996, Leonid Gorbenko, the new governor of the region, asked that a department of the Russian Security Council be opened in Kaliningrad becaue of its strategic location, adding darkly that he could "easily understand why German Chancellor Helmut Kohl supports Japan's claims on the Kurile islands."[57] Thus, Kaliningrad's future status remains unclear. Given Russia's military withdrawal from central Europe, its concerns about NATO expansion, and the persistent influence of nationalist forces in domestic politics, it is unlikely that the military status of Kaliningrad will be changed, especially if this involves lessening the military presence there. Poles and Lithuanians point to these uncertainties to request greater security guarantees from the West; it was one of the reasons pushing the Poles toward demanding full NATO membership and the Lithuanians to signing the NATO–Baltic Charter in January 1998. As Russia redefines its interests after the collapse of communism, Kaliningrad's status remains hostage to the broader problems of the Russian transition.[58] In the longer run, its position will become more complex as NATO expands to include Poland and possibly the Baltic states. Ultimately, however, the resolution of the problem will depend on multilateral, as opposed to bilateral, Russian-German relations.

Economic Ties

Economic relations between Germany and Russia have been less fraught than issues involving politics and security, but the implementation of the unification agreements and the economic difficulties in Russia nevertheless present enormous challenges to Bonn as it seeks to fulfill its economic side of the unification bargain.

Historical memories and the reality of postwar Soviet-German economic ties contributed to Moscow's expectation that Germany would not only be Russia's number one economic partner, but also encourage its allies to be more forthcoming. Thus, on top of the considerable costs of unification, Germany was now being asked for additional contributions for the creation of a new market society. It realized that its financial and trade resources were its most important means of influencing the political and economic situation in Russia. But it was also wary of the risks of being too deeply involved in a crisis-ridden economy. Bonn realized that it could never meet Russian expectations, which were unrealistic to begin with.

The scale of Russia's economic transition is clear when one realizes that the Russians have not only had to create a market economy, but have virtually had to build an economy from scratch. The USSR did not have an economy in the Western sense of the word. Rather, their system was a political pump for the distribution of resources by bureaucratic means and allocation was based on the Communist Party's political priorities. The system was not run by supply and demand, but according to the *nomenklatura*'s wishes. The original aim of the command economy's inventors in the 1930s was to replace the market with a system of state agencies that would allocate supplies, labor, and capital, decide production quotas, and determine prices: that was the supreme accomplishment of the Soviet economic system.[59] Underneath that official system, however, was a thriving unofficial economy accounting for up to 30 percent of production. The black market was the Russians' only previous experience of a market, which is one of the reasons that it has been so difficult to create legitimate (and taxpaying) private businesses.

By the time that the Soviet Union collapsed, Germany had provided $52.2 billion in aid, most of which had gone to Russia. This included $23 billion in credit and export guarantees; $11.4 billion in grants, including humanitarian and technical assistance; $4.5 billion as Germany's contribution to the $24 billion of G-7 aid for Russian reforms, $2.4 billion in energy investment projects; and $10.7 billion to cover the GDR's transfer ruble balance.[60] This was much more than any other country had provided. As the collapse took place and there was concern about whether Russians would survive a harsh winter, Germany was in the forefront of providing humanitarian assistance. It was instrumental in persuading the European Community to provide ECU 20 million in food relief to the USSR late in 1991, and it contributed to subsequent EC TACIS aid programs. Evaluating these efforts, Russian commentators revealed a mixture of gratitude and criticism: what was needed, they argued, were not handouts but help in rebuilding the economy.[61]

After the fall of the USSR, the only substantial new aid pledge was DM 550 million to the Yeltsin government in December 1992, in return for a Russian promise to withdraw its troops from East Germany four months earlier than had originally been planned. By April 1993, Germany, with its DM 80 billion for the CIS countries, was by far the largest aid donor—the next was the United States, with DM 13.5 billion, followed by Japan and France at DM 4 billion, and Britain at DM 1 billion.[62] Germany had also agreed in December 1992 to defer the $11 billion Russian debt owed to the GDR for eight years and had made other financial concessions. Despite all this German largesse, the Russians remained disappointed. Critics of German policy, including a Russian team led by presidential advisor and Deputy Head of the Institute of Europe Sergei Karaganov, claimed that Germany's credits and other financial assistance during and after the Gorbachev era only led the Soviet Union closer to the financial abyss. They accused Germany of determining the major direction of Western aid in the years to come, although they realized that Germany could not be blamed for this policy: "Moscow was only too eager to take up loans; indeed it even begged for them."[63] By 1994, one Russian commentator reiterated this critique: if Germany had been willing to give large sums during the period of "Gorbymania," then surely it should now be willing to give much more, now that Russia had really embarked on reforms.[64]

The major bilateral economic relationship between 1992 and 1996 involved implementing the unification agreements. But the German government assisted the Russian transformation in other ways. It was a leading voice in the establishment of a center to employ Russian nuclear scientists, so as to deter them from selling their services to Third World countries seeking to acquire nuclear weapons. It also provided assistance in dismantling nuclear weapons. Together with France, it opened an Office for Nuclear Reactor Security Matters in Moscow, to refurbish Russian reactors. The nuclear dimension was one that caused Germany a great deal of concern, since it was near enough to Russia to suffer the consequences of another Chernobyl disaster. In addition to training Russian managers in Germany, the German government sent experts to advise Russia on developing a new legal system and commercial code, and the *Treuhandanstalt*, which was responsible for privatizing East Germany industry, also sent advisors.

Another form of technical assistance was the move to Moscow by Wolfgang Kartte, who had headed the Federal Cartel Office for sixteen years and was Germany's top expert on competition. He advised the Russians on privatization and the creation of a market economy, traveling regularly not only through Russia but also to the other CIS states.[65] The major government-financed German political Foundations, the Adenauer-, Ebert-, and Naumann-Stiftungen, provided technical and political assistance programs. There were also subnational contacts. German Länder established offices in different regions of Russia, to promote trade and democratization. Sister-city projects between German and Russian cities provided a range of exchanges for adults and young people. Germany was, moreover, instrumental in pushing for a relaxation of COCOM controls and for admission of Russia and other former communist countries to this body. Russia was invited to attend COCOM meetings, "one of the biggest recent sensations," as a Russian commentator gleefully noted, after years of being COCOM's prime target.[66]

Multilateral Ties

Germany was determined not to give the impression of seeking a unilateral role in Russia, and increasingly sought to Europeanize its relations with Russia, to include it both in European and international structures. Multilateral ties would relieve Germany of what it viewed as a substantial and open-ended economic burden, and would possibly curb a reassertion of imperial interests by anchoring Russia firmly in what the Moscow leadership called the "community of civilized nations."

Kohl became the chief spokesman encouraging the G-7 nations to invite the USSR to their annual meeting in 1991. To some extent this was out of self-interest. German unification was proving to be much more expensive than most people had predicted—or than Kohl had promised in his successful re-election campaign in 1990. In view of these strains on the German economy and body politic, Bonn argued that its partners must assume a greater share of the burden of stabilizing the USSR. The stress on multilateral action was also related to Germany's broader quest not to be singled out as the country designated to be the paymaster for rebuilding the postcommunist states.

Kohl and his advisors also believed that it was important to invite Gorbachev, if not to become a member of the exclusive G-7 club, then at least to be a guest at its dinner. On the face of it, the notion of admitting the USSR to an organization of the world's richest countries was highly questionable. The Soviet Union was a potentially significant economic power, but the state of its economy hardly qualified it for membership in the G-7. But since the G-7 also represented a political club whose international weight was disproportionately important, Moscow wanted to be accepted as member of the club and an invitation would, Kohl believed, strengthen Gorbachev's commitment to continued reforms.

Kohl secured an invitation for Gorbachev to attend the 1991 London summit—the first time that a Soviet leader had ever attended a G-7 meeting. But Gorbachev did not succeed in obtaining fresh loans or a promise of massive Western aid.[67] He gained a Western commitment to assist the Soviet Union in its transition with technical advice and to grant associate status to the USSR in the International Monetary Fund and the World Bank. This was evidence of the desire of the industrialized nations to buttress Gorbachev's fortunes less than a month before the putsch. In November, the G-7 agreed to reschedule the Soviet Union's hard currency debt and give relief on interest payments, to the distress of German banks and the USSR's major creditors, who were owed a total of DM 60 billion. Despite this support from the G-7, it was too late for Gorbachev to reap political gains: neither Western assistance nor political commitments could produce greater domestic support. Some of Gorbachev's supporters, probably engaging in wishful thinking, have argued the opposite: if the G-7 had offered Gorbachev the $15 billion he sought at the London summit, then the coup might never have taken place and the Soviet Union might have stayed together. After all, if the main justification for Gorbachev's foreign policy and the loss of the Soviet empire was that it would bring concrete Western support, where was this Western quid pro quo? Similar charges were subsequently also made by Yeltsin supporters.

After the Soviet collapse, Germany tried to persuade its allies to assume more of the burden of assisting Russia and to admit Russia to the exclusive club of the world's wealthiest industrial countries. More than its partners, Germany realized that Russia expected to be rewarded for renouncing communism and the Soviet Union and helping to end the Cold War. In January 1992, the United States sponsored a Coordinating Conference on Assistance to the New Independent States in Washington, in which Germany was an active participant. The World Bank was appointed to lead multilateral donor coordination. In April 1992, the G-7, again with a little prodding from Germany, announced a $24 billion assistance package for Russia. A year later, just before Yeltsin's referendum on his economic reforms, it offered a $43.4 billion assistance plan, including $14.2 billion in currency stabilization efforts. The package also included a $15 billion Paris Club debt rescheduling that allowed Russia to repay its debts due in 1992 and 1993 over the next ten years. This was important for Germany, to whom Russia owes half of its total external debt, or about $40 billion. In June 1994, a further rescheduling of Russia's $80 billion debt was announced, as well as a G-7 commitment to bring Russia into the General Agreement on Tariffs and Trade. By having Russia associated with the G-7, the West was sending an important political signal to Yeltsin—that it was willing to welcome Russia as an associate member of the club.

The 1992 G-7 summit was in Munich, and Kohl and Finance Minister Theo Waigel had a major hand in setting the agenda for the talks. The April agreement to provide $24 billion in aid for reform was tied to the provision that Russia accept strict IMF conditionality in implementing its reforms, thus committing itself to extensive currency stabilization efforts. The IMF had agreed, just prior to the summit, to release its first $1 billion credit installment to Russia. The G-7 also agreed to support efforts within the CIS to improve safety conditions at nuclear reactors. Speaking at a press conference with Yeltsin after the summit was over, Kohl announced a ten-point "Help for Self-Help" program that the G-7 had agreed upon in their discussions with Yeltsin, including debt rescheduling, export credits, and high-technology cooperation. Russian commentary on the G-7 summit was generally positive.

By the time of the 1993 Tokyo summit, Russia's economic problems, particularly its high inflation rate (about 17 percent in the month of April) and failure to meet IMF conditionality had raised questions about the advisability and feasibility of multilateral aid programs. The Tokyo G-7 summit, to which Russia was again invited (after pressure on the reluctant Japanese from Kinkel and other German officials), reiterated its support for his reforms and attempts to bring inflation under control. It also stressed the need to create a legal system in Russia and consolidate political reforms, and promised further assistance.[68] At the Naples G-7 summit in 1994, Russia's debt was again rescheduled, money for the refurbishing of nuclear reactors was promised, and the G-7 agreed to bring Russia into the GATT. Finance Minister Waigel stressed that "Russia cannot yet be included" fully in the G-7, but it was a part of the political dialogue, which "corresponds to Russia's importance and its role in the world."[69] A major change occurred in IMF policy in 1995 when the organization decided that Russia was worth the risk of much larger loan, and granted a $6 billion standby facility with monthly IMF monitoring. In 1996, fearful that the Communists might win the presidential election, the IMF granted an unprecedented $10.1 billion facility, also with monthly monitoring. Thus, although Germany's desires for larger-scale IMF assistance were not initially realized, by 1996 the IMF had a major stake in the outcome of the Russian transition.

The 1997 summit in Denver elevated Russia to a new status. By this time, Yeltsin had recovered from heart surgery, promoted Chubais and Nemtsov, who promised further economic reforms, and signed the NATO-Russia Founding Act. His reward was a promise of Russian membership in what was now to become the G-8, and prospective membership in the World Trade Organization, the Paris Club, and other international economic bodies from which Russia had hitherto been excluded. After seven years of being a marginal participant in international economic institutions, in May 1998, Russia became a full participant at the Birmingham G-8 summit.

Germany also worked hard to promote closer EC-Russia ties. The EC was involved in humanitarian and technical assistance to Russia, but

Yeltsin favored a new EC-Russia agreement that would be more comprehensive than the 1989 USSR-EC treaty. Negotiations began in November 1992 and Germany shepherded them through. The key issue was the
degree to which the EC was willing to open its markets to Russia and
change Russia's status from that of a state-trading country to a market
economy, which would bring it more benefits. As Russians and Eastern
Europeans frequently reiterated, one of the most important ways to assist
their economic transitions was to open European markets to their goods.
The market question was highly problematic for the EC, given its restrictive Common Agricultural Policy, and its fears of possible loss of employ-
ment as a result of competition from former communist countries.[70] The
Partnership and Cooperation Agreement between Russia and the re-
named European Union was finally signed at the EU's Corfu summit in
June 1994. The EU promised to move toward freer trade with Russia
after 1998, but the conditions under which this would happen were
never clearly defined. Moreover, the agreement with Russia was of far
more modest dimensions than the Association Agreements—a prelimi-
nary step toward eventual full EU membership—that the EU had signed
with the Central and Eastern European and Baltic states.

The major lesson that Germany, like its Western partners, learned from
its experience with aid was that its impact was only marginal, given the
enormous problems of the economic transition. Certain types of aid, particularly humanitarian aid, were quite effective, especially when German
officials were able to monitor the entire process from Germany to the
end-user. Technical assistance, especially when carried out on a small
scale, was also effective. However, too much of the initial aid fell into the
wrong hands and disappeared down a "black hole." It was impossible to
account for much of it, and some made its way to Cypriot, Swiss, or
Caribbean bank accounts. The Russians' attitude toward assistance was
ambivalent: they disliked the humiliation of having to ask for aid, but
they realized that they needed it; yet they remained suspicious that the
old *nomenklatura* was pocketing most of it. Had Germany not given so
much aid and had it not persuaded its Western partners to share some of
the burdens, however, Russia would undoubtedly have been worse off in
the first post-communist years. Yet, no amount of Western aid could
solve Russia's economic problems. The private sector was much more
important in the long run.[71]

The Private Sector

The real source of Russian disappointment was not in German government or multilateral involvement, which remained sizable largely for po-

litical reasons, but in the private sector. Although German-Soviet trade had been declining in the Gorbachev era, officials hoped that, after unification, trade between eastern Germany and Russia would be the mainstay of a revived German-Russian trade relationship.[72] This, however was not to be. With the disappearance of the GDR, the restructuring of its economy, and the collapse of the USSR, trade between Russia and eastern Germany quickly declined. United Germany after 1992 was Russia's most important trade partner, accounting for 17 percent of total foreign trade turnover. The complementary pattern of German-Russian trade had not changed: the bulk of German imports were raw materials, particularly oil and gas, and the bulk of German exports were manufactured goods. The situation was particularly difficult for Russia, since the production of its prime hard currency earner, oil, had fallen precipitously during and after the Soviet collapse. Russia also inherited a sharply deteriorating foreign trade situation from the Soviet Union.[73]

In the Soviet era, most West German–Soviet trade had been supported by government-backed Hermes export credit guarantees, and there had been few problems with Russia meeting its repayment schedules. By the time of the Soviet collapse, Russia was no longer in a position to pay back its debts, and Hermes guarantees became controversial. In January 1992, the economics and finance ministers, after some disagreements, concurred that the CIS states would receive DM 5 billion in new credit guarantees. Even this sum was not enough for eastern German textile manufacturers, who called the decision a "death sentence."[74] The granting of Hermes credit guarantees continued to be a problem, given the Russian economic weakness, leading some German entrepreneurs to opt for "goods for goods," as opposed to credits, that is, barter rather payment.

In the Soviet period, the most important aspect of German-Soviet economic relations was energy trade, and this continued in the post-Soviet era. Eastern Germany was particularly dependent on Soviet oil supplies and there was concern that with falling oil production, Russia would not be able to fulfill its obligations. Russia maintained its oil deliveries, choosing to cut exports to CIS nations, for whom it was more difficult to pay in hard currency. Gas exports also caused concern. In 1990, Germany received 40 percent of its natural gas supplies from Russia. After the collapse of the USSR, Gazprom, then led by Viktor Chernomyrdin, demanded higher prices for gas sold to eastern Germany. The situation was complicated by the fact that Ruhrgas, which had hitherto had a monopoly on the major Soviet–West German gas deals, was now in intense competition with its rival company, Wintershall, for the eastern German gas market and for new deals with Russia. Russian officials threatened to stop gas supplies to Germany and the pro-Yeltsin newspaper *Rossiskaia gazeta* talked about the "first step toward liberation from our slavish dependence on Ruhrgas." After a visit by the German economics minister, a compromise was finally reached. Wintershall and the eastern German supplier agreed on a gas price that was acceptable to their Russian partners.[75] German firms continued to invest in the energy sector, although they were more cautious than their American counterparts. A major reason was the uncertainty over who was responsible for which deals in which regions of Russia.

Energy deals highlighted both continuity with the Soviet past and the extent of postcommunist change. In 1997, in a deal similar to those first signed in the 1970s, Gazprom and Mannessmann signed a DM 25 billion deal to construct three gas pipelines from the Yamal Peninsula to Frankfurt-an-der-Oder, with a capacity of 51 billion cubic meters of gas. This was a classic pipe-for-gas deal. By then however, in a reversal of the pre-1989 situation, Gazprom itself was also actively investing in the German energy infrastructure. It has entered into a number of joint ventures with Wintershall, and this German-Russian energy partnership will increase in the future. Indeed, German private investment in Russia was, by 1997, smaller than Gazprom's investments in Germany.

German firms became active in telecommunications, using their experience from modernizing the GDR's antiquated telecommunications system and building satellites, telephone networks, and other communications infrastructure.[76] Mercedes-Benz entered into a joint venture to produce and sell buses, and its automobiles soon became favorites among the new Russian rich.[77] Many German firms employed eastern Germans for their businesses in Russia, because they spoke Russian and were familiar with the market. But the frustration quotient was high. Interminable delays and confusion about the chain of command deterred some would-be investors. Political uncertainties added to German hesitations, as did Russia's liquidity problems and the absence of an enforceable commercial legal system. Russian commentators were well aware of the reasons for German hesitation to invest. They appreciated German uncertainty about how the economy was being organized and they realized that it was up to Russia to put its house in order if it wanted to attract more German investment.[78]

New Issues: The Transition from Past to Future

The issues that preoccupied Germany and Russia from 1992 to 1997 were largely legacies of the Cold War. In addition to security-related problems, there was the Russian refusal to return cultural artifacts taken by the Soviets from Germany at the end of the war. The 1990 German-

Soviet treaty included an article to the effect that, "Both sides agree that art treasures which disappeared or were unlawfully misappropriated, which are now in their territory, will be returned to their owner or owners or successors."[79] The historical symbolism and questions about who really won the war have made the question of "stolen art" particularly sensitive. If Russia is unable to keep even the cultural spoils of a war in which 27 million Soviet citizens died, then what indeed is left of the victory over the Nazis? As a German official admitted, "Russia was defeated in war [1918] and in peace [1991]. Winning World War II is the one thing that gives the Russians a sense of self-confidence and pride. To take this away from them would be quite unbearable."[80] Early in 1997, both legislative houses in Moscow passed a law claiming that the cultural artifacts are Russian property and cannot be returned to Germany. Yeltsin, who was eager to compromise with the German government, vetoed the legislation. However, both the Duma and the Federation Council overrode Yeltsin's veto, leading to a stalemate.[81] At the same time, the German government returned to Russia a mosaic that had been part of the famed Amber Chamber in the prerevolutionary Tsarskoe Selo palace outside St. Petersburg, which disappeared during World War II and was subsequently discovered in Germany.[82] The Russian parliament has refused to be similarly generous.

Beyond issues of cultural artifacts that wound national pride, however, is an agenda of new, post–Cold War issues. Economic and social problems largely beyond the control of governments will increasingly affect German-Russian ties. As Russian foreign policy becomes increasingly "privatized," with a multitude of nongovernment actors pursuing their own agendas, it has become more difficult for Germany to engage in a coherent dialogue with Russia.

One major new problem in the bilateral relationship was potentially lethal, a product of the breakdown of central control in Russia. Russians began to sell nuclear materials to various international bidders and some of this material found its way to Germany. In 1992, German police seized enriched uranium originating in Russia. The German and Russian intelligence services began to cooperate in trying to stop not only the illegal export of nuclear materials, but also of conventional weapons and drugs. They also signed an agreement to cooperate in combating terrorism.[83] Bernd Schmidbauer, coordinator of the German Foreign Intelligence Service, and his Russian counterpart, Evgenii Primakov, visited each other's headquarters and agreed to open cooperation bureaus, something unthinkable only three years before, when the KGB still existed.[84] In August 1994, a series of seizures of large amounts of nuclear material by the German authorities prompted intense discussion between the two sides, involving their respective domestic intelligence services too. The issue of nuclear smuggling caused considerable tension in the relationship and was symptomatic of broader German concerns about the extent to which Russia's domestic woes, including the exponential growth of organized crime, were being exported to Germany and could undermine German stability.

The problem of the growing role of Russian organized crime in Germany is probably the most graphic example of "privatized" foreign activity. Even if one discounts the more lurid tales, it is undeniable that in major cities like Berlin and Frankfurt, Russian criminals are active and impinge on many aspects of German daily life. Substantial numbers of "new" Russian businessmen, blue-collar migrants, criminals, and students have come to Germany in the past five years. Some are engaged in legitimate business activities, but others have exported their organized crime networks and practices. Moreover, a significant proportion of Russian flight capital, some of which is the product of money laundering, drug trafficking, and other criminal activities, has found its way into German banks. These large sums of money and the people who control them have the potential to affect German society and financial stability in a number of ways. Thus, complex societal interactions—which governments can only partially control—will influence German-Russian relations in the postcommunist era in ways that are not amenable to traditional diplomatic solutions.

Probably the biggest question mark that hangs over Russian-German relations as they enter the twenty-first century and the unification agenda is completed is the issue of generational change. The men who fought the Cold War and united Germany were products of the Second World War and their political consciousness was profoundly affected by it. But Gorbachev, Yeltsin, and Kohl are the last of that generation. The Germans who initiated the first steps toward rapprochement with the USSR in the 1960s and 1970s approached Moscow with a mixture of guilt for the devastation of the war, a sense of responsibility for making amends, and a commitment to reviving traditional ties. Moreover, Kohl and his generation feel a profound sense of gratitude toward Gorbachev and the Russian people for making unification possible. The older generation in Russia has feared Germans and has also experienced a continuing sense of pride for defeating Germany in 1945.

Once this generation is gone, this special relationship will no longer exist. Younger Germans will not feel the same sense of responsibility or engagement in Russia. It could become "just another country," reasonably far away and potentially troublesome. Younger Russians will also have more distanced feelings about Germany. However obstructionist the *Germanisty* were in 1989–90, they were very knowledgable about Germany, and no younger generation of German experts has as yet replaced them in the foreign policy establishment. Without the commitment and mutual love-hate relationship that created a powerful symbiosis for their predecessors, the next generation of Russian and German leaders may be at once more detached and more willing to reexamine the entire basis of their relationship.

The Lessons of Unification

The way in which unification was negotiated continues to influence Russian-German relations. The difficulty of completing troop withdrawals on time and the shortage of housing led Russian officials to increase their criticisms of both Gorbachev and Shevardnadze and to seek compensation for these problems. Grachev claimed that fifteen rather than four years would have been an appropriate time frame for troop withdrawals. Because of Germany's desire to accelerate the withdrawals, Yeltsin adopted Gorbachev's tactics and secured more money from Bonn. Even after the troops were withdrawn, Russians continued to utilize the unfinished agenda to secure German economic concessions. Germany was reluctant to give more money, but it rarely said "no" outright. Nevertheless, given the enormous task of trying to undo forty-five years of Soviet domination in eastern Germany, the Germans achieved most of what they wanted by 1994. The unresolved issues did not threaten their security. They were secondary problems that were part of the more general challenge of reintegrating the unraveling political fabric of postcommunist Europe. The Russians were less clear about how to evaluate postunification relations because it was difficult to decouple the collapse of communism in Europe and in the USSR from the birth pains of the new Russia. Defining criteria for success in a transitional and unpredictable environment was almost impossible.

As Germany grappled with its new Ostpolitik, it realized that it had become the easternmost outpost of stability in Europe, the dividing line between stability and instability. It sought to play down its unique burden by stressing the Europeanness of its new identity and its new relationship with Russia. Germany's President Roman Herzog emphasized this at the farewell ceremonies for the Russian troops: "We can now enter together, in close partnership with our European partners and neighbors, a new era of European politics, of European cooperation."[85] Germany sought to define its new eastern identity in all-European terms. Russia was less interested in the all-European aspect of German-Russian relations, because it was not yet a member of any multilateral European club save the OSCE. As it sought to redefine its identity as a great power in Europe, it preferred traditional bilateral relations in which it could have more influence. "The Russian-German partnership" wrote a former diplomat, "is the guarantee of Europe's security and blossoming in the near future."[86]

By 1997, the most important elements of the unification agenda had been completed. From the German point of view, the withdrawal of Russian troops was the major success. But a new agenda, involving everything from the smuggling of nuclear material to international organized crime and drug trafficking, increasingly influenced the relationship. From the Russian point of view, the implementation of the unification agreements was more complex. Massive troop withdrawals exacerbated domestic political, economic, and social problems, reinforcing Russia's sense of humiliation and vulnerability. German economic assistance went some way toward alleviating Russian economic problems; but it was not sufficient to compensate for the strategic losses caused by unification.

By the late 1990s, Russians who emphasized the positive aspects of the relationship stressed that ties wth Germany were normalized now that all the major issues had been resolved. Certainly, if one compares bilateral German-Russian ties with those between the United States and Russia, the relationship is less complex and less tense. The United States and Russia face serious difficulties over conventional and strategic arms control, NATO enlargement, Russia's role in the CIS and the Caspian Sea basin, Bosnia, and Russian disappointment that a strategic partnership with America has not materialized. The relationship with Germany is less burdened with conflicts. There are no issues comparable to tensions over arms control or feelings of humiliation because of the way that Germany has treated Russia. Perhaps because Russia does not look to Germany to validate its status as a major power as it does to the United States, its expectations are of a different order of magnitude.

As a Yeltsin national security advisor wrote, Germany was an alternative partner to the United States and could form a strategic partnership with Russia. Given Germany's key role in Europe and NATO, Germany and Russia could form a new relationship that was different from Rapallo and could help Germany achieve its political goals in Europe: "In Germany," he concluded, "more clearly than anywhere else, they understand the risk of excluding Russia from Europe."[87]

Although these sentiments found a positive echo in some German circles, they also reflected a degree of Russian wishful thnking.[88] Most Russians still do not appreciate the extent to which Germany is a European power committed to further European integration and to a prosperous, democratic East-Central Europe—all of which diminish the attraction of a German-Russian strategic partnership for Bonn.

Both Germany and Russia, therefore, face the problem of fashioning the new German-Russian relationship in a way that enhances, rather than diminishes, Russian self-confidence and contributes toward a mutually acceptable redefiniton of Russia's postimperial identity. Russia's inclusion in multilateral European structures is the answer. As German President Roman Herzog has said, "Europe and Germany need Russia."[89] But before Russia can be accepted as a member of the club, it has to agree to play by the club's rules. That requires considerable domestic change. The transition will take much longer than anyone initially realized, because expectations were unrealistic in 1992. And the United States' role in redefining European security architecture forces a weakened Russia to respond to an agenda set by Washington, in which Germany plays a limited role.

Seven

National Identity and Foreign Policy after Communism

The peaceful development of Russia is the
decisive factor for lasting stability in Europe.
There is no other land whose development will
have more influence on the shaping of
international relations, on the future of Europe
or on the world. . . . As long as Russia does
not answer the central question of whether it
wants to be a nation-state or an empire; as
long as Russia places a higher value on its role
as a global actor than on its efficient
administration, on a modern economic
structure and a system of social security; and as
long as Russia does not know where its limits
are, Russia will not find itself or come to
peace.

   (*Karl Lamers, CDU-CSU foreign policy
spokesman, June 1995*)[1]

They say of Russia that it belongs neither to
Europe nor to Asia, that it is a special world.
So let it be. But we must also prove that
mankind, in addition to its two sides defined
by the words "East" and "West," possesses a
third side.

   (*Pyotr Chadaaev*)[2]

SINCE THE FALL of communism, Russia and Germany have wrestled with central existential questions, redefining their national identities, national interests, roles in Europe, and concepts of citizenship. These issues are much more problematic for Russia, which has lost an empire and never previously developed a national, as opposed to imperial, identity, than for Germany, which redefined its national identity after its defeat in 1945. Both Germany and Russia have been subject to pressure from their

neighbors and partners to reorient their foreign policies. But whereas
Germany has had the security of a firm alliance system and is integrated
into all the major democratic international structures, Russia has none of
these advantages. It has lost its former allies and the security of its previous multilateral structures, and has had to battle the specter of isolation
and marginalization from the "civilized" world. How are both countries
to reconceptualize their respective roles in Europe under these circumstances and to what extent will they be integrated into new structures?
These questions will, in the long run, be much more important for Europe's future than the bilateral Russian-German relationship alone. We
cannot understand the roles that both countries will play without first
examining how they have reassessed their national identities and foreign
policies since 1991. This chapter will trace the evolution of German and
Russian foreign policy approaches and practices since German unification
and the Soviet collapse.

Russian Dilemmas

In 1996, Boris Yeltsin created a commission to collect suggestions for
what the new Russian national idea should be. This might appear curious
to someone from a country with well-entrenched foreign policy, but it
reflected the current reality: Russia had no national idea. After the
breakup of the Soviet Union, Russia faced a major crisis in defining how
its foreign policy should evolve. On the one hand, it became the international legatee of the Soviet Union, heir to the USSR's permanent seat on
the U.N. Security Council, to most of its military forces, to its foreign
policy institutions—and to its debts. But Russia's position and interests
in the world were very different from those of the Soviet Union, and its
major foreign policy goals were radically transformed. The new Russia
had rejected the USSR's ideology and mission and no longer had the
global capabilities of the Soviet Union. But the most dramatic change
was that Russia's most important and complex relations were now with
the new countries that came into existence in 1991. These are the states
of the former Soviet Union, the *blizhnee zarubezhe*, or "near abroad."[3]
Given Russia's economic weakness, its diminished capacity for power
projection, and the demise of East-West confrontation, its relations with
the far abroad underwent a transformation of a lesser order of magnitude
than in its relations with, say, Ukraine, whose very existence was a blow
to Russian identity and represented a reversal of the gains of World War
II.[4]

Russia's simultaneous quadruple transition—from totalitarianism to
democracy, from centrally planned to market economy, from imperial to

postimperial state, and from unitary to federal state—add up to a daunting and unprecedented challenge. But the area in which perception has until recently lagged most behind reality is that of foreign policy. Many Russians have rejected communism, the bankrupt state-run economy, and Russia's messianic global role with its expansionist ideology. But many have also not accepted the breakup of the Soviet Union. They feel humiliated and diminished by it. For over four hundred years, Russia dominated its neighbors. Russia's boundaries today are those of the mid-seventeenth century, before Russia took over Ukraine and began the expansion that ultimately led to the creation of the vast tsarist empire and its successor, the Soviet Union. Centuries of empire have left a far-reaching psychological legacy that cannot be discarded overnight. The major challenge for Russia is to find a new identity as a nonimperial, major regional power whose interests are determined by nonideological factors. It has to do this in an era when the rebirth of nationalism and ethnicity is the central and often destabilizing factor in all the former communist countries. Accepting the loss of territory, prestige, and influence abroad has been very painful.

In grappling with these realities, the Russian elite first looked to history to seek precedents for a noncommunist foreign policy identity. But the tsarist empire offered little guidance. After all, it was characterized by constant expansion, growing military might, and dominance not only of its neighbors but also of east-central Europe. Russian imperial identity and the concept of Russian nationhood developed as a result of the conquest of adjacent territories. Indeed, there has never been a Russian national identity that is separate from that of an occupying power vis-à-vis its subjects. The Soviet empire, with its manichean, dialectical world view, its "internationalist" and imperialist goals offered even less guidance for developing a postimperial Russian identity that does not view Russia as superior to its neighbors.[5] It is unclear to many Russians what it means to be a Russian without playing the role of "big brother" to neighboring nations.

One element of historical continuity that influences the development of Russian foreign policy and has direct implications for Germany is the debate about Russia's geohistorical place. For centuries, Russians have debated among themselves whether they are part of Europe and should share European culture, or whether as Slavs they are something different and unique with roots both in Europe and Asia and should therefore pursue their own distinctive path in order to fulfill their historical destiny. In the nineteenth century, these two points of view were expressed in the struggle between the Westernizers, who wanted to transform Russia into an industrialized, democratic state that respected the rule of law, and the Slavophiles. The latter believed that Russian pre-Enlightenment culture and religion were superior to those of the decadent West, and idealized rural life and the organic connection between the tsar, the Orthodox Church, and the peasants. In the post-Soviet era, the intelligentsia again initially divided into two camps over the interests and direction of future Russian foreign policy that echo this previous debate, the Atlanticists and the Eurasianists. The Atlanticists urged that Russia do everything necessary to integrate with the West and become a Western democracy, finally rejecting centuries of "uniqueness" that had left the country poor and authoritarian. The Eurasianists countered that it was futile to try and integrate with a West that would not accept Russia as an equal; they urged that Russia carve out a new role in Asia and the southern Newly Independent States and not seek to become a market-oriented democracy. It should instead pursue a policy of state capitalism.

Russia's first foreign minister, Andrei Kozyrev, a former member of the Soviet diplomatic service who was forty-one when Yeltsin appointed him, embodied these Russian dilemmas. By the time he resigned in December 1995, he was being criticized by both the Westernizers and the Eurasianists. Between 1992 and 1995, he reflected an Atlanticist, pro-Western orientation. For the first time in centuries, Russia no longer espoused an alternative international system but had accepted the Western-dominated international order with its own rules of the game. But Kozyrev increasingly became more assertive about Russia's right to a sphere of influence in the former Soviet states. There was a brief honeymoon period with the West in the first eight months of 1992, during which Russia harbored illusions about how much the West would help it and the West harbored illusions about how speedily Russia would become a democracy. After this Russia began to reassert its right to great power status—whatever that meant for an unstable, economically weak country with a vast nuclear arsenal and a military that was in the midst of dissolution and a major identity crisis.[6] In an early interview, Kozyrev stated, "Our aim is to enter the community of civilized nations of the northern hemisphere."[7] Kozyrev explained his convictions in a pragmatic way: "Our choice is . . . to progress according to generally accepted rules. They were invented by the West, and I'm a Westernizer in this respect. . . . The West is rich, we need to be friends with it. . . . It's the club of first-rate states Russia must rightfully belong to."[8] Answering critics who claimed that accepting the West's rules was a humiliation, Kozyrev argued that by entering Europe as a "normal, democratic power," Russia would have a far greater chance of influencing the course of events in Europe than did its Soviet predecessor, because it now sought cooperation, not military domination.[9]

Beyond a general commitment to the West, a major Russia foreign policy priority is relations with the former Soviet states. When Presidents Yeltsin, Leonid Kravchuk of Ukraine, and Stanislau Shushkevich of Belarus created the CIS in a hurried, ill-planned meeting, at a hunting lodge outside Minsk in December 1991, none of them had any clear concept of how the CIS would function and what its agenda would be. Yeltsin and Kozyrev initially did not believe that the Soviet Union would break up into fifteen separate states, but rather hoped for a new confederation among the republics of the Soviet Union. But that was not the Ukrainian agenda. Ukraine from the beginning saw the Belovezhsk Agreement creating the CIS as a means to achieving total independence from Russia and had no interest in future integrative structures. Eventually, the CIS extended to all of the former Soviet republics, minus the Baltic states. It soon became clear that even though the CIS continued to exist, Russia's bilateral ties with the CIS countries would be much more important than the multilateral organization that had no constitution or treaty framework. Kozyrev from the start emphasized the need to create "a zone of good-neighborliness all along Russia's borders," always mindful of the disastrous Yugoslav example as war among the nationalities there spread to Bosnia. He also reiterated the need to defend "the rights, lives and dignity of ethnic Russians in states of the former USSR," although he advocated doing this by diplomacy rather than military means.[10]

Since Russians had largely defined who they were in contrast to their neighbors whom they occupied, the breakup of the USSR created a major new problem—the Russian diaspora, scattered throughout the Newly Independent States. The old Soviet passports had been stamped with a person's nationality and most Soviet citizens of mixed ethnic background had tried to secure Russian nationality, since this was usually a prerequisite for career advancement. Now, all of a sudden, being Russian guaranteed nothing. Russians—unlike, for instance the Armenian or Jewish diasporas—had no experience of surviving as a nation without a state and there was little solidarity and no organizational links among the large Russian minorities in Ukraine, Kazakhstan, Latvia, or Estonia. The issue of the 25 million Russians in the NIS became a focus of Russia's search for a new identity. There were two central questions: how were the new governments to treat their Russian minorities, and what should the relationship of these minorities be to Moscow? Different states responded in varied ways to the first issue. Estonia, for instance, in which Russians formed almost 40 percent of the population, disenfranchised its Russian citizens, making Estonian citizenship available only to those who qualified in terms of residency and command of the Estonian language. Ukraine, by contast, continued to function with a well-integrated Russian population. Within Russia, the answers to the second question also differed. Initially, even the most pro-Western elements adopted an extraterritorial definition of nationality, suggesting that Russians living in Ukraine owed their primary loyalty to Moscow, not Kiev. The Russian government also insisted on the introduction of dual citizenship for the Russian diaspora. Eventually, the dual citizenship idea was dropped, and the Russian population in the different NIS states realized that it either had to adopt the citizenship of the country in which it lived or migrate back to Russia.

Beyond the Russian diaspora lay the issue of what Russia's role in the CIS should be. As violence spread in a number of post-Soviet states— Moldova, Georgia, Armenia, Azerbaijan, Tajikistan—Kozyrev became increasingly assertive about Russia's right to a peacekeeping role in the CIS. "Russia carries a special responsibility for maintaining peace and stability in this huge area."[11] Since the West was unwilling to become involved in conflicts in the former Soviet states, it de facto recognized Russia's special role as a peacekeeper in the region. The semiofficial Council for Foreign and Defense Policy in 1992 published its first view of what Russian foreign policy should be, on the first anniversary of the failed putsch. It proclaimed Russia a "medium power," saying that Russia, like Germany, would be preoccupied with itself for the next few years, but that a purely Eurocentric orientation was insufficient. Russia's security would largely be determined by the success or failure of domestic reform. Arguing that Russia had lost its "German inheritance" and that its relations with Germany were no longer "special," it said that the future of Russian-German relations would largely depend on Russia's ability to regulate its relations with the European successor states.[12] The 1992 document attacked Russian policy toward the West as being too one-sided and sycophantic. But by 1994, when the council's second major platform was published, the emphasis had changed. In the group's estimation, Russia's chief foreign policy problem was not the West, but the neglect of the CIS. In order for Russia to reclaim its rightful position as a global power capable of defending its own interests, it must concentrate on rebuilding an integrated economic space within the former Soviet Union.[13] In other words, Russia had to accept a reduced role, loss of empire, and more responsibility for the CIS. The new Russian identity would be defined by reform of its ties to the former Soviet states.

Most opposition to the official foreign policy came from those who refused to accept the end of the Soviet Union. Their major criticisms were directed toward relations with the near, as opposed to the far, abroad. Evgenii Ambartsumov, a prominent foreign policy intellectual, early on declared that Russia should announce its own "Monroe Doctrine," declaring the entire geopolitical space of the former Soviet Union to be a sphere of its vital interests.[14] On the extreme right, the newspaper *Sovetskaia Rossiia* published a typical broadside in 1992 : "Democracy is profoundly inimical to our national culture, it tramples down everything it comes into contact with, in the name of some world order or another.

And in general all these phenomena—democracy, globalism, Zionism, and cosmopolitanism—are identical twins."[15] These ideas were taken up by Vladimir Zhirinovsky, head of the woefully misnamed Liberal Democratic Party, and others in the bitter December 1993 election campaign. Opposition to a pro-Western policy and advocacy of a revival of empire have remained part of the debate as Russia slowly moves toward more political and economic reform. Kozyrev's policies came under increasing criticism as real partnership with the West did not materialize, and he was blamed for neglecting Russia's interests in the CIS and Asia. He resigned under pressure at the end of 1995, keeping a seat in the Duma from the Murmansk district. He faded into obscurity quite rapidly, having never had a power base other than his support from Yeltsin, so that when that support eroded, he had no allies.

Kozyrev was replaced in January 1996 by Evgenii Primakov, who had a much firmer base in the foreign policy establishment than did his predecessor. An expert on the Middle East from the Caucasus, he had served as a journalist, head of the Academy of Science's Institute for World Economy and International Relations, Gorbachev advisor, and head of the FSB, the post-Soviet foreign intelligence service. He was well connected in intelligence and security circles. He represented the new Russian foreign policy consensus, which was a synthesis between the Atlanticist and Eurasianist positions. The new consensus stresses that Russia remains a great power. It has reconciled the primacy of integration with the West with the view that Russia's interests lie in the Eurasian realm by arguing that Russia should cooperate with the West where appropriate, while seeking a selective, pragmatic and "equal" partnership and integration into the world economy. But Russia will simultaneously pursue its interests in the CIS, regarding itself as the rightful hegemonic power in the former Soviet space. Russia should pursue two strategies—integration with the West and a selective, largely economic reintegration with some CIS states coupled with closer ties with Asia and the Middle East. Ultimately, Russia seeks both membership in the Western club and a privileged role in Eurasia.[16]

In a more democratic Russia, public opinion has also played a role in the debate about national identity. Polling data reveals continuing divisions among the Russian population about Russia's identity and role, with younger and better-educated people more able to accept the fall of the USSR and the need for creating a Western-style democracy. In an extensive 1997 survey conducted by the Institute of Sociological Analysis, in which respondents could choose up to three statements with which they agreed, 52 percent of those polled (post-Soviet individualists) agreed with the statement, "Russia should become a state whose strength and power is guaranteed by the prosperity of its citizens"; 41 percent (democratic Westernizers) agreed with the statement, "Russia should become a state with a market economy, democratic freedoms, and observance of human rights"; 35 percent (internationalists) agreed with the statement, "Russia must be a multinational state of people with equal rights"; 21 percent (*derzhavniki*) believed that "Russia should be a strong military power"; 19 percent (unifiers) believed that Russia should recreate voluntarily the Soviet Union; 16 percent (Russian nationalists) believed that Russia should be a state of the Russian people; 13 percent (Orthodox Christians) believed that Russia should become an Orthodox Christian state; 12 percent (socialist restorers) believed that Russia should return to a socialist system; and only 7 percent (imperialists) agreed with the statement "Russia must be reborn as a strong military empire in the borders of the former USSR." Thus, one of the first major surveys on these issues revealed that the majority of Russians have rejected the Soviet and imperial legacies as a guide for the future.[17] Moreover, most of the foreign policy elite agree that Russia should define its national interests in terms of the success of its domestic political and economic evolution which will determine how its foreign policy develops.[18]

Foreign Policymaking in the New Russia

Another challenge for the new Russian foreign policy was institutional, and involved creating structures for the making and implementation of policy. By a decree of December 18, 1991, the Russian Federation assumed control over the daily operations of its Soviet predecessor and over its staff, assets, structures, and missions abroad.[19] The demise of the CPSU Central Committee's International Department appeared to leave the Ministry of Foreign Affairs as the most important source of foreign policymaking. But given Yeltsin's desire for a strong presidential system, it was inevitable that he would create his own foreign policymaking apparatus. In June 1992, he announced the creation of the Security Council, supposedly modeled on the United States' National Security Council but which some feared might in fact become another Politburo that would wield too much power—although that has not so far happened.[20] The question of personnel was also crucial. How many Soviet diplomats—who were used to dealing with the far, as opposed to the near, abroad and had diplomatic experience in the communist system—should be kept and how many inexperienced younger people, untainted by years of service in the *nomenklatura* and perhaps open to more equal dealings with the CIS, should be brought in?

One immediate problem faced the Foreign Ministry: impoverishment. Under communism, government bureaucracies had been overstaffed and comparatively well off. Now all of them had to cope with diminished means, as questions about the whereabouts of the vast CPSU assets were raised. Officials reported that the Russian Foreign Ministry, now housed in the Stalinist wedding-cake Soviet Foreign Ministry building, faced a grave currency crisis of its own, with a shortfall of 30 percent of the funds needed to operate at home and abroad.[21] In the first two years after the collapse of the USSR, twice as many people left the ministry as took new positions there.[22] Morale fell as people were fired and old-line specialists were no longer consulted. This was particularly true of the old German hands, most of whom had worked in the party, as opposed to the state, apparatus. Moreover, bright, ambitious young people no longer viewed the diplomatic service in a weakened Russia as an avenue for career advancement and gaining international experience; instead they went into the burgeoning private sector.

From 1992 until the attack on the Russian parliament in October 1993, foreign policymaking became more diffuse and contentious. President Yeltsin sometimes took contradictory stands, most notoriously when he appeared to promise Polish President Lech Wałęsa in September 1993 that Poland could eventually join NATO, only to reverse himself after returning home from his trip and talking to his advisors. The Security Council, Foreign Ministry, Defense Ministry, intelligence services, and parliament all played a role in formulating policy; but there were no generally accepted rules of the game because the whole process had to reinvent itself. Yeltsin also developed his own personal staff in the Kremlin, led by Yuri Baturin, which advised him on foreign policy and wrote most of his speeches. But the chain of command was not clearly established. In the United States, the cacophony of inputs into foreign policy nevertheless has some elements of predictability, and there is a regularized process of interagency discussions. In Russia, by contrast, it was much harder to predict which agency or individual would have what input or influence on any particular decision in Russia. No regularized interagency process had evolved by the late 1990s. The area of greatest weakness was relations with the CIS, where officials struggled to develop a concept of how these relations should be conducted, particularly in view of the fact that the former Soviet republics were far less prepared than was Russia to carry out an effective foreign policy with viable institutions.

After the October 1993 assault on the Congress of People's Deputies, and following the December 1993 elections which returned a large number of anti-Yeltsin deputies to the newly formed Duma, the foreign policymaking process remained fragmented. In 1994, the Security Council was reorganized and expanded, but its powers were also limited because of Yeltsin's predilection for listening to a small group of his own advisors. By late 1994, General Aleksandr Korzhakov, head of the Presidential Security Service and very close to Yeltsin but greatly criticized by the liberals, had become influential in both domestic and foreign policy decisions, possibly more influential than the Kremlin staff. Korzhakov's rise and fall (in 1996 he was abruptly dismissed, only to go on to write a nasty memoir about his erstwhile boss adorned with unflattering photographs) highlighted the lack of clear lines of authority in Russian foreign and security policy decision making and the continuing importance of informal channels of communication.[23] After the invasion of Chechnya in December 1994, the domestic politics of Russian foreign policy became even more contentious.

During the campaigns for the December 1995 Duma elections and the June 1996 presidential elections, the question of Russia's links both to the West and to the CIS became an issue. Yeltsin and his team were accused of neglecting the CIS and kowtowing to the West, and yet public opinion surveys showed that foreign policy issues had a low priority for most voters, whose main concerns were economic and social. After Yeltsin's reelection in July 1996, General Aleksandr Lebed was briefly placed in charge of the Security Council; yet there were many other individuals and institutions that had an input into foreign policy. The Defense Council, which included political, military, and economic officials, was created and abolished in 1998. Part of the presidential apparatus, it emerged as the key bureaucracy for coordinating defense policy, especially military reform. The Duma continued to have veto power over some foreign policy decisions such as the START treaties, but had very little power to initiate foreign policy. By 1998 the two key foreign policy institutions were the Kremlin and the Ministry of Foreign Affairs, but foreign policy lacked coherence. The economic reformers promoted by Yeltsin in the spring of 1997 took a more pragmatic attitude toward many foreign policy issues than did their more geopolitically minded counterparts in the Foreign and Defense Ministries, and tensions between the presidential apparatus and the traditional ministries grew. Russia remained a weak state primarily preoccupied with its own domestic upheavals, particularly the declining economy and the conflict between the legislature and the executive. It sought to utilize its weakness and power to disrupt European security as a means of bargaining with the West and securing concessions, and sometimes it succeeded. But it also realized that the outside world could have only a limited impact on its domestic economic and political problems.

If Russians themselves were conflicted about who they were and what their foreign policy should be, the West was also divided in its evaluation of how to respond to Russia. Western governments favored cooperation with the Yeltsin government and constantly encouraged it to proceed with its reforms. But as Russia became more assertive about its rights in the CIS, and refused to compromise on issues of concern to the West—for instance, nuclear reactor sales and arms sales to the Third World, especially to rogue states—Western voices became more critical, raising the specter of a reborn aggressive Russia without communist ideology. The head of a major German think tank cautioned that the lessons of German-Russian history were twofold: cooperate as closely as possible with the Russians, and hold the Russians as far as possible at arm's length.[24] Despite the general Western realization that Russia wanted to play a more effective and constructive international role, there was continuing caution because of the unpredictability of changes in officials and policies.

Germany from the Rhine to the Spree

Germany in 1990 was a country with new borders. As a result of unification, it had lost its central postwar mission—the pursuit of unification. Since 1945, Germany had successfully redefined its national identity and interest as a country firmly embedded in Western structures. For forty years, the Federal Republic had concentrated on building democracy, eschewing a major international role and overcoming its Nazi past. It had pursued a limited foreign policy, circumscribed by four-power occupation rights, and focusing on NATO, the European Community, and Ostpolitik. But with unification came new questions about Germany's foreign policy that were also old questions. What was Germany's rightful place in Europe? What should its role in Europe be?

The second German unification in 1990 differed in two major respects from the first in 1871: it was achieved peacefully, and Germany was a democracy. For the first time since 1871, Germany and its neighbors had no territorial grievances against each other. Moreover, Russian power was now further away from Germany than at practically any other time in history. During the Cold War, West Germany had Soviet troops on its borders. After August 1994, Germany was separated from Russian troops by Poland, the Baltic States, Belarus, and Ukraine, a comfortable buffer of at least 700 miles.

In the effort to redefine German identity, the more immediate past of the Third Reich was a powerful antimodel. But the legacy of the pre-Nazi imperial era was also no guide. Before and after the unification of 1871, Germany's place in the center of Europe, the *Mitellage*, was a constant source of dispute and insecurity, both to Germany and its neighbors. Whether weak or strong, Germany had always destabilized Europe. Since 1945, the imperial and Nazi concepts of *Lebensraum* and prosperity through conquest of territory have been thoroughly discredited; indeed there is very little left in Germany of Prussian authoritarianism and militarism.[25] Postwar West Germany also became comfortable with the Cold War stalemate, during which there were no wars in Europe, and the experience of a post–Cold War Europe in which wars have again broken out is particularly disturbing for Germans. Their post–World War II history gives some guidance as to what their country should be, but their prewar history offers powerful reminders of what it must never again become.

It is, therefore, not surprising that a country that twice this century almost destroyed Europe through war and Holocaust and subsequently was so successful as a peaceful nation—an "economic giant and political dwarf"—should be wary of changing its foreign policy or its attitude toward the use of military force. The idea of creating a new national identity was problematic. As one politician put it, "German policy cannot appeal to a national dream as [American policy] can. There is no German dream. There is only a German nightmare. People talk about returning to normalcy now that the Wall is down. What does 'normalcy' mean in German history? And what does 'return' mean?"[26]

West Germany's official postwar goal was unification. It realized that goal, but it proved to be very expensive. Germany was now the central state in Europe on the border of two worlds, one prosperous and stable, the other unstable and in the throes of political and economic convulsions. Despite their postwar successes, many Germans remained uneasy about how durable their own achievements were. Could the unstable East jeopardize what Germany had achieved through its integration into the stable West? Could the fall of communism undo the gains of the Cold War?

Germany would ideally have liked to continue its pre-unification policies in the postunification period. Its leaders made it quite clear that the achievement of full sovereignty and the addition of 16 million Germans to West Germany in 1990 should in no way change the direction or definition of foreign policy. It was a traditionally reluctant international player, whose public had internalized civic and nonviolent values. From 1949 to 1990, West Germany had limited sovereignty, was closely integrated into NATO, and never systematically developed an autonomous concept of national security or national interest. The European Community had in part been created for the precise purpose of giving Germany a European identity within a democratic framework. After 1990, given the enormous burdens of unification, Germany became more self-preoccupied and introspective, wary of conducting a major debate on its foreign policy role lest it unleash unwelcome ghosts of foreign adventures past. The leitmotiv of German diplomacy, one that reassured German leaders, was continuity, a theme constantly stressed by politicians from all the major parties. Surely the pledge of continuity was the ultimate assurance of *Berechenbarkeit* (predictability), the highest virtue in German eyes?

But Germany's neighbors and partners would not allow it the luxury of continuity. Whereas the outside world offered no systematic prescriptions for what it thought postcommunist Russian foreign policy should be, Germany's partners and allies had definite ideas about how they thought German foreign policy should evolve. They demanded that Germany assume international responsibilities commensurate with its new status, be they in Western Europe, east-central Europe and Russia, or outside Europe. Initially, Germany did not share its partners' perception that unification had radically altered Germany's international status. But since the pillar of German foreign policy was integration into the Western alliance, Bonn was obliged to take seriously its allies' pressure to contemplate changes in foreign policy.

The first major question that the new Germany faced concerned the nature of its national interests. Like Russia, Germany had in the past also experienced a debate (albeit on a smaller scale) similar to that between Slavophiles and Westernizers: was Germany fully a part of the Western European world or did its geographical *Mittellage* also predestine it to a political *Mittellage* between East and West, a special understanding for and connection with Slavs and other peoples to the East, and a special role in the East? In the 1990s, the latter view was held by a few people from the older generation, both on the right and remnants of the SED. Younger Germans felt no organic connection with the East. Most Germans rejected nationalism for a vague European identity; East Germans, having been denied viable expressions of national self-consciousness, felt themselves to be less European and more German.

When the German capital moves to Berlin in the year 2000, the political center of gravity will be a mere fifty miles from Poland, but far away from France, which is so close to Bonn.[27] The geographical reality of moving the capital from Western Europe to *Mitteleuropa* will have long-term political repercussions. The symbolism of the shift from the Rhine to the Spree has major implications for Germany's view of its place in Europe. With the Iron Curtain gone, Germany will now be a central European power once again. Few West Germans question the government's commitment to strengthen European unity, help stabilize east-central Europe and Russia, and play a major role in the North Atlantic alliance. More complex are the questions of what role, if any, Germany should play outside Europe and how it should regard the use of the German military in foreign policy. Will the postunification Berlin republic regard the use of force differently from the pre-unification Bonn republic?

These debates took place against the background of the growing costs of unification. As in Russia, domestic politics played an increasing role in determining foreign policy in the 1990s and domestic preoccupations also distracted leaders from focusing on foreign policy issues. On October 3, 1990, Germans in both parts of the country had celebrated the unification of their country with great fanfare and rejoicing. By the second anniversary of unification, commemorations were already marked by expressions of frustration, betrayal, and despair in the east, and in the west by indifference to and resentment at the resources transfered to the new Länder. In the 1990s, the prevailing complaint was *Politikverdrossenheit*, or "disenchantment with politics," a general political malaise and cynicism accompanied by a weakening of the old party system. By October 1994, largely fueled by East German discontent at the results of unification, the neocommunist PDS secured thirty seats in the Bundestag, winning a clear majority in three Berlin districts. Kohl's 1990 election campaign promises of a quick and relatively painless path to unification proved quite unrealistic. The psychological wall between East and West Germany would outlast the Wall's physical destruction by decades. As the East German poet Rainer Kunze wrote, "As we razed [the Wall] we had no idea how high it is within us."[28]

The price of unification had a direct impact on German foreign policy, diminishing the means available to Bonn to expend abroad. Contrary to the government's own predictions, the reconstruction of the eastern German economy—which turned out to be in much worse shape than most outsiders had realized—caused significant strains on Bonn's budget. Despite the relative success of the overhaul, unemployment in the east rose to 40 percent in some areas. But the burdens of unification were not only felt in the east. Western Germans—again contrary to what was initially promised them—had to pay higher taxes to offset the expenditures there. The astronomical costs of unification coincided with, though they did not necessarily cause, the fraying of the once prosperous German welfare state, with its generous vacations, short work days, and worker-friendly policies. Although many European states began to experience a crisis in their welfare states, Germans—particularly in the western part of the country—tended to blame their social and economic woes on unification. Despite the problems, it was generally agreed that Germany's economic difficulties were only temporary, and that once the eastern German economy had been rebuilt, economic performance would significantly improve. Nevertheless, this was the first time since the postwar *Wirtschaftswunder* that Germany had to question seriously its economic performance. The preoccupation with the eastern Länder dominated politics in Germany, and this reinforced its desire not to take on new foreign policy responsibilities.

But international events did not allow Bonn the luxury of focusing on domestic problems. First came the Gulf crisis. When the Gulf War broke out, the coalition states sought Germany's assistance, and in continuity with its past, Bonn offered checkbook diplomacy instead of troops. It contributed a total of DM 18 billion to the war effort, but was criticized by its allies for abdicating responsibility and not doing more, considering how dependent it was on Middle East oil.[29] On the other hand, there was vocal opposition to the war within Germany, a reflection of the discomfort Germans felt with the realization that the end of the Cold War would bring violence, in contrast to the peaceful days of nuclear deterrence and East-West tensions.

The next major foreign policy issue was the war in the former Yugoslavia. In this instance, Germany was criticized for doing too much and reasserting its power in a heavyhanded and unilateral way. In December 1991, Germany prevailed on its reluctant European Community partners to recognize Slovenia and Croatia as independent states. Germany was criticized for taking actions that facilitated the spread of the war to Bosnia; but it has resolutely defended its action as the only correct one in face of Serbian aggression.[30] At the time, Germany's neighbors viewed the recognition of Croatia and Slovenia as the beginning of a new trend of German assertiveness and desire for hegemony, but in retrospect it appears to have been an exception rather than the start of a new pattern of international behavior. The contrast between German inaction in the Gulf War and activism in Yugoslavia highlighted the ambiguity that both the Germans and their partners felt about the new, larger FRG assuming greater international responsibilities.

Despite Germany's assertiveness in the Yugoslav question, Bonn refused until 1995 to participate in the international peacekeeping forces there. The issue of the use of troops outside of Germany became the major symbol of Germany's foreign policy dilemmas. As one politician explained, "We were there [in Yugoslavia] fifty years ago, that's enough." On the other hand, after insisting that Germany become a pacific, demilitarized society so that a Third Reich could never again reappear, American and European protests against Germany's unwillingness to commit its troops to multinational forces had an ironic ring.

Nevertheless, Chancellor Kohl was well aware that more was expected from Germany. His government began to question the conventional wisdom that the German Basic Law prevented the use of Bundeswehr troops outside of Germany. After a heated internal debate, in July 1994 the Federal Constitutional Court handed down its decision on this controversial issue: German military forces may participate in multinational military operations within the framework of the United Nations outside of NATO territory if such operations are approved by the Bundestag "in principle" prior to deployment. Welcoming the decision, Foreign Minister Kinkel said, "We have now finally achieved clarity. . . . But we will not move away from the 'culture of restraint.' There will be no militarization of German foreign policy."[31]

The question of what Bundeswehr troops could and should do may have been legally resolved, but politically, the issue remains controversial. Germany has become a successful example of a *Zivilmacht*, a civilian power in which the use of military force is not a defining element of its statehood—one that could be a new model for postcommunist Russia. The vast majority of Germans believe that the Federal Republic should stay out of international conflicts: the country they would most like to emulate is neutral, prosperous, tranquil Switzerland. A small minority, mainly outside Germany, has argued that in order to maintain international equilibrium in the post–Cold War world, Germany should become a nuclear power, an issue that could become more salient as Germany continues to redefine its national interests. But the nuclear option is anathema to most Germans.[32] The majority accepts the desirability of remaining a *Zivilmacht* that focuses on a political-economic international role.[33]

Germany's major foreign policy focus, and one that embodied the most continuity, remained Europe. Chancellor Kohl had repeatedly said that in order to prevent a renationalization of German politics, post-unification Germany must remain embedded in a unified Europe, committed to further European integration. Germany viewed its primary role as the anchor of the European Community. It was a major initiator of the Single European Act, culminating in the Maastricht Treaty of December 1991, which committed the European Community to moving toward far deeper integration, including creating a common currency. Unlike most of its European Union (EU) partners, Germany favored both widening the community—admitting new members, including the east-central European countries—and deepening it by enhancing the powers of the European Union over those of national states, and developing a viable common foreign and security policy. A number of countries have expressed reservations about Maastricht, especially about the desirability of a single European currency and other provisions. By the end of the EU's intergovernmental conference in 1997, the German public had become more skeptical about the common currency, but Kohl himself remained a strong champion of further integration. The major problem for Germany was the fraying of the Franco-German partnership and concern that France would not support the reorganization and expansion of the EU. The problems of unification and general European economic difficulties have lengthened the timetable for closer European integration and the

rapid admission of the Višegrad countries. But Germany, for both historical and pragmatic reasons, remains the EU's major advocate—and
paymaster.

The fall of communism and German unification also transformed Germany's Ostpolitik. Prior to 1989, the major goal of Ostpolitik was to
attenuate the division of Germany, but now the stakes had completely
changed. Germany was in many ways the big winner in the Cold War.
After all, it was finally united and gained many new opportunities for
expanding its presence in east-central Europe. But after the fall of communism Germany also faced more direct dangers from the east than did
its European partners, since instability on its eastern borders could
threaten its own stability.[34] A *Zwang nach Osten* (need to help the East),
rather than any imagined *Drang nach Osten* (desire to dominate East),
was the major consideration. Germany no longer feared enemies to its
east; rather, it faced needy friends, all of whom were competing for German largesse. Whereas before 1989 Ostpolitik had been driven by the
desire to overcome Germany's division, after 1990, the goal was to stabilize its neighbors in east-central Europe as well as the former Soviet states
so that they did not threaten European—and German—security. The
chief German fear was hoards of unwelcome refugees all seeking the
good life in Germany. Russia remained the key country, because without
a successful Russian transition, it would be difficult for east-central Europe to prosper. The enemy was no longer Soviet military might or the
power to intimidate through the threat of force. Now the enemy was
poverty, the breakdown of societal structures, and disorder. Germany was
more aware of the challenges facing these countries in transition because
of its own experience of unification.

The other major issue influencing the redefinition of foreign policy
were the problems of antiforeigner violence, migrants, and asylum
seekers. Germany was and remains the great magnet for refugees from
the ex-communist countries and the Third World fleeing political persecution or seeking a better life. After the fall of communism it rapidly
became the front-line state in this respect because of its geographic location, its prosperity, its liberal asylum laws—until they were tightened in
1993 as a response to domestic unrest. During the Cold War West Germans welcomed *Gastarbeiter* (guest workers) from Yugoslavia or Turkey
in their midst, for sound economic reasons. But after unification, with
high unemployment in the East and general bitterness over the costs of
unification, German attitudes changed dramatically, and outbreaks of violence against foreigners occurred in both eastern and western Germany.

After another heated internal debate, the government changed the liberal asylum laws, which had initially been a reaction to the Nazi past. In
July 1993, the Bundestag passed a law stipulating that from that point
on, Germany would not accept asylum seekers who had entered Germany

through neighboring countries that had been declared stable, such as Poland or the Czech Republic. In order to be granted asylum, people would have to demonstrate genuine persecution and the impossibility of returning to their country of origin. This new law placed strains on Poland and the Czech Republic, through which many migrants from parts further East sought entrance to Germany.[35] As a result of the new asylum law, they heavily reinforced their eastern borders, demanded visas for entry from countries to their east and south, and turned back many would-be migrants.

German public opinion polls revealed that although most Germans realized that their position in the world had changed as a result of unification, many of the policies they favored were a product of the Cold War era. Objective circumstances and subjective perceptions were not in harmony, as was also the case in Russia. Unification had not given East Germans much input unto foreign policy, and the foreign policy elite remained almost exclusively West German. Unlike Russia, which had to create new foreign policy institutions, the new, bigger united Germany kept the same institutions and personnel. However, after Klaus Kinkel replaced Hans-Dietrich Genscher as foreign minister, Germany no longer articulated as distinct a foreign policy vision as it had when Genscher pursued his goals of closer ties with the USSR and east-central Europe, even to the point that he had come in for criticism in the West. Kinkel's major tasks included reorienting Germany's multinational policies in NATO and Bosnia, including German participation in peacekeeping efforts there, and preparing Germany for a permanent seat on the United Nations Security Council. But Kinkel was cautious about pursuing too assertive a foreign policy: "A natural and normal national consciousness is healthy and important because it is the prerequisite for a multinational policy," he explained. "However, it always has to be taken into account that Germany fared well with a policy of prudent reserve after World War II."[36] East Germans, who had lived in a highly militarized society for so long, were much more averse to the idea of the use of force or membership in military alliances such as NATO than were West Germans. They were also less pro-American and less pro-European. But overall, Germans after unification remained overwhelmingly pro-Western, pro-American, pro–European integration, and aware that they had a vital interest in ensuring stability in the East. The "culture of reticence," the aversion to using force, remained deeply embedded in German political life. Although younger people were more open to the idea of assuming the same burdens as other NATO members, most Germans remained averse to engaging in any explicit discussions of German national interests.[37] Nevertheless, Germany's commitment to obtain a permanent seat on the Security Council, which would institutionalize its role as a major international player, reflects a new consensus among officials that Germany must develop a more dynamic foreign policy profile that reaches beyond Europe.

In a conversation with the author, some young diplomats who had completed their training in the German Foreign Ministry in 1997 (only 1 out of 23 of them from the eastern part of Germany) reflected continuing ambivalence about Germany's foreign policy identity and role. "We are prisoners of the present," declared one, "we can't imagine how our policy will change, but we know that it must." Reticent about defining national interest, they agreeed that Germany has no national idea, ideology, or real mission. Perhaps, they speculated, Germany's current mission was to act as a democratizing force in east-central Europe. They professed a European identity, but expressed considerable resentment against French attempts to bend Germany to their will, and against American paternalism. When asked about Germany's foreign policy priorities, some cited Russia, others Europe, and others global ecological issues. What emerged from the discussion was a vague sense of lack of full independence of action—that Germany could be a more powerful international player—but an unwillingness to take specific actions to make Germany more influential. There was a consensus that Germany has historically democratic roots, but there was always the danger that some form of nineteenth-century nationalist romanticism could one day reassert itself both domestically and internationally.

In the search for new roles and identities, Germany has many advantages over Russia. Its population and resources have grown, but its membership in the EU and NATO continue to provide the basic framework within which it makes foreign policy decisions. It has made allies out of former enemies in the Soviet Union and Eastern Europe. It has become a successful democratic, capitalist state, one of the burgeoning economies in the new global system. It can be more assertive about its interests now that the Soviet enemy has disappeared and it no longer depends on the United States for its security. But it remains firmly embedded in European and transatlantic structures.

The same cannot be said of Russia. Russia has lost all of its allies and multilateral structures, as well as territory, resources, and prestige. Integration into broader European and transatlantic structures would help define its future orientation and goals. But because Russia is unaccustomed to a non-hegemonic role and is not yet ready or able to be a full participant in European security structures, its role in future postcommunist arrangements in Europe remains in doubt. Yet its relationship to these emerging structures will have a major impact on how Europe evolves in the next decades.

Eight

Russia and Germany in the New Europe

We supported Germany's unification and
agreed to the dissolution of the Warsaw Pact
because we believed that a new era had
dawned, an era of partnership. The old NATO
is an anachronism. It was established for
confrontations. Its eastward expansion will
create nothing but a system of first-class,
second-class, and third-class states.
  (*General Valery Manilov, Deputy Chief of
  Staff of the Russian Federation, 1997*)[1]

The process of European integration should
not stop at the reunification of Germany; it
should go on. Only then will Europe be a safe
place for Germany. Only then will Germany be
a safe place for Europe.
  (*Václav Havel, 1990*).[2]

RESTRUCTURING European security after communism—in the midst of
political turmoil, economic dislocation and ethnic conflict—has been
enormously challenging. In retrospect, the creation of NATO and the
Warsaw Pact, facing each other across the Fulda Gap, appears straight-
forward compared to the task of crafting and reorganizing institutions
that could guarantee security not against a known, predictable enemy,
but against disparate ethnic and religious groups. These groups, fighting wars in the name of historical vindication, did not threaten major
cities with nuclear weapons, but had the potential to undermine security through refugees, terrorism, and unpredictable acts of violence.
Thus, Germany and Russia had to look beyond their bilateral relationship to the countries that lay between them, from Ukraine to the Czech
Republic. Both had to reassess their relations with east-central Europe.
Each country has its own nightmare. For Germany, it is being destabilized under the influence of an inherently unstable environment; for

Russia, it is being excluded from a European security system that could be directed against it.

While Germany has been the prime mover in the search for a more secure Europe and Russia has responded to an agenda set by the West, east-central Europe continues to demand the fastest possible access to Western institutions, primarily NATO and the European Union. East-central Europe recognizes that Russia and Germany are the two major powers that will affect its political and economic development in the twenty-first century, just as they did in the twentieth century. The countries that lie between Germany and Russia have approached the problem of European security by seeking to join existing Western institutions because this offers the quickest road to stability. After an initial flurry of speculation about reorganizing European security after the fall of communism, the discussion evaporated in the face of so many obstacles and in the past five years there has been little discussion of creating new institutions. In a chaotic situation, few statesmen or thinkers can make the leap of imagination necessary to envisage entirely new European security structures in whose creation the former communist states would have as much of say as would the West. But the basic asymmetry involved in the West setting the criteria for admission to its clubs has sharpened suspicions on both sides of what once was the Iron Curtain and complicated Russia's attempts to devise a democratic, nonimperial foreign policy.

Discussions about the future of Russian-German relations and their impact on European security inevitably raise questions about whether historical ghosts will reappear. Will Europe be dominated by either Germany or Russia or some partnership between the two? Will a new Russo-German rivalry arise, compromising Europe's ability to proceed with further democratic transformation and integration? Today, Germany does not have the will and Russia lacks the resources to dominate central Europe in the way either country previously did. West Germans have engaged in the process of *Vergangenheitsbewältigung*—confronting and overcoming the past. East Germans have only recently begun this process and in their case they have a dual history to confront—the Nazi and communist pasts. Most Germans today realize that the search for hegemony over the lands to their east helped cause two world wars in the twentieth century, with devastating consequences and that Germany in 1945 lay prostrate and internationally outcast because of the atrocities to which it had subjected the peoples of Europe. Thus, most Germans view central and east-central Europe today as partners in the process of European integration, rather than as countries they could occupy and dominate.

The Russians, however, have a far more difficult conceptual task: they have barely begun to confront and deal with their history, let alone overcome it. They have only recently embarked on the search for a "usable" past, in which their admittedly brief and intermittent periods of creating a more pluralist system and eschewing foreign expansion could be a guide to a future democratic Russia. The lack of a consensus on what caused communism's defeat and how the peoples of the former Soviet Union should go about dealing with the past means that only some in the Russian political elite—mainly those engaged in the private sector— have fully accepted that the domination of east-central Europe was detrimental to their national interests. Despite the facts that by 1985, maintaining the empire was becoming more costly, east-central Europe was a net economic drain on Soviet resources, and its governments enjoyed very little legitimacy, the Warsaw Pact nations were viewed as part of the USSR's security glacis and the bedrock of the Soviet global empire. Without east-central Europe, Russia is hardly a great power. Thus, Russia will for the foreseeable future be limited in its ability to reassert influence in east-central Europe not by conviction but by lack of resources. This is not a prescription for longer-term stability. But just as the desire for empire intensifies as the initial conquest of empire succeeds (or, as the French would say, *L'appétit vient en mangeant*) it is possible that the rejection of empire can become an acquired taste too, if the loss of empire is perceived to contribute to a country's material and political well-being.

Russia and East-Central Europe

Since the fall of the Soviet Union, Russia's European policy has gone through a number of phases. Even during the last year of the USSR, there was a major debate on how important and valuable east-central Europe was to the USSR. Specialists in the Foreign Ministry and the foreign policy think tanks argued that Soviet security had been enhanced by the fall of unpopular East European regimes, because Moscow no longer needed to prop them up. Moscow should seek to establish new, more equal relations with an east-central Europe whose ties to the West would not harm the Soviet Union. Opponents of this view in the International Department of the Central Committee (under Falin) and the military argued that the USSR should use whatever levers it possessed to preserve Soviet interests in the region, retain the region as a buffer zone between the West and the USSR, and prevent the emergence of closer security ties between the West and east-central Europe.[3] There were fundamental differences over Eastern Europe's future ties with the West.

Since 1991, both the Gorbachevian internationalist stress on the common European home and the hardline refusal to give up east-central Europe as a buffer protecting Russia from the West have been rejected. Now there is a more differentiated emphasis on Russia's state interests that divides Europe into three different regions—Western Europe, east-central Europe, and the European CIS states—eschewing any utopian vision of a merging of the three.[4] The Russian political class has accepted that east-central Europe can no longer be a Russian sphere of influence, but it is unwilling to concede that Russia has no interests in the region. Vladimir Lukin, former Russian ambassador to the United States and subsequent chairman of the Foreign Affairs Committee of the State Duma, put it succinctly: "Russia, by virtue of its size and resources, remains a Great Power with many legitimate interests in adjacent regions."[5]

But what are "legitimate interests"? From the point of view both of Russian-German relations and of European security, the major questions concern Russia's interest in east-central Europe, with which it has found it difficult to develop a postimperial relationship. After the unification of Germany and the collapse of the Warsaw Pact and the CMEA, Soviet relations with east-central Europe atrophied, largely because the countries of the area, having just liberated themselves from communism, reoriented their economies and precipitously severed many of their links with Moscow. They shared one goal—to become part of Western structures as quickly as possible in order to prevent any future Russian attempts to dominate them again. For their part, Soviet and then Russian officials focused on developing a new relationship with the West and with the CIS states, largely neglecting east-central Europe. This was part of Kozyrev's attempt to join Western structures and reject previous Russian policies. The apparent disinterest in east-central Europe coincided with the brief honeymoon period with the West in 1992. The semiofficial Foreign Policy and Defense Council, in its first articulation of Russia's national interests, downplayed the significance of east-central Europe, saying that "these countries will not assume any priority status in Russian politics" because they had little to contribute to Russia's economic improvement. The report concluded that "any effort to include these countries in the list of Russian priorities would be unrealistic."[6] But that assessment changed after it became clear that east-central Europe sought rapid membership in Western institutions, particularly NATO, from which Russia was excluded.

Although no responsible politicians or foreign policy commentators are calling for the restoration of the Soviet empire in east-central Europe, Russia has stressed that it does have legitimate security interests in the region and regrets the lack of a more dynamic relationship. A 1993 Ministry of Foreign Affairs document claimed that with the creation of a new group of states located between Russia and the former Warsaw Pact states, Russia's interest in east-central Europe had increased. The region "retains its interest for Russia as an historically formulated sphere of influence." The main danger now was that the West might try to exclude

Russia from the region.⁷ Russia's major concern is to ensure that east-central Europe does not threaten Russian territorial and economic security by joining an alliance that could be directed against Moscow.⁸ Its focus is damage limitation, not any new policies toward the area. It seeks to minimize east-central Europe's ties to Western European or transatlantic structures that exclude Russia. The goal is to limit Western political-military penetration and preserve strong Russian ties to the region. Russia believes that it has the right to participate in decisions affecting east-central Europe's security.⁹ As a Yeltsin spokesman put it, "Russia considers itself to be a great power and the successor to the Soviet Union and all its might. Everybody clearly understands that Russia cannot and does not want to wait in the entrance hall of the 'European house' and to ask permission to enter."¹⁰

Concerns about east-central Europe involve a range of issues from security to economics. The precipitous rupture of economic ties hurt Russia's economy, although Moscow rapidly sought to expand economic links with the West. By 1997, the share of trade with former CMEA countries and the CIS in Russia's overall foreign trade had fallen drastically. The European Union was Russia's most important trading partner, accounting for 40 percent of Russia's overall trade. But there were many connections between Russia and its former allies, ranging from intelligence links to culture and education, not all of which were ruptured after the collapse of the USSR. In this situation, where the general post-communist chaos complicated the task of formulating a coherent Russian hierarchy of interests in central and east-central Europe, ties with the region became ad hoc and contradictory, wavering between conciliation and confrontation.

Russia's approach to east-central Europe was also influenced by electoral considerations. It hardened around the time of the December 1993 Duma elections, when politicians warned that east-central Europe should not try to solve its security problems at Russia's expense, reiterating that the area remained in Russia's sphere of "vital interest." During the 1996 presidential election campaign, opposition to NATO enlargement was expressed by candidates from all parties, with implied threats by some candidates to deploy more nuclear weapons targeted against east-central European states that joined. But public opinion data show that few Russians favor the reabsorption of the region, particularly by force. True, resentment also remains against the east-central European countries. Many Russians believe that they were exploited economically by these countries during the Soviet period. They point to fifty years of economic, military, and political support for the region and complain that east-central Europeans have not only failed to show them gratitude for this, but have rejected them completely in favor of the West. Yet there is no stomach for pressuring east-central Europe or for costly foreign initiatives that would drain scarce resources away from Russia's own difficult domestic reconstruction.

Both Russia and east-central Europe have more recently realized that the rupture of their political and economic ties after 1989 was counterproductive for both sides, and that it is in their interests to rebuild relations, albeit slowly and on a more equal footing than previously. The coming to power of former Communists in Poland and Hungary and the prospect that those countries will join NATO has also shifted the balance. "Poland cannot turn its back on the East," said former Polish Foreign Minister Andrzej Olechowski, urging closer economic and political links with Moscow.[11] Hungary, under Prime Minister Gyula Horn (who, as foreign minister in 1989, helped bring down the Berlin Wall) has also made a concerted effort to improve ties with Moscow and has discussed issues of European security extensively with the Kremlin.[12] Russia remains a promising market for many east-central European products, especially in the absence of a more open EU market. This revival of Russian–east central European economic ties could have positive economic effects; but the uncertainty about Russia's future political direction and ambitions has also reinforced the conviction in east-central Europe that it must actively pursue its Western options and press for closer integration into Europe at the same time as it pursues ties with Russia. Historical memories of Russian domination remain very powerful. By the same token, Russia's major goal is not to be excluded from decisions about European security that involve east-central Europe.

Since there are no postwar precedents for a "normalization" of Russian ties with the region that do not involve Russian hegemony, the search for normalization may be a process of decades rather than years, given how important this region was for Soviet foreign policy. Surprisingly little has been written by Russian experts or officials on the subject of relations with east-central Europe.[13] Annual surveys by the Foreign Ministry barely mention the area. Conceptually, it is perhaps too difficult to conceive of a more equal relationship with the region. Inasmuch as normal relations would be more equal, it is also up to the east-central European countries to present Russia with clear guidelines of how they view the future of their respective relations. Yet these countries are too preoccupied with being admitted to Western structures to focus on redefining their ties with Russia.

One Russian scholar has proposed a new way in which Russia could become productively involved with east-central Europe. It could form multilateral partnerships, the most promising one being a German-Polish-Russian triangle that would involve mutually reinforcing political, economic, and security interests. Given Germany's interest in both Poland

and Russia and its desire not to see Russia isolated from the rest of Europe, this could be a model for future Russian-German relations and for Russian ties with the region.[14] So far, such innovative suggestions have not been taken up by officials. On the other hand, a working group at the Russian Academy of Science's Institute of Europe met in 1997 to examine Russia's relations with east-central Europe and came to the conclusion that these relations were not important. The region was no longer a sphere of Russian interest and Western Europe was of much more importance for Russia than Eastern Europe.[15] There is as yet no "new thinking" on east-central Europe and no consensus on what Russia's future relations with the countries in the region might become. The same, however, cannot be said of Germany, which has replaced Russia as the major European power in the region.

Germany and East-Central Europe

During the negotiations over German unification, Foreign Minister Genscher tried on numerous occasions tried to assuage the concerns of Germany's neighbors about what its postunification policies would be. "Our aim," he said, "as Thomas Mann wrote as early as 1952, is to create not a German Europe but a European Germany." The October 1994 election, which narrowly returned the CDU-CSU-FDP coalition to power, was fought largely on domestic issues and revealed no great public interest in Germany assuming more international responsibilities.

As Germany debates its role in Europe in the next century, its primary concerns are European integration and relations with its neighbors to the east. After unification and the collapse of communism, Bonn reassessed its ties with east-central Europe. Whereas it had been reticent about east-central Europe and careful to calibrate its ties to the region with Moscow during the Cold War, it no longer had to worry that a more assertive relationship with the region would be viewed with suspicion in the USSR. Moscow no longer had any proprietary claims there. Bonn realized that its longer-term future lay not only in the EU, but also to the east, and it wanted, for the first time in decades, to have normal relations with all its neighbors. Germany, as Chancellor Kohl said, "cannot remain indefinitely the eastern border of stability." It has, therefore, done a great deal to help stabilize the region and has focused particularly on the relationship with Poland, where it has actively pursued reconciliation. Germany has also been a major proponent of the closer integration of east-central Europe with Western Europe. Bonn believes that only by tying the region firmly to European structures can the end results of the difficult transition there be assured. Without successful outcomes in east-central Europe, Germany's own security would be seriously threatened.

By the late 1990s, a new consensus was forming in Germany as it prepared to move its capital east to Berlin: its future prosperity depended largely on a more concentrated mix of diplomacy and investments in the East. There was broad agreement within the population that Germany had a "special responsibility" toward east-central Europe, to guarantee its stability and ensure that Germany was no longer the frontline state between two antagonistic blocs. NATO enlargement was one aspect of this new strategy, but there were sound economic reasons too. Traditionally, east-central Europe had been Germany's major trade partner, but after 1945, economic ties had atrophied until the new Ostpolitik of the 1970s. After the fall of communism, these ties were revived at an accelerated pace. Germany now accounts for one-third of east-central Europe's trade with the West. In 1996, Germany's trade with the region reached $89 billion, up 11 percent over the previous year.[16] According to a Bundesbank report, "The central and east European economic area is already more important as an export market for Germany than the United States."[17]

Germany is also a major investor in east-central Europe, creating about 500,000 new jobs in the area between 1990 and 1996. Indeed, German unification had a positive impact on the economies of the region by providing an outlet for its exports and a source of private investment. Thus, Germany has made a significant contribution to the stabilization and transformation of east-central Europe.[18] The region has always been a natural market for German exports. Today, it is a source of cheap, educated, productive labor and as such has added attraction for German investors and entrepreneurs. In addition, Germany's cultural impact in the area is growing. The Goethe Institute estimates that out of 20 million foreigners studying German around the world, 15 million are in east-central Europe.[19] This active German role is the object of both approval and concern in east-central Europe. As one Czech official put it, "The only thing we fear more than German economic domination is the absence of German economic domination."[20]

Germany is the largest aid donor to east-central Europe. From 1989 to 1993, Germany spent a total of DM 41.1 billion ($24.2 billion) in grants, credits, export guarantees, transfer ruble credits (sums owed by the former GDR), and commitments to the European Bank for Reconstruction and Development and the International Monetary Fund for east-central Europe. As Chancellor Kohl said, opening up Western markets to goods from these countries is of "strategic importance." "In the final analysis," he observed, "opening our markets contributes more to the success of economic reforms and consequently to stabilization than economic aid, know-how, and loans."[21]

In the interwar period, as in other periods of German history, Germany used its close economic ties with east-central Europe as a form of political influence and leverage. The question that some in this region are now asking is how and whether economic influence translates into political influence. Clearly, there is a correlation; but since Germany is a member of the EU, it sees its role in east-central Europe not in a strictly bilateral sense but as part of a multilateral EU policy of stabilizing the region and contributing to its economic growth. While east-central Europe views German policies as those of a national state, the Germans do not perceive it that way. They are convinced that Germany's role must be within multilateral structures only; otherwise they could encounter negative reactions. Thus, concerns about the political implications of German economic activities in east-central Europe should be balanced by the realization that as long as the EU survives and prospers, Germany's ability to dominate politically will be strictly limited. Moreover, if east-central Europe is able to make the transition to a functioning democratic, market-oriented region and institutionalize the rule of law, then its vulnerability to outside influences will be considerably lessened.

Nevertheless, there remains a fundamental asymmetry in Russian and German power and influence in east-central Europe. Russia exercises some economic influence, but its major power lies in the long and potentially menacing military-political shadow that it casts over the region. Its role is at best neutral. Germany is much more engaged in east-central Europe than is Russia, with far more economic influence. The emerging democracies in the region have accepted that Germany's role is benign and has assisted their transitions; indeed, they look to Germany to protect them from future Russian designs. Given their twentieth-century experience, fear of Russia dwarfs fear of Germany.

NATO Enlargement

Origins and Questions

German unification and the Soviet collapse left a security vacuum in the heart of Europe. The Warsaw Pact was gone, and each former member had to fend for itself, left with armed forces trained in the Soviet system that had no new mission. East-central European countries, fearing a rebirth of Russian designs, wanted to join Western security structures as soon as possible. Russia had lost its allies and was unsure about its future security arrangements, but it knew that it did not want to be excluded from any new system that included its former Warsaw Pact allies. From the Soviet point of view, there was an implicit understanding in 1990 that in return for permitting unification, Germany would ensure that the USSR would be included in European security structures that would replace those of the Cold War. Moreover, at least from Gorbachev's point of view, the Two Plus Four agreements ensured that NATO would not extend eastward.[22] In the postcommunist world, these conflicting perceptions presented Germany and its allies with a major dilemma: was it possible to create structures that could simultaneously reassure and satisfy the security needs of both east-central Europe and Russia? In postcommunist Europe, the old security alliances whose rationale was that of containing Soviet power have proven ill-suited to resolving the ethnic conflicts that emerged as the major threat to European security after the demise of Yugoslavia and the USSR. Yet it was equally difficult to contemplate creating entirely new structures in the heterogeneous patchwork that was postcommunist Europe.

NATO was not originally designed to deal with civil wars, because its major mission was to contain Soviet power. But the spread of the carnage of ethnic cleansing in Yugoslavia forced the United States and its allies to rethink NATO's mission. For years, those contemplating the future of Yugoslavia had posed the question, "After Tito, what?" The answer turned out to be far more grisly than could have been imagined, as postcommunist Yugoslavia erupted into a bloody civil war. Initially, the United States hoped that its European allies would intervene and stop the conflict in their own backyard. But the allies were divided, and lacked the will to take the necessary actions. France and Germany disagreed on what to do, and Germany was wary of intervening without a broader multilateral structure. It became increasingly clear that the United States would have to become involved, and NATO appeared to be the most appropriate institution to coordinate the Western intervention. Moreover, some American defense officials had begun to realize that new challenges in Europe, combined with continuing dangers from the Middle East which the Gulf War had dramatically brought home, necessitated a rethinking of NATO's mission. A consensus began to develop that unless NATO were willing to operate out of area—both geographically and functionally—it might go out of business.

NATO began its operations in the Yugoslav war after prevailing on its members to support intervention, and Russia became involved early on via the Contact Group—the United States, Russia, Germany, Britain, and France—which met regularly to discuss the situation. There were often disagreements between Russia and the other members of the group, but it inaugurated an important process of post–Cold War cooperation. The 1995 Dayton Accords, brokered by Assistant Secretary of State Richard Holbrooke, which brought a cease-fire to Bosnia and introduced the multinational Bosnia Implementation Force, were a recognition of NATO's new mission, one that also involved Russian cooperation in the peacekeeping endeavor. Russian troops joined those from other nations, operating under NATO command. Indeed, IFOR and its successor SFOR (Stabilization Force) surprised many by proving to be an effective vehicle for Russian-NATO cooperation, even though the Russians periodically complained that they were not always consulted on important decisions and despite the persistence of differences over how to treat the Bosnian Serbs. But as other ethnic conflicts within the former Soviet Union—most notably Nagorno-Karabakh, Georgia, and Tajikistan—intensified and Russia began to play a more prominent "peacekeeping" role in the CIS, it became clear that the perceptions and definitions of threats to European security had changed so radically that the old European and transatlantic structures would have to further rethink their roles and modus operandi.

The outbreak of the civil war in Yugoslavia and of ethnic conflicts in other parts of the postcommunist world, plus the uncertainty of the Russian transition, placed the issue of future European security structures on the front burner earlier than some Western countries might have chosen. The United States was dismayed that its European allies were not willing or able to intervene early in the Yugoslav civil war because of fundamental differences of opinion. The countries of east-central Europe became increasingly concerned about their vulnerability in a Europe in which they were not included in any military alliances and in which they viewed Russia as a potential threat. Moreover, as former Communists were elected in Hungary and Poland and nationalist voices grew louder, disillusionment that the overthrow of communism had not brought the populations of east-central Europe more concrete gains spread. The NATO allies, especially Germany, were determined to preserve the progress that had been made in the region and prevent it from sliding back into authoritarianism and instability.

Thus, the initial postcommunist debate about whether NATO still had any utility was soon superseded by a general consensus in the West and east-central Europe that NATO was the most appropriate forum for reorganizing European security. The alliance had declared its mission to be as political as it was military, it had a proven record, and it was constitutionally entitled to expand. Several avenues were tried, the initial ones being designed to include as many ex-communist states as possible without giving them any major influence in NATO affairs. First, the North Atlantic Cooperation Council was created in December 1991. All the ex-Soviet states (including the non-European ones) were eligible to join, and the NACC provided a forum for discussing issues of mutual concern. Much more substantive was the Partnership for Peace (PfP), which was officially announced at the January 1994 NATO summit. PfP is an outreach program focusing on defense and military cooperation and on the democratization of postcommunist armed forces. It involves joint exercises and the possibility of eventual full NATO membership for some.[23] States whose goal was full NATO membership could begin to shape their own military organizations and doctrines to conform to NATO standards. Any postcommunist country could join, enabling them not only to engage in joint maneuvers and planning sessions with NATO, but also to consult with NATO in times of crisis.[24] It was an infinitely flexible program, which could constantly be upgraded to involve closer levels of cooperation. In other words, PfP provided some of the benefits of NATO membership, but without the critical security guarantees that came with Article Five of the NATO treaty, providing that if a member country were attacked, NATO would come to its defense. Some American officials intended PfP to be an alternative to NATO expansion, placating the east-central Europeans by giving them a close partnership with NATO, while avoiding the issue of full membership. But from the point of view of east-central Europe, PfP was insufficient because the countries in the region sought full NATO membership to ensure their inclusion in Western security structures that could protect them from external aggressors.

Russia, however, was from the outset much more skeptical about PfP because PfP did not give it a privileged role and because it offered east-central European states the possbility of eventual NATO membership. Russia was not prepared to accept that NATO would continue and grow if the Warsaw Pact was dead. Even in its weakened post-Soviet condition, Russia remained concerned—one might even say obsessed—with securing recognition as a great power on a par with the United States, as opposed to, say, Germany. At a May 1994 NATO meeting, Defense Minister Pavel Grachev formally proposed that if Russia joined PfP, it should have a special role and special relations with NATO. Germany was the ally most willing to accept that Russia deserved a special role and should not be humiliated by being treated on the same level as, say, Moldova. But the United States insisted that Russia not receive special treatment, and Grachev was informed that Russia would sign the accord on the same basis as the other twenty states already in PfP.[25]

Russia initialed the PfP agreement on June 22, 1994, but also presented its own document clarifying its interpretation of PfP, which requires a commitment to democratization of civil-military relations and of society. Not surprisingly, Russia's attitude toward the program remained ambivalent. Some officials were against Russia joining PfP. When Kozyrev signed the agreement in June 1994, he also signed a bilateral protocol envisaging Russia-NATO cooperation beyond the PfP program, saying that the protocol "reflects the status of Russia as a superpower."[26] In December 1994, in response to Western criticism of Russia's invasion of

Chechnya, Kozyrev announced that Russia was withdrawing from PfP. He linked Russia's refusal to proceed with PfP to NATO's decision to enlarge: "Hasty expansion of NATO and scheduling this process will create a new situation. This will be an obvious departure from the partnership we agreed upon."[27] Russia did finally accede to PfP in the spring of 1995, but as Yeltsin's advisory Foreign Policy and Defense Council warned, "The 'Partnership for Peace' Program will only play a positive role if it prevents the enlargement of NATO."[28] Russia's participation in PfP remained ambivalent, and by 1998, Russia had not been as active a participant in the program as had the countries of east-central Europe.

The Drive to Enlarge

The Partnership for Peace program had hardly begun when the debate leaped forward to NATO enlargement. The origins of the decision to enlarge NATO were complex, involving both U.S. and German domestic politics and alliance politics. On the U.S. side, although ethnic East European votes played a role, one should not exaggerate their importance in influencing the decision. The policies that drove enlargement were conceived and executed by officials who were responsible for foreign, not domestic policy. Moreover, the process by which the initial debates about the future of NATO evolved into a consensus on NATO enlargement within the U.S. bureaucracy was highly complex, involving different institutions and officials. There were, however, a few key players in the initial decision to enlarge and its subsequent implementation—Strobe Talbott, Anthony Lake, and Richard Holbrooke on the American side, and Helmut Kohl and Defense Minister Volker Rühe on the German side.

German and American officials both argue that their respective leaders initially conceived the idea. Certainly, Rühe and his chief of planning Ulrich Weise played an important role. Germany is the country most directly affected by uncertainties both in east-central Europe and in the former Soviet Union. Given Germany's shift in emphasis toward intensifying ties with east-central Europe and Bonn's preoccupation with not being the westernmost outpost of stability in Europe, it was logical that Germany do the utmost possible to guarantee that its eastern neighbors remained on a democratic, market-oriented path. Because of its troubled historical relations with Poland, German officials felt a particular obligation to assist Poland in its transition. Rühe viewed Poland as the most important country in east-central Europe and resolved to do all he could to ensure its inclusion in Western structures. But Rühe was also influenced by domestic considerations. During the Genscher era, the Foreign Ministry had largely eclipsed the Defense Ministry in many of the most important foreign policy decisions, but now that Genscher was gone, Rühe saw an opportunity to reassert his own ministry's influence. He also had his own political ambitions, and launching a new initiative might promote these. In the first speech by a major Western official on this subject, given at the International Institute for Strategic Studies in London in March 1993, he had called for early NATO enlargement. As he later explained,

> Now that [the states of Eastern Europe] have liberated themselves from Soviet hegemony, the time has come to extend them benefits, help them live by Western standards, consolidate freedom, democracy and the rule of law. . . . *This is the very essence of the concept of extending NATO and the European Union to the East.* Without democracy, stability and free market economy, this geographic part of Europe will remain vulnerable to the old problems of conflicting historical resentments, ambitions, and territorial and ethnic disputes. . . . *We cannot save reform in Russia by placing reform in Central and East-Central Europe at risk.*[29]

Rühe, however, insisted from the beginning that NATO enlargement would not be an open-ended process and that Russia itself would not be a candidate for eventual membership.

Soon after Rühe's March speech, NATO enlargement emerged as a focus of discussion among officials in the new Clinton administration. As the first post–Cold War president, Clinton came into office convinced that the Cold War–era international institutions would have to be adapted to fit the new times, and his appointments to key policymaking positions reflected this conviction. Strobe Talbott, the first U.S. ambassador-at-large to the Newly Independent States, was a Russia expert who had translated Khrushchev's memoirs while a Rhodes Scholar at Oxford, as well as a seasoned diplomatic correspondent and columnist for *Time* magazine. He had also reported from Belgrade in the early 1970s, and had traveled extensively around Eastern Europe. "I spent time in Poland after the 1970 Gdańsk riots and in Czechoslovakia a few years after the Soviet invasion," he recalls, "and I understood East European concerns about the Soviet Union very well." But he also realized the necessity of promoting democracy within Russia and including it in the postcommunist security architecture. Talbott was instrumental in pursuing a policy of engagement with the former Soviet Union, emphasizing support for democracy and the transition to a market economy. Nevertheless, Clinton and Talbott feared that NATO would atrophy in the new era if it did not assume new responsibilities and develop a new mission: "How could NATO survive if it did not take in new members?"[30]

By mid-1993, some of Talbott's colleagues favored a "fast-track" approach to NATO enlargement; but he believed that a rapid enlargement of NATO that neglected Russia's concerns about being excluded from the new security might endanger the administration's new policy toward Russia. The best solution was to proceed with NATO enlargement in a way that convinced Russia that its interest would be served by NATO's new role. The process should be open-ended and Russia should be eligible for eventual membership. As he subsequently wrote, "The enlargement of NATO is not a new issue. From its inception, NATO brought in new members for reasons, and with consequences, that strengthen the case for doing so again. . . . In Hungary and Poland, the prospect of NATO membership has helped to solidify the national consensus for democratic and market reforms."[31]

President Clinton's national security advisor, Anthony Lake, was another key figure. Head of policy planning at the State Department under President Carter and subsequently an academic, he did not initially focus on European issues, having come from a background of specializing in democratization in Africa and Asia. But his focus began to change in April 1993, after President Clinton had met one-on-one with the leaders of Eastern Europe prior to the opening ceremonies of the U.S. Holocaust Museum. The two leaders who made the greatest impression on Clinton were Czech President Václav Havel and Polish president Lech Wałęsa, both of whom carried great moral authority. They argued that the only way to prevent future catastrophes in Europe was to admit their countries into democratic Western institutions, particularly NATO. Including them in structures that demanded democratization and prior agreement to renounce any irridentist territorial claims before membership would greatly lessen the likelihood of authoritarian leaders coming to power again. Lake found these arguments convincing. He viewed NATO as an institution that could promote democracy in the region by guaranteeing security. Security, argued Lake, favors democracy, whereas insecurity favors rabble-rousers, nationalists, and authoritarians.[32]

By the fall of 1993, therefore, NATO enlargement was being discussed in the White House, the State Department, and the Department of Defense. But at this point the Defense Department and some officials in the State Department were skeptical or even opposed to the idea.[33] The issue had also attracted the attention of people in the policy community at large. Three analysts at the RAND Corporation who were researching an article for *Foreign Affairs* on why NATO should be enlarged[34] had conversations with officials from the German Defense Ministry's Planning Staff and realized that they agreed on this issue. Eventually Rühe commissioned a longer study from RAND on the modalities of NATO enlargement, possibly the first time that a foreign government had commissioned a RAND study.[35] The study not only discussed how to expand

NATO, but also addressed the question of how to deal with Russia. Anticipating that Russia would respond negatively to NATO enlargement, it advocated a number of ways to defuse Russian opposition: a NATO-Russia Treaty, a NATO-Russia joint council, modifications in the CFE Treaty, and economic compensation, such as inviting Russia to play a larger role in the G-7. It also discussed giving Ukraine its own treaty with NATO. Most of these suggestions eventually became Western policy. Yet, when the study was initially presented to the German Defense and Foreign ministries in 1993–94, there was considerable opposition. Moreover, when the study was discussed at the White House, a Clinton advisor said, "Everyone in Washington thinks you are crazy except for two people." Those two were President Clinton and Anthony Lake.[36]

By the summer of 1994, the White House and State Department were actively pushing for a consensus on NATO enlargement, viewing it as a continuous process from which no country, including Russia, should be excluded. Talbott was instrumental in bringing Richard Holbrooke, then ambassador to Germany, back to Washington as assistant secretary of state for Europe. An investment banker and long-time foreign policy specialist who had been assistant secretary for Asia under President Carter, Holbrooke was determined to resolve two major issues: ending the bloodshed in Bosnia and ensuring that NATO was enlarged. For Holbrooke, this latter issue was linked with a concept that he had already actively promoted during his year in Bonn: that of cooperation through a strategic triangle between Washington, Bonn, and Moscow. This, he believed, was the only way to secure peace and stability in east-central Europe. To this end a series of meetings had been held between American, German, and Russian officials in Bonn. At one memorable dinner, the distinguished historian Fritz Stern declared in the course of proposing a toast to the assembled officials that if such a meeting had taken place in 1914, the First World War might never have broken out. In any case, Holbrooke came to Washington convinced that the only way to manage potential future conflicts in the explosive region of east-central Europe was to anchor German-Russian cooperation in a U.S.–led framework.[37]

The initial interest in enlarging NATO, therefore, emerged in both Germany and America, though for different reasons. The United States viewed NATO expansion both as necessary for Europe as part of an ongoing process of broadening the alliance's functional mission, and as a means of ensuring its own future role in Europe. Germany was more concerned about the geographical imperatives for enlargement as a means of stabilizing east-central Europe. In the United States, the State Department was more enthusiastic than was the Defense Department. In Germany, the Ministry of Defense was more enthusiastic than the Foreign Ministry. But the coincidence of interests between the German Defense Ministry, the U.S. State Department, and the White House ensured that the project would proceed.

By January 1994, the NATO alliance, under pressure from the United States, committed itself to prepare studies on how and when to expand. Thus, the decision had, in principle, been taken, although there remained considerable dissent within the government and there had been little discussion within the broader public in the United States or Europe on the desirability or feasibility of NATO expansion. The initial study was completed by the fall of 1995. It identified the major purpose of expansion: "NATO enlargement will be a further step towards the Alliance's basic goal of enhancing security and stability throughout the Euro-Atlantic area, within the context of a broad European security architecture based on true cooperation; it will threaten no-one."[38]

The alliance was initially split over how to proceed, and the arguments divided themselves roughly into three schools of thought. The first favored slow expansion. Assuming that east-central Europe's major problems are economic and political, proponents of this view favored EU expansion first, rather than NATO expansion, since the EU would address the most important aspects of the domestic transition. Moreover, there was the question of the "haves" and "have-nots." Including east-central Europe but excluding the Baltic states or Rumania and Slovenia raised serious questions about equity and new divisions in Europe. The second school emphasized the fragility of the transitions in east-central Europe and the link between security and democracy. It argued that rapid NATO expansion was imperative not only to ensure successful transitions but also to guarantee that Germany did not face new temptations if the security vacuum in east-central Europe continued. Indeed, some argued that NATO expansion was aimed as much at containing Germany as containing Russia.[39] A third school of thought held that preparations for NATO expansion should take place, but that NATO should only be expanded if Russia did begin to pose a threat to east-central Europe, either because it moved in an authoritarian direction domestically or if it harbored territorial designs on the area.[40] Meanwhile, the PfP program should be given a chance to work and expand cooperation between Eastern Europe and NATO.

There were a number of counterarguments to the idea of early expansion of NATO so as to shore up east-central Europe's transitions, and these began to surface in the United States and Europe after the basic decisions had been made. If, as was argued by its proponents, the major danger facing east-central Europe was the fragility of its transitions, then surely the EU—a political-economic organization—not NATO—a primarily military organization—would be a far more effective institution for assisting the area economically and politically. Second, expansion of NATO might lead to the rise of anti-Western, nationalist forces and provoke a Russian counterreaction, since it would redivide Europe, this time on the Polish-Russian frontier in Kaliningrad, instead of the Elbe River. Despite official pronouncements from NATO, it was clear that the subtext for NATO expansion was to protect east-central Europe from revived Russian imperial designs. As Talbott had written in explaining NATO expansion, "among the contingencies for which NATO must be prepared is that Russia will abandon democracy and return to the threatening patterns of international behvior that have sometimes characterized its history, particularly during the Soviet period."[41] NATO expansion, opponents argued, would intensify Russian desires to exercise more influence over the CIS, and over Ukraine in particular. A Ukraine with NATO at its borders would be more vulnerable to Russian pressure. Moreover, the problem of the Baltic states—which were far more vulnerable to Russian pressure than east-central Europe, and which were not seen as prospective full NATO members—remained unresolved. It was also highly questionable whether a truly viable European security system could exist if it excluded Russia, especially a Russia whose government had explicitly renounced its Soviet past. Russia should be part of the solution, not isolated on the other side of a new East-West divide. There was much that could be done to upgrade and strengthen PfP.

The initial decision to enlarge NATO was also taken without a full discussion of the costs of enlargement both to the existing NATO allies and to the new member countries, struggling to improve their economic performance. In an age of economic recession in many NATO countries, cutbacks in defense budgets and increasing unwillingness to send troops abroad, how likely was it that German or American legislators would support sending troops to defend Poland against Russia, if they were unable or unwilling to send them to keep the peace in Yugoslavia? As one European skeptic remarked, comparing the difficulties of EU expansion to NATO expansion, "If we won't buy [east-central Europe's] strawberries or steel, are we going to defend their territorial integrity?"

By 1997, critics of NATO enlargement were becoming increasingly vocal, largely because of the feared negative effect on a Russia struggling to democratize. As George F. Kennan, architect of the containment policy, wrote in an article entitled "A Fateful Error," "Such a decision may be expected to inflame nationalistic, anti-Western and militaristic tendencies in Russian opinion; to have an adverse effect on the development of Russian democracy; to restore the atmosphere of cold war to East-West relations, and to impel Russian foreign policy in directions decidedly not to our liking."[42] Kennan was joined by a diverse group of senior statesmen from both the left and right of the political spectrum, including Paul

Nitze, one of the founding fathers of postwar American policy toward the USSR, and other officials from the Reagan administration who opposed NATO enlargement for a variety of reasons. Some suspected that its main goal was to preserve NATO's bureaucracy and institutions, rather than face the real question of whether Europe and the United States still needed NATO. Other private task forces and groups within the foreign policy establishment reflected mixed views, but there was certainly no consensus within the United States on this most important change in policy toward east-central Europe and Russia since the end of the Cold War. Indeed, the Defense Department, which had initially opposed NATO enlargement, remained skeptical, because of its concern with the cost and military logistics of bringing these fledgling democracies into NATO.[43]

There was also initially no consensus in Germany over enlargement. Rühe had linked his plea for NATO enlargement to a commitment to building a strategic partnership with Russia, although he emphasized that Russia should not be able to veto NATO expansion. The German Foreign Ministry and the chancellor, however, were initially more cautious about enlargement, emphasizing the importance of not taking any actions that would provoke Russia, especially during the 1996 presidential election campaign. At a conference in Munich in February 1996, Kohl advocated moving slowly on expansion, precisely because of its psychological effects in Russia, pointing out that Yeltsin had serious and legitimate concerns about what NATO enlargement would mean.[44] The German Foreign Ministry was more skeptical about enlargement than was the Defense Ministry. Germany, which also gave much more overt official support to Yeltsin's 1996 candidacy than did the United States, was acutely conscious of the need to balance its interests in stabilizing east-central Europe against its interests in stabilizing Russia, and realized the inherent contradiction between the two if Russia were isolated from a new European security order. Chancellor Kohl himself initially was noncommittal on the timing of expansion, although the German government agreed in principle with NATO enlargement. Kohl viewed himself as one of Yeltsin's chief partners in the West and also as a mediator between the United States and Russia. Only after it was clear that NATO and Russia would sign their own agreement—a policy actively promoted by Kohl and Kinkel—did the German consensus on NATO enlargement become stronger.[45]

Chancellor Kohl was instrumental in 1996 in persuading a reluctant France to support NATO enlargement. Through his discussions with President Chirac, reinforced by an ongoing Franco-German dialogue, he was able to secure French approval of the plan, after the French had rebuffed the United States on this issue. Kohl was also a key figure in persuading Yeltsin to sign on to the NATO-Russia Joint Council in

1997. Kohl and Clinton both used their close ties to Yeltsin to overcome his objections. They both were in frequent telephone contact with each other and with Yeltsin and reiterated that the NATO-Russia Council would serve Russia's interests. This was indeed an example of the new strategic triangle.[46]

But the major reason why Germany has not seen a public debate similar to that in the United States—all major political parties, including many of the Greens, support NATO enlargement—is because east-central Europe is in Germany's backyard and its problems and potential are much better known to Germans, who are directly affected by events in the region, than to Americans, who are not. Moreover, the SPD, like other leftist parties in Europe, went from criticizing NATO during the Cold War to supporting it enthusiastically once the war in Bosnia began to intensify and no European country was willing to intervene. The party's foreign policy spokesman, Karsten Voigt, argued that without NATO enlargement, Germany's Ostpolitik would become bilateralized, focusing on German-Polish or German-Czech ties and thereby risking further tensions in Europe because of Germany's more assertive role. It was much better to embed German Ostpolitik within NATO structures.[47] A continuation and expansion of NATO would, moreover, ensure that European security policy did not become renationalized and that NATO would eventually be able to take on new tasks outside its traditional area of operation.[48] Indeed, the German Bundestag ratified NATO enlargement before the U.S. Senate did so in 1998.

Russian Views

The Russian approach to NATO expansion, by contrast, has not been ambivalent, but crystal clear. With the exception of a few pro-Western intellectuals, opposition to NATO enlargement has extended across the entire political spectrum since October 1993, when Yeltsin had to disavow what he had said to Polish President Wałęsa the previous August, when a joint declaration of the two presidents had characterized Poland's decision to join NATO as one "taken by a sovereign Poland in the interests of overall European integration that does not go against the interests of other states including Russia.[49] Once Yeltsin had changed his tune, Foreign Minister Kozyrev summarized the altered Russian attitude as follows: "The future of East-Central Europe lies in its transformation . . . not into some kind of buffer zone but into a bridge connecting the East and the West of the continent."[50] Kozyrev's successor, Evgenii Primakov, was equally outspoken in his criticism of NATO enlargement, calling it a mistake—"probably the worst since the end of the Cold War." Likewise, First Deputy Defense Minister Andrei Kokoshin termed NATO expansion "unacceptable"; he pointed out that "Russia's firm position on NATO expansion has already yielded certain fruit. It is stimulating differences on this question in political circles in Germany, France, and other countries."[51]

Opposition to NATO enlargement came both from the conservatives and reformers in Russia. Conservatives claimed that the West was treating Russia like a "neo–banana republic." Or, as Nikolai Portugalov put it, "NATO has not fundamentally changed since its founding forty-eight years ago. It was, is, and remains a military alliance directed against the Soviet Union and now Russia; and an efficient instrument of American hegemony in Europe."[52] The State Duma formed an Anti-NATO Association in January 1997, claiming that NATO enlargement would jeopardize Russia's security and national interests because Western military power would now be at Russia's borders. A lone dissenter was former minister of finance and Duma member Boris Fyodorov. Rather than complain, he urged, Russia should submit its own application to join NATO.[53]

But criticism of NATO enlargement has been equally vocal from the democratic side. The recurrent theme among pro-reform Russians is that NATO expansion will have undesirable effects on Russian domestic politics, causing a psychological shock to those who were used to viewing the organization as the major enemy of the USSR, particularly the Russian military and antireform nationalists. Moreover, military reformers claimed that NATO enlargement would have an adverse effect on their attempts to restructure and downsize the Russian military.[54] Yeltsin's Council on Foreign and Defense Policy published a report on NATO in the summer of 1995 stressing that Russia's primary national interest was to achieve economic, political and social stability, and that "precisely from this point of view—the political-psychological—NATO enlargement goes against the national interests of Russia."[55] Yet during the December 1995 Duma and the June 1996 presidential election campaigns, public opinion data indicated that the vast majority of Russians were not bothered by NATO enlargement. What primarily concerned them was their own economic and social situation and rising crime rates. A February 1997 poll showed that 49 percent of Russians were indifferent to the prospect of NATO expansion, and that younger people cared less about the issue than did older Russians.[56] The fury about NATO expansion was an intra-elite, not a national, polemic.

Another theme that reoccurred in critiques from both conservatives and reformers was that NATO expansion violated not only the spirit but also the letter of the Final Settlement on Germany. Aleksandr Lebed referred to secret Central Committee documents showing that Kohl had promised Gorbachev at Stavropol that NATO "would not intentionally

move eastward." Primakov asserted that Mitterrand, Baker, and Hurd
had promised the USSR that NATO would not expand eastward. A
Yeltsin foreign policy advisor and director of international coverage for a
major television network quoted in detail documents from the Ministry
of Foreign Affairs archives showing that promises to this effect had been
made not only in 1990, but also in 1991. He concluded, after extensive
citations, that the lesson to be drawn from this was "that one must not
decide such important questions as the structure of European security on
the level of oral assurances and agreements, inasmuch as this is fraught
with potential political crises."[57] And a former diplomat claimed that
NATO enlargement violated Article 5 of the September 1990 Treaty on
the Final Settlement on Germany, which states that foreign troops and
nuclear weapons would not be deployed in the eastern part of the country. This meant, he continued, that NATO structures could not move
eastward.[58] Some Western diplomats, most notably former American ambassador to the USSR Jack Matlock, supported these claims. Nothing
explicit was said about NATO not expanding beyond the GDR in 1990,
and the Soviets implicitly chose to understand that this had been promised them. Thus, the linkage of NATO expansion to broken promises
made at the time of German unification remained a focus of the Russian
critique, connected to the broader issue of the West's not delivering on
promises made at the dawn of the postcommunist era.

The NATO-Russia Founding Act—A New Opportunity?

Both the Russian critique and opposition to NATO enlargement within
the United States and other NATO countries had an impact on Western
policy. By 1996, concerned over the resurgence of Communists in
Russia, and sensitive to criticism that NATO enlargement (or "adaptation" as it was now called) could have deleterious consequences for its
relations with Russia, the Clinton administration, backed by Germany,
focused on crafting a NATO-Russia Charter that would give Russia a
special relationship with NATO, though not membership in the organization for the forseeable future. Russian officials were initially lukewarm
to the idea, insisting that NATO was an antiquated organization and that
a such a charter would do little to mitigate their exclusion from membership in the new enlarged NATO. By the fall of 1996, the Russian government reluctantly decided that it would have to accept NATO expansion
(although it did not say so publicly) and try to obtain the best deal possible from NATO. During Yeltsin's eight-month absence from the Kremlin
following his heart attack on the eve of the final round of presidential
elections and his subsequent open-heart surgery and bout with double

pneumonia, virtually no progress was made on working out the terms of a NATO-Russian agreement, even though the German and American governments tried to move along the process. American officals praised Kohl for his efforts to persuade Yeltsin. But in the absence of their president, no one in the Russian government was willing to take the risk of signing on to an agreement that could have major negative domestic repercussions. Only after Yeltsin returned to the Kremlin and appointed his new reform team did the negotiations begin in earnest. Western officials realized that in order to assuage the Russian feelings of humiliation it was important to link Russia to NATO through an agreement that granted Russia special conditions—unlike the PfP. But the major problem initially was Russia's inability to offer concrete proposals for such a charter. Russian spokesmen were quite articulate in discussing what they did *not* want, but were largely unable to produce definite suggestions for what they *did* want. This reflected a much deeper problem in Russian foreign policy—Moscow's inability to formulate consistent, coherent policies.

During the spring of 1997 Yeltsin, influenced by Chubais and other economic reformers who were more interested in joining the West economically than quarreling over NATO enlargement, gave the green light to his foreign minister to negotiate the charter with NATO. At the Helsinki summit in March 1997, President Clinton persuaded his skeptical Russian interlocutors that a NATO-Russian agreement could bring significant benefits to Russia. But Yeltsin and Primakov remained highly crticial of NATO enlargement and stressed that the charter with NATO was a separate issue from that of enlargement. During the intense months of negotiation, Russia responded to an agenda largely set by NATO and had to give up some of its initial demands, particularly that the Charter be legally binding. NATO negotiators were surprised by the ease and speed with which they were able to conclude negotiations, after so much prior Russian prevarication. In this sense, the negotiations over the NATO-Russia Charter resembled those over German unification: the West was dealing with disorganized, sometimes intransigent Russian negotiators who eventually showed considerable flexibility and pragmatism and dropped their initally nonnegotiable demands. But in 1989–90, the West only had to persuade two people, Gorbachev and Shevardnadze, while in 1996–97, there were more players involved. In the NATO case, the timing was largely determined by the Russian wish to declare victory and participate in a NATO summit that was to meet before the one inviting new east-central European members, as well as for Yeltsin and Primakov to be feted alongside the major Western leaders.[59]

The NATO-Russia Founding Act was signed in Paris on May 27, 1997. Much of the treaty repeated language about cooperation and settling conflicts by peaceful means that was to be found in other post–Cold War accords. The new clauses provided for consultation and cooperation in the new Russia-NATO Permanent Joint Council to be created at NATO headquarters, thereby giving Russia a voice, but not a vote, in NATO affairs. The Joint Council meets monthly at the ambassador level and more or less frequently at higher and lower levels of representation. The Founding Act laid out future areas for cooperation, including crisis management, preventative diplomacy, joint operations, peacekeeping, arms control, nonproliferation, and disaster situations. The act stressed that NATO has "no intention, no plan, and no reason" to deploy nuclear weapons on the territory of new members or to change its nuclear policy; pledged both sides to work together to revise the treaty on Conventional Forces in Europe; and reiterated that NATO would carry out defense missions by reinforcement rather than permanently stationing substantial combat forces in new member countries.[60] The Founding Act, therefore, represented a compromise on the part of NATO, which had not initially wanted to pledge that it would not deploy nuclear weapons or combat forces in the new member countries, and also on the part of Russia, which had wanted a legally binding statement promising this. Yeltsin described the accord as "a victory for reason," although he also said "Russia still views negatively the expansion plans for NATO."[61] Chancellor Kohl said that the agreement opened a new chapter in European history, and Defense Minister Rühe described it as a "revolutionary change" in the face of Europe. Shortly thereafter, Ukraine also signed a treaty with NATO, intended to enhance its security against possible Russian countermeasures after NATO expanded.

Russian commentary on the NATO-Russia Act and the events leading up to it was, as expected, mixed and contradictory. *Izvestiia*, in two different articles, quoted Ministry of Foreign Affairs officials as saying "We got everything we wanted," and cited confidential documents showing that NATO "made maximum concessions" to Russia. But Andranik Migranian, a critic of Yeltsin although a member of his Council on Foreign and Defense Policy, likened the NATO-Russia Founding Act to such fateful events as the Congress of Vienna, Versailles, and Yalta, because it froze a particular correlation of forces—in this case the postcommunist one, at a point where Russia was very weak and threatened Russia's future relations with its CIS neighbors. And Communist leader Gennadi Ziuganov opined, "This is more a treaty of complete capitulation than an agreement."[62] Most critics used the opportunity to criticize Yeltsin and his new team for conceding too much to NATO. But former Prime Minister Yegor Gaidar congratulated Clinton: "He has managed to pull off the seemingly impossible: to implement NATO enlargement without causing irreparable damage either to democratic elements in Russia's political establishment or to U.S.–Russian relations."[63]

A few weeks after the act was signed, NATO, at its Madrid summit on July 8, 1997, agreed to admit a "first tranche" of three new members,

Poland, the Czech Republic, and Hungary, by the year 1999, fifty years after its founding. As a result, the alliance's outer borders moved 450 miles further east. Russia sent a low-level delegation to the conference. After all the furious negotiations and hubbub surrounding the meeting, the conference itself was somewhat anticlimactic, especially because of last-minute wrangling over whether Slovenia and Rumania should also be admitted—a position promoted by France, but not supported by some other NATO members. The United States vetoed the proposal for a variety of reasons, one of which was the desire not to further antagonize Russia. Germany was divided over admitting more members. The other quid pro quo to Russia was an invitation to the Denver G-8 summit, where it was promised almost full membership in the club and in other Western financial institutions. Thus, by the end of 1997, the Russian economic reformers who were more interested in the G-8 than in NATO could claim some success.

As Russia looked to its role in Europe in the next millenium, the major question was how it would participate in the new NATO-Russia Joint Council and how much of a say it would have in NATO affairs. The "second tranche" of enlargement, particularly the issue of whether the Baltic states would join, will also preoccupy Russia. Since for the foreseeable future it was unlikely that any new institutons dealing with European security would be created, the closest it could approach a partnership with the West would be through its role in the new NATO. Russia now had an opportunity to play a more active and positive role in European developments, even if it was not a NATO member, but it was largely up to the Russian government to take full advantage of the flexible—but still vague—NATO-Russia Act. Active participation required training more officials in NATO-related affairs and achieving a consensus within the government and among various ministries and Yeltsin's own national security staff over what Russia's goals in the Joint Council would be. In theory, Russia could play a largely obstructionist role in the council, seeking to bloc further expansion of NATO or further extension of its role in Bosnia; or it could remain largely passive, failing to make use of the council at all. But if it were inclined to take a more active role, there are a number of issues where it could gain from such cooperation, including implementing PfP activites; increasing interoperability; joint peacekeeping in the CIS and elsewhere; standardization of armaments; and further activities in Bosnia. It could also use the forum to discuss broader issues of arms control and increasing its role in European affairs. Some of these issues have already been taken up in NATO-Russian "Sixteen Plus One" meetings prior to the Founding Act, and there are many areas where Russia and NATO have cooperated de facto. But ultimately, Russia's willingness and ability to use the NATO opportunity to participate more fully in European affairs will depend on domestic developments, and particularly on the outcome of its own ambitious plans for military reform, which are threatened by lack of funds. This is the first real chance that Russia has had since German unificaton and the collapse of communism to play a more active role in Europe. The opportunity is Russia's to seize or to forfeit. It is, paradoxically, the first opportunity for a new Russian role in postcommunist European security that approaches what Gorbachev had initially expected from German unification, although certainly not in the form that he envisaged.

In the longer run, active Russian participation might have an impact on developments within NATO itself, although no current or future members are willing to concede to Russia any power of veto. But the question of further enlarging NATO to include the Baltic states or even Ukraine, and future NATO reform, will be issues in which Russia has a vital stake. It is not inconceivable that Russia itself might one day join NATO, although such a NATO would look entirely different than it does at the end of the twentieth century.

Alternatives

From the Russian point of view, the OSCE is a far more desirable institution with which to regulate European security than is NATO, for the obvious reason that Russia and the United States have an equal role in the OSCE. Germany has also emphasized that the OSCE—an all-European institution that includes Russia and the other post-Soviet states— remains a valuable and important organization that must concern itself with European security, especially with ethnic conflicts. Indeed, some in the Foreign Ministry, reflecting the Genscherite tradition, believe that not enough was done after the collapse of communism to upgrade the OSCE as a serious institution for regulating European security. This was largely because of American skepticism about the efficacy of the organization. The inability of the OSCE to intervene to defuse the Yugoslav crisis increased American doubts. In December 1994, the OSCE agreed to strengthen its consultative mechanisms and clarify its operational mandate. It seeks greater power in organizing and monitoring peacekeeping missions using troops from member states.

Russia has been a vociferous proponent of upgrading OSCE as an alternative to NATO expansion. For Russia, an upgraded OSCE could give Moscow a degree of influence over security arrangements in Europe while confirming Russia's role as the main player in CIS security. At the December 1994 meeting, however Russia's plans for an enhanced role for OSCE were rebuffed. Clearly, a fifty-three-member organization representing nearly a billion people that has extended the definition of Europe to include Central Asian states, and in which every member state has an equal vote, cannot be as effective as a smaller, integrated military organization like NATO. Russia has repeatedly advocated reorganizing the OSCE to form a directorate composed of the most important members, similar to the United Nation's Security Council, that would run the day-to-day affairs of the organization. This would enable it to act more effectively than in the current situation where Malta has an equal voice with that of the United States or Russia. Officially, the United States and its European allies have not endorsed the idea of an OSCE directorate; but experts on both sides of the Atlantic are still debating its merits. It would not, however, be a substitute for NATO.[64]

The other major institution—arguably the most important one—that could make a significant contribution toward stabilizing east-central Europe is the European Union. Germany took the lead in urging the speedy enlargement of the EU to include the Višegrad states, realizing that the EU could make a more significant contribution toward stabilizing east-central Europe than could NATO. Indeed, it promised during its presidency of the EU in the second half of 1994 to make this its first priority. However, a number of factors prevented Germany from achieving its goal. France and other southern European countries objected to the inclusion of the Višegrad countries in a short period of time because of their own economic needs, which they believed would be neglected were rapid accession to occur. There were other divisions within the EU that pushed back the timetable for east-central Europe's accession. A major stumbling block remained the EU's refusal to open its markets to goods from the region. At its Luxembourg summit in December 1997, the EU finally agreed on the modalities of expansion by up to eleven members by early in the next century. Poland, the Czech Republic, Hungary, Slovenia, Estonia, and Cyprus will be the first candidates to be invited. On the face of it, Russia should be less troubled by EU expansion than it is by NATO expansion, because the EU does not involve military structures. But if Central Europe were to be fully integrated while Russia remained largely outside the EU, then Russia might react negatively to its exclusion from the economic benefits that its erstwhile CMEA partners would enjoy.

Russia's slow integation into European structures accelerated in February 1996, when it became a full member of the Council of Europe, despite other members' misgivings about its conduct in Chechnya. This entailed a formal commitment by Russia to implement democratization and human rights measures to live up to the norms of the council and has proved a useful venue for Russian politicans to participate in the broader European dialogue on democratization.[65] Russia has also moved closer to the EU, although it has not taken full advantage yet of its treaty with the organization. Whereas for Russia the economic dimension of relations with the EU is paramount, the EU is more interested in the political side and is more reserved about economic relations. After all, only 3 percent of the EU's foreign trade is with Russia, whereas nearly 40 percent of Russia's foreign trade is with the EU. Russia wants the EU to open its markets more quickly; the EU is wary of protectionist Russian policies. So far, the EU-Russia agreement has laid a framework for improved ties but not yet for partnership, and Russia, unlike the east-central European countries, has no prospect of EU membership.[66]

The debate over NATO, OSCE, EU, and other organizations will continue. After all, there is no consensus on what the real threat to European security is, beyond general concerns about Russian unpredictability and ethnic conflict. Given the uncertainties in Russia, the CIS, and east-central Europe, it is perhaps too early to redesign European security architecture. But it is evident that Europe, west, central, and east, will not be secure unless Russia is a part of the cooperative framework in which security is assured and extended eastward. However difficult it is, Russia must be an active participant in European security structures and that process will be slow and evolutionary. It was unrealistic to expect that immediately following the end of East-West ideological confrontation, Russia would become a compliant Western partner because its economic needs were so great. It still views itself as a major European power with certain entitlements, despite its economic difficulties. It fears a new dividing line in Europe and wants to be partners with the West, but it will not be a compliant ally. It will continue to pursue its own interests and will, therefore, be a rival as well as a partner. Germany has realized this sooner than has the United States, because its expectations from the fall of communism were more realistic than those of America. But Germany's concerns about its immediate neighbors to the east necessitate a delicate balancing act between reassuring its near abroad and engagement with Russia.

At the end of the twentieth century, Russia remains in a European no-man's-land. It seeks closer integration with Europe, but is wary of compromising too much. It is not fully part of any organization except for the OSCE. It stands outside Europe's door, with one foot in and the other outside. As long as its domestic situation is uncertain and the struggle between reformers and those who despise the new groups continues, and as long as it fails to reform its military, it cannot fully become part of Europe. The most that the West can do is to support Russian democratization efforts—including the as yet unsuccessful attempts to establish the rule of law—and leave the door open for future Russian entry. But Russian actions will also determine how long that door remains open and whether the new, larger Europe is willing and able to accept Russia when and if it is ready to join.

Both Russia and Germany will have a major impact on European developments in the twenty-first century. The head of the Duma's international affairs committee, Vladimir Lukin, has said that the future of these relations depends on whether Germany follows a policy of integrating or "Germanizing" Europe, which will partly depend on how Russia deals with east-central Europe: "our task is to form reliable guarantees against Russian and German great power chauvinism."[67] Are either of these likely in the next century? History, geography, and technological change—but, above all, internal developments—will all influence the future of Russian-German relations and their impact on their European neighbors.

Nine

Russia and Germany in the Twenty-First Century

> Every German frontier is artificial, therefore
> impermanent; that is the permanence of
> German geography.
>   (*A. J. P. Taylor, 1951*)[1]

> The Germans and the Russians are the two
> European peoples who squandered their
> opportunities in the twentieth century.
>   (*François Furet, 1991*)[2]

GIVEN the dizzying pace of negotiations on German unification and the uncertainties surrounding the creation of the new Federal Republic of Germany and the collapse of the USSR, it is remarkable how far not only Germany but also Russia have come toward stabilizing their post–Cold War institutions. Despite the dislocations and unexpected costs of unification, Germany has gradually begun to play a more active role in Europe and overseas. Its postwar democratic body politic has been robust enough to withstand the price and burdens of unification and is ready to move on to the next stage of European integration—one that will, eventually, also include the countries of east-central Europe. Russia, too, has with great difficulty managed to emerge from the collapse of the Soviet Union without reverting to authoritarian rule or experiencing civil war, although the invasion of Chechnya is a reminder of the weakness of the current quasi-federal system. Despite the vacillation between more or less reformist policies, the overly powerful presidential system, the emergence of competing financial-political groups, and the growth of crime, Russia has experienced dynamic economic growth in some sectors and the commitment to pluralism and competition within the system remains strong. Although Russia remains a weak state that is far too dependent on the rule of one man, there are enough encouraging signs that given its intellectual and economic potential, it may eventually emerge as a viable post-Communist state with a commitment to further democratization.

Thus, the prospects for continued German-Russian cooperation in a more democratic Europe are better now than at any time in this century. As Germany and Russia continue to redefine their roles and identities in

Europe, the past has become less relevant to the future than either country initially hoped or feared. The century began with German-Russian rivalry leading to World War I. In the interwar years, German-Russian military and political cooperation enabled both countries to recover from the war's devastation. But their cooperation threatened the integrity and independence of east-central Europe, and led to the invasion of Poland, its renewed partition in 1939, and then to the outbreak of the Second World War. After Hitler's defeat, the USSR's relations with West Germany were frosty; its relations with the GDR, while officially warm and fraternal, were fraught with tensions. Once détente began, Moscow embarked on cooperative relations with both Germanies, but remained wary of the inter-German rapprochement that ultimately led to the fall of the GDR. Since unification, the historical cycle of mutual cooperation, conflict, and suspicion has been broken. Bilateral relations are as close as they have ever been, and for the first time ever, neither Germany nor Russia threatens the countries that lie between them. Moreover, the bilateral relationship itself is becoming less critical, as German-Russian relations now operate within several multilateral structures—the G-8, the Bosnia forces, NATO, the EU, the OSCE, and the United Nations. The more embedded these ties are in broader structures, the more difficult it becomes to rupture and radically change them.

If the past has little relevance for the current relationship, how is one to envision what might happen in Germany and Russia and between the two countries in the next century? Germans and Russians have barely recovered from the shock of the unanticipated fall of communism and reunification of Germany.

As Germans and Russians contemplate their futures, they raise both old and new questions. Russians still debate whether they belong in the West or somewhere between Asia and Europe, although the Russian government has made it clear that the West will continue to be its most important partner. Germans puzzle over what it means to be Europe's central power, an increasingly ethnically heterogeneous nation-state integrated into European structures.[3] Most favor continuity with past policies and no major redefinition of national interests.[4] A minority on the left and right question whether Germany should and will in the future remain embedded in European structures and the transatlantic alliance.[5]

Despite the difficulties of forseeing what might happen in Germany and Russia and between Berlin and Moscow in the next decades, there are compelling reasons for looking into the future. Russia and Germany will between them dominate the European continent in the next century, and how and where they exercise influence will have a significant impact not only on developments inside Europe but also on relations between Europe and the United States and on the multilateral structures within which they operate. A Europe in which both Germany and Russia were prosperous, democratic countries would look very different from a Europe in which both Germany and Russia had fallen on hard economic times and were governed by right-wing nationalist coalitions seeking foreign adventures to distract from domestic problems. Two major factors will determine which Europe emerges: what happens inside Russia and its neighbors, and how the process of further European integration and EU enlargement proceeds.

This chapter offers future scenarios for domestic developments within Germany and Russia and explores how these different scenarios might affect bilateral relations between the two countries and, ultimately, their respective roles in Europe. The scenarios suggest different ways of looking at future developments in Europe, depending on whether Germany and Russia both prosper politically and economically or whether only Germany succeeds in doing so. They are based on what has happened in both countries since the fall of communism and on the broader European environment that will shape both countries. Scenarios are not predictions. They are structures for identifying and thinking about the main issues and organizing one's thoughts.

German Futures

"Prisoners of the Present"—European Germany

There are many indications that Germany is recovering from the economic, social, and psychological costs of unification in a way that will leave intact its postwar identity as a "civilian power" with a stable democratic political system. Germany will be a major European power in the next century, but its influence will derive from its economic and political rather than its military assets. Nevertheless, there will also be economic constraints on what Germany can do. There will be strong efforts to slim down the bountiful postwar West German welfare state and to make Germany more competitive internationally. Austerity is already the new mantra, and, before Germany has fully recovered from unification, it will have experienced more belt tightening. The social market economy, conceived by Chancellor Ludwig Erhard, produced postwar West Germany's economic miracle. But in the era of unification, an aging population, generous benefits, and the unexpected costs of absorbing eastern Germany threatened the comfortable postwar welfare state. Nevertheless, since most European Union members have also been forced to cut back on their welfare systems and lessen state subsidies, Germany does not face this problem alone.

A Berlin Wall still runs across Germany today, but now it is psychological and social. As one bitter joke goes, when the East Germans began to chant in 1989, "We are one people," the West Germans responded, "So are we." Nevertheless, eventually the psychological Berlin wall will disintegrate, and current feelings of resentment against the *Besserwessis* and inferiority vis-à-vis the West will decline.[6] Germany will in time also absorb its immigrants, including those from former communist states. It will develop a new identity as an ethnically heterogeneous country with a sizable immigrant population.

A reasonably prosperous, democratic Germany will maintain both its European and regional identities. Bavarians and Saxons may well continue to feel more Bavarian or more Saxon than German; but in a future integrated Europe, local and regional identity could reinforce European-ness, as opposed to Germanness. A democratic, stable German society will view its international role as that of a civilian, nonnuclear power and a primarily European actor. It will continue to project its economic power eastward in Europe as part of its major postunification task, that of creating a stable buffer zone to its east, with its eastern neighbors integrated into both the EU and NATO. It will eventually be surrounded by a group of reasonably stable, prosperous east-central European states, although some postcommunist states, particularly in the Balkans, may become neither prosperous nor stable.

The prerequisite for this self-confident, democratic, European Germany is a European Union that continues to prosper and expand. Germany's initial integration into the European Community in 1957 and its reconciliation with France in 1963 were essential for the development of a European, nonnationalist identity, which enabled it to become a civilian power anchored in multilateral structures. Since becoming chancellor in 1982, Helmut Kohl has made Europe his major task—integration, the establishment of a common currency, and more recently, the widening and deepening of the EU to include east-central European and Baltic members and create a common foreign and security policy. This commitment to European integration and diminishing the national powers of its member states will outlive Helmut Kohl's tenure, because it is broadly accepted by the German populace as the best way to ensure that Germany is never again tempted by nationalist yearnings. A wider and deeper EU will create a multilateral Ostpolitik that will facilitate both the integration of east-central Europe and closer cooperation with Russia. It will provide the necessary context for an active, European Germany.

But will the European Union be able to restructure itself sufficiently to complete a successful enlargement? How successfully will the euro replace national currencies and how will the Central Bank work? The populations in most European countries, especially Germany, have become increasingly skeptical about whether they want a common European currency. Moreover, in recent years, the EU has been reluctant to reform itself institutionally or radically rethink its outdated common agricultural policies which are major barriers to further enlargement.[7] Germany has a vital interest in internal EU reform, but is only one of many players in complicated negotiations. It certainly has the largest stake in EU adaptation but cannot guarantee a successful outcome.

Nationalist Germany

It is extremely difficult to imagine that Germany, which has been so successful as a democratic polity and market economy in the postwar and postunification years, could experience a drastic reversal of fortune and contemplate renouncing its current system. But given the costs of unification, the relative weakness of political parties, and questions about what will happen once Helmut Kohl is no longer chancellor, there is a remote possibility that Germany might enter a period of economic and political stagnation. This could occur if structural economic and political reforms within the country are not undertaken more vigorously and Germany does not become more competitive internationally and is unable to adapt to the process of globalization. A long period of stagnation in Germany could begin a process of reevaluating the postwar system.

Unless there are major changes both in the international economy and within Europe, Germany will remain committed to European integration and to democratizing the former communist states. There is only a very slight chance of external developments seriously threatening a peaceful, prosperous German future. But, if there were to be a major worldwide recession, coupled with the failure of east-central Europe to progress in its transition, the serious weakening of the European Union, and the outbreak of more conflicts in the Balkans, Germany might change dramatically. The economic situation might deteriorate sharply, and with rising unemployment and contracting welfare benefits, each part of Germany would blame the other for its problems. Anger against foreigners and immigrants would rise. Old-fashioned nationalism might arise from the ashes of a failing Europe. Nationalism would involve demanding "German jobs for Germans," asserting Germany's unique role in Europe, its right to a place in the sun (or at least in Eastern Europe) and its rejection of the Western-imposed culture of restraint on the part of a civilian power. A younger generation, no longer influenced by the Second World War or the Cold War, would replace the postunification leadership.

If such a Germany were to elect a right-wing nationalist government, the entire postwar policy of *Westbindung* (integration into the West) would be challenged and foreign policy could be renationalized. The new leaders might reopen questions of postwar borders and of nuclear weapons. After all, who is to say that the loss of territories to the USSR and Poland in 1945 was permanent? It could be just a temporary aberration, similar to losses of German territory in past centuries. And who is to say that Germany must for ever remain a nonnuclear state and that it needs NATO to guarantee its security?

A nationalist German government could both withdraw from NATO or render it ineffective and seek to regain Kaliningrad, the rest of East Prussia, Silesia, and Pomerania, perhaps even the Sudetenland. An economically weaker Germany might also view military rearmament as a means of jump-starting the economy. It could become a nuclear power. Such a Germany would once again become preoccupied with the politics of resentment. It would be the *Zentralmacht Europas* searching for a new, military role and national power projection. However, such a Germany would only be conceivable if all the carefully constructed postwar multilateral European and transatlantic structures no longer operated to restrain European nationalism and irredentism. It would mean that fifty years of democratization and the entire postwar security system in Europe had failed. It is, therefore, a highly remote possibility.

Russian Futures

Russia Muddles Along and Upward

It is much more challenging to predict Russia's future than Germany's, and the possibilities for darker scenarios are significantly greater. We only have the evidence of less than a decade of postcommunist transformation, balanced against centuries of authoritarian government and the absence of the rule of law. Nevertheless, it is astounding how much has changed in Russia since Mikhail Gorbachev resigned on Christmas Day 1991. The Russian Federation is such a multifaceted mosaic that it is difficult to generalize about its entire vast area. But evidence from the past few years indicates that Russia will continue to muddle along and that, in a few years, it will probably "muddle upward". Its economic and social situation will improve as long as the post-Yeltsin administration remains committed to reforms and to redistribution of resources so that those who have so far been bypassed by the economic revolution come to believe that democracy and capitalism will indeed improve their lives.

Considerable progress has already been made toward the consolidation of a postcommunist system with distinct channels of power and authority and means of assuring checks and balances. Out of the continuing disorganization and instability in Russia, a new system has emerged, one that will enable Russia to continue its development for some time without any major upheavals.[8] Despite the strong presidency enshrined in the Yeltsin constitution of 1993—some Russians speak of its "tsarist" character—considerable obstacles to the reimposition of authoritarian rule exist. No single group on the Russian scene is able to secure a monopoly on power, and thus, the various "oligarchs"—the financial conglomerates and the politicians and media groups whom they support—will continue to vie for power within a system that has already developed some recognizable rules of the game. This system is lopsided and will continue to lack effective judicial institutions and the rule of law for some time. Moreover, its unruly legislature is weak, thus reinforcing executive power. Soviet structures still persist in this hybrid system, both in the enduring power of the old *nomenklatura* and in the ways in which different regions of Russia and different parts of the economy are run. Behind the facade of chaos, however, is a network of competing interest groups both within the executive branch and outside the government that will ensure competition within the political system and the growth of civil society, albeit one based on personal ties and not on the rule of law.

Russia's market economy will continue its uneven growth, corruption will persist as a major feature of that economy and of society as a whole, and foreign economic involvement will be important for Russian economic development, although investors will remain hesitant as long as organized crime remains endemic to the system. Democratic institutions and civil society will coexist and compete with the power of old and new oligarchs, some of them connected to organized crime. But, as Russia for the first time in its history produces a middle class with a commitment to the development of more viable political parties and the rule of law, the power of these conglomerates may also diminish. In a Russia that muddles along, power will become increasingly decentralized, regional political and economic diversity will grow, the center will become weaker, but the federation will probably stay together. There will be continued political maneuverings and rivalries in the post-Yeltsin era, but the clock cannot be turned back to the communist era. Russia will remain a weak, pluralist state and a partial democracy.

In a Russia that muddles along, foreign policy will still be based on weakness rather than strength. Relations with the CIS will be varied and Russia will stress closer economic integration with selected states. By 1997, a new pragmatism and activism in ties with the CIS has emerged. Russia's most important partner remains Ukraine, whose economic and political transition lags behind that of Russia and whose preoccupation with future Russian designs on its territory have, until recently, defined relations. But the 1997 treaties regulating the Black Sea Fleet and recognizing Ukraine's borders signal a willingness on both sides to improve ties. Similarly, the 1997 union with Belarus, which did not go nearly as far as some nationalists wanted, signaled a more reserved approach toward reintegration. While relations with the Slavic Newly Independent States will improve, Russia's ties with the Transcaucasian and central Asian states will be determined by a number of military and economic factors. Energy considerations will be crucial in determining ties with Azerbaijan and central Asia, especially as the Caspian Sea projects develop, but the Russian government will have to contend with its private energy companies, who do not necessarily share the geopolitical concerns of the government, or at least of the Foreign and Defense ministries. Indeed, the increasing role of private groups in formulating Russian's foreign policy is likely to shift its ties with the CIS in a generally more pragmatic direction.

Russia's military involvement in some CIS states will continue, as will its insistence on its right to play a "peacekeeping" role in countries like Tajikistan or in the Nagorno-Karabakh conflict. Moreover, the refusal of the world community to participate in Russian peacekeeping activities in the CIS will guarantee that Russia will continue to play this role for a long time. Nevertheless, it is unlikely that the issue of the Russian diaspora in the CIS will prompt military intervention by Moscow. Despite all the early militant rhetoric about protecting fellow Russians in the "near abroad" and demanding dual citizenship for them, the story of Russia's relations with its diaspora is that menacing words about coming to their aid have not been matched by deeds, because action is too costly and because the Russian people do not have the stomach for any more political upheavals. Russians in Russia and the CIS might have nostalgia for the Soviet Union, but they are not going to pay with money—or with their lives—to restore it

Russian foreign policy will remain a cautious mixture of partnership with the West combined with the assertion of Russia's right to its own unique interests and policies. Its relationship with east-central Europe will remain tentative, and the debate about how significant this area is for Russia—as opposed to the CIS, about whose importance there is less debate within Russia—will continue. Russia will not have the means to pursue a more assertive foreign policy, nor will it have a coherent strategy. But it will continue to seek a great-power role in Europe, albeit an ill-defined one. Under the best of circumstances, it will have to make do with a fluctuating relationship both with the West and with Asia. Its domestic challenges will not give it the luxury of defining a dynamic new role in the postcommunist world. Policies will be reactive, rather than proactive.

While it is most likely that Russia will continue to muddle along for a few decades, it is also possible that it could "muddle upward," that its economic fortunes could improve sufficiently to create a more stable and democratic society. In 1996, Russia was the best-performing emerging market, until it was adversely affected by the 1997 Asian financial crisis and the 1998 near collapse of the financial system because of revenue shortages. If the current Russian government and its successors are able to harness Russia's burgeoning market society in such a way that growth rates begin to rise, taxes are collected, and the new wealth is no longer confined to a tiny group of people, then foreign investment will increase and Russian flight capital will return. A more stable and prosperous economy will then provide the framework for a society that does begin to operate on the basis of laws as opposed to personal ties, and where people begin to accept both the rights and the responsibilities that are part of a viable democratic society. Military reform might succeed, and the army become smaller, all-volunteer and more effective. As the old *nomenklatura* generation passes from the scene, newer, postcommunist structures will arise in the hybrid society and will change it. In a Russia that is "muddling upward," Russia will still remain a partial democracy, but the economy will have turned the corner and political and social evolution will have reached the point where the possibility for a return to authoritarianism is less than it is while Russia merely muddles along.

In a more self-confident Russia, foreign policy would be more coherent. Economic interests would become more important vis-à-vis classical military and security interests. The role of nongovernment actors in foreign policy would become more regularized, with the rules of the game for the government and the private sector more clearly delineated. Russian foreign policy would become more active both within the CIS and in Asia and both Western and east-central Europe, although Russia would still be limited in its global reach. The old asymmetry between Russia's military and its economic strength would no longer define its national identity or its national interests in the way it did under communism and since the USSR's collapse. In a few decades, the old obsession with military power and prestige, born of a traditional inferiority complex, might have diminished. A Russia that is "muddling upward" might begin to break away from its centuries-old cycle of authoritarianism, uprisings, and repression.

Authoritarian Russia

Despite the impressive progress that Russia has already made away from communism and a state-run economy, democratic structures are not well enough entrenched to prevent a return to authoritarian political rule. True, there is no possibility that the communist system would be brought back. But if the economic situation does not improve, the society becomes more pervaded by crime, and people continue to experience significant hardships; if corruption at the top is perceived to be the cause of the nonpayment of wages to a significant percent of the population; if the post-Yeltsin struggle for power destabilizes the country significantly; if instability on the periphery spills over into the Russian Federation; if military reform does not proceed and the army remains impoverished and humiliated; and if both foreign investment and IMF involvement significantly decline, then a populist figure who promises to clean up corruption, bring back stability, pay people the wages they deserve, end the power of financial conglomerates, and restore Russia's dignity at home and abroad might come to power by electoral means.

Such a leader might, in the name of cleaning up corruption and tackling problems of crime and insecurity, restrict civil liberties with the consent of those who elected him, because, for them, too much freedom means instability, unpredictability, lawlessness, crime, and economic inequalities. An authoritarian Russian ruler would gain control over and suppress the media and rescind some economic reforms. Russia would nevertheless retain an overwhelmingly private, as opposed to state-controlled economy, but an authoritarian regime would institutionalize economic corruption at the highest levels. The leader would also seek to impose more centralized rule on the Russian regions—although that would be extremely difficult, given how far decentralization has already gone—and would put more pressure on the CIS states to reintegrate. He would have the support of those parts of the military who want to recapture past Soviet glories and to gain more resources.

Foreign policy rhetoric in an authoritarian Russia would become more nationalist, expansionist, and Eurasian, and Russia would withdraw from further arms control negotiations and be more assertive about its interests in relations with a variety of countries, irrespective of how its Western partners view them. Nevertheless, Russia's foreign policy would still be affected by the country's depleted resources. Attempts to reintegrate the CIS by force would be constrained by limited capabilities. Despite its weakened military, Russia could become more menacing internationally, withdrawing from commitments to the West, looking increasingly to Asia, and adopting a more aggressive nuclear policy. Alternatively, authoritarian Russia could become more isolationist, although dependence on the international economy would limit its ability to retreat from the world. But, as long as the EU and NATO survive and prosper, and as long as Germany remains firmly anchored in transatlantic structures, an authoritarian Russia's ability to influence European developments will be limited.

Germany, Russia, and the Future

Europe's future will largely depend on whether Germany and Russia continue on their present path, and on how Russia completes its transition away from communism. If Germany emerges successfully from unification as a self-confident, European power and faces a Russia that continues to muddle along, Berlin will pursue its involvement in Russia in order to promote stability, but it will also support policies that seek to contain the effects of Russian instability or future disintegration. These policies would include intensified involvement in east-central Europe, assuring its membership both in NATO and the European Union. German economic involvement in Russia would continue to provide significant support for Russia's transition, and the bilateral relationship would remain strong.

A Russia that muddles along will push for greater German involvement and seek to block German actions to strengthen European security that do not include Russia—particularly further extensions of NATO. It will continue to act unilaterally in foreign policy, dealing with potential security threats on its own, because it will have no security partners beyond general agreements with the West.[9] The German-Russian relationship will continue to be of central importance for Russia, but of less importance for Germany if the consolidation of east-central Europe and its integration into NATO and the EU proceeds well. The German-Russian relationship will not endanger European stability or east-central Europe's sovereignty.

As Germany recovers fully from unification and Russia begins to "muddle upward," German-Russian relations will improve, the level of their economic and political interactions will rise and the German-Russian relationship would become more symmetrical. But as long as Russia has only one foot in Europe, German policy will continue to focus on promoting the recovery of east-central Europe and will remain cautious about Russia. The prospect of continuing German-Russian cooperation against a background of enduring German concerns about Russia's stability is the most likely for the next decade, at least.

A stable, prosperous Germany and a stable, prosperous Russia that is "muddling upward" opens new possibilities. Russia and Germany could cooperate with other European countries in a variety of ways that no one can currently envisage. This benign collaboration would extend to multilateral structures, including the European Union, NATO, and the OSCE. If Russia were to become truly democratic then the division of Europe—attenuated but not obliterated by the fall of communism—would finally be overcome. In this new world order historical ghosts would evaporate, and the twentieth century would indeed have been laid to rest.

A European Germany would face difficult choices if Russia became more authoritarian. It would be less inclined than the United States to rupture ties with Moscow, because it has a long-term stake in a stable Russia. Germany would argue that it had to remain involved in Russia in order to mitigate the new rulers' ambitions, and it would continue its economic commitments, particularly if the new regime promised to safeguard foreign investments. At the same time, NATO and EU enlargement would be accelerated, because east-central Europe and the Baltic states would feel threatened by Russian ambitions. Russia might well take at least symbolic military action against these moves. It would counter NATO enlargement with an assertive military posture in the CIS, especially Ukraine. But east-central Europe's independence would be guaranteed by NATO. The Yalta era is over.

In the extremely unlikely event that Germany became more nationalistic, then Russian-German relations would begin to cast a more sinister shadow over Europe. East-central Europe would be particularly vulnerable to German pressure, although the German economy would also be weak. Germany would look to Russia as a market for increased arms sales in return for Russian raw materials, reviving traditional trade patterns. A more nationalist Germany could affect a Russia that is muddling along in two different ways. Fearing possible German designs on Russian territory, Russia might seek to ally with Germany's former NATO partners against Germany. Alternatively, it might seek to placate Germany by forming a partnership that involved economic concessions in return for territorial restraint. Whatever Russia tried to do, a nationalist Germany would have a negative influence on Russia's ability to emerge from muddling along to a more viable democratic market society.

The very worst outcome for Europe would be one in which both Germany and Russia returned to nationalism and authoritarianism. If both countries were to move in more militaristic directions, partly as a result of failed economic policies, then Europe would again revert to the battleground it was for centuries, and face both German and Russian hegemony—and nuclear weapons. The historical model of malevolent, as opposed to benign, collaboration would be revived. It would be back to the future. The first issue that Germany and Russia would confront is whether to divide east-central Europe or fight over it. Since both countries would be trying to improve their economic situations, they might initially agree to divide the area into spheres of influence The region would then be subject to the same kind of pressures that it has experienced for centuries, unless NATO without Germany would be able to defend it.

This last scenario is highly unlikely because Germany is a satiated, stable democracy and because Russia is unlikely to have the will or the means to become an aggressive military power for a long time. It is far more probable that a self-confident Germany within a more integrated Europe will continue to coexist and cooperate with a Russia lurching unevenly toward democracy and a growing market economy, while east-central European countries pursue their paths toward democracy as members of the transatlantic security community and partners in shared Western values.

The relationship between Russia and Germany will also be influenced by the role of the United States. After all, NATO enlargement, the Bosnia forces, and the NATO-Russian relationship are means of assuring that Washington remains as involved as Berlin in the evolution of postcommunist Europe. As long as America continues to play a leading role in Europe, it will act as a stabilizing force and an anchor of European security. If it were to withdraw into isolationism, then both the domestic and the international situation in Europe could seriously deteriorate.

The irony in the post–Cold War situation is that the United States has finally realized what presidents Wilson and Roosevelt both dreamed of as the outcome of the two world wars: a Europe of independent countries voluntarily pursuing integration and no longer threatened by Germany or Russia seeking to impose their spheres of influence; an open world trading system; a global economy that encompasses all the countries of Europe; peaceful multilateral structures; and growing economic prosperity. Yet it is unclear whether the United States will remain willing or able to play a leadership role in this new, more unified Europe in the next century. Public opinion is divided over whether America should expend resources and send its young men and women to help keep the peace in Europe. Yet, without U.S. leadership of and partnership with its allies in Europe, the democratizing Europe that has taken so long to create might not remain in being.

As Germany and Russia enter the next millennium, they will both be part of an international economic system that limits any single country's ability to operate nationally. Moreover, Europe will no longer determine the world's fate in the twenty-first century as it did in the first half of the twentieth; and the power of the United States, which has dominated the world in the second half of this century, could be challenged by Asia's growing might sometime during the next. In the twenty-first century, when new global actors will emerge, the Russian-German relationship and its impact on Europe will no longer have the power to disrupt the lives of hundreds of millions of people. Instead, ties between Moscow and Berlin will occupy a central, but not decisive, place in the evolution of the world after communism.

Notes

Preface

1. Quoted in Wladimir S. Semjonow, *Von Stalin bis Gorbatschow: Ein halbes Jahrhundert in diplomatischer Mission 1939–1991* (Berlin: Nicolai Verlag, 1995), 205. Semenov served in the Soviet embassy in Berlin during the Nazi era, in the Allied Control Commission in postwar Berlin, and as ambassador to the Federal Republic prior to Gorbachev's accession.

Chapter One
Comrades in Misfortune

1. W. I. Lenin, *Werke*, vol. 27 (Berlin [east], 1960), 149, quoted in Semjonow, *Von Stalin bis Gorbatschow*, 204.

2. Quoted in Andrei Gromyko, *Memories* (London: Hutchison, 1989), 316.

3. Vasili Klyuchevsky, *Peter the Great* (New York: Vintage Books, 1961), 263.

4. Walter Laqueur, *Russia and Germany* (New Brunswick, N.J.: Transaction Publishers, 1990), 53.

5. Quoted in Nicholas Riasanovsky, *Russia and the West in the Teaching of the Slavophiles* (Cambridge, Mass.: Harvard University Press, 1952), 60–61.

6. Laqueur, *Russia and Germany*, 57.

7. Adam B. Ulam, *The Bolsheviks* (New York: Praeger, 1976), 75.

8. Jürgen Kuczynski and Grete Wittkowski, *Die deutsch-russischen Handelsbeziehungen in den letzten 150 Jahren* (Berlin: Verlag die Wirtschaft, 1947), 24, 45, 67.

9. George F. Kennan, *Russia and the West under Lenin and Stalin* (Boston: Little, Brown, 1960), 201.

10. Even after unification and united Germany's inclusion in NATO, some of the *Germanisty* still believe that a Rapallo-type relationship will reemerge in the twenty-first century. Author's interview with Nikolai Portugalov, former advisor to the CPSU Central Committee, Moscow, July 1997.

11. Werner Beitel and Jürgen Nötzhold, *Deutsch-Sowjetische Wirtschaftsbeziehungen in der Zeit der Weimarer Republik* (Ebenhausen: Stiftung Wissenschaft und Politik, 1977), 57–66.

12. Dimitri Volkogonov, the military historian, using newly opened archives, describes how closely Stalin read Hitler's writings. See Dimitri Volkogonov, *Stalin:Triumph and Tragedy* (Rocklin, Calif.: Prima Publishing, 1995), 352.

13. Author's interview with Wolfgang Schnurr, economic attaché at the German embassy in Moscow from 1937 to 1941, Bonn, October 1980.

14. Volkogonov, *Stalin: Triumph and Tragedy*, 387, 499.

15. According to Volkogonov, there was discussion just prior to the German invasion that the USSR should attack Germany first, but Stalin demurred. He

even refused to put troops on alert on the Western frontier because he feared "provoking" Hitler. Ibid., 398–402.

16. Tony Judt, "The Rediscovery of Central Europe," *Daedalus* (Winter 1990) 119, no.1: 23–54.

17. For discussion, see Zbigniew Brzezinski, *The Soviet Bloc: Unity and Conflict* (Cambridge, Mass.: Harvard University Press, 1967), and Daniel Yergin, *Shattered Peace* (Boston: Houghton Mifflin, 1977).

18. Gromyko, *Memories*, 112. See also I. S. Kremer, *FRG: Etapy "Vostochnoi Politiki"* (Moscow: Mezhdunarodnie Otnosheniia, 1986), 9–10.

19. According to Sergei Kondrashev, a KGB officer in the Berlin station in 1945, and Daniil Melnikov, in charge of anti-Nazi propaganda during the war, in 1945 Stalin argued in favor of a united, neutral Germany which he could control. Kondrashev interview in BBC television series, *Messengers from Moscow*. Author's interviews with Daniil Melnikov, July 1974, September 1986. See John Lewis Gaddis, *We Now Know* (Oxford: Oxford University Press, 1997), 113–121, for a discussion of how the new documents prove that Stalin actively pursued a unification strategy, but apparently failed to understand how the behavior of Soviet troops in Germany undermined his plans.

20. For discussion, see Thomas E. Wolfe, *Soviet Power and Europe* (Baltimore: Johns Hopkins University Press, 1970), 27–31, and Victor Baras, "Stalin's German Policy after Stalin," *Slavic Review*, 37 no. 2 (June 1978): 259–67. Gaddis, in *We Now Know*, 127–29, argues that new documents show that Stalin was more serious about the 1952 note than historians have so far believed.

21. Minutes of conversation between Stalin and leaders of the SED found in the Russian archives, quoted in Cold War International History Project (Washington) *Bulletin*, no. 4 (Fall 1994): 48.

22. Under the Hallstein Doctrine, the Federal Republic, as the sole representative of the German nation, refused to have diplomatic relations with any country (except for the USSR) that recognized the GDR. The Hallstein Doctrine was first implemented in 1957, when Yugoslavia established diplomatic relations with the GDR. It was finally abrogated in 1967, when the FRG established diplomatic relations with Rumania.

23. See Angela Stent, *From Embargo to Ostpolitik: The Political Economy of West German–Soviet Relations, 1955–1980* (Cambridge: Cambridge University Press, 1980).

24. See Wolfe, *Soviet Power in Europe*, chap. 6, for a discussion of the abortive Khrushchev visit.

25. See Erwin Weit, *Eyewitness* (London: Andre Deutsch, 1973). Weit was Polish leader Władisław Gomułka's interpreter and witnessed many tense scenes between Khrushchev and Ulbricht.

26. For a discussion of the debates surrounding the Khrushchev moves, see Michael J. Sodaro, *Moscow, Germany and the West From Khrushchev to Gorbachev* (Ithaca, N.Y.: Cornell University Press, 1990), chap.2. According to Vladimir Semenov, then deputy foreign minister, neither Adenauer nor Khrushchev was interested in German unification. Khrushchev suggested to Semenov that he might appoint his son-in-law, Aleksei Adzhubei, editor of *Izvestiia*, as foreign minister. Semenov suggested that this would not be a good idea, whereupon

Khrushchev sent Adzhubei to West Germany to prepare his 1964 visit without consulting Semenov, who was in charge of German affairs in the Foreign Ministry. See Semjonov, *Von Stalin bis Gorbatschow*, 305–6.

27. Julij A. Kwizinskij, *Vor dem Sturm* (Berlin: Siedler Verlag, 1993), 165, 170.

28. See Angela Stent, "Soviet Policy toward the German Democratic Republic," in *Soviet Policy in Eastern Europe*, ed. Sarah M. Terry (New Haven, Conn.: Yale University Press, 1984), chap. 2.

29. "Über Massnahmen zur Gesundung der politischen Lage in der DDR," notes of a meeting between Grotewohl, Oelssner, Ulbricht, Malenkov, Beria, Molotov, Khrushchev, Bulganin, Mikoyan, Kaganovich, Semenov, and Grechkov, Moscow, June 3 and 4, 1953, in SAP, J PA J NL 2/32 *Dokumente*.

30. For an eyewitness account of the 1953 revolt and Beria's downfall, see Semjonow, *Von Stalin bis Gorbatschow*, 294–300. It remains unclear, however, exactly what Semenov's relationship was with Beria, whom he clearly feared. Gaddis, *We Now Know*, 129–31, argues that Beria, had he succeeded Stalin, would have proposed uniting Germany without a communist government there.

31. Hope H. Harrison, "New Evidence on Khrushchev's 1958 Berlin Ultimatum," Cold War International History Project *Bulletin*, no. 4, (Fall 1994): 35–39. Gerhard Wettig, "Die Sowjetische Politik während der Berlin-Krise 1958–1962," *Deutschland Archiv*, no. 3 (1997): 383–99, gives a comprehensive account of the new archival material on this issue.

32. See Michael J. Sodaro, "Ulbricht's Grand Design: Economy, Ideology and the GDR's Response to Détente, 1967–1971," *World Affairs*, 142, no. 3 (Winter 1980): 147–68.

33. J. L. Gervin, cited in Robert Legvold, "The Russian Question," in *Russia and Europe: Emerging Security Agenda*, ed. Vladimir Baranovsky (Oxford: Oxford University Press, 1997). Legvold gives an illuminating analysis of the similarities between the traditional "German question" and the current "Russian question."

Chapter Two
Prelude to Unification

1. Conversation between Brezhnev and Honecker, July 28, 1990, *Auf höchster Stufe: Gespräche mit Erich Honecker*, ed. Jochen Staadt (Berlin: Transit, 1994), 13.

2. Honecker conversation with Konstantin Rusakov, October 21, 1981, ibid., 40.

3. Ibid., 61.

4. Georgi Arbatov, former Central Committee member and head of Moscow's USA and Canada Institute, stresses how important the German initiatives were. See Georgi Arbatov, *The System* (New York: Random House, 1992), 171.

5. See F. Stephen Larrabee, "The Politics of Reconciliation: Soviet Policy toward West Germany, 1961–1972" (Ph.D. dissertation, Columbia University, 1977), and Arnulf Baring, *Machtwechsel: Die Ära Brandt-Scheel* (Stuttgart: Deutsche Verlagsanstalt, 1982), 2.

6. Arbatov, *The System*, 71; Kwizinskij, *Vor dem Sturm*, 221; Valentin Falin, *Politische Erinnerungen* (Munich: Droemer Knaur, 1993), 117.

7. Baring, *Machtwechsel*, 244. These secret Soviet-FRG contacts were conducted through Sven Backlund, Swedish consul general in Berlin, and Pyotr Abrasimov, Soviet ambassador in East Berlin.

8. See Egon Bahr's speech at the Tutzing Evangelical Academy, July 15, 1963, in *Die Deutsche Ostpolitik 1961–1970*, ed. Boris Meissner (Cologne: Verlag Wissenschaft und Politik, 1970), 45–48.

9. Timothy Garton Ash, *In Europe's Name* (New York: Random House, 1993), 203.

10. Treaty between the Federal Republic of Germany and the Soviet Union, Moscow, August 12, 1970, in U.S. Senate, Committee on Foreign Relations, *Documents on Germany 1944–1970* (Washington, D.C.: U.S. Government Printing Office, 1971), 864–66.

11. Baring, *Machtwechsel*, 357.

12. Ibid., 354.

13. See Stent, *From Embargo to Ostpolitik*, 163–68.

14. In 1972, the SPD won 271 seats in the Bundestag, as opposed to 224 in 1969.

15. *Kommunist*, no. 5 (1969): 9, 24; *Neues Deutschland* March 26, 1969.

16. See Fred Oldenburg, "Eine endliche Geschichte," *Deutschland Archiv* no. 2 (1995): 164–65. Ulbricht was understandably furious when his opponents in the Politburo likened his errors, in 1971, to those of Khrushchev. In an outraged letter, he told his accusers exactly what he thought of Khrushchev. See Ulbricht's "An Genosse Hans Rodenberg," October 23, 1971, in SAP, J PA J NL 2/32. In an additional insult, Ulbricht was accused at an SED Central Committee meeting in 1970 of being an early Dubček supporter. See "Zur Korrektur der Wirtschaftspolitik Walter Ulbrichts auf der 14. Tagung des ZK der SED 1970," in SAP J PA J NL 2/32. Zdeněk Mlynář, a key figure in the Prague Spring, paints an unflattering portrait of Ulbricht and Polish leader Gomułka as "hostile, vain, and senile old men," who were from the outset highly critical of Dubček and urged the Kremlin to take firm action. See Zdeněk Mlynář, *Nightfrost in Prague* (New York: Karz Publishers, 1989), 153–56.

17. See Ulbricht's lengthy (four hours and twenty minutes) exchange with Gromyko, "Stenografische Niederschrift des Gespräches des Genossen Walter Ulbricht mit dem Genossen Andrej Gromyko," February 24, 1970, in SAP, JIV 2/201/1108

18. See Larrabee, "The Politics of Reconciliation," chap. 4.

19. William E. Griffith, *The Ostpolitik of the Federal Republic of Germany* (Cambridge, Mass.: MIT Press, 1978), 198.

20. Melvin Croan, *East Germany: The Soviet Connection*. Washington Papers, no. 36 (Beverly Hills, Calif.: Sage Publications, 1976), 26.

21. "Zur korrektur der Wirtschaftspolitik Walter Ulbrichts auf der 14. Tagung des ZK der SED 1970."

22. Brezhnev to Honecker, July 28, 1970, SAP, J PA J NL 2/32.

23. "Vermerk über die gemeinsame Besprechung der Delegation des ZK der KPSU mit der Delegation des ZK der SED am 21.8.1970" (Moscow), SAP, J PA NL 2/32.

24. Letter to Brezhnev and the Soviet Politburo from the SED Politburo (minus Ulbricht), January 21, 1971, SAP, J PA NL 2/32.

25. "Rede des Genossen Walter Ulbricht auf der Sitzung der Bezirksleitung in Leipzig, 21.11.1970," SAP J PA NL 2/32.

26. The Quadripartite Agreement was the first agreement since Berlin was divided to regulate ties between the western and eastern halves.

27. "Zu dem Gen. L. I. Breschnew," August 1970, SAP J PA NL 2/32.

28. According to Yuli Kvitsinsky, who was then working in the Foreign Ministry, the GDR-FRG agreements were negotiated without consultation with the Soviet leadership, arousing considerable suspicion in Moscow. See Kwizinskij, *Vor dem Sturm*, 260.

29. See Stent, "Soviet Policy toward the German Democratic Republic," 33–60.

30. Helmut Schmidt, *Grand Strategy for the West* (New Haven, Conn.: Yale University Press, 1984), 54.

31. For details, see Stent, *From Embargo to Ostpolitik*, 202–7.

32. Kremer, *FRG: Etapy "Vostochnoi Politiki,"* 162.

33. Ibid., 134–36. The Soviets claimed that the agreement applied only to West Berlin; the Americans, French, and British argued that it applied to the whole of Berlin.

34. For the Alastair Buchan Memorial Lecture, see *Helmut Schmidt: Perspectives on Politics*, ed. Wolfram F. Hanrieder, (Boulder, Colo.: Westview Press, 1982), chap. 2.

35. See Walter F. Hahn, "West Germany's Ostpolitik: The Grand Design of Egon Bahr," *Orbis* 16, no. 4 (1974): 859–80. See also Egon Bahr, *Was wird aus den Deutschen?* (Reinbeck bei Hamburg: Rohwolt, 1982).

36. Stent, "Soviet Policy toward the German Democratic Republic," 44–47.

37. Ibid.

38. Wjatscheslaw Keworkow, *Der geheime Kanal* (Berlin: Rohwolt, 1995), 151, 179–180. Erich Mielke, the East German Stasi (secret police) chief, apparently even complained that Brezhnev had sent Brandt a more lavish birthday gift (two kilos of caviar) than he had sent to Honecker. Such was the stuff of GDR-Soviet ties. Egon Bahr, in an afterword to Keworkow's book, writes that a major change during this period was that Moscow's view of the FRG was now shaped more by West German than by East German sources. Clearly, the GDR was losing its role as the chief Soviet interlocutor on the situation in the Federal Republic.

39. Kwizinskij, *Vor dem Sturm*, 260–66

40. Ronald D. Asmus, "The Dialectics of Détente and Discord: The Moscow–East Berlin–Bonn Triangle," *Orbis* 28 (Winter 1985): 743–74.

41. A. James McAdams, "Inter-German Detente: A New Balance," *Foreign Affairs* 65, no. 2 (Winter 1986) 141–43.

42. See Stent, "Soviet Policy Toward the German Democratic Republic," 57.

43. Ibid.

44. Falin, *Politische Erinnerungen*, 239.

45. For a representative view of these issues by a respected conservative scholar, see Boris Meissner, "Die deutsch-sowjetischen Beziehungen seit dem Zweiten Weltkrieg," *Osteuropa* 35, no. 9 (1985): 644–45, when he writes that the 1970 treaty was "a noticeable success for Soviet diplomacy."

46. For more on this debate, see Sodaro, *Moscow, Germany and the West From Khrushchev to Gorbachev*, chap. 9.

47. See Arbatov, *The System*, 203–6. He quotes a "leading arms designer responding to the question about whether the Soviet military really anticipated that there would be a nuclear war. "No," he answered, "If anything, the military leaders are convinced there won't be a nuclear war. And that's exactly the reason why they go on happily building the most dangerous new weapons systems available."

48. *Krasnaia zvezda*, May 9, 1984.

49. *Pravda*, July 27, 1984.

50. See the remarks by Vadim Zagladin, first deputy chief of the International Department of the Central Committee, CPSU, and by Lev Bezymensky, in *Zukunft Europas: Probleme der politischen und militärischen Entspannung: UdSSR und Bundesrepublik Deutschland*, Bergedorfer Gesprächskreis, Protokoll no. 75 (Hamburg: Körber Stiftung, 1984) 25, 83.

51. *Pravda*, January 27, 1986.

52. See Oldenberg, "Eine endliche Geschichte," 15–16, who quotes SED archives on these issues.

53. The author attended a conference run by the Hanns Seidel–Stiftung, an organization of the Bavarian CSU, shortly after the granting of loan, which had caused a mild sensation in both Germanies. At the conference, CSU officials took a hard line on the Soviets, and had some difficulty defending the decision to help Honecker, a man whom they reviled.

54. Hans-Dietrich Genscher, "How Will East-West Relations Develop in 1984?" (March 30, 1984), speech distributed by the German embassy, Washington, D.C.

55. Richard Löwenthal, "The German Question Transformed," *Foreign Affairs* 63, no. 2 (Winter 1984–85): 313.

56. Ash, in *In Europe's Name*, demonstrates the many ways in which successive West German governments' dealings with the GDR served to bolster its legitimacy. Craig Whitney, in *Spy Trader* (New York: Times Books, 1993) details how the East and West Germans dealt secretly with each other on questions relating to espionage. Some have argued that the West German foreign ministry archives, which now house the East German foreign ministry archives, are not being opened because they would reveal a variety of dealings with the GDR that Bonn would rather not publicize.

57. For the documentary evidence from the archives, see Fred Oldenburg and Gerd-Rüdiger Stephan, "Honecker kam nicht nach Bonn," *Deutschland Archiv*, no. 8 (August 1995): 791–806.

Chapter Three
Rethinking the German Question

1. Georgi Shakhnazarov, *Tsena svobody* (Moscow: Rossika, 1993), 119.

2. Mikhail Gorbachev, *Zhizn' i reformy*, vol. 2 (Moscow: Novosti, 1995), 152.

3. Eduard Shevardnadze, *The Future Belongs to Freedom* (New York: Free Press, 1991), 31. Shevardnadze writes that he knew as early as 1986 that German

unification was inevitable. This may be a post facto rationalization, but Shevardnadze does seem to have been more prescient than many others around Gorbachev.

4. George F. Kennan ("X"), "The Sources of Soviet Conduct," reprinted in *Soviet Foreign Policy. Classic and Contemporary Issues,* ed. Frederic Fleron, Erik P. Hoffmann, and Robbin F. Laird (New York: Aldine de Gruyter, 1991), 316. This book also contains a good selection of the main arguments about the nature of Soviet foreign policy.

5. John Lewis Gaddis, discussing the meaning of newly released Soviet archives in *We Now Know,* stresses the importance of ideological factors in guiding Soviet policy during the Cold War.

6. See Robert Legvold, "The Revolution in Soviet Foreign Policy," *Foreign Affairs: America and the World 1988/89* 68, no. 1 (Winter 1988–89): 821–98; Seweryn Bialer, "New Thinking and Soviet Foreign Policy," *Survival* 30, no. 4 (July/August 1988): 291–309.

7. Author's interview with Mikhail S. Gorbachev, Moscow, July 1996.

8. Mikhail S. Gorbachev, *Perestroika* (New York: Harper and Row, 1987), 140–41.

9. Ibid., chap. 3. Vadim Medvedev, "Velikii Oktiabr' i Sovremennyi Mir," *Kommunist,* no. 2 (1988): 3–18.

10. Eduard Shevardnadze, "The 19th All-Union CPSU Conference: Foreign Policy and Diplomacy," *International Affairs,* no. 10 (Moscow) (October 1988): 1–34. For a critical analysis of efforts to reform the Foreign Service, see Yevgenii Shmagin and Igor Bratchikov, "Perestoika in the USSR Foreign Ministry," ibid., no 3 (March 1989): 42–53.

11. For the origins of this term (it was used by Brezhnev during his 1981 visit to Bonn) and a discussion of its significance, see Hannes Adomeit, "Gorbatschows Westpolitik," *Osteuropa* 38, no. 6 (1988): 418–46.

12. Yurii Zhukov, "What Kind of Dialogue for Europeans?" *International Affairs* (Moscow), no. 7 (July 1987): 93.

13. Mikhail Amirdzhanov and Mikhail Cherkasov, "Our Common European Home," ibid., no. 1 (January 1989): 28.

14. Vladimir Baranovskii, "Stroitel'stvo 'Obshchego evropeiskogo doma': politicheskie i ekonomicheskie aspekty" (Institute of World Economy and International Relations, Moscow, 1987, mimeographed).

15. Nikolai Portugalov, "Bonn Goalkeepers," *New Times,* no. 22 (1987): 12.

16. Cited in Neil Malcolm, "The 'Common European Home' and Soviet European Policy," *International Affairs* (London) 65, no. 4 (1989): 659–76.

17. *Pravda,* April 28, 1985.

18. See Karen Dawisha, *Eastern Europe, Gorbachev and Reform* (Cambridge: Cambridge University Press, 1989), 202–6.

19. *Pravda,* February 25, 1986.

20. Aleksandr Yakovlev, interviewed in *Die Zeit,* May 12, 1989. In the 1970s and 1980s, Western observers had worried about the "Finlandization" of Western Europe, fearing that Western Europe would go too far in accomodating Soviet demands. Now Yakovlev was proposing a new idea—the "Finlandization" of Eastern Europe, implying more domestic autonomy.

21. Shakhnazarov, *Tsena svobody*, 95–100, stresses how long it took for Gorbachev to realize the full implications of what was happening in Eastern Europe. Other Soviet participants in the events leading to German unification are less charitable, describing Gorbachev as a "provincial politician" who did not understand the situation in Eastern Europe and did not pay enough attention to it.

22. Angela Stent, "Doctrinal Discord," *New Republic*, January 8 and 15, 1990.

23. Author's conversation with Rafael Fyodorov, Central Committee headquarters, Moscow, September 1989.

24. Gorbachev, *Perestroika*, 177.

25. Author's conversation with Gorbachev, Moscow, July 1996.

26. Günter Schabowski, *Der Absturz* (Berlin: Rohwolt, 1991), 197.

27. Quoted in Peter Bender, *Deutsche Parallelen* (Berlin: Siedler Verlag, 1989), 125.

28. Ibid., 211. In November 1985, as part of a general Politburo shakeup, Honecker had fired the East Berlin party boss, Konrad Naumann, who had opposed his commitment to inter-German détente, and replaced him with Schabowski. See Bundesminister füer innerdeutsche Beziehungen, *Informationen*, December 12, 1985, 12–13, 20–21.

29. Gorbachev, *Zhizn' i reformy*, 1:155–56.

30. TASS, quoted in Wolfgang Seiffert, "Die Deutschlandpolitik der SED im Spannungsfeld der Sowjetischen Interessenlage," *Deutschland Archiv*, no. 3 (March 1987): 280.

31. Ilse Spitmann, "Gorbatschow besucht die SED," ibid., no. 5 (May 1986): 449–51.

32. Schabowski, *Der Absturz*, 214.

33. Elizabeth Pond, *Beyond the Wall* (Washington, D.C.: Brookings Institution, 1993), 81–82.

34. Gorbachev, *Zhizn' i reformy*, 2: 405, 407. Gorbachev's depiction of the close Brezhnev-Honecker relationship contrasts with descriptions of a tense relationship between the two in the memoirs of a number of other Soviet and East German officials.

35. An incident described by Helmut Kohl shows vividly just how close these ties were. He recalls the first time he met Honecker, at Andropov's funeral in 1984. In order to have a conversation that the KGB might not be able to understand, he proposed to Honecker that they speak *pfälzisch*, the dialect spoken both in Kohl's home town of Ludwigshafen and in Honecker's Saarland birthplace, Becksbach. Honecker laughed loudly at this suggestion, and they conducted an intense conversation, discovering that they had many common acquaintances from their home towns which were only eighty kilometers apart. Helmut Kohl, *Ich wollte Deutschlands Einheit* (Berlin: Propyläen-Verlag 1996), 54.

36. *Neues Deutschland*, September 11, 1987.

37. Alexander Tolpegin, "Realities and Illusions," *New Times*, no. 38 (1987): 4. Kochemasov also notes that not once during the summit did Kohl raise the question of human rights in the GDR or of the Berlin Wall. Wjatscheslaw Kotschemassow, *Meine letzte Mission* (Berlin: Deitz, 1994), 271.

38. See, for instance, the bitter attack in a letter to Honecker of December 1,

1986, by Hermann Axen, the party secretary responsible for international affairs, on an article by Soviet Central Committee official Vadim Zagladin, responsible for the international communist movement, that was published in the West German communist party's theoretical journal, *Marxistische Blätter*. After attacking Zagaldin's undialectical thinking, Axen complains that Gorbachev promised a joint SED-CPSU analysis of the international communist movement, but the International Department of the CPSU had done nothing to promote this project. Zentrales Parteiarchiv, Berlin, Büro Hermann Axen. IV 2/2.035/63.

39. Kotschemassow, *Meine letzte Mission*, 132.

40. Honecker, cited in Günter Schabowski, *Das Politburo* (Reinbek bei Hamburg: Rohwolt, 1990), 34. Hager in *Neues Deutschland*, April 10, 1987.

41. Author's conversation with Gorbachev, Moscow, July 1996.

42. See, for instance, Doris Cornelsen, "Die Lage der DDR-Wirtschaft zur Jahreswende 1987/88," Deutsches Institut für Wirtschaftsforschung, *Wochenbericht*, no. 5 (1988): 59–67.

43. Hans-Dieter Schulz, "In der Welt ohne Beispiel: Sowjethandel der DDR: Qualität stärker steigern als Quantität," *Deutschland Archiv*, no. 12 (December 1985): 1249–50.

44. Heinrich Machowski, "Grundzüge der neuen sowjetischen Aussenwirtschaftspolitik," *Aus Politik und Zeitgeschichte*, November 7, 1987, 21–23.

45. Kotschemassow, *Meine letzte Mission*, 85–86.

46. Shakhnazarov, *Tsena svobody*, 122.

47. See A. James McAdams, *Germany Divided* (Princeton, N.J.: Princeton University Press, 1993), 180.

48. Daniel Küchenmeister, "Wann Begann das Zerwürfnis zwischen Gorbachev und Honecker? *Deutschland Archiv*, (January 1993): 30–40.

49. Author's conversation with Igor Maxymichev, Moscow, July 1996.

50. Schabowski, *Der Absturz*, 217. See also Hamilton, "Division, Revolution, Unification," 24, 25, and McAdams, *Germany Divided*, 180.

51. "Einschätzung der Rede M. Gortbatschows auf der XIX. Parteikonferenz der KPSU," Zentrales Parteiarchiv, Büro Hermann Axen, IV 2/2.035.

52. Author's interviews with Igor Maximychev and Nikolai Portugalov, Moscow, July 1997. Markus Wolf, in *Spionagechef im Geheimen Krieg* (Munich: List Verlag, 1997), 435, claims that even at the Eleventh SED Party Congress, Gorbachev and his advisors were rethinking their German priorities.

53. See Gorbachev's interview in *Der Spiegel*, October 24, 1988. See also Gorbachev, *Zhizn' i reformy*, 1:165–67.

54. Shakhnazarov, *Tsena svobody*, 120.

55. Nikolai Portugalov told the author that the ideal of the *Germanisty* was the period of the Soviet-German military collaboration during the 1920s. In his unpublished memoirs (p. 1), he states that they wanted to restore a geostrategic alliance with a united Germany and considered "the one-sided Soviet fixation with the USA for better or worse as a fatal flaw."

56. Kwizinskij, *Vor dem Sturm*, 427. See also Gorbachev, *Zhizn' i reformy*, 2:702. He praises Strauss as a strong "realist."

57. Hans-Dietrich Genscher, *Erinnerungen* (Berlin: Siedler, 1995), 493–502.

58. Nikolai Portugalov, "Cloudy with Sunny Intervals," *New Times*, no. 31

(1986) 14. In conversations with the author, Portugalov claimed that he did not believe much of what he wrote about Germany, knowing the reality to be very different, and another German expert, Daniil Melnikov, echoed this sentiment. One assumes, however, that these articles served some purpose for the USSR.

59. See Pond, *Beyond the Wall,* 51–52. See also Genscher, *Erinnerungen,* chap. 15.

60. Joan F. Mcintyre, "Soviet Attempts to Revamp the Foreign Trade Sector," in U.S. Congress, Joint Economic Committee, *Gorbachev's Economic Plans,* vol. 2 (Washington, D.C., 1987), 466–99.

61. Otto Wolff von Amerongen, *Der Weg nach Osten* (Munich: Droemer Knaur, 1992), 182–84.

62. See Iu. Borko, "O nekotorykh aspektakh izucheniia protsessov zapadnoevropeiskoi integratsii," *MEMO,* no. 2 (1988) 35–50; compared to Iu. Shishkov, "Evropeiskoe soobshchestvo na perelomom rubezhe," ibid., no. 6 (1986): 40–53.

63. Thane Gustafson, *Gorbachev's Dilemmas* (Cambridge, Mass.: Cambridge Energy Research Associates Private Report, 1989).

64. "Die Perestroika greift noch nicht," Deutsches Institut für Wirtschaftsforschung, *Wochenbericht,* no. 33 (1988): 425–22; "Ost-West Handel stagniert," ibid., no. 46 (1987): 628–34.

65. Oleg Bogomolow, "Perestroika und die Aussichten für die Wirtschaftsbeziehungen zwischen Ost und West," *Europa-Archiv,* 43, no. 16 (1988): 449–58.

66. Wolff, *Der Weg nach Osten,* 179.

67. Gorbachev depicts a nervous Späth almost begging for a summit and reproaching the Soviet leader for visiting France and Great Britain before West Germany. See Gorbachev, *Zhizn' i reformy,* 2:153–54.

68. Marie Lavigne, "Prospects for Soviet Trade Reform," Paper presented at the Institute for Defense Analysis, Alexandria, Va. (February 23, 1989), 30.

69. Kwizinskij, *Vor dem Sturm,* 396–97.

70. Ibid., pp. 408–11; Genscher, *Erinnerungen,* 502–8.

71. *Newsweek,* October 27, 1986, p. 29.

72. In his memoirs, Gorbachev characterizes Kohl's statement by claiming that Kohl likened new political thinking to Goebbels's propaganda. Gorbachev, *Zhizn' i reformy,* 2:152.

73. "Opasnii atavizm," *Pravda,* November 27, 1986.

74. Kwizinkij, *Vor dem Sturm,* 419–21; Dettmar Cramer, "Der Bundespräsident in der Sowjetunion," *Deutschland Archiv* (August 1987) 792–94. In his memoirs, Anatoly Cherniaev, a major Gorbachev advisor, interprets Gorbachev's remarks thus: "History, as we see, decided much earlier than in a hundred years. But something is more important: Gorbachev did not exclude the reunification of Germany. And his signal was understood." Anatoly Cherniaiev, *Shest' let s Gorbachevym* (Moscow: Progress, 1993), 154.

75. Gorbachev evaluates the summit very positively, implying that the West Germans had finally come round to the Soviet view of the world. Gorbachev, *Zhizn' i reformy,* 1:154–56.

76. *Pravda,* October 30, 1988. COCOM was the NATO-led coordinating

committee based in Paris that regulated technology transfer to communist countries. For a full account of the summit, see "Dokumente zum Besuch von Bundeskanzler Helmut Kohl in Moskau vom 24. bis zum 27. Oktober 1988," *Europa-Archiv* 43, no. 21 (1988): D615–D634.

77. Nikita Zholkver, "The Frontier," *New Times*, no. 32 (1986): 21.

78. "UdSSR Sprecher zum Status von Berlin (West)", Bundesminister für innerdeutsche Beziehungen, *Informationen*, no. 20, October 30, 1987, 11.

79. *FAZ*, January 20, 1988.

80. Some Soviet diplomats, in retrospect, regretted that the four-power mechanisms were not used more actively in Berlin. See Igor Maksimychev, "A Missed Chance of Four-Power Cooperation in Berlin," *International Affairs* (Moscow), no. 4–5 (1995): 108–111.

81. *Pravda*, October 24, 1988.

82. See the forum on the accord in *Deutschland Archiv* (September 1985) 912–48.

83. For the text of the original statement, see *Neues Deutschland*, August 28, 1987.

84. For the final text, see "Das gemeinsame Papier von SED und SPD und die Reaktion der SED," *Deutschland Archiv*, (January 1988): 86–108.

85. Olga Alexandrova, *Die neuen sozialen Bewegungen im Westen aus der Sicht der sowjetischen Ideologie und Gesellschaftswissenschaft*, BIOST, Bericht Nr. 57, (Cologne, 1988).

86. Fred Oldenburg, "'Neues Denken' in der Sowjetischen Deutschlandpolitik?" *Europa-Archiv* 42 (November 1987): 1154–60.

87. V. I. Dashichev, "Nekotorye aspekty 'Germanskoi Problemy,'" unpublished ms., November 21, 1987, given by Dashichev to the author.

88. Author's conversations with Dashichev and Yuri Davydov of the Institute of the USA and Canada, Moscow, July 1995, the only participant to support Dashichev's views. See also Viacheslav Dashichev, "Soviet Policy and German Unification," Paper presented to the XVIth World Congress of the International Political Science Association (Berlin, August 21–25, 1994).

89. Gorbachev, *Zhizn' i reformy*, 2:409 ff. He attributes this phrase to disgruntled members of the SED Politburo.

Chapter Four
Wir Sind Ein Volk

1. Helmut Kohl's press conference, Moscow, 1988, cited in *Financial Times*, August 28, 1990.

2. *Neues Deutschland*, January 20, 1989.

3. Igor Maksimychev and Hans Modrow, *Posledny god GDR* (Moscow: Mezhdunarodnie Otnoshenia, 1993), 27.

4. See the works by Baker, Cherniaev, Falin, Genscher, Gorbachev, Kießler and Elbe, Kwizinskij, Kotschemassow, Schäuble, Teltschik, Waigel, and Zelikow and Rice cited below.

5. For details, see Eugene B. Rumer, *The German Question in Moscow's "Com-*

mon European Home": *A Background to the Revolutions of 1989*, A RAND Note, N-3220-USDP (Santa Monica, Calif.: RAND Corporation, 1991), 14–15.

6. James A. Baker III, *The Politics of Diplomacy* (New York: Putnam, 1995), 159.

7. Don Oberdorfer, *The Turn* (New York: Poseidon Press, 1991), 350–52; policy statement by Chancellor Helmut Kohl on the NATO summit in Brussels and on the visit by President George Bush to the Federal Republic of Germany, Bonn, June 1, 1989, *Statements and Speeches* 12, no. 13, June 5, 1989 (New York: German Information Center); Genscher, *Erinnerungen*, 614–24

8. In his memoirs, Gorbachev vividly depicts the emotions he felt at this West German outpouring. Enthusiastic crowds in Bonn's Rathausplatz called out to him, "Gorbi! Make love, not walls," and urged him to continue his policies. Gorbachev, *Zhizn' i reformy*, 2:706.

9. *Der Spiegel*, June 5 and 12, 1989. When the author interviewed young professional Germans in July 1989 about why their views of Gorbachev were so much more positive and enthusiastic than their evaluations of Kohl or Bush, she was told, "We started off with different expectations and standards for Gorbachev."

10. "Obraz Nemtsa i FRG v SSSR," *Moskovskie novosti*, June 18, 1989.

11. Gorbachev, *Zhizn' i reformy*, 2:158–59.

12. *New York Times*, June 14, 1989.

13. Wolff von Amerongen, *Der Weg nach Osten*, 181.

14. For Gorbachev's speech to the Ostaussschuss, and other documents from the summit, see "Der Besuch des sowjetischen Partei-und Staatschefs Michail Gorbatschow in der Bundesrepublik Deutschland im Juni 1989," *Europa-Archiv*, 44, no. 13 (1989): D371–19.

15. See Magarditsch A. Hatschikjan and Wolfgang Pfeiler, "Deutsch-sowjetische Beziehungen in einer Periode der Ost-West Annäherung, *Deutschland Archiv*, no. 8 (August 1989): 883–89, for details of all these agreements and problems over Berlin.

16. Genscher, *Erinnerungen*, 23, quotes Shevardnadze as placing this declaration in the context of a recognition that the GDR was in serious trouble.

17. For the text of the Joint Declaration, see Karl Kaiser, *Deutschlands Vereinigung* (Bergisch Gladbach: Gustav Lubbe Verlag, 1991), 143–48.

18. See Hannes Adomeit, "Gorbachev and German Unification," *Problems of Communism* 39, no. 4 (July–August 1990): 1–23.

19. *Pravda*, June 16, 1989.

20. Genscher, *Erinnerungen*, 628.

21. Kwizinskij, *Vor dem Sturm*, 433.

22. These rumors have been circulated by both Russians and Germans. Gorbachev also fueled them inasmuch as he subsequently told people that Kohl made promises that were never delivered.

23. Kohl, *Ich wollte Deutschlands Einheit*, 44.

24. Kotschemassow, *Meine letzte Mission*, 62–63.

25. Genscher, *Erinnerungen*, 589.

26. Author's interview with Gorbachev, Moscow, July 1996; Sergei Tarasenko, quoted in Hamilton, "Division, Revolution, Unification," 24.

27. Charles Gati, *The Bloc That Failed* (Bloomington: Indiana University Press, 1992), 167–68.

28. Sodaro, *Moscow, Germany and the West*, 375.

29. *Pravda*, June 29, 1989.

30. "Vstrecha M. S. Gorbacheva s E. Honekkerom," *Vestnik MID* (July 1989): 1–3.

31. Jonathan Greenwald, *Berlin Witness* (University Park: Pennsylvania State University Press, 1993), 52–53.

32. Kotschemassow, *Meine letzte Mission*, 156.

33. Only 10–12 percent of those who went to the polls voted against the SED and allied parties, but the regime reflexively felt the need to report that 98.5 percent of the population had voted for the SED.

34. Vyacheslav Dashichev, "Changing Europe: Soviet and American Approaches" (Institute of The World Socialist Economic System, Moscow, September 1989, mimeographed).

35. Adomeit, "Gorbachev and German Unification," 6.

36. Schabowski, *Der Absturz*, 222.

37. Genscher, *Erinnerungen*, 637–41.

38. Gyula Horn, *Freiheit, die ich meine: Erinnerungen des ungarischen Außenministers, der den Eisernen Vorhang öffnete* (Hamburg: Hoffmann und Campe, 1991), 327.

39. Kohl, *Ich wollte Deutschlands Einheit*, 75, took this to mean that Gorbachev had already given the Hungarians his assent.

40. Kochemasov describes the Soviet concern about and discomfort with the Hungarian decision. Kotschemassow, *Meine letzte Mission*, 163–64. He also says that both the West Germans and Hungarians knew very well what the consequences of these actions might be. But, says Kochemasov bitterly, Bonn had paid DM 800 million for this "service." Ibid., 188.

41. Schabowski, *Der Absturz*, 222; Reinhold Andert and Wolfgang Herzberg, *Der Sturz* (Berlin and Weimar: Aufbau-Verlag, 1990), 66.

42. Genscher, *Erinnerungen*, 648–50. According to *Der Spiegel*, October 9, 1989, Genscher used British publisher Robert Maxwell as an intermediary to thank Honecker for permitting the Prague standoff to be peacefully resolved and to ask that the GDR allow the same treatment for new potential emigrants. Honecker replied through Maxwell that he very much wanted to preserve good relations with the Federal Republic.

43. "He said to me several times, 'Tolya, I don't want to go. I will be in a spurious, embarrassing position. I don't want to go, but on the other hand I don't want to embarrass Honecker by just not showing up.'" Transcript of talk by Anatoly Cherniaev, Cold War Endgame: Conference held at Princeton University, March 29, 1996 (unpaginated).

44. Falin, *Politische Erinnerungen*, 484; Shakhnazarov, *Tsena svobody*, 123.

45. Gorbachev had become so popular and the Soviet Union appeared to be so benign in contrast to the GDR that GDR refugees even sought asylum in the Soviet embassy in East Berlin as a means of emigrating to West Germany!

46. Gorbachev, *Zhizn' i reformy*, 2:934.

47. *Pravda*, October 7, 1989.

48. Gorbachev, *Zhizn' i reformy*, 2:935, confirms that he was referring to the Soviet situation when he spoke these words, but he went on to tell Honecker, "Life demands courageous decisions from you."

49. Schabowski, *Der Absturz*, 241–42; Egon Krenz, *Wenn Mauern fallen* (Berlin: Paul Neff Verlag, 1990), 96. For a text of the Gorbachev-Honecker discussions, see *Der Spiegel*, September 16, 1991, 101–10. Kochemasov, in *Meine letzte Mission*, 163–68, criticizes Gorbachev for not being more honest with Honecker about Soviet views of what was happening in the GDR.

50. Falin, *Politische Erinnerungen*, 487. Maxymichev claims that although he and others in the 150-person Soviet embassy in East Berlin (the largest Soviet embassy in the world) understood the real situation, they never sent any honest cables to Moscow because "The ambassador only told Moscow what the Kremlin wanted to hear." Author's conversation with Maxymichev, Moscow, July 1996.

51. Author's conversations with people involved in the October 1989 Leipzig demonstration, Leipzig, March 1990.

52. Krenz, *Wenn Mauern fallen*, 134–40. In 1992, Krenz somewhat modified his story. See Egon Krenz, "Annmerkung zur Öffnung der Berliner Mauer im Herbst 1989," *Osteuropa* 42 (April 1992): 364–69.

53. Kotschemassow, *Meine letzte Mission*, 168–69. See also the article by Stanislav Kondrashev in *Izvestiia*, April 29, 1990. Brandt (*SZ*, December 14, 1989) and others have claimed that Soviet troops were given the order already in August not to interfere with expressions of domestic discontent in Eastern Europe.

54. Jeffrey Gedmin, in *The Hidden Hand* (Washington, D.C.: American Enterprise Press, 1992), 101–2, gives credence to all of these reports.

55. One of the more surprising comments comes from the former director of the Central Intelligence Agency, who claims that Krenz "made common cause with the marchers, joining the revolt." See Robert M. Gates, *From the Shadows* (New York: Simon and Schuster, 1996), 468.

56. Pond, *Beyond The Wall*, presents the most persuasive and balanced argument on these issues, chap. 9.

57. Igor Maximytscjew, "Die Maueröffnung," *Deutschland Archiv*, no. 11 (1994): 1141–42.

58. Schabowski, *Der Absturz*, 261.

59. Kotschemassow, *Meine letzte Mission*, 176.

60. Shakhnazarov, *Tsena svobody*, 124.

61. This account is taken from Krenz's notes on the meeting, cited in Philip Zelikow and Condoleeza Rice, *Germany Unified and Europe Transformed* (Cambridge, Mass.: Harvard University Press, 1995), 86–92.

62. Krenz, *Wenn Mauern fallen*, 149–50; Krenz, "Annmerkung zur Öffnung der Berliner Mauer im Herbst 1989," 366–67. Maxymitschew, "Die Maueröffnung," 1143, cites messages from Gorbachev stressing his satisfaction with the meeting.

63. On the same day, Todor Zhivkov, Bulgaria's longtime leader, was ousted in a Soviet-backed palace coup, but the breaching of the Wall was so dramatic and symbolic of the demise of the Cold War that the world scarcely noticed the fall of the first Balkan domino.

64. Kwizinskij, *Vor dem Sturm*, 13.

65. Markus Wolf, *In eigenem Auftrag*, (Munich: Schneekluth, 1991), 146. Wolf writes that, during this July trip to Moscow, he was surprised by how much his interlocutors were concerned with the question of German unification.

66. Maximytschew, "Die Maueröffnung," 1145.

67. Ibid., 239.

68. Kotschemassow, *Meine letzte Mission*, 186–87.

69. Igor Maksimychev, "Berlinskaia stena," *Nezavisimaia gazeta*, November 10, 1993; and "Was ist bei euch los?" *Der Spiegel*, October 31, 1994.

70. TASS in English, November 9, 1989, cited in FBIS-SOV-89-216, November 9, 1989, 28.

71. Schabowski, *Der Absturz*, 307–8. He also says that in reading out the law, he was surprised to find West Berlin mentioned and wondered whether the Soviets knew about it. Krenz, *Wenn Mauern fallen*, chap. 3, claims that Schabowski made a mistake in saying that the law would go into effect immediately. The text of the law ibid., 180–81.

72. Schabowksi, *Der Absturz*, 309–10; Krenz, *Wenn Mauern fallen*, 183.

73. Hans-Hermann Hertle, "Kontrollen Eingestellt—nicht mehr in der Lage—Punkt," interview with Harald Jaeger, *Deutschland Archiv*, no. 11 (1995): 1126–34.

74. ADN in English, November 14, 1989, in FBIS-SOV-89-218, November 14, 1989, 35.

75. Falin, *Politische Erinnerungen*, 488–89.

76. Maximytscjew, "Was ist bei euch los?" 46.

77. Maksimychev, "Berlinskaia stena."

78. Interview with Eduard Shevardnadze, "Otstavka bol'she, chem zhizn'," *Literaturnaia gazeta*, April 10, 1991. Some of the reformist Soviets have explicitly claimed that Falin and other old German hands tried to stop the Wall from being opened.

79. Maksimychev, "Berlinskaia stena,"; Hans-Hermann Hertle, "Ein Stein vom Herzen," *Der Spiegel*, November 4, 1994, 40–41.

80. This was later confirmed by Krenz in an interview. See David Pryce-Jones, *The Strange Death of the Soviet Empire* (New York: Henry Holt, 1995), 266.

81. Cherniaev, talk at Cold War Endgame Conference, claims that Defense Minister Marshal Yazov never raised the issue of using Soviet troops against East Germany because he knew that Gorbachev would not have permitted it.

82. Krenz, "Annmerkung zur Öffnung der Berliner Mauer im Herbst 1989," 368–69.

83. Shakhnazarov, *Tsena svobody*, 124.

84. Author's interview with Gorbachev, Moscow, July 1996.

85. Michael Beschloss and Strobe Talbott, *At the Highest Levels*, (Boston: Little, Brown, 1994), 132.

86. Cherniaev, *Shest' let s Gorbachevym*, 305, gives a transcript of the phone conversation between Kohl and Gorbachev.

87. Horst Teltschik, *329 Tage*, (Berlin: Siedler Verlag, 1991), 19–201; Kwizinskij, *Vor dem Sturm*, 15. Kvitsinsky says of the November 10 gathering that he could physically feel that reunification was happening and that the GDR on longer existed.

88. Kohl, *Ich wollte Deutschlands Einheit*, 131–32, notes that hardliners in the KGB and Stasi were deliberately feeding Gorbachev misinformation about how things were completely out of control in Berlin, hoping to use this to justify military intervention.

89. Teltschik, *329 Tage*, 63.

90. Margaret Thatcher, *The Downing Street Years* (London: Harper Collins, 1995), 782, argues that she opposed unification and believed that a united Europe would augment, not check, German power.

91. For the text of the plan, see Kaiser, *Deutschlands Vereinigung*, 158–68.

92. See the interview with Deutsche Bank President Alfred Herrhausen in *Der Spiegel*, November 20, 1989.

93. Genscher attributes Kohl's moves in part to jealousy over Genscher's own role in defusing the refugee situation in Prague and in part to preempt both the FDP and the SPD. Genscher, *Erinnerungen*, 669–74. Baker, *The Politics of Diplomacy*, 116, remarks that "we would have preferred to have heard about the plan before it was announced."

94. Teltschik, *329 Tage*, 52–53, 58.

95. Cherniaev, *Shest' let s Gorbachevym*, 305–9; Gorbachev, *Zhizn' i reformy*, 2:712–14.

96. Genscher, *Erinnerungen*, 687.

97. Beschloss and Talbott, *At the Highest Levels*, 157; Oberdorfer, *The Turn*, 383.

98. Cherniaev, talk at Cold War Endgame Conference. Anatoly Dobrynin, *In Confidence* (New York: Random House, 1995), 630, confirms that the fact that Gorbachev had not rejected unification was not lost on President Bush.

99. Zelikow and Rice, *Germany Unified and Europe Transformed*, 130.

100. Pavel Palazchenko, *My Years With Gorbachev and Shevardnadze* (University Park, Pa.: Pennsylvania State University Press: 1997), 185–91.

101. For text of Shevardnadze's speech, see "Evropa: Vremia peremen," *Pravda*, December 20, 1989.

102. Dashichev, "Soviet Policy and German Unification," 25.

103. Kotschemassow, *Meine letzte Mission*, 212.

104. Gregor Gysi, *Das war's noch lange Nicht* (Düsseldorf: Econ, 1995), 110.

105. TASS, December 12, 1989, quoted in *The Soviet Union 1990/91*, BIOST, Sonderveröffentlichung, (Cologner, February 1992), 102.

106. Genscher, *Erinnerungen*, 693.

107. Maksimychev, "A Missed Chance of Four-Power Cooperation in Berlin," 108–15.

108. Throughout this period, the armed forces newspaper, *Krasnaia zvezda*, as might have been expected, stressed the importance of communism in the GDR and the dangers of West German neofascism. See *Krasnaia zvezda*, December 6 and 30, 1989, and January 9, 1990.

109. Wolfgang Schäuble, minister of the interior in the FRG, who was largely responsible for negotiating the internal details of unification, recalls that, when he first proposed immediate currency and economic union between the two German states in the middle of December, his colleagues' reaction was reserved. After all, economic union meant finally "thinking the unthinkable," and they were not

ready for that. See Wolfgang Schäuble, *Der Vertrag*, (Stuttgart: Deutsche Verlag-sanstalt, 1992), 21–22.

110. Eberhard Schneider, "Der Letzte Parteitag der SED," BIOST, Bericht Nr. 19 (1990): 51.

111. *Pravda*, February 7, 1990.

112. For accounts of this meeting, see Shakhnazarov, *Tsena svobody*, 125, Cherniaev, *Shest' let s Gorbachevym*, 346–47; and Gorbachev, *Zhizn' i reformy*, 2:714–715. It is notable that these crucial decisions on German unity were made by an ad hoc committee, and not by an established institution such as the Polit-buro. According to Cherniaev, Princeton Cold War Endgame Conference talk, this was the date on which the Soviet leadership agreed to unificaton.

113. Cited in Pond, *Beyond the Wall*, 171.

114. Author's interview with Maximychev, Moscow, July 1996.

115. Kohl, *Ich wollte Deutschlands Einheit*, 254.

116. Gorbachev, *Zhizn' i reformy*, 2:714–17. Palazchenko, *My Years with Gor-bachev and Shevardnadze*, 172. Baker, *The Politics of Diplomacy*, 205, recalls that at this meeting, Gorbachev was much more relaxed about unification than was Shevardnadze, who seemed very preoccupied with domestic problems.

117. TASS international service, February 12, 1990, cited in FBIS-SOV-90-029, February 12, 1990, 44.

118. Teltschik, *329 Tage*, 137–43. Kohl, *Ich wollte Deutschlands Einheit*, 275, describes the look of "disgust" on Falin's face. He assumed, from the reaction of some of those at the meeting, that the Politburo had not been consulted about this decision.

119. For the communiqué, see Kaiser, *Deutschlands Vereinigung*, 192–93. Genscher notes the contrast between this cordial meeting and his acerbic recep-tion by Gorbachev on December 5. Genscher, *Erinnerungen*, 722–24.

120. *Die Welt*, March 19, 1990.

121. Even Shakhnazarov, in a conversation with the author in June 1995, ad-mitted that things did not turn out the way that the Kremlin would have wished in Germany. But, he added, at least this German unification, unlike the previous one, was peaceful.

122. Heym quoted in Hamilton, "Division, Revolution, Unification," p. 87.

123. Quoted in Vitaly Ganushkin and Anatoly Kovrigin, "The Colours of So-cialism," *New Times*, no. 42, October 17–23, 1989.

Chapter Five
United Germany and NATO

1. Beschloss and Talbott, *At the Highest Levels*, 198.

2. In a conversation with the author.

3. Beschloss and Talbott, *At the Highest Levels*, 240.

4. As the U.S. ambassador in Moscow noted, "In early 1990, most Western diplomats in Moscow, including myself, had little hope that Gorbachev could agree to a summary disolution of the GDR and a united Germany in NATO and survive politically with enough authority to keep perestroika alive." Jack F. Matlock, Jr., *Autopsy on an Empire* (New York: Random House, 1995), 383.

5. Falin, *Politische Erinnerungen*, 490.

6. Maksymichev and Modrow, *Posledny god GDR*, 105–6.

7. Zelikow and Rice, *Germany Unified and Europe Transformed*, 251.

8. Thatcher, *The Downing Street Years*, 791, 796.

9. Gorbachev's aide, Sergei Tarasenko, was particularly forthcoming on the internal Soviet divisions, especially in conversation with Frank Elbe, head of the German Foreign Ministry's planning staff. Author's conversations with participants in the Two Plus Four negotiations.

10. Author's conversations with American and German officials who participated in the negotiating process.

11. See Wolfgang Venohr, ed., *Die deutsche Einheit kommt bestimmt* (Bergisch Gladbach: Gustav Lubbe Verlag, 1982). This collection of essays by writers from the left and right foresaw a confederation between the two Germanies that would opt for neutrality.

12. See Angela Stent, "Western Europe and the USSR," in *Areas of Challenge for Soviet Foreign Policy in the 1980s*, ed. Gerrit W. Gong, Angela E. Stent, and Rebecca V. Strode (Bloomington: Indiana University Press, 1984), 14–15. In 1972, for instance, Brezhnev intervened to counter the possible passage of the Mansfield Amendment calling for the withdrawal of U.S. troops from Europe by agreeing to enter talks on mutually balanced force reduction in Europe. Matlock, *Autopsy on an Empire*, 383.

13. See Yergin, *Shattered Peace*, 64–65, 95–97.

14. Zelikow and Rice, *Germany Unified and Europe Transformed*, 183.

15. This was not the view of the *Germanisty*. They believed that a neutral, united Germany would naturally be drawn back into an alliance with Russia. Author's conversations with Falin and Portugalov.

16. As Matlock points out, "Gorbachev could have played a spoiler's role in the negotiations on German unity and actually improved his political position at home." *Autopsy on an Empire*, 387.

17. Cherniaiev, *Shest' let s Gorbachevym*, 346–47; Aleksandr Galkin and Anatoly Cherniaev, in "Pravdu, i tol'ko pravdu," *Svobodnaia Mysl'*, no. 2–3, (1994): 25, argue that Mitterrand and Thatcher wanted Gorbachev to take a hard line with the Germans to "pull their chestnuts out of the fire."

18. Gorbachev interview on Moscow Radio, February 20, 1990, in FBIS-SOV-90-035, February 21, 1990, 50.

19. There was considerable disagreement within the State Department and between the State Department and the National Security Council over whether the Two Plus Four mechanism was either appropriate or desirable. Zelikow and Rice detail these disagreements in *Germany Unified and Europe Transformed*, 167–68, 194–95. See also Robert Hutchings, *American Diplomacy and the End of the Cold War* (Baltimore: Johns Hopkins University Press, 1997), 112–113.

20. Genscher, *Erinnerungen*, 714–15.

21. Genscher's speech to the Evangelische Akademie in Tutzing, January 31, cited ibid., 714. Later on, the Soviets claimed that they had taken this to mean that NATO would not expand into other countries.

22. Robert Blackwill, "German Unification and American Diplomacy," *Außenpolitik*, 45, no. 3 (July 1994): 211–25.

23. Baker, *The Politics of Diplomacy*, 204–5; Baker, talk at Cold War Endgame Conference.

24. Falin, *Politische Erinnerungen*, 491. Galkin and Cherniaev, in their highly critical review of Falin's book, deny that his statements are accurate; "Pravdu, i tol'ko pravdu," 26–27. Baker also stresses that Gorbachev was more receptive to Two Plus Four than was Shevardnadze.

25. Shevardnadze, *The Future Belongs to Freedom*, 134.

26. Palazchenko, *My Years with Gorbachev and Shevardnadze*, 175–76.

27. For Genscher's side of the story—and his wariness of Kohl and his advisors—see Genscher, *Erinnerungen*, 724–730.

28. Teltschik, *329 Tage*, 122.

29. For the details of internal unification, see Wolfgang Schäuble, *Der Vertrag*.

30. Author's interview with Gerhard Stoltenberg, Washington, October 3, 1995; for a broader discussion of the Stoltenberg/Genscher argument, see Richard Kießler and Franz Elbe, *Ein runder Tisch mit scharfen Ecken* (Baden-Baden: Nomos, 1993) 82–25.

31. See Stephen F. Szabo, *The Diplomacy of German Unification* (New York: Saint Martin's Press, 1992), 72–76; Pond, *Beyond the Wall*, 192–97. The U.S. negotiators, mainly based in the Department of State, largely excluded the Defense Department from their deliberations.

32. Shevardnadze interview in *Neue Berliner Illustrierte*, March 7, 1990, in FBIS-SOV-90-046, March 7, 1990, 39. This was, of course, aimed at an East German audience.

33. Gorbachev, *Zhizn' i reformy*, 2:721.

34. Palazchenko, Bessmertnykh and Tarasenko quotes from their talks at Cold War Endgame Conference.

35. Teltschik, *329 Tage*, 201. At this point, even those identified with a pro-Gorbachev position were advocating a solution other than full participation of a united Germany in NATO's military structures. See Sergei Karaganov, "Zhizn' bez strakha," *Moskovskie novosti*, April 1, 1990.

36. The author asked several Soviet participants in the negotiations why the French option was never consistently pursued and never received a clear answer. The *Germanisty* blame Gorbachev, Shevardnadze, and Cherniaev for being both too pro-American and too "provincial."

37. Robert Zoellick, chief counselor to Baker, claims that the U.S. was amazed that the Soviets did not pursue the French solution, that is, that united Germany could not remain in NATO's integrated military command, and that they did not insist that united Germany should have no NATO nuclear weapons on its soil. These proposals could have caused serious difficulties in the U.S.-German relationship. Talk at Cold War Endgame Conference.

38. Gates, *From the Shadows*, 491.

39. Falin interview with Pryce-Jones, *The Strange Death of the Soviet Empire*, 277, 292.

40. Author's conversation with Gerhard Stoltenberg.

41. Dobrynin, *In Confidence*, 628, 636.

42. For an extensive discussion from the point of view of a communist critic, see Yegor Ligachev, *Inside Gorbachev's Kremlin* (New York: Pantheon, 1993).

Although Ligachev criticizes all aspects of Gorbachev's domestic policies, he barely mentions Germany. For many critics, foreign policy was far less important than domestic politics.

43. Teltschik, *329 Tage*, 212–13.

44. At his Camp David meeting with Bush in late February, Kohl was confident: "Everyone is confused but me," he said, noting that even if Gorbachev failed, his successor would have to pursue similar policies. Baker, *The Politics of Diplomacy*, 232–34.

45. Genscher, *Erinnerungen*, 728, confirms this, although he says he was willing to consider different rules for NATO structures on the territory of the GDR. Kohl, at Camp David, had said that "NATO units, including Bundeswehr forces dedicated to NATO, cannot be stationed on GDR soil." Baker, *The Politics of Diplomacy*, 237.

46. Genscher recalls that, at the "Open Skies" conference, the Dutch and others of Germany's neighbors unsuccessfully tried to reopen the question by saying that every NATO member should have a say in German unification. This infuriated the West German Foreign Ministry. Genscher, *Erinnerungen*, 729. But a Polish delegation did attend a special Two Plus Four meeting dealing with the German-Polish border. See Rice and Zelikow, *Germany United and Europe Transformed*, 217–22.

47. Teltschik, *329 Tage*, 192, 206.

48. Kwizinksij, *Vor dem Sturm*, 31.

49. Stent, *From Embargo to Ostpolitik*, chap. 7.

50. *Der Spiegel*, May 28, 1990.

51. Teltschik, *329 Tage*, 204, 221, 226–27, 230–37.

52. Ash, *In Europe's Name*, 118.

53. See Hannes Adomeit, "Gorbachev, German Unification and the Collapse of Empire," *Post-Soviet Affairs* 10, no. 3 (July–September 1994): 222–24. Adomeit also speculates that Gorbachev may have been a "devious tactician" who deliberately left the economic linkage until the last moment, when the West Germans were forced to concede more. But there is little evidence to support a Machiavellian interpretation of the disorganized Soviet strategy.

54. Heinrich Machowski of the DIW, quoted in Frederick Kempe, "Bonn Offers Moscow Huge Credit, Seeking to Ease Unification Jitters," *Wall Street Journal*, June 22, 1990.

55. Hutchings, *American Diplomacy and the End of the Cold War*, 118, points out that few outside the U.S. government believed these were realistic goals. Some believed that insistence on NATO membership would create obstacles to German unification.

56. For details of the evolution of U.S. strategy, see Zelikow and Rice, *Germany Unified and Europe Transformed*, chaps. 4–7.

57. See Angela Stent, "East-West Technology Transfer and the Western Alliance," in *Trade, Technology and Soviet–American Relations*, ed. Bruce Parrott (Bloomington: Indiana University Press, 1985), 283–323.

58. Baker, *The Politics of Diplomacy*, 254.

59. Szabo, *The Diplomacy of German Unification*, 86; Zelikow and Rice, *Germany Unified and Europe Transformed*, 263–64.

60. Baker, *The Politics of Diplomacy*, 251–52; Kohl, *Ich wollte Deutschlands Einheit*, 394.

61. Beschloss and Talbott, *At the Highest Levels*, 219.

62. Gorbachev, *Zhizn' i reformy*, 2:722–23; Cherniaev, *Shest' let s Gorbachevym*, 348–49, Baker, *The Politics of Diplomacy*, 253.

63. Gorbachev, *Zhizn' i reformy*, 2:723; Cherniaev, *Shest' let s Gorbachevym*, 348; Baker, *The Politics of Diplomacy*, 253.

64. Thatcher, *The Downing Street Years*, 805–6.

65. Blackwill, "German Unification and American Diplomacy." Beschloss and Talbott, *At the Highest Levels*, 220; Zelikow and Rice, *Germany Unified and Europe Transformed*, 276–78.

66. Genscher, *Erinnerungen*, 256.

67. Ibid., 801–4.

68. For the full text of the London Declaration, see Kaiser, *Deutschlands Vereinigung*, 241–46.

69. Beschloss and Talbott, *At the Highest Levels*, 237; Blackwill, "German Unification and American Diplomacy."

70. Ibid.; Kießler and Elbe, *Ein runder Tisch mit scharfen Ecken*, 131.

71. *Izvestiia*, May 7, 1990.

72. Teltschik, *329 Tage*, 285–86. It was his impression that the old German hands in Moscow were still trying to sabotage progress on this whole issue.

73. *Berliner Zeitung*, May 4, 1990.

74. Kwizinskij, *Vor dem Sturm*, 34.

75. Genscher, *Erinnerungen*, 805–14, 819–23.

76. Some of the American participants believe that there was a secret negotiating channel between Dieter Kastrup, political director in the Foreign Ministry, and the Soviet side that was activated during periods of particular difficulty.

77. Shevardnadze, *The Future Belongs to Freedom*, 141.

78. Shevardnadze's speech in *Izvestiia*, July 5, 1990.

79. "Otvety E. A. Shevardnadze na voprosy zapadogermanskoi Gazety 'Welt am Sonntag,'" *Vestnik MID*, July 31, 1990, 25.

80. Genscher, *Erinnerungen*, 831, criticizes those present who wrote about this dispute; but he agrees that it took place.

81. Teltschik, *329 Tage*, 316–38. Genscher, *Erinnerungen*, 830–51. Officials in the German Foreign Minstry claim that they knew in advance of the meeting that Gorbachev had changed his mind on NATO, but that the Chancellor did not know. Kohl, *Ich Wollte Deutschlands Einheit*, 425–36, stresses that Gorbachev bargained very hard before finally conceding.

82. Shevardnadze, *The Future Belongs to Freedom*, 142.

83. Gorbachev, *Zhizn' i reformy*, 2:725. In his memoirs, Gorbachev highlights the importance of the natural splendor of their surroundings in enabling the two sides to reach closure of unification.

84. Falin interview with David Pryce-Jones, *The Strange Death of the Soviet Empire*, 292–93. Of course, Falin was not part of the Caucasus meeting. Gorbachev took only Shevardnadze and Cherniaev with him. Maximychev, in a conversation with the author, has a similarly condescending and critical view of Gorabchev and Shevardnadze.

85. Falin, *Politische Erinnerungen*, 493–98. Falin remains embittered by what he sees as a sell-out by the USSR. He reflects a view common in some Soviet quarters that some kind of "secret deal" was made between Kohl and Gorbachev and that Gorbachev profited personally from it. Author's conversation with Valentin Falin, Berlin, August 1992. Falin also regards Shevardnadze as "an agent of American influence" (Beschloss and Talbott, *At the Highest Levels*, 240). Portugalov, in a conversation with the author, Moscow, July 1997, highlighted the fact that the *Germanisty* were largely anti-American.

86. Galkin and Cherniaev, "Pravdu, i tol'ko pravdu," 28.

87. Dobrynin, *In Confidence*, 636.

88. For the text of the press conference, see *Pravda*, July 18, 1990.

89. Those most involved in the negotiations in Washington were somewhat disappointed when Kohl did not call them from the USSR telling them about the Caucasus breakthrough; but they were willing to attribute this to the lack of communication facilities. The East Germans were angry that neither the Soviets nor the West Germans had informed them of what had transpired.

90. Teltschik, *329 Tage*, 346. One can speculate that had Saddam Hussein invaded Kuwait earlier than August 1990, U.S. attention would indeed have been diverted.

91. Bundesministerium für Wirtschaft, *Der deutsche Osthandel* (Bonn, 1991), 50–51.

92. Interview with Wilhelm Christians in *New Times*, no. 45 (1990): 23.

93. *Der Spiegel*, no. 41, October 15, 1990.

94. Kwizinskij, *Vor dem Sturm*, 59.

95. Teltschik, *329 Tage*, 359–63; Kohl, *Ich wollte Deutschlands Einheit*, 467–68.

96. Author's conversations with American and German negotiators. The Western negotiating teams were constantly surprised by how badly prepared the Soviet team was.

97. Genscher, *Erinnerungen*, 865–73. Kohl, *Ich Wollte Deutschlands Einheit*, 469.

98. For the text of the treaty, see Kaiser, *Deutschlands Vereinigung*, 260–68.

99. Zelikow and Rice, *Germany Unified and Europe Transformed*, 184; Kiessler conversation with author, Bonn, June 1997.

100. For the text, see Kaiser, *Deutschlands Vereinigung*, 334–42.

101. For the text, see FBIS-WEU-90-219, November 13, 1990, 16–20.

102. Dobrynin bitterly confirms this: "No small part in the downgrading of [the International] Department was played by Shevardnadze, who wanted to monopolize foreign policy and avoid competition from our department. Thus the department, and I as its head, were no longer actively involved in foreign policy on a daily basis." Dobrynin, *In Confidence*, 628.

103. Falin, *Politische Erinnerungen*, 497–98; Kwizinskij, *Vor dem Sturm*, 66–68.

104. Ibid., 82–85.

105. Indeed, after the collapse of the USSR, a number of Soviet German experts, including Falin and Fyodorov, resettled in Germany, the country whose unification they had tried so hard to prevent. They apparently enjoyed more support from Germans than from Russians.

106. Fred Oldenburg, "Sowjetische Europa-Politik und die Lösung der deutschen Frage," *Osteuropa* 41, no. 8 (August 1991): 770–71.

107. For retrospective accounts of the Western strategy and achievements, see Thomas Risse, "The Cold War's Endgame and German Unification," *International Security* 21, no. 4 (Spring 1997): 159–85; Stephen Szabo, "A Second Look at the Diplomacy of German Unification," *German Politics and Society* 15, no. 4 (1997): 130–39.

108. Author's conversations with Hans Misselwitz, former parliamentary state secretary in the GDR Foreign Ministry and with the last GDR foreign minister, Markus Meckel, Washington, D.C., 1991 and 1993.

109. Nevertheless, Shevardnadze confided in Baker that although he had no objection to a united Germany being in NATO were Kohl, Genscher, or Brandt to lead the country, he had major fears about the next generation of Germans, possibly Republikaner (the extreme right-wing party) coming to power and leading a more aggressive Germany. Baker, *The Politics of Diplomacy*, 230.

110. Gorbachev, *Zhizn' i reformy*, 2:178–79.

111. Ibid.

112. Galkin and Cherniaev, "Pravdu, i tol'ko pravdu," 29. They enumerate all the Soviet gains from Germany: support of their troops, housing construction for their officers in the USSR, credits, humanitarian assistance, and active support on international fora, especially the G-7.

113. Dobrynin, *In Confidence*, 636. Maksimychev, "Kliuch k svobode."

114. Dobrynin, *In Confidence*, 630.

115. Author's conversation with Shakhnazarov, Moscow, June 1995.

Chapter Six
Implementing Unification

1. "Zu jedem Kampf bereit," interview with Yeltsin, *Der Spiegel*, April 25, 1994.

2. "Erklärung des Bundeskanzlers zur aktuellen Lage in Rußland," in Presse- und Informationsamt der Bundesregierung, Bonn, *Bulletin*, (hereafter *Bulletin*) March 16, 1993, 192.

3. *SZ*, March 22, 1994.

4. Genscher, *Erinnerungen*, 973–74.

5. After the coup and the subsequent banning of the Communist Party and thus of its Central Committee, Nikolai Portugalov, now an unemployed *Germanist*, claimed that of the 150-member International Department of the Central Committee, one-third favored the coup, one-third opposed it and one-third would have gone either way. Falin made his opposition clear—after the coup had failed. *New York Times*, September 4, 1991.

6. Boris Pankin, *The Last Hundred Days of the Soviet Union* (New York: I. B. Taurus, 1996), 127–32.

7. Genscher, *Erinnerungen*, 976.

8. K. Viatkin, "Rossiia i Germaniia: Potentsial sotrudnichestva," *MEMO*, no. 4 (1994): 104.

9. Yeltsin quotes this and other disparaging remarks about him in Boris Yeltsin, *The Struggle For Russia* (New York: Random House, 1994), 25.

10. Iurii Shpakov, "Trudnii gost'," *Moskovskie novosti*, December 1, 1991, 4. For the text of the agreements, see "Besuch des Präsidenten von Rußland," *Bulletin*, November 25, 1991, 1081–88.

11. Statement of Chancellor Kohl to the Moscow press, ibid., December 22, 1992, 1268.

12. See Kohl's statement, ibid., March 16, 1993, 192, in which he credited Yeltsin for the "trusting and friendly" relations between the two countries; and ibid., April 29, 1993, 294, for the statement welcoming the results of the referendum.

13. "Kohl: Wir setzen auf Jelzin," *FAZ*, September 23, 1993.

14. For a fuller discussion of these issues see Angela Stent and Lilia Shevtsova, "Russia's Election: No Turning Back," *Foreign Policy*, no. 103 (Summer 1996): 92–109.

15. In a discussion with the author, Gorbachev referred dismissively to the "Boris-Helmut sauna friendship," which has clearly affected his view of Kohl since unification.

16. *Die Welt*, April 20, 1997, described the idea of an updated Rapallo as "dangerous," because it threatened to undermine Germany's transatlantic ties.

17. RFE/RL Daily Report, September 5, 1994; DDP/ADN in German, July 28, 1994, in FBIS-SOV-94-146, July 29, 1994, 7.

18. Author's conversation with diplomats involved in the troop withdrawal negotiations, Berlin, June 1995.

19. Ulrich Brandenburg, "The 'Friends' Are Leaving: Soviet and Post-Soviet Troops in Germany," *Außenpolitik* (English Edition) 44, no. 1, (1993): 77–88.

20. Author's conversation with Major-General Hartmut Foertsch, Washington, D.C., December 1991.

21. Author's conversation with Gerhard Stoltenberg, Washington, D.C. October 1995.

22. *Frankfurter Rundschau*, February 11, 1992.

23. Claus J. Duisberg, "Germany: The Russians Go," *The World Today*, 50, no. 10 (October 1994): 193.

24. *Die Welt*, April 17, 1993.

25. Interview with General Burlakov, *Berliner Zeitung*, September 1, 1993.

26. Ibid., December 31, 1993.

27. One Russian official claimed that "leading personnel of the trade administration of the Western group" had transferred DM 17 million to overseas bank accounts. *Die Welt*, June 3, 1994.

28. RFE/RL Daily Report, January 4, 1994.

29. *Izvestiia*, January 28, 1994 and March 11, 1994; *Krasnaia zvezda*, April 1, 1994; RFE/RL Daily Report, September 15, 1994.

30. *Nezavisimaia gazeta*, September 15, 1994.

31. Falk Bommsdorf, "Befreier und Besatzer," *Die Zeit*, February 25, 1994.

32. Helmut Domke, "Beim Abschied der Allierten die gemeinsame Ebene suchen," *Berliner Zeitung*, March 4, 1994.

33. General Burlakov addressing President Yeltsin, August 31, 1994, on Russian television, in FBIS-SOV-94-169, August 31, 1994, 9–10.

34. Yeltsin's speech at the Berlin Schauspielhaus, August 31, 1995, in FBIS-SOV-94-169, August 31, 1994, 3.

35. Author's conversation with General Klaus Naumann, Washington, D.C., October 1994.

36. See Gabriel al Salem, "Invitation to Interfere" (M.A. thesis, Georgetown University, 1994), 22 ff.; Konstantin Isakov, "Ethnic Germans in the USSR," *New Times*, no. 14 (1989): 27–31.

37. ITAR-TASS, October 6, 1992, quoted in FBIS-SOV-92-195, October 7, 1992, 4.

38. *Die Welt*, March 1, 1993.

39. *SZ*, April 7, 1993.

40. ITAR-TASS, March 15, 1994, in FBIS-SOV-94-051, March 16, 1994, 20; RFE/RL Daily Report, March 17, 1994.

41. Pavel Shinkarenko, "Nemtsi na Volge," *Rossiskie vesti*, August 4, 1992.

42. *Rossiskaia gazeta*, June 23,1992.

43. The head of the German desk in the Russian Foreign Ministry confirmed to the author that the Volga Republic will not be restored. He likened it to Birobidjan, created by Stalin in extremely inhospitable territory as the Jewish Autonomous Republic, where very few Jews ever lived. The solution, he argued, was to create German autonomous regions in a number of different areas. Author's interview with Igor Bratchikov, Moscow, July 1996.

44. *Die Welt*, January 20, 1992; *SZ*, June 3, 1992.

45. German Information Service, New York, *Deutschland-Nachrichten*, September 5, 1997

46. *Kaliningradskaia oblast': Segodniia, zavtra* (Moscow: Carnegie Endowment for International Peace,1995), 27.

47. Countess Marion Dönhoff, for instance, the publisher of *Die Zeit* had originally come from this area. She proposed joint Russian-German-Polish-Lithuanian "condominium" over the Königsberg area in order to bring in investments and develop it. See Marion Gräfin Dönhoff, "Königsberg: Signal der Versöhnung?" *Die Zeit*, November 15, 1991.

48. *Kaliningradskaia oblast'*, 27.

49. When asked by the author about the consulate issue, a Russian Foreign Ministry official countered, "Why should Germany want to open a new consulate when the German Foreign Ministry is cutting back on expenditures? Why is more German aid going to Kaliningrad than to Omsk, with far more ethnic Germans?"

50. *Der Spiegel*, March 21, 1993, 145.

51. *Frankfurter Rundschau*, January 12, 1994.

52. *Izvestiia*, April 9, 1994.

53. Priit J. Vesilind, "Kaliningrad: Coping with a German Past and a Russian Future," *National Geographic*, March, 1997, 120.

54. *Krasnaia zvezda*, March 19, 1994; *Komsomolskaia pravda*, March 22, 1994; Radio Mayak, March 29, 1994, in FBIS-SOV-94-061, March 30, 1994, 27.

55. This was evident in the author's discussions in the Russian Foreign Ministry and the German Embassy in July 1996, Moscow.

56. *Kaliningradskaia oblast'*, 25. This scholarly and detailed monograph also does not differentiate between individual and government proposals.

57. Moscow NTV in Russian, June 23, 1996 (from Internet); Moscow Interfax, October 31, 1996 (from Internet).

58. For a broader discussion of these issues with various viewpoints, see *Die Zukunft des Gebiets Kaliningrad (Königsberg)*, Sonderveröffentlichung BIOST, *Bericht* (Cologne, July 1993).

59. Yergin and Gustafson, *Russia 2010*, chap. 4.

60. *German Support for the Transition to Democracy and Market Economy in the Former Soviet Union* (New York: German Information Center, June 1992).

61. See for instance, Yuri Popov, "Western Aid: How It Is distributed," *Rossiskie vesti*, May 15, 1992, 3.

62. "Deutschland trägt die Hauptlast der westlichen Rußland-Hilfe" *FAZ*, April 8, 1993.

63. Sergei Karaganov, *Whither Western Aid to Russia?* (Gütersloh: Bertelsmann Foundation Publishers, 1994), 28.

64. Evgenii Bovkun, "Nemetskaia pomoshch': Den'gi, istrachennye vpustuiu," *Izvestiia*, April 6, 1994.

65. Author's conversation with Wolfgang Kittl, Ministry of Economics, Bonn, October 1993. For articles on Kartte's activities, see Martina Ohm, "Vom Platz der Luftbrücke ins Weiße Haus," *Der Tagesspiegel*, April 8, 1993; Boris Lysenko, "V. Kartte: Opora reform," *Izvestiia*, July 28, 1992.

66. Aleksandr Anichkin, "Priglashenie v Klub izbrannikh," *Izvestiia*, June 16, 1992.

67. See Heinrich Vogel, "The London Summit and the Soviet Union," *Außenpolitik* (English edition) no.4 (1991): 315–25.

68. For the text of the G-7 summit declarations, see "Wirtschaftsgipfel Tokio: Politische Erklärung, in *Bulletin*, July 16, 1993.

69. *Welt am Sonntag*, July 10, 1994.

70. *SZ*, November 11, 1993, 23.

71. For a fuller discussion of these issues, see Angela Stent, "Russia's Economic Revolution and the West," *Survival 37*, no.5 (Spring 1995): 121–43.

72. Author's interview with Wolfgang Heitland, Federal Economics Ministry, Bonn, October 1993.

73. "Rußland: Schwieriger außenwirtschaftliche Neubeginn," Deutsches Institut für Wirtschaftsforschung, *Wochenbericht*, July 23, 1992, 378–83.

74. *FAZ*, January 23, 1992; *SZ*, January 23, 1992.

75. *Handelsblatt*, February 5 and 20, 1992; *Die Welt*, February 4, 1992. ITAR-TASS reported that Germany was now paying higher gas prices, see FBIS-SOV 92-049, March 12, 1992, 30.

76. *Die Welt*, January 7, 1992; *Izvestiia*, May 30, 1992; *Kommersant*, May 25–June 1, 1992.

77. *Izvestiia*, May 25, 1992; *Frankfurter Rundschau*, April 10, 1993. By 1994, the largest Mercedes-Benz dealership outside Germany was in Moscow; and the lead man promoting Mercedes was former Ambassador Andreas Meyer-Landrut.

78. Evgenii Bovkun and Viktor Tolstov, "Biznesmen iz Germanii primet predlozheniie iz Rossii," *Izvestiia*, February 28, 1992; Vadim Markushin, "Nam pomogaiut, potomy chto khotiat pomoch' sebe," *Krasnaia zvezda*, March 31, 1993.

79. Quoted in *The Economist*, December 24, 1994.

80. In a conversation with the author, Bonn, June 1997.

81. Moscow Interfax, May 14, 1997, in FBIS-SOV-97-134, May 14, 1997. During his meeting with Yeltsin in November 1997, Kohl reiterated that this matter was of great importance to the German government. German Information Center, New York, *Deutschland-Nachrichten*, December 5, 1997, no. 1.

82. The "Amber Chamber" was created in 1716 and presented by King Friedrich Wilhelm I of Prussia to Peter the Great, who had it installed at Tsarskoe Selo.

83. *NZZ*, October 3, 1992.

84. *SZ*, February 16, 1993.

85. "Rede von Bundespräsident Roman Herzog anläßlich der Verabschiedung der russischen Streitkräfte aus Deutschland in Berlin am 31. August 1994," in *Europa-Archiv* 49, no. 19 (1994): 561–62.

86. Igor Maximychev, "The German Factor in European Security," *International Affairs* (Moscow) 43, no. 11 (1997): 61.

87. S. Kortunov, "Rossiia ishchet soiuznikov," *Mezhdunarodnaia zhizn'*, no. 5 (1996): 21.

88. A clear example of this "old" and wishful thinking is Igor Maksimychev, *Ob'edineniia Germania kak faktor evropeiskoi bezopasnosti* (Moscow: Institut Evropy, 1997).

89. German Information Center, New York, *Deutschland-Nachrichten*, September 5, 1997.

Chapter Seven
National Identity and Foreign Policy after Communism

1. Karl Lamers, "Bonn to Moscow: Our Tolerance Is Limited," *Wall Street Journal*, June 19, 1995.

2. Quoted in Andranik Migranian, *Rossiia v poiskakh identichnosti* (Moscow: Mezhdunarodnie Otnosheniia, 1977), 18.

3. The "near abroad" is a Russian invention, disliked by the other Newly Independent States. They feel that this puts them in a category that differentiates them from the "far abroad," the outside world, implying that Russia views them differently than other European or Asian countries and has a proprietary interest in them.

4. For a more extensive discussion of these themes, see Angela Stent, Thane Gustafson, and Daniel Yergin, "The Return of a Great Power," in Yergin and Gustafson, *Russia 2010*, chap. 15.

5. After all, in 1928 Stalin proclaimed that an internationalist was one who "unreservedly, wholeheartedly supports the Soviet Union" because it was the motherland of socialism—a very specific definition of an "internationalist."

6. See Hannes Adomeit, "Russia as a Great Power," *International Affairs* 71, no. 1 (January 1995): 35–68.

7. Interview with Andrei Kozyrev in *New Times*, no.3 (1992): 20–24.

8. Interview with Andrei Kozyrev, *Moscow News*, June 7–14, 1992, 14; Kozyrev quoted in Moscow Interfax, November 25, 1992, in FBIS-SOV-92-229, 16.

9. Andrei Kozyrev, *Preobrazhenie* (Moscow: Mezhdunarodnie Otnoshenia, 1995), 203. This book is a reflection of his Atlanticist views.

10. Interview with Kozyrev, *Rossiskie vesti*, December 3, 1992.

11. Kozyrev article, ibid., February 9, 1994.

12. "Strategiia dlia Rossii," *Nezavisimaia gazeta*, August 19, 1992.

13. Strategiia dlia Rossii II, ibid., May 14, 1994.

14. *Izvestiia*, August 8, 1992, 6.

15. *Sovetskaia Rossiia*, July 4, 1992.

16. See Stent and Shevtsova, "Russia's Election: No Turning Back," 92–109.

17. See T. I. Kutkovets and I. M. Kliamkin, *Russkie idei*, nos. 1–2 (January–February 1997).

18. See the roundtable discussions on national interest and foreign policy in "Natsional'nie interesy vo vneshnei politike Rossii," *Mezhdunarodnaia zhizn'* 3 (1996): 3, and *Rossiia: Desiat' voprosov o samom vazhnom* (Moscow: Carnegie Center, 1997), chap. 10.

19. See *Rossiskaia gazeta*, December 24, 1991.

20. For a discussion of the evolution of the Security Council—which turned out to be weaker than many had hoped or feared—and other institutions, see Jan S. Adams, "The Russian National Security Council," *Problems of Post-Communism* 43, no. 1 (January–Feburary 1996) 35–42; and F. Stephen Larrabee and Theodore W. Karasik, *Foreign and Security Policy Decisionmaking under Yeltsin* (Santa Monica, Calif.: RAND Corporation, 1997).

21. Gennadi Charodeev, "I u MIDa net deneg," *Izvestiia*, May 4, 1992; ibid., June 1, 1992.

22. "Foreign Policy of Russia in 1996 and 1997," *International Affairs* (Moscow) 43, no. 2. (1997): 62–69.

23. Larrabee and Karasik, *Foreign and Security Policy Decisionmaking under Yeltsin*, 29. See also Aleksandr Korzhakov, *Boris Yeltsin: Ot rassveta do zakata* (Moscow: Interbook, 1997) for lurid accounts of Yeltsin's personal weaknesses.

24. Michael Stürmer, "Deutsche Interessen", in *Deutschlands Neue Außenpolitik*, ed. Karl Kaiser and Hanns W. Maull (Munich: R.Oldenbourg Verlag, 1994), 58.

25. Jonathan Dean, *Ending Europe's Wars* (New York: Twentieth Century Fund, 1994), 152.

26. Confidential conversation with the author.

27. In 1992 the Bundestag, after a heated debate, voted to move the capital of a united Germany from provincial Bonn to cosmopolitan Berlin, shifting Germany's center of gravity considerably to the East. The majority for Berlin was small, and the PDS vote was decisive in securing Berlin. The move, which was repeatedly postponed, was to be completed by the end of the millennium.

28. Cited in Hamilton, "Division, Revolution, Unification," p. 24.

29. Karl Kaiser and Klaus Becher, *Deutschland und der Irak-Konflikt* (Bonn: Europa-Union Verlag, 1992), 47.

30. See "Recognition of the Yugoslav Successor States," Position Paper of the German Foreign Ministry, March 10, 1993, New York, *Speeches and Statements* German Information Center, 16 no. 10.

31. *The Ruling of the Federal Constitutional Court On the Deployment of the German Armed Forces.* (New York: German Information Center, July, 1994).

32. The most articulate—and notorious—exposition of the position that Germany should become a nuclear state was John Mearsheimer, "Back to the Future: Instability in Europe After the Cold War," *International Security* 15, no 1 (Summer 1990) 5–56. He later made the same argument for Ukraine maintaining its nuclear arsenal. See his "The Case for a Ukrainian Nuclear Deterrent," *Foreign Affairs* 72, no.3 (Summer 1993): 50–66.

33. The most articulate exponent of this theory is Hanns Maull, "Zivilmacht Bundesrepublik Deutschland: Vierzehn Thesen für eine neue Deutsche Außenpolitik," *Europa-Archiv* 47, no. 10 (1992): 269–78; and Hanns Maull, "Großmacht Deutschland: Annmerkungen und Thesen," in *Die Zukunft der deutschen Außenpolitik*, vol. 1: *Grundlagen*, ed. Karl Kaiser and Hanns Maull (Bonn: Europa-Union Verlag, 1993), 53–72, in which he argues that Germany cannot become a "normal" power for a long time.

34. See F. Stephen Larrabee, *East European Security after the Cold War*, (Santa Monica, Calif.: RAND Corporation, 1993), 124–27.

35. *Foreigners in Germany and the New Asylum Law* (New York: German Information Center, June 1994).

36. Interview with Klaus Kinkel, *Welt am Sonntag*, July 21, 1996.

37. See Ronald D. Asmus, *German Strategy and Opinion after the Wall 1990–1993* (Santa Monica, Calif.: RAND, 1994), for the full results of this major public opinion survey.

Chapter Eight
Russia and Germany in the New Europe

1. Interview in *Die Woche*, March 21, 1997.

2. Václav Havel, "The Chance that Will Not Return," *U.S. News and World Report*, February 26, 1990.

3. Larrabee, *East European Security after the Cold War*, 155.

4. See S. Neil Macfarlane, "Russian Conceptions of Europe," *Post-Soviet Affairs* 10, no 3 (1994): 234–69; and Iurii P. Davydov, "Rossiia i Evropa v novom izmerenii," *SShA: Ekonomika, politika, ideologiia*, no. 5 (1995): 21–32.

5. Vladimir Lukin, quoted in Angela Stent, Thane Gustafson, and Daniel Yergin, "The Return of a Great Power," in Yergin and Gustafson, *Russia 2010*, 255. Lukin has also criticized Gorbachev for not discussing the future of Soviet–East European ties with Kohl before unification and for a lack of vision of how these ties should evolve. See V. P. Lukin and A. I. Utkin, *Rossiia i zapad* (Moscow: Sampo, 1995), 29–30.

6. *Nezavisimaia gazeta*, August 19, 1992.

7. Ministry of Foreign Affairs, "Foreign Policy Concept of the Russian Federation," in FBIS-SOV-93-037, March 23, 1993, 1–2.

8. See Allen Lynch, "After Empire: Russia and Its Neighbors," *RFE/RL Research Report* 3, no. 12 (March 25, 1994): 10–17.

9. MacFarlane, "Russian Conceptions of Europe," 254–60.

10. Cited in Suzanne Crow, "Russia Reasserts Its Strategic Agenda," *RFE/RL Research Report* 2, no. 50 (December 17, 1993): 1–8.

11. *New York Times*, June 9, 1994.

12. Conversation with Hungarian Foreign Minister László Kovács, Washington, D.C., October 1995.

13. A recent piece by Yuriy Davidov, "Russian Security and East-Central Europe," in *Russia and Europe: Emerging Security Agenda*, ed. Vladimir Baranovsky (Oxford: Oxford University Press, 1997), chap. 17, paints a somber picture.

14. V. Baranovskii, "Mikromodel' evropeiskoi bezopasnosti?" *MEMO* no. 6 (1996): 40–50.

15. Author's conversation with Igor Maximychev, a member of this working group, Moscow, July 1997.

16. *The Week in Germany* (New York: German Information Center, April 25, 1997), 5.

17. *Washington Post*, July 21, 1997.

18. Heinrich Machowski and Wolfram Schrettl, "The Economic Impact of Unified Germany on Central and East-Central Europe," in U.S. Congress, Joint Economic Committee, *East-Central European Economies in Transition* (Washington, D.C.: U.S. Government Printing Office, 1994), 412–40.

19. *Washington Post*, July 21, 1997.

20. Rita Klímová, first postcommunist Czech ambassador to the United States, in conversation with the author, Berlin, 1991.

21. *The Stabilization of Central and East-Central Europe* (New York: German Information Center, April 1994), 2.

22. Author's interview with Gorbachev, Moscow, July 1996. The United States and its allies deny that this promise was ever made. Nevertheless, Gorbachev and many others in the foreign policy establishment, including many of Gorbachev's critics, share this view and therefore it plays a significant political role.

23. For the Partnership for Peace Framework Documents, see James W. Morrison, *NATO Expansion and Alternative Future Security Alignments*, McNair Paper no. 40 (Washington, D.C.: National Defense University, April 1995), 139–41.

24. For more details on the program, see Catherine McArdle Kelleher, *The Future of European Security* (Washington, D.C.: Brookings Institution, 1995), chap. 4.

25. *Krasnaia zvezda*, May 24, 1994; Kelleher, *The Future of European Security*, chap. 4.

26. *Rossiskaia gazeta*, June 22, 1994; ITAR-TASS, June 21, 1994, in FBIS-SOV-94-120, June 22, 1994, 5.

27. Kozyrev interview with Interfax, November 30, 1994, quoted in RFE/RL *Daily Report*, no. 226, December 1, 1994

28. "Rossiia i NATO," *Nezavisimaia gazeta*, June 21, 1995.

29. "America and Europe: Common Challenges and Common Answers," text of lecture by Volker Rühe at Georgetown University, March 2, 1993, 9–10.

30. Author's conversation with Strobe Talbott, Washington, D.C., January 1998.

31. Strobe Talbott, "Why NATO Should Grow," *New York Review of Books*, August 10, 1995: author's conversation with Talbott, Washington, D.C., January 1998.

32. Author's conversation with Anthony Lake, Washington, D.C., January 1998.

33. For a discussion of the way in which a consensus within the government was forged, see James M. Goldgeier, "NATO Expansion: Anatomy of a Decision," *Washington Quarterly* 21 (Winter 1998): 85–102.

34. Ronald Asmus, Richard Kugler, and F. Stephen Larrabee, "Building A New NATO," *Foreign Affairs* 72, no. 4, (1993): 28–40

35. It is instructive that Rühe did not ask the Ebenhausen-based Stiftung Wissenchaft und Politik, the German equivalent of RAND, to carry out his study. Apparently, he had more confidence in the American analysts.

36. Bruce Clark, "How the East Was Won," *Financial Times*, July 5 and 6, 1997; author's conversations with people involved in the NATO enlargement decision.

37. Author's conversations with Richard Holbrooke and Fritz Stern, January 1998.

38. *Message on the Study of NATO Enlargement* (Brussels: NATO Headquarters, September 20, 1995), 1.

39. Former Secretary of State Henry Kissinger argued this point in various publications. Holbrooke did not share this view. Some Russians made exactly the opposite point: NATO expansion was a cover for German ambitions in the east and would facilitate German domination of the region. Author's conversation with Yeltsin advisor Sergei Kortunov, Moscow, June 1995. But, in a conversation with Polish Foreign Minister Dariusz Rosati in Washington in October 1997, the author was told: "Germany is now a peace-loving, democratic society—it's nice to be in the same alliance with Germany."

40. For a fuller exposition of these schools of thought and their prescriptions, see Ronald D. Asmus, Richard L. Kugler, and F. Stephen Larrabee, "NATO Expansion: The Next Steps," *Survival* 37, no. 1 (Spring 1995) 7–33. The authors were analysts at the RAND Corporation who had worked closely with the German Defense Ministry. Asmus became deputy assistant secretary of state for NATO enlargement in 1997.

41. Talbott, "Why NATO Should Grow," 5.

42. *New York Times*, February 5, 1997.

43. See for instance Council on Foreign Relations Task Force, *Should NATO Expand?* (New York: Council on Foreign Relations, 1995); Council on Foreign Relations Task Force, *Russia, Its Neighbors and An Enlarging NATO* (New York: Council on Foreign Relations, 1997); and United States Institute of Peace, *Managing NATO Enlargement* (Washington, D.C.: United States Institute of Peace, April 1997).

44. Kohl's speech to the Thirty-third Munich Conference on Security Policy, in *Bulletin*, February 14, 1996, 165–68.

45. For an eloquent German case against NATO expansion, see Karl-Heinz Kamp, "The Folly of Rapid NATO Expansion," *Foreign Policy*, no. 98 (Spring 1995): 116–31.

46. Author's conversations with officials involved in the enlargement negotiations.

47. Author's conversation with Karsten Voigt, Bonn, July 1997.

48. See Karl Kaiser, "Reforming NATO," *Foreign Policy*, no. 103 (Summer 1996): 128–43.

49. ITAR-TASS, August 25, 1993.

50. Quoted in Crow, "Russia Asserts Its Strategic Agenda," 2.

51. *Krasnaia zvezda*, February 7, 1996.

52. *Sovetskaia Rossiia*, October 31, 1996; author's conversation with Portugalov, Moscow, July 1997.

53. *Rossiiskie vesti*, March 26, 1997.

54. Nikolai Pishchev, "Dal'nii pritsel NATO," *Nezavisimaia gazeta*, April 4, 1997.

55. "Rossiia i NATO," ibid., June 21, 1995.

56. *New York Times*, May 28, 1997.

57. Aleksei Pushkov, "Bezopasnost," *Nezavisimaia gazeta*, March 19, 1997.

58. Aleksandr Lebed's article in *Izvestiia*, May 27, 1997; Primakov quote in *Die Presse*, September 1, 1996; Iu. O. Rachmaninov, "Nekotorie soobrazheniia o rasshirenii NATO," *SShA: Ekonomika, politika, ideologia*, no. 2 (1997): 57.

59. Author's conversation with German and American officials who participated in these discussions and with Russian analysts, Washington, Bonn, and Moscow, June–July 1997.

60. *New York Times*, May 28, 1997. For the text of the NATO-Russia Founding Act, see FBIS-SOV-97-102, May 27, 1997.

61. *Washington Post*, May 28, 1997.

62. *Izvestiia*, May 16, 1997; March 19, 1997; Migranian in *Nezavisimaia gazeta*, May 27, 1997; Ziuganov quote in FBIS-SOV-97-136, May 16, 1997.

63. Yegor T. Gaidar, "A View from Russia," *Foreign Policy*, no. 109 (Winter 1997–98): 66.

64. For a Russian view of the relationship between NATO and OSCE by the deputy foreign minister, see N. Afanas'evskii, "Lissabonskii sammit OBSE," *Mezhdunarodnaia zhizn'* no. 1 (1997): 11–13.

65. V. Lukin, "Vot my i v Sovete Evropy," ibid., no. 3 (1996): 24–28; Iu. Ushakov, "39-i chlen Soveta Evropy," ibid., 29–35.

66. See Heinz Timmermann, "Die Europäische Union und Rußland–Dimensionen und Perspektiven der Partnerschaft," *Integration*, no. 4 (1996): 195–207; Jürgen Nötzhold, "Rußland als Partner der europäischen Union," *Europäische Rundschau*, no. 1 (1997): 27–37.

67. Lukin speech in *Interfax*, August 22, 1994, in FBIS-SOV-94-163, August 23, 1994, 3.

Chapter Nine
Russia and Germany in the Twenty-First Century

1. A. J. P. Taylor, *The Course of German History* (London: 1951), 13.

2. François Furet, "Das Rätsel eines Zerfalls," *Schweizer Monatshefte* 71, no. 2 (1991): 117.

3. Hans-Peter Schwarz, *Die Zentralmacht Europas* (Berlin: Siedler, 1994), chap. 1.

4. For more discussion of these ideas, see Timothy Garton Ash, "Germany's

Choice," *Foreign Affairs* 73, no. 3 (July–August 1994) 65–81. See also Arnulf Baring, ed., *Germany's New Position in Europe: Problems and Perspectives* (Oxford: Berg, 1994).

5. See for instance, Jürgen Habermas, *Die Normalität einer Berliner Republik* (Frankfurt: Suhrkamp, 1993), 167–88, and the collection of essays edited by Rainer Zitelman et al., *Westbindung: Chancen und Risiken für Deutschland* (Frankfurt: Propyläen-Verlag, 1993).

6. "Besserwessis" is a pun on "Wessis" (West Germans) and "Besserwisser" (know-it-alls).

7. For further discussion, see Werner Weidenfeld, ed., *A New Ostpolitik—Strategies for a United Europe* (Güetersloh: Bertelsmann Foundation Publishers, 1997).

8. For more on the emergence of a new hybrid system, see Stent and Shevtsova, "Russia's Elections: No Turning Back."

9. For a fuller discussion of Russian foreign policy options, see Legvold, "The Russian Question."

Bibliography

Archives and Official Documents

Bulletin (Bonn).
Bundesarchiv, Bonn. Stiftung Archiv der Parteien und Massenorganisationen der DDR.
Bundesminister für innerdeutsche Beziehungen. *Informationen.*
Bundesministerium für Wirtschaft. *Der deutsche Osthandel 1990.*
"Treaty between the Federal Republic of Germany and the Soviet Union, Moscow, August 1970." In U.S. Senate, Committee on Foreign Relations, *Documents on Germany, 1944–1970.* Washington, D.C.: U.S. Government Printing Office, 1971.
The Week in Germany. The German Information Center of New York.
Zentrales Parteiarchiv, Sozialistische Einheitspartei Deutschlands, Berlin. Zentralkomitee der SED, Büro Hermann Axen.

Newspapers and Magazines

Berliner Zeitung
Financial Times
Frankfurter Allgemeine Zeitung
Frankfurter Rundschau
Handelsblatt
Izvestiia
Kommersant
Komsomolskaia pravda
Krasnaia zvezda
Literaturnaia gazeta
Moscow News
Moskovskie novosti
Neue Berliner Illustrierte
Neue Zürcher Zeitung
Neues Deutschland
New York Times
Newsweek
Nezavisimaia gazeta
Pravda
Rossiskaia gazeta
Rossiskie vesti
Segodniia
Sovetskaia Rossiia
Soviet News
Der Spiegel
Süddeutsche Zeitung
Wall Street Journal
Washington Post
Die Welt
Welt am Sonntag
Die Zeit

News Agency Dispatches

ADN
DDN/ADN
FBIS
Interfax (Moscow)
ITAR-TASS
TASS

Interviews

The author conducted interviews with the following.

Rudolf Adam
Joachim von Arnim
Robert Blackwill
Igor Bratchikov
Yuri Davydov
Frank Elbe
Valentin Falin
Hartmut Förtsch
Rafael Fyodorov
Otto von der Gablentz
Yegor Gaidar
Mikhail Gorbachev
Wolfgang Heitland
Eberhard Heyken
Richard Holbrooke
Wolfgang Ischinger
Sergei Karaganov
Richard Kiessler
Wolfgang Kittl
Klaus-Peter Klaiber
Sergei Kortunov
Evgenii Korzhakin
Anthony Lake

Igor Maximychev
Markus Meckel
Hans Misselwitz
Klaus Neubert
Martin Ney
Hans-Jochen Peters
Nikolai Portugalov
Dariusz Rosati
Reinhard Schäfers
Georgi Shakhnazarov
Galina Starovoitova
Fritz Stern
Gerhard Stoltenberg
Ernst von Studnitz
Dieter Stüdemann
Strobe Talbott
Horst Teltschik
Günther Verheugen
Karsten Voigt
Otto Wolff von Amerongen
Grigory Yavlinsky
Robert Zoellick

Books and Articles

Adomeit, Hannes. "Gorbachev and German Unification." *Problems of Communism* 39, no. 4 (1990): 1–23.

———. "Gorbachev, German Unification and the Collapse of Empire." *Post-Soviet Affairs* 10, no. 3 (July–September 1994): 197–230.

———. "Gorbatschows Westpolitik." *Osteuropa* 38, no. 6 (1988): 418–34.

———. "Russia as a Great Power." *International Affairs* 71, no. 1 (January 1995): 35–68.

Alexandrova, Olga. "Die neuen sozialen Bewegungen im Westen aus der Sicht der sowjetischen Ideologie und Gessellschaftswissenschaft." BIOST Bericht, no. 57. Cologne, 1988.

Al Salem, Gabriel. "Invitation to Interfere." M.A. thesis, Georgetown University, 1994.

Amirdzhanov, Mikhail, and Mikhail Cherkasov. "Our Common European Home." *International Affairs*, no. 1 (1989): 28–33.

Andert, Reinhold, and Wolfgang Herzberg. *Der Sturz.* Berlin and Weimar: Aufbau-Verlag, 1990.

Arbatov, Georgi. *The System.* New York: Random House, 1992.

Ash, Timothy Garton. "Germany's Choice." *Foreign Affairs* 73, no. 3 (July–August 1994): 65–81.

———. *In Europe's Name*. New York: Random House, 1993.

Asmus, Ronald D. "The Dialectics of Detente and Discord: The Moscow/East Berlin/Bonn Triangle." *Orbis* 28, no. 4 (Winter 1995): 743–74.

———. *German Strategy and Opinion After the Wall, 1990–1993*. Santa Monica, Calif.: RAND, 1994.

Asmus, Ronald D., Richard Kugler, and F. Stephen Larrabee. "Building a New NATO." *Foreign Affairs* 72, no. 4 (1993): 28–40.

———. "NATO Expansion: The Next Steps." *Survival* 37, no. 1 (Spring 1995): 7–33.

Bahr, Egon. *Was wird aus den Deutschen?* Reinbeck bei Hamburg: Rohwolt, 1992.

Baker, James A., III. *The Politics of Diplomacy*. New York: Putnam, 1995.

Baranovskii, Vladimir. "Mikromodel' evropeiskoi bezopasnosti." *MEMO*, no. 6 (1996): 40–50.

———. "Stroitel'stvo obshchego evropeiskogo doma: politicheskie i ekonomicheskie aspekty." Institute for World Economy and International Relations, Moscow, 1987. Mimeographed.

Baranovsky, Vladimir, ed. *Russia and Europe: Emerging Security Agenda*. Oxford: Oxford University Press, 1997.

Baras, Victor. "Stalin's German Policy after Stalin." *Slavic Review* 37, no. 2 (June 1978) 259–67.

Baring, Arnulf, ed. *Germany's New Position in Europe: Problems and Perspectives*. Oxford: Berg, 1994.

———. *Machtwechsel: Die Ära Brandt-Scheel*. Stuttgart: Deutsche Verlagsanstalt, 1982.

Beitel, Werner, and Jürgen Nötzhold. *Deutsch-Sowjetische Wirtschaftsbeziehungen in der Zeit der Weimarer Republik*. Ebenhausen: Stiftung Wissenschaft und Politik, March 1977.

Bender, Peter. *Deutsche Parallelen*. Berlin: Siedler Verlag, 1989.

Bergedorfer Gesprächskreis. *Zukunft Europas: Probleme der Politischen und Militärischen Entspannung: UdSSR und Bundesrepublik Deutschland*. Protokoll, no. 75. Hamburg: Körber-Stiftung, 1984.

Beschloss, Michael, and Strobe Talbott. *At the Highest Levels*. Boston: Little, Brown, 1993.

Bialer, Seweryn. "New Thinking and Soviet Foreign Policy." *Survival* 30, no. 4 (July–August 1988): 291–309.

Blackwill, Robert. "German Unification and American Diplomacy." *Außenpolitik* 45, no. 3 (July 1994): 211–25.

Bogomolow, Oleg. "Perestroika und die Aussichten für die Wirtschaftbeziehungen zwischen Ost und West." *Europa Archiv*, no. 16 (1988): 449–58.

Borko, Iu. "O nekotorykh aspektakh izucheniia protsessov zapadnoevropeiskoi integratsii." *MEMO*, no. 2 (1988): 35–50.

Brandenburg, Ulrich. "The 'Friends' Are Leaving: Soviet and Post-Soviet Troops in Germany." *Außenpolitik* 44, no. 1 (1993): 76–87.

Brzezinski, Zbigniew. *The Soviet Bloc: Unity and Conflict*. Cambridge, Mass.: Harvard University Press, 1967.

Bullock, Alan. *Hitler and Stalin: Parallel Lives.* New York: Knopf, 1992.

Cherniaev, Anatoly. *Shest' let s Gorbachevym.* Moscow: Progress, 1993.

Cold War Endgame: Conference Held at Princeton University, March 29, 1996. Unpaginated transcripts of talks by participants.

Cold War International History Project (Washington). *Bulletin,* no. 4 (Fall 1994).

Cornelsen, Doris. "Die Lage der DDR-Wirtschaft zur Jahreswende 1987/1988." Wochenbericht. Berlin: Deutsches Institut für Wirtschaftsforschung, May 1988.

Council on Foreign Relations Task Force. *Russia, Its Neighbors and an Enlarging NATO.* New York: Council on Foreign Relations, 1997.

————. *Should NATO Expand?* New York: Council on Foreign Relations, 1995.

Cramer, Dettmar. "Der Bundespräsident in der Sowjetunion." *Deutschland Archiv* (August 1987): 792–93.

Croan, Melvin. *East Germany: The Soviet Connection.* The Washington Papers. Beverly Hills, Calif.: Sage, 1976.

Crow, Suzanne. "Russia Reasserts its Strategic Agenda." *RFE/RL Research Reports* 2, no. 50 (December 17, 1993): 1–8.

Dashichev, Vyacheslav. "Changing Europe: Soviet and American Approaches." Unpublished manuscript, Institute of the World Socialist Economic System, September 1989. Mimeographed.

————. "Nekotorye Aspekty Germanskoi Problemy." Unpublished manuscript, November 27, 1987, in the possession of the author.

————. "Soviet Policy and German Unification". Paper presented to the XVI World Congress of the International Political Science Association, Berlin, August 21–25, 1994.

Davydov, Iuri. "Rossiia i Evropa v novom izmerenii." *SShA: Ekonomia, Politika, Ideologiia,* no. 5 (1995): 21–32.

Dawisha, Karen. *Eastern Europe, Gorbachev, and Reform.* Cambridge: Cambridge University Press, 1990.

Dean, Jonathan. *Ending Europe's Wars.* New York: Twentieth Century Fund, 1994.

Dobrynin, Anatoly. *In Confidence.* New York: Random House, 1995.

"Dokumente zum Besuch von Bundeskanzler Helmut Kohl in Moskau vom 24. bis zum 27. Oktober 1988." *Europa-Archiv* 43, no. 21 (1988).

Falin, Valentin. *Politische Erinnerungen.* Munich: Droemer Knaur, 1993.

Foreigners in Germany and the New Asylum Law. New York: German Information Center, June 1994.

Furet, François. "Das Rätsel eines Zerfalls." *Schweizer Monatshefte* 71, no. 2 (1991).

Gaddis, John Lewis. *We Now Know.* Oxford: Clarendon Press, 1997.

Ganushkin, Vitaly, and Anatoly Kovrigin. "The Colours of Socialism." *New Times,* no. 42, October 17–23, 1989.

Gates, Robert M. *From the Shadows.* New York: Simon and Schuster, 1996.

Gati, Charles. *The Bloc that Failed.* Bloomington: Indiana University Press, 1990.

Gedmin, Jeffrey. *The Hidden Hand.* Washington, D.C.: AEI Press, 1992.

"Das gemeinsame Papier von SED und SPD und die Reaktion der SED." *Deutschland Archiv* (January 1988): 86–91.

Genscher, Hans-Dietrich. *Erinnerungen.* Berlin: Siedler, 1995.

————. "How Will East-West Relations Develop in 1984?" Speech distributed by the German Embassy, Washington, D.C. March 30, 1984.

German Support for the Transition to Democracy and the Market Economy in the Former Soviet Union. New York: German Information Center, June 1992.

Goldgeier, James M. "NATO Expansion: The Anatomy of a Decision." *Washington Quarterly* 21, no. 1 (Winter 1998): 85–101.

Gompert, David C., and F. Stephen Larrabee, eds. *America and Europe.* Cambridge: Cambridge University Press, 1997.

Gorbachev, Mikhail. *Perestroika.* New York: Random House, 1987.

————. *Zhizn' i reformy.* 2 vols. Moscow: Novosti, 1995.

Greenwald, Jonathan. *Berlin Witness.* University Park, Pa.: Penn State University Press, 1993.

Griffith, William E. *The Ostpolitik of the Federal Republic of Germany.* Cambridge, Mass.: MIT Press, 1978.

Gromyko, Andrei. *Memories.* London: Hutchinson, 1989.

Gustafson, Thane. *Gorbachev's Dilemmas.* Cambridge, Mass.: Cambridge Energy Research Associates Private Report, 1989.

Gysi, Gregor. *Das war's noch lange nicht.* Düsseldorf: ECON, 1995.

Habermas, Jürgen. *Die Normalität einer Berliner Republik.* Frankfurt: Suhrkamp, 1993.

Hahn, Walter F. "West Germany's Ostpolitik: The Grand Design of Egon Bahr." *Orbis* 16, no. 4 (1974): 159–80.

Hamilton, Daniel. "Division, Revolution, Unification." Unpublished ms. 1993.

Hanrieder, Wolfram F. *Helmut Schmidt: Perspectives on Politics.* Boulder, Colo.: Westview Press, 1982.

Harrison, Hope H. "New Evidence on Khrushchev's 1958 Ultimatum." Cold War International History Project *Bulletin*, no 4 (Fall 1994) 35–39.

Hatschikjan, Magarditsch, and Wolfgang Pfieler. "Deutsch-sowjetische Beziehungen in einer Periode der Ost-West-Annaeherung." *Deutschland Archiv*, no 8, August 1989: 883–89.

Hertle, Hans-Hermann. "Ein Stein vom Herzen." *Der Spiegel*, November 14, 1994, 40–43.

————. "Kontrollen Eingestellt—nicht mehr in der Lage—Punkt." Interview with Harald Jaeger. *Deutschland Archiv*, no. 11 (1995).

Horn, Gyula. *Freiheit, die ich meine: Erinnerungen des ungarischen Außenministers, der den Eisernen Vorhang Öffnete.* Hamburg: Hoffmann und Campe, 1991.

Hutchings, Robert L. *American Diplomacy and the End of the Cold War.* Baltimore: Johns Hopkins University Press/Woodrow Wilson Center Press, 1997.

"Interview with Andrei Kozyrev." *New Times*, no. 3 (1992).

"Interview with Wilhelm Christians." *New Times*, no. 45 (1990): 23.

Isakov, Konstantin. "Ethnic Germans in the USSR." *New Times*, no. 14 (1989): 27–29.

Joffe, Josef. "After Bipolarity: Germany and European Security." In *European Security After the Cold War.* London: International Institute for Strategic Studies, 1994.

Kaiser, Karl. *Deutschlands Vereinigung.* Bergisch Gladbach: Gustav Lubbe Verlag, 1991.

Kaiser, Karl, and Klaus Becher. *Deutschland und der Irak-Konflikt.* Bonn: Europa-Union Verlag, 1992.

Kaiser, Karl, and Hanns W. Maull. *Deutschlands neue Außenpolitik, vol. 1: Grundlagen.* Munich: R. Oldenbourg Verlag, 1994.

Kaiser, Karl, and Hanns W. Maull, eds. *Die Zukunft der deutschen Außenpolitik.* Bonn: Europa-Verlag, 1993.

Kaliningradskaia oblast': Segodnia, zavtra. Moscow: Carnegie Endowment for International Peace, 1995.

Kamp, Karl-Heinz. "The Folly of Rapid NATO Expansion." *Foreign Policy*, no. 98 (Spring 1995): 116–31.

Karaganov, Sergei. *Whither Western Aid to Russia.* Gütersloh: Bertelsmann Foundation Publishers, 1994.

Kelleher, Catherine McArdle. *The Future of European Security.* Washington, D.C.: Brookings Institution, 1995.

Kennan, George. *Russia and the West under Lenin and Stalin.* Boston: Little, Brown, 1960.

———. "The Sources of Soviet Conduct." In *Soviet Foreign Policy: Classic and Contemporary Issues*, ed. Frederic Fleron, Erik P. Hoffmann, and Robbin F. Laird, 313–26. New York: Aldine de Gruyter, 1991.

Keworkow, Wjatschelaw. *Der geheime Kanal.* Berlin: Rohwolt, 1995.

Kießler, Richard, and Frank Elbe. *Ein runder Tisch mit scharfen Ecken.* Baden Baden: Nomos, 1993.

Klyuchevsky, Vasili. *Peter the Great.* New York: Vintage Books, 1961.

Kohl, Helmut. *Ich wollte Deutschlands Einheit.* Berlin: Propyläen-Verlag, 1996.

Kortunov, S. "Rossiia ischet soiuznikov." *Mezhdunarodnaia zhizn'*, no. 5 (1996): 11–30.

Korzhakov, Aleksandr. *Boris Yeltsin: Ot rassveta do zakata.* Moscow: Interbook, 1997.

Kotschemassow, Wjatscheslaw. *Meine letze Mission.* Berlin: Deitz, 1994.

Kozyrev, Andrei. *Preobrazhenie.* Moscow: Mezhdunarodnie otnosheniia, 1995.

Kremer, I. S. *FRG: Etapy "Vostochnoi Politiki."* Moscow: Mezhdunarodnie otnosheniia, 1986.

Krenz, Egon. *Wenn Mauern fallen.* Berlin: Paul Neff Verlag, 1990.

Kuczynski, Jürgen and Grete Wittkowski. *Die deutsch-russischen Handelsbeziehungen in den letzten 150 Jahren.* Berlin: Verlag Die Wirtschaft, 1947.

Küchenmeister, Daniel. "Wann begann das Zerwürfnis zwischen Gorbatschow und Honecker?" *Deutschland Archiv* (January 1993): 30–39.

Kutkovets, T. I., amd I. M. Kliamkin. *Russkie idei.* Moscow: Institute of Sociological Analysis, 1997.

Kwizinskij, Julij A. *Vor dem Sturm.* Berlin: Siedler Verlag, 1993.

Laqueur, Walter. *Russia and Germany.* New Brunswick, N.J.: Transaction Publishers, 1990.

Larrabee, F. Stephen. *East European Security after the Cold War.* Santa Monica, Calif.: RAND, 1994.

———. "The Politics of Reconciliation: Soviet Policy toward West Germany, 1961–1971." Ph.D. dissertation, Columbia University, 1977.

Larrabee, F. Stephen, and Theodore W. Karasik. *Foreign and Security Policy Decisionmaking under Yeltsin.* Santa Monica, Calif.: RAND Corporation, 1997.

Lavigne, Marie. "Prospects for Trade Reform." Paper presented at the Institute for Defense Analysis, Alexandria, Va., February 23, 1989.

Legvold, Robert. "The Revolution in Soviet Foreign Policy." *Foreign Affairs* 68, no. 1 (Winter 1988–89): 82–98.

Ligachev, Yegor. *Inside Gorbachev's Kremlin.* New York: Pantheon, 1993.

Lowenthal, Richard. "The German Question Transformed." *Foreign Affairs* 63, no. 2 (Winter 1984–85): 303–15.

Lukin, Vladimir. "Vot my i v Sovete Evropy." *Mezhdunarodnaia zhizn'*, no. 3 (1996): 24–28.

Lukin, Vladimir, and A. I. Utkin. *Rossiia i zapad.* Moscow: Sampo, 1995.

Lynch, Allen. "After Empire: Russia and its Neighbors." *RFE/RL Research Report* 3, no. 12 (March 25, 1994): 10–17.

McAdams, A. James. *Germany Divided.* Princeton, N.J.: Princeton University Press, 1993.

———. "Inter-German Detente: A New Balance." *Foreign Affairs.* 65, no. 2 (Winter 1986): 136–53.

Macfarlane, S. Neil. "Russian Conceptions of Europe." *Post-Soviet Affairs* 10, no. 3 (1994): 234–69.

Machowski, Heinrich. "Grundzüge der neuen sowjetischen Außenwirtschaftspolitik." *Aus Politik und Zeitgeschichte.* November 7, 1987.

Machowski, Heinrich, and Wolfram Schrettl. "The Economic Impact of Unified Germany on Central and Eastern Europe." In U.S. Congress, Joint Economic Committee, *East-Central European Economies in Transition.* Washington, D.C.: U.S. Government Printing Office, 1994.

McIntyre, Joan F. "Soviet Attempts to Revamp the Foreign Trade Sector." In U.S. Congress, Joint Economic Committee, *Gorbachev's Economic Plans,* 2:489–503. Washington, D.C., 1987.

Maier, Charles S. *Dissolution.* Princeton, N.J.: Princeton University Press, 1997.

———. *The Unmasterable Past: History, Holocaust, and German National Identity.* Cambridge, Mass.: Harvard University Press, 1988.

Maksimychev, Igor. "The German Factor in European Security." *International Affairs* (Moscow), no. 11 (1997): 51–63.

———. "A Missed Chance of Four-Power Cooperation in Berlin." *International Affairs* (Moscow), nos. 4–5 (1995).

Maksimychev, Igor, and Hans Modrow. *Posledny god GDR.* Moscow: Mezhdunarodnie otnosheniia, 1993.

Malcolm, Neil. "The 'Common European Home' and Soviet European Policy." *International Affairs* (London) 65, no. 4.

Matlock, Jack F., Jr. *Autopsy on an Empire.* New York: Random House, 1995.

Maull, Hanns. "Großmacht Deutschland: Annmerkungen und Thesen." In *Die Zukunft der deutschen Außenpolitik,* ed. Karl Kaiser and Hanns Maull. Bonn: Europe-Union Verlag, 1993.

Maximytschew, Igor. "Die Maueröffnung." *Deutschland Archiv,* no. 11 (1994): 1137–57.

————. "Was ist bei euch los?" *Der Spiegel*, October 31, 1994.

Mearsheimer, John. "Back to the Future: Instability in Europe after the Cold War." *International Security* 15, no. 1 (Summer 1990): 5–56.

————. "The Case for a Ukrainian Nuclear Deterrent." *Foreign Affairs* 72, no. 3 (Summer 1993): 50–66.

Medvedev. Vadim. "Velikii Oktiabr' i sovremennyi mir." *Kommunist*, no. 2 (1988): 3–18.

Meißner, Boris. *Die Deutsche Ostpolitk, 1961–1970.* Cologne: Verlag Wissenschaft und Politik, 1970.

————. "Die deutsch-sowjetische Beziehungen seit dem Zweiten Weltkrieg." *Osteuropa* 35, no. 9 (1985): 631–51.

Migranian, Andranik. *Rossiia v poiskakh identichnosti.* Moscow: Mezhdunarodnie Otnosheniia, 1997.

Mlynář, Zdeněk. *Nightfrost in Prague.* New York: Karz Publishers, 1989.

Morrison, James W. *NATO Expansion and Alternative Future Security Alignments.* McNair Paper 40. Washington, D.C.: National Defense University, April 1998.

"Natsional'nye interesy vo vneshnei politike Rossii." *Mezhdunarodnaia zhizn'*, no. 3 (1996).

Nötzhold, Jürgen. "Rußland als Partner der europäischen Union." *Europäische Rundschau*, no. 1 (1997): 27–37.

Oberdorfer, Don. *The Turn.* New York: Poseidon Press, 1991.

Oldenburg, Fred. "Eine endliche Geschichte." *Deutschland Archiv*, 1995.

————. "Neues Denken in der sowjetischen Deutschlandpolitik?" *Europa-Archiv* 42, no. 11 (November 1987).

————. "Sowjetische Europa-Politik und die Lösung der deutschen Frage." *Osteuropa* 41, no. 8 (August 1991): 751–73.

"Ost-West-Handel stagniert." Deutsches Institut für Wirtschaftsforschung, *Wochenbericht*, no. 46 (1987).

"Otvety E. A. Shevardnazde na voprosy zapadnogermanskoi Gazety 'Welt am Sonntag.'" *Vestnik MID*, July 31, 1990.

Palazchenko, Pavel. *My Years with Gorbachev and Shevardnadze.* University Park, Pa.: Penn State University Press, 1997.

Pankin, Boris. *The Last Hundred Days of the Soviet Union.* New York: I. B. Taurus, 1996.

"Die Perestroika greift noch nicht." Deutsches Institut für Wirtschaftsforschung, *Wochenbericht*, no. 33 (1988).

"Policy statement by Chancellor Helmut Kohl on the NATO Summit in Brussels and on the Visit by President George Bush to the Federal Republic of Germany, Bonn, June 1, 1989." German Information Center, New York, *Statements and Speeches* 12, no. 13 (June 5, 1989).

Pond, Elizabeth. *Beyond the Wall.* Washington, D.C.: Brookings Institution, 1993.

Portugalov, Nikolai. "Bonn Goalkeepers." *New Times*, no. 22 (1987): 12.

————. "Cloudy with Sunny Intervals." *New Times*, no 31 (1986): 14.

Pryce-Jones, David. *The Strange Death of the Soviet Empire.* New York: Henry Holt, 1995.

Rakhmaninov, Iu. O. "Nekotori soobrazheniia o rashirenii NATO." *SShA: Ekonomika, Politika, Ideologiia*, no. 2 (1997): 56–60.

Riasanovsky, Nicholas. *Russia and the West in the Teaching of the Slavophiles.* Cambridge, Mass.: Harvard University Press, 1952.

Risse, Thomas. "The Cold War's Endgame and German Unification." *International Security* 21, no. 4 (Spring 1997): 159–85.

Rossiia: Desiat' voprosov o samom vazhnom. Moscow: Carnegie Center, 1997.

Rühe, Volker. "America and Europe: Common Challenges and Common Answers." Lecture given at Georgetown University, March 2, 1995.

The Ruling of the Federal Constitutional Court on the Deployment of the German Armed Forces. New York: German Information Center, July 1994.

Rumer, Eugene B. "The German Question in Moscow's 'Common European Home': A Background to the Revolutions of 1989." RAND Note N-3220-USDP. Santa Monica, Calif.: RAND Corporation, 1991.

Schabowski, Günter. *Der Absturz.* Berlin: Rohwolt, 1991.

———. *Das Politburo.* Reinbek bei Hamburg: Rohwolt, 1990.

Schäuble, Wolfgang. *Der Vertrag.* Stuttgart: Deutsche Verlagsanstalt, 1992.

Schmidt, Helmut. *Grand Strategy for the West.* New Haven, Conn.: Yale University Press, 1984.

Schneider, Eberhard. "Der letzte Parteitag der SED." BIOST, no. 19 (1990).

Schulz, Hans-Dieter. "In der Welt ohne Beispiel: Sowjethandel der DDR: Qualität stärker steigern als Quantität." *Deutschland Archiv*, December 1985.

Schwarz, Hans-Peter. *Die Zentralmacht Europas.* Berlin: Siedler, 1994.

Seiffert, Wolfgang. "Die Deutschlandpolitik der SED im Spannungsfeld der sowjetischen Interessenlage." *Deutschland Archiv*, March 1987.

Semjonow, Wladimir. *Von Stalin bis Gorbatschow: Ein halbes Jahrhundert in diplomatischer Mission 1939–1991.* Berlin: Nikolai Verlag, 1995.

Shakhnazarov, Georgi. *Tsena svobody.* Moscow: Rossika, 1993.

Shevardnadze, Eduard. "The 19th All-Union CPSU Conference: Foreign Policy and Diplomacy." *International Affairs* (Moscow), no. 10 (October 1988): 58–64.

———. *The Future Belongs to Freedom.* New York: Free Press, 1991.

Shmagin, Yevgeni, and Igor Bratchikov. "Perestroika in the USSR Foreign Ministry." *International Affairs* (Moscow), no. 3 (March 1989): 42–53.

Sodaro, Michael J. *Moscow, Germany and the West From Khrushchev to Gorbachev.* Ithaca, N.Y.: Cornell University Press, 1990.

———. "Ulbricht's Grand Design: Economy, Ideology and the GDR's Response to Detente, 1967–1971." *World Affairs* 142, no. 3 (Winter 1980): 147–68.

Spitmann, Ilse. "Gorbatschow besucht die SED." *Deutschland Archiv*, May 1986.

Staadt, Jochen, ed. *Auf höchster Stufe: Gespräche mit Erich Honecker.* Berlin: Transit, 1994.

Stent, Angela. "Doctrinal Discord." *The New Republic*, January 5 and 18, 1990.

———. "East-West Technology Transfer and the Western Alliance." In *Trade, Technology and Soviet-American Relations*, ed. Bruce Parrott, 283–323. Bloomington: Indiana University Press, 1985.

———. *From Embargo to Ostpolitik: The Political Economy of West German–Soviet Relations, 1955–1980.* Cambridge: Cambridge University Press, 1981.

———. "Russia's Economic Revolution and the West." *Survival* 37, no. 5 (Spring 1995): 121–63.

———. "Soviet Policy toward the German Democratic Republic." In *Soviet Policy in Eastern Europe*, ed. Sarah M. Terry. New Haven, Conn.: Yale University Press, 1984. Pp. 33–60.

———. "Western Europe and the USSR." In *Areas of Challenge for Soviet Foreign Policy in the 1980s*, ed. Gerrit W. Gong, Angela E. Stent, and Rebecca V. Strode, 1–52. Bloomington: Indiana University Press, 1984.

Stent, Angela, and Lilia Shevtsova. "Russia's Election: No Turning Back." *Foreign Policy*, no. 3 (Summer 1996): 92–109.

Szabo, Stephen F. *The Diplomacy of German Unification*. New York: St. Martin's Press, 1992.

———. "A Second Look at German Unification." *German Politics and Society* 15, no. 4 (1997): 130–39.

Talbott, Strobe. "Why NATO Should Grow." *New York Review of Books*, August 10, 1995.

Taylor, A. J. P. *The Course of German History*. New York: Putnam, 1979. 1951.

Teltschik, Horst. *329 Tage*. Berlin: Siedler Verlag, 1991.

Thatcher, Margaret. *The Downing Street Years*. London: HarperCollins, 1995.

Timmermann, Heinz. "Die Europäsche Union und Rußland—Dimensionen und Perspektiven der Partnerschaft." *Integration*, no. 4 (1996): 195–207.

Tolpegin, Alexander. "Realities and Illusions." *New Times*, no 38 (1987): 4–5.

Ulam, Adam. *The Bolsheviks*. New York: Praeger, 1976.

United States Institute of Peace. *Managing NATO Enlargement*. Washington, D.C.: April 1997.

Ushakov, Iu. "39-i chlen Soveta Evropy." *Mezhdunarodnaia zhizn'*, no. 3 (1996): 29–35.

Venohr, Wolfgang, ed. *Die deutsche Einheit kommt bestimmt*. Bergisch Gladbach: Gustav Lubbe Verlag, 1982.

Viatkin, K. "Rossiia I Germaniia: Potentsial sotrudnichestva." *MEMO*. no. 4 (1994).

Vogel, Henirich. "The London Summit and the Soviet Union." *Außenpolitik* (English edition) 42, no. 4 (1991).

Volkogonov, Dimitri. *Stalin: Trimuph and Tragedy*. Rocklin, Calif.: Prima Publishing, 1995.

"Vstrecha M. S. Gorbacheva s E. Honekkerom." *Vestnik MID*, July 1989.

Weidenfeld, Werner. *A New Ostpolitik—Strategies for a United Europe*. Gütersloh: Bertelsmann Foundation Publishers, 1997.

Weit, Erwin. *Eyewitness*. London: Andre Deutsch, 1973.

Wettig, Gerhard. "Die Sowjetische Politik während der Berlin-Krise 1958–1962." *Deutschland Archiv*, no. 3 (1997): 383–99.

Whitney, Craig. *Spy Trader*. New York: Times Books, 1993.

Wolf, Markus. *In eigenem Auftrag*. Munich: Schneekluth, 1991.

———. *Spionagechef im Geheimen Krieg*. Munich: List Verlag, 1997.

Wolfe, Thomas E. *Soviet Power and Europe*. Baltimore: Johns Hopkins University Press, 1970.

Wolff von Amerongen, Otto. *Der Weg nach Osten*. Munich: Droemer Knaur, 1992.

Yeltsin, Boris. *The Struggle for Russia*. New York: Random House, 1994.

Yergin, Daniel. *Shattered Peace*. Boston: Houghton Mifflin, 1977.

Yergin, Daniel, and Thane Gustafson. *Russia 2010*. New York: Vintage, 1994.

Zelikow, Philip, and Condoleeza Rice. *Germany Unified and Europe Transformed*. Cambridge, Mass.: Harvard University Press, 1995.

Zholkver, Nikita. "The Frontier." *New Times*, no. 32 (1986): 21–25.

Zhukov, Yuri. "What Kind of Dialogue for Europeans?" *International Affairs* (Moscow), no. 7 (1987): 92–101.

Zilteman, Rainer, et al. *Westbindung: Chancen und Risiken für Deutschland*. Frankfurt: Propyläen-Verlag, 1993.

Die Zukunft des Gebiets Kaliningrad (Königsberg). Sonderveröffentlichung BIOST, *Bericht*. Cologner, July 1993.

Index

ABOUT THE AUTHOR

Angela E. Stent is Professor of Government at Georgetown University. Her previous books include *From Embargo to Ostpolitik* and *Areas of Challenge for Soviet Foreign Policy in the 1980s.*